AF324062

Services
Trade Reform
Making Sense of It

World Scientific Studies in International Economics
(ISSN: 1793-3641)

The complete list of the published volumes in the series can be found at
http://www.worldscientific.com/series/wssie.

28 World Scientific Studies in International Economics

Services Trade Reform

Making Sense of It

Philippa Dee

The Australian National University, Australia

World Scientific

NEW JERSEY · LONDON · SINGAPORE · BEIJING · SHANGHAI · HONG KONG · TAIPEI · CHENNAI

Published by

World Scientific Publishing Co. Pte. Ltd.

5 Toh Tuck Link, Singapore 596224

USA office: 27 Warren Street, Suite 401-402, Hackensack, NJ 07601

UK office: 57 Shelton Street, Covent Garden, London WC2H 9HE

Library of Congress Cataloging-in-Publication Data
Dee, Philippa S.
   Services trade reform : making sense of it / by Philippa Dee.
    p. cm. -- (World scientific studies in international economics ; v. 28)
   Includes bibliographical references.
   ISBN 978-9814508742 (hardcover : alk. paper)
   1. Service industries--Government policy. 2. International trade. I. Title.
II. Series: World scientific studies in international economics ; v. 28.
   HD9980.6.D44 2013
   382'.3--dc23
                            2013019824

British Library Cataloguing-in-Publication Data
A catalogue record for this book is available from the British Library.

In-house Editor: Monica Lesmana

Typeset by Stallion Press
Email: enquiries@stallionpress.com

Printed in Singapore by World Scientific Printers.

Preface

With the Doha Round of multilateral trade negotiations moribund, it is time to reconsider the future of trade negotiations as an impetus for reform. Services trade is a leading-edge behind-the-border issue, so a services perspective offers critical insights into the future of trade negotiations more generally. My own thinking on these issues results from a long sequence of analytical, empirical and policy-related work on services issues, from both academic and government perspectives. The purpose of this book is to trace my thinking on how to make sense of services trade reform, and what this means for the future of trade negotiations more generally.

I would like to thank, without implication, my fellow travellers on this intellectual journey. I would like to start with 'the services team' who worked with me at the Australian Productivity Commission in the 1990s. Some of them are listed as co-authors of particular chapters — Alexis Hardin, Leanne Holmes, Kevin Hanslow and Tien Phamduc. Others appear in the bibliography, the stalwarts being Greg McGuire, Duc Nguyen-Hong and the irrepressible 'KK' Kalirajan (the latter two sadly died too young), along with Richard Adams, Samantha Doove, Owen Gabbitas, Joe Owen, Mick Schuele and Tina Smith. During our pioneering work on measuring barriers to services trade, I used to joke that like all seminal researchers, they could look forward to being famous for getting it not quite right the first time around. I am grateful that they embraced the chance of possible infamy with such enthusiasm, and brought their professionalism in the area of microeconomic reform to bear in this new area.

I would also like to thank the academics with whom we collaborated in those early endeavours. The first joint research project between the Productivity Commission, the University of Adelaide and the Australian National University was headed by Christopher Findlay, who also led two subsequent services projects. Christopher has been a valued collaborator — he co-authored two chapters in this volume and appears prominently in the bibliography. Other early collaborators were Alexandra Sidorenko, who also co-authored a chapter here, and Tony Warren. It was with these researchers that I began to explore the general policy implications of our early analytical and empirical work.

I would like to thank the researchers who helped me to test my understanding of services issues in particular contexts. Three appear as co-authors here — Ndiame Diop of the World Bank, Hildegunn Nordås of the OECD and Anne McNaughton of the Law Faculty at the Australian National University. Peter Drysdale, also of the Australian National University, encouraged me to understand the political economy of any given situation and its implications for institution-building. Working with the Economic Research Institute for ASEAN and East Asia in Jakarta has allowed me to develop an even deeper understanding of the links between services trade policy and domestic reform — thanks to Ponciano Intal and Dionisius Narjoko for facilitating that ongoing collaboration.

Much of the material in this book is reproduced with the permission of the original publishers, and I thank them accordingly. Some chapters have been edited to remove major repetition, such as descriptions of model frameworks or previous research. In the interests of keeping the chapters self-contained, some minor repetition of arguments remains.

I would like to dedicate this book to the late, great Richard Snape. Ever the gentleman, Richard was one of a generation of Australian trade economists who eschewed narrow specialization. He understood theory, policy, and institution-building, and saw his role as spanning all three. He encouraged our early efforts at the Productivity Commission. Were he alive today, I hope he would see this contribution as following in his footsteps.

Philippa Dee
Australian National University

Contents

List of Tables

List of Figures

Abbreviations

ABARE	Australian Bureau of Agricultural and Resource Economics
ADBI	Asian Development Bank Institute
AFAS	ASEAN Framework Agreement on Services
APEC	Asia-Pacific Economic Cooperation
ARF	ASEAN Regional Forum
ASEAN	Association of South East Asian Nations
ASEAN+3	A group of countries comprising the ten members ASEAN plus China, Japan and the Republic of Korea
ASEAN+6	A group of countries comprising the ten members ASEAN plus Australia, China, India, Japan, the Republic of Korea and New Zealand
AUSFTA	Australia–US Free Trade Agreement
B2B	Business-to-business
BAPPENAS	*Badan Perencanaan dan Pembangunan Nasional* (National Development Planning Agency)
BEP	Baltagi, Egger and Pfaffermayr
BOD	Board of Directors
BOP	Balance of payments
CACM	Central American Common Market
CAFTA	Central America Free Trade Agreement
CARICOM	Caribbean Community
CARIFORUM	Forum of the Caribbean Group of African, Caribbean and Pacific (ACP) States
CEFTA	Central European Free Trade Agreement
CEPII	*Centre D'études Prospectives Et D'informations Internationales*
CER	Closer Economic Relations
CES	Constant elasticity of substitution
CET	Constant elasticity of transformation
CGE	Computable general equilibrium
cif	cost, insurance and freight
COMESA	Common Market for Eastern and Southern Africa
CSI	Coalition of Service Industries

CUSTA	Canada–US Free Trade Agreement
DFAT	Department of Foreign Affairs and Trade
EAS	East Asian Summit
EC	European Commission
EEA	European Economic Area
EEC	European Economic Community
EFTA	European Free Trade Association
ERIA	Economic Research Institute for ASEAN and East Asia
ESCAP	Economic and Social Commission for Asia and the Pacific
EU	European Union
EV	Equivalent variation
FATS	Foreign affiliate trade statistics
FDI	Foreign direct investment
fob	free on board
FTA	Free Trade Agreement
FTAP	GTAP with foreign direct investment
G20	Group of Twenty (Argentina, Australia, Brazil, Canada, China, France, Germany, India, Indonesia, Italy, Japan, the Republic of Korea, Mexico, Russia, Saudi Arabia, South Africa, Turkey, the United Kingdom, the United States and the European Union)
GAFTA	Greater Arab Free Trade Area
GATS	General Agreement on Trade in Services
GATT	General Agreement on Tariffs and Trade
GDP	Gross domestic product
GEMPACK	General Equilibrium Modelling Package
GNP	Gross national product
GTAP	Global Trade Analysis Project
HO	Heckscher–Ohlin
IC	Industry Commission
ICAO	International Civil Aviation Organization
ICT	Information and communications technology
IMF	International Monetary Fund
INS	*Institut National de la Statisique*
ITU	International Telecommunications Union
KLEMS	Capital, Labour, Energy, Materials, Services Database
LAIA	Latin American Integration Association
LDCs	Least developed countries
MA	Market access
Mercosur	*Mercado Común del Sur* (Southern Common Market)
MFN	Most-favoured nation
MIT	Massachusetts Institute of Technology
NAFTA	North American Free Trade Agreement

NBER	National Bureau of Economic Research
NEDA	National Economic and Development Authority
NPER	National Professional Engineers Register
NT	National treatment
OECD	Organization for Economic Co-operation and Development
ONH	*Office des Huiles*
PC	Productivity Commission
PDR	People's Democratic Republic
PSTN	Public switched telephone network
PTA	Preferential Trade Agreement
QR	Quantitative restriction
SAPTA	South Asian Preferential Trade Agreement
s.d.	standard deviation
SPARTECA	South Pacific Regional Trade and Economic Cooperation Agreement
STAN	Structural Analysis Database
TRIMS	Agreement on Trade Related Investment Measures
UNCTAD	United Nations Conference on Trade and Development
US	United States
USTR	United States Trade Representative
VSAT	Very small aperture terminal
WTO	World Trade Organization

Chapter 1

Making Sense of Services Trade Reform

Philippa Dee

1.1 Introduction

To make sense of services trade reform, this book starts from analytical frameworks and finishes with policy recommendations about how and where to undertake reform in the future. It aims to show policy makers how to approach the economics and politics of services trade reform domestically, consistent with relevant special features of services trade. It aims to show analysts the full policy implications of those special features, including what they mean for how services reform should be treated in the future in national and international forums.

In covering such broad territory, the book draws together published material that previously has been widely scattered across place and time. The book therefore also presents a journey in thinking about services trade reform — my own thinking, and that of fellow travellers, both co-authors and other scholars writing concurrently. In the early days, there were things we got right analytically, but a few we got wrong (though those ideas persist in some circles today). This introductory chapter therefore needs to sort the wheat from the chaff. It also provides an overview of how the core good ideas have persisted in subsequent thinking about policy reform, policy forums, and what it takes politically to achieve reform.

Forming a bridge between the analytical frameworks and the policy implications is a series of chapters giving applications of computable general equilibrium (CGE) modelling to services trade. Such material often elicits groans from both pure analysts and pure policy wonks. Nevertheless, many of the policy insights into services trade reform hinge on empirical issues. The discipline of CGE modelling has helped to identify those empirical issues. It has also been part of the solution, in conjunction with econometric studies of services industry performance that have formed the inputs into the CGE modelling. This volume gives a sample of CGE applications, while a recent volume (Dee 2013b) gives the state of the art in the econometric studies. The lessons from CGE modelling are then incorporated into the discussion of policy implications.

1.2 Wheat and Chaff

The insight that has proved most deeply influential in shaping thinking about the economics and politics of services trade reform is that services trade barriers are not always purely discriminatory. Some of the key barriers to services trade protect incumbents from any competition, be it from foreign providers or from domestic new entrants. Drake and Nicolaïdis (1992) document how this was one of the 'special features' of services trade recognized by the epistemic community of policy specialists, academics, industry specialist and others whose intellectual leadership promoted acceptance of services as a legitimate multilateral trade issue, and ultimately influenced the design of the General Agreement on Trade in Services (GATS), under the World Trade Organization.

The GATS provisions on national treatment dealt with discrimination against foreign services and service suppliers, both at and behind the border. But the GATS also recognized a category of quantitative barriers to 'market access' that could affect domestic and foreign suppliers equally. It also recognized that domestic regulations more broadly could impede services trade, and that disciplines should eventually be negotiated to minimize their incidental impact on trade.

Richard Snape (1998, p. 284) noted how, as a result of these latter features, services trade negotiations would differ from the previous 'core business' of goods trade negotiations under the General Agreement on Tariffs and Trade (GATT):

> The GATT is almost entirely concerned with relations between us and them; these provisions of the GATS are not concerned with us and them but between 'some of us' on the one hand and 'the rest of us and them' on the other.

I had the honour of working with Richard while he was Deputy Chairman of the Australian Productivity Commission. At the time he expressed some unease at this extension of multilateral disciplines into the realm of domestic competition policy. To a large extent, the policy insights in this book vindicate his unease — for a variety of reasons, trade negotiators tend to continue to operate on an 'us and them' basis, and this can lead to bad economics and unhelpful political economy. More on this later.

Drake and Nicolaïdis (1992, p. 77) document how during the Uruguay Round negotiations, which established the architecture of the GATS, the classical liberal approach of the United States Trade Representative (USTR) favoured the 'us and them' approach to services:

> The popular beltway discourse on 'fair trade' was interpreted to mean that discrimination was the chief problem and that national treatment was the primary solution.

The European Community saw non-discrimination as only part of the solution, and advocated a managed approach that would balance progressive liberalization of market access with respect for policy objectives.

The idea that services trade reform is *really* only about national treatment persists in some circles today. It clearly still flavours USTR's negotiating stances, and is sometimes implicit in the approach of the OECD towards services trade issues — as reflected in my own contribution to an OECD project that is reproduced here in Chapter 7. In their recent work on quantifying services trade barriers, Borchert, Gootiiz and Mattoo (2012a, 2012b) acknowledge in principle that barriers can be non-discriminatory, but in practice their data is heavily biased towards discriminatory measures. And the very recent application by Miroudot, Sauvage and Shepherd (2010) of Dennis Novy's (2009) analytical framework to measuring services trade barriers also presumes either that the only barriers that matter are discriminatory, or that the non-discriminatory barriers (equivalent to barriers on 'internal trade') do not change when the discriminatory ones do. Clearly this is not true, since most services trade reform has occurred unilaterally as part of a domestic regulatory reform agenda (see Chapter 14).

The chaff in our initial approach to services trade barriers was the joint presumption that (a) barriers should be modelled as a 'tax equivalent' (as opposed to a 'productivity equivalent'), and (b) at least some of that tax burden should fall on stocks of foreign direct investment. Consider the second presumption first.

One of the other 'special features' of services trade recognized by the epistemic community was that services could be delivered in a number of ways, often involving the cross-border movement of the producer or consumer. Sampson and Snape (1985) developed one of the early taxonomies, which is reflected in the GATS' four modes of supply. One of these modes is the permanent commercial presence of a service supplier in the territory of the consumer.

Initially we thought that at least some barriers to commercial presence should be modelled as a tax on stocks of foreign capital, probably because we were implicitly thinking those services were delivered by foreign direct investment (FDI). In fact, those services are delivered by the activities of foreign affiliates. The distinction is the same as that between FDI statistics and Foreign Affiliate Trade Statistics (FATS). The services are not delivered by the capital stock of a foreign affiliate, but by its output — produced in turn by its capital stock (only some of which may be foreign-financed), along with labour (only some of which may be expatriate) and material and service inputs (which may be sourced locally, from the parent company, or from independent foreign suppliers). And barriers to establishing a commercial presence are typically barriers to presence, rather than to capital intensity. Thus while artificial barriers to entry may allow returns to incumbent foreign affiliates to be inflated, there is no reason why they should also distort capital–labour ratios. In more recent applications (eg Chapters 6 and 7), I have modelled tax effects of barriers to commercial presence as falling on the *output* of foreign affiliates, rather than on their capital stocks, although the rents still flow to affiliate owners. In the original modelling treatments in Chapters 4 and 5, where taxes fell on capital stocks, the allocative efficiency losses associated with services trade barriers may have been overstated, but otherwise the impact of this treatment would have been relatively minor.[1]

A more important question is whether it was appropriate to treat services trade barriers as having *only* tax effects. Clearly they also have the potential to raise real resource costs. This was suggested by some of the early econometric efforts to measure the impact of services trade barriers on price–cost margins (eg Kalirajan 2000). It turns out that this issue also has a crucial impact on the economics and politics of services trade reform, as demonstrated in many of the remaining chapters in this volume.

It is clearly an empirical question whether services trade barriers add to costs or to price–cost margins, although the issue has often been decided on *a priori* grounds. When Deardorff and Stern (2005) argued that services trade barriers should be modelled via a 'tariff equivalent', they not only ruled out the possibility of cost effects, they also presumed that barriers operated 'at the border' rather than 'behind the border', and furthermore, that they were purely discriminatory. At the opposite extreme, Hertel (2000) assumed services trade barriers added entirely to costs. Konan and Maskus (2006) adopted an arbitrary half-and-half treatment. Theory might nevertheless suggest that artificial *entry* barriers might create rents and/or add to fixed costs, while barriers to *operation* might add to variable costs (eg Chapter 6, Hoekman 2006, Mattoo and Sauvé 2010). Yet recent examples show that these distinctions are not clear-cut in practice (eg Dinh 2013) — there is no substitute for careful econometric analysis.[2]

---

[1] At the Productivity Commission, our initial decision to treat some services trade barriers as taxes on FDI capital was influenced by discussions with Richard Snape. We were not alone — Petri (1997) also had this treatment, for example.

[2] Dee (2013b) presents some second-generation estimates of the effects of services trade barriers on industry performance, testing whether they affect costs or price–cost margins. The final chapter of that volume uses these estimates as inputs into CGE modelling of the effects of services reform in APEC economies.

Thus the two distinctions with the greatest analytical (as opposed to descriptive) power that emerge from the theoretical and empirical analysis of services trade barriers are:

- whether the barriers are discriminatory or non-discriminatory; and
- whether they affect costs or price–cost markups.

1.3 Tracing Through the Policy Implications

Our very earliest thinking about services trade barriers identified the possibility that their potential to be non-discriminatory might create 'second-best' problems that did not arise with goods trade. Chapter 2 in this volume was originally written while we were still scoping analytical frameworks, yet it identified the possibility for second-best efficiency losses if services trade liberalization applied national treatment without also attending to behind-the-border non-discriminatory measures. At that time we understood the theoretical possibility, but did not have a sense of its empirical importance. Chapter 11 gives a more complete discussion of possible principles for piecemeal reform of services trade, drawing on a greater body of empirical work and a longer history of services trade negotiations and unilateral reform. The guidelines in that chapter differ in important respects from the more preliminary guidelines we offered in Chapter 2, because they also take into account that some barriers will affect costs rather than price–cost margins.

Chapter 3 outlines some of the key issues facing those who want to build empirical models of services trade, based on our first experience with doing so. The analytical issues have not changed greatly over time, although there is now more scope to calibrate some of the behavioural parameters (as in Chapter 7). Data remains problematic. Not only to CGE modellers have to contend with the dearth of bilateral data on cross-border services trade, they also face a lack of data on commercial presence — both the extent of foreign ownership, and the costs and sales structures of foreign affiliates. My solutions to these problems have changed over time. I have been able to simplify the original data construction methods (described in Chapter 4) somewhat by the judicious use of FATS data for US affiliates kindly supplied by Michael Ferrantino of the US International Trade Commission. The new method is described in Chapters 6 and 7, and can be applied flexibly to create models with any dimensionality of sectors or regions.

Our first CGE modelling treatment of services trade reform was rather stylized, in that we had only one aggregate services sector, and our characterization of services trade barriers for that entire sector was an application of empirical results for banking and telecommunications. Nevertheless, the first modelling applications revealed some useful new insights. A key one was that, to the extent that barriers to commercial presence did raise price–cost margins, then services trade liberalization would affect welfare not just through its allocative efficiency effects, but also through the way it redistributed barrier rents across countries. The results in Chapter 4 suggested that services trade liberalization could even be detrimental to major FDI exporters, for this reason. This result was somewhat surprising, if not implausible to some, given that the United States, a major FDI exporter, was at that stage also the biggest *demandeur* for services trade liberalization. Our analytical point had a counterpart in the economics and politics of tariff-jumping FDI, though of course our modelling results overstated the case because we had treated *all* services trade barriers as creating rents. But Drake and Nicolaïdis (1992) also document how the United States' initial enthusiasm for multilateral services trade reform subsequently dampened on a number of fronts. Instead, the United States (along with other countries) has sought expanded market access on a preferential basis through free trade agreements (FTAs), which incidentally have the potential for at least some rent preservation (see Chapter 10).

In Chapter 5, we tested whether the Stolper–Samuelson and Rybczynski theorems from goods trade theory applied in our empirical CGE model of services trade. Because we treated some services trade barriers as affecting foreign affiliates' price of capital, the Stolper–Samuelson theorem could not hold: the movement of relative factor prices was dominated by the removal of barriers to capital movement. The critical assumptions of the Rybczynski theorem were not met in the model, because products and services were treated as imperfect substitutes. Nevertheless, we could show that the model displayed the same underlying economic forces that lead to the Rybczynski result under its special set of assumptions.

While this exercise was largely a consistency check on the model, it did reveal an important empirical insight. Our analysis of input–output tables showed that in both developed and developing countries, the biggest direct and indirect users of services tended to be other services sectors. At a time when some of the 'hype' about multilateral services trade liberalization was about the spillover benefits to manufacturing, our data and modelling suggested that the biggest beneficiaries from services trade reforms could be other services sectors. Much of the hype about spillovers was being generated from the EU, where political constraints at the national and supra-national level were making merchandise trade liberalization on a stand-alone basis particularly difficult. Yet it is revealing that in subsequent Doha Round negotiations, services were essentially sidelined. Services' potential role as a deal-maker in the Doha Round is examined more broadly in Chapter 9.[3]

Over time the modelling of services trade liberalization became less stylized. Models were purpose-built with flexible dimensionality, trade barrier estimates became available for each sector separately, and reform scenarios were devised to reflect feasible next steps. Chapter 6 presents one such exercise for (pre-Arab spring) Tunisia. At that time, feasible next steps in services were likely to come from further bilateral trade negotiations with the EU in a Euro–Med context.

To a CGE modeller, what matters about trade negotiations is not the commitments that are made on paper, but how they translate into changed policies on the ground. My first experience with modelling the outcome of a trade agreement was examining the likely effects of Vietnam's WTO accession, along with two Vietnamese colleagues, one of whom was directly involved in the accession negotiations (Dee, Le and Dang 2005). The services offers were essentially a multilateralization of the commitments that Vietnam had made in its Bilateral Trade Agreement with the United States. To model their

---

[3] Subsequent modelling analysis has nevertheless confirmed the importance of services–manufacturing linkages, especially via logistics services, to the countries now involved in Factory Asia — see Dee (2012b).

impact, we needed to compare them to Vietnam's actual policies on the ground. This comparison revealed two things that surprised us all:

- how little difference the offers made to the totality of restrictions affecting services trade — many commitments merely bound the *status quo*, and a few involved backward steps;
- how the few real differences were almost exclusively about granting national treatment, ie removing discrimination against foreign suppliers, rather than tackling the plethora of non-discriminatory restrictions.

As a result, the modelled gains from Vietnam's WTO accession in services were essentially trivial, and furthermore, involved a crowding out of Vietnamese-owned businesses — and this from an agreement that was being touted (along with Chinese WTO accession) as one of the big success stories of services trade negotiations.

The discipline of CGE modelling provided a real insight that continues to be underappreciated — what matters about trade agreements is not what they promise on paper but what they deliver on the ground, and in services, they often deliver very little. The evidence is surveyed in in Chapters 10 and 14.

The Tunisian case in Chapter 6 is not quite as bleak as the Vietnam example. It also provides empirical evidence for two other propositions about services trade reform — the lack of gains from reciprocity, and the way that tackling non-discriminatory barriers can help to guard against the crowding out of domestic activity. Both themes recur in later chapters.

As the CGE modelling of services trade reform became less stylized, it also began to incorporate new empirical evidence about which barriers created rents and which raised real resource costs.[4] Where barriers are found to raise real resource costs, they are modelled as a 'productivity equivalent' rather than a 'tax equivalent'; liberalization then frees the excess resources and yields a productivity gain. But as those lobbying for

---

[4] As noted, the most up-to-date and comprehensive modelling evaluation using such evidence is the final chapter in Dee (2013b).

services trade liberalization know, productivity gains are often seen as problematic, because they involve doing more with less. So as a response to the unemployment created by the global financial crisis, is it at all possible that services trade reform can contribute to job growth? The answer offered in Chapter 7, perhaps surprisingly, is 'yes'.

The employment effects of liberalizing FDI in services are summarized in Figure 7.4 of Chapter 7. Two key mechanisms contribute to positive employment outcomes. When services are made cheaper, people will tend to buy more of them. Econometric evidence suggests that this scale effect is likely to be substantial, because demands for services appear to be reasonably price responsive. Furthermore, as foreign-invested firms expand, their labour intensity is likely to increase. This reflects their ability to attract additional labour, relative to additional FDI capital (this being far less mobile than debt or other financial instruments). Indirect econometric evidence allowed a very rough calibration of these effects.

Yet the Doha Round negotiations have been unable to deliver a comprehensive trade agreement which, as a 'single undertaking', would have included services trade reform. Multilateral discussions have now moved to the possibility of a plurilateral WTO agreement on services. The struggle at the moment is about whether the provisions in that agreement would be preferential — granted only to other plurilateral partners — in the same way that the subset of services provisions in FTAs that imply real liberalization have tended to be.[5]

Our first analysis of possible reasons for the disappointing services outcomes in the WTO pointed to an absence of gains from reciprocity in services. In Chapter 8 we attributed the disappointing progress to this lack of reciprocity, rather than to any architectural flaws in the GATS. However, we also noted that the economics and political economy of services trade reform were deeply domestic, and it was unlikely that

---

[5] The slightly awkward language is intentional. Baldwin (2011) has argued that 21st century FTAs are now largely non-preferential, including in their services provisions. However, those services provision that do more than bind the *status quo* (or in many cases, less than the *status quo*) are largely preferential. For example, see the recent evidence on the ASEAN Framework Agreement on Services in Chapter 14, as well as in Dee (2013c).

foreign *demandeurs* would want reforms in a sequence that was in the best interests of the home country. The final section of that chapter is subtitled 'Back to Basics — Services Trade Liberalization as Domestic Microeconomic Reform'. This was again influenced by my experience at the Australian Productivity Commission where, by the 1990s, the economic debate had turned from at-the-border to behind-the-border issues, particularly in infrastructure services industries. Looking at Australia's catalogue of unilateral microeconomic reforms through a GATS lens, we found that the reforms were overwhelmingly about market access and domestic reform, rather than national treatment. This gave us a strong hint of the necessity of treating services trade liberalization within a broader domestic microeconomic reform context.

The arguments for why there are so few gains from reciprocity in services are developed further in Chapter 9. This also elaborates how political economy considerations and GATS architecture (specifically, a request-and-offer negotiating modality) contribute to services trade negotiations being conducted primarily on an 'us and them' basis. Our prognosis at the time was that services negotiations were unlikely to be a deal-maker in the Doha Round when there were so many reasons for them to be seen as a negative-sum game. As my co-author wrote, the question then was not what services could do for the WTO and its negotiations, but what the WTO and its principles could do for services reform. A suggested answer is offered in the next section.

So much for arguments about why there is so little progress on services in trade negotiations — what about the evidence? My first survey of the available evidence on (a) whether the services provisions of FTAs are GATS-plus, and (b) whether they do anything more than simply bind the *status quo*, is shown in Chapter 10. A more recent survey is included as part of Chapter 14. As summarized recently by Francois and Hoekman (2010), the answer is that with the possible exception of the EU, most services policy reform has been unilateral. If trade negotiations were going to contribute positively, they would have focused on the non-discriminatory restrictions on market access, both to minimize the chances of second-best welfare losses, and to counter the political economy fears about the crowding out of domestic activity

(Chapter 11).[6] Yet by and large, trade negotiations have not done this, so the useful work has been done unilaterally.

1.4 How to Achieve Services Trade Reform in Future

I have sometimes characterized the removal of non-discriminatory restrictions on market access as 'easy' in political economy terms (or easier than focusing on national treatment), because it can counter the political economy fears about crowding out domestic activity. Yet that is not the whole story, because removing non-discriminatory restrictions on market access will threaten the vested interests of incumbent services suppliers. In some countries, these are the most powerful vested interests of all.

It is not enough to say that services trade reform is a domestic issue, and leave it at that. The critical next question is what can possibly help policy makers to counter the powerful vested interests that stand in the way of domestic services reform? That is the topic of the last three chapters of this volume.

Again, my background at the Australian Productivity Commission is relevant. That organization has played a powerful albeit indirect influence over the years in shaping the Australian debate in favour of domestic reform. And while its institutional model has been successfully exported to New Zealand, our near neighbour in many senses of the word, it is unlikely that the model can be exported to other countries whose current political systems and institutional structures reflect a rather different history. But can it be home-grown? With the encouragement of Peter Drysdale of the Australian National University, I started to 'deconstruct' the Productivity Commission model to see whether (a) elements of its success could be found embodied in existing institutions in other countries, and (b) whether those elements could in turn account for some of the success in implementing reforms in those countries.

---

[6] Note that there is no safeguard mechanism for services in the GATS. Nor would it help, for while it would guard against crowding out, it would do little to discourage the 'us and them' approach to negotiations.

Those efforts, and the thinking behind them, are summarized in Chapter 12 (for East Asia) and Chapter 13 (for South Asia). The hypothesis is that a critical element in reform success is a policy review process (structured, *ad hoc* or even accidental) that is independent, takes an economy-wide view, and operates so that the debates among stakeholders are carried out publicly, rather than behind closed doors. The process is important not just for the *technical solution* it may provide. It is also a *strategy* to deal with vested interests, by exposing their special pleading and providing a forum in which countervailing interests can marshal on a self-selected basis. Such processes have been found to contribute to reform action in both East and South Asia. The two studies (Dee 2010a, 2012a) also discuss how regional forums can help to strengthen indigenous capacities for such policy reviews.

What about the EU? Surely this is an example of a trade agreement that has delivered services policy reform? My legal co-author of Chapter 14 argues that the EU is far from a trade agreement in the conventional sense — it is a *sui generis* legal system. And the enforcement mechanisms used by the European Court of Justice clearly played a significant role in promoting domestic reform within the EU. But those mechanisms are not unique — the WTO Appellate Body has somewhat similar powers and functions. Instead, what we find in Chapter 14 is that the EU's success was because *domestic* constituents were empowered to take action against uncompetitive regulation. Thus the EU promoted economic reform in sensitive, behind-the-border areas because it overcame the problem of loss of sovereignty by internalizing the political battle to domestic interests, and yet still provided a non-political frame of reference for the debate. This is precisely the role that has been played in Australia by the Productivity Commission.

Returning to the question posed at the end of Chapter 9, what can the WTO (or trade agreements generally) and their principles do for services reform? And what is the future role of the WTO in behind-the-border issues more generally? The question is more critical now that the Doha Round is moribund.

I do not think that the answer lies in extending the WTO negotiating mandate to a deeper or broader set of behind-the-border issues. The experience to date with services trade reform demonstrates that when such issues are dealt with in a trade negotiating framework, they are typically dealt with on an 'us and them' basis, and this is not conducive to fundamental reform. This situation is not likely to change in the future, for the following reason.

In much of East and South Asia, some of the biggest economic problems currently are caused by the poor economic performance of incumbent services suppliers, which are often State-owned. Their dominance and lack of competitiveness is a drag on economic growth and a source of structural imbalances. In least developed countries, their performance is often a barrier to entry into regional production networks, because many of the incumbents operate in key parts of the logistics chain. The privileged position of incumbents has often been established by political corruption of various kinds, and the maintenance of their position elicits and encourages further corruption on an ongoing basis. Their crowding out of other domestic activity, including small and medium enterprises (either directly or through their privileged access to credit), is a key source of growing inequality.

Will trade negotiations help? The difficulty remains that trading partners have an interest in getting a slice of the incumbents' action, but not necessarily in unleashing the full forces of domestic competition.[7] Are these trade partners likely to forgo short-term national interests in the future in order to help these countries promote deeper reform and hence generate greater global gains? While there are a few hopeful signs, the overall track record in forums ranging from Doha negotiations (on trade) to Kyoto negotiations (on climate change) is not good.[8]

The best strategy for many developing countries may therefore be to delay trade negotiations in services while they get their domestic houses in order. This will require deep domestic reforms that establish the conditions for contestability more generally. Only once those conditions are established will it be in the interests of these countries to return to the

---

[7] Indirect evidence of this is the finding by Huang (2005) that foreign firms enjoy significant regulatory advantages (as perceived by the firms themselves) over domestic firms.

[8] As noted in Chapter 10, one apparently hopeful sign is the recent recommitment to the most-favoured nation principle in the trade policy announcement of the Australian Government (DFAT 2011).

trade negotiating table to trade concessions on national treatment. While Baldwin (2011) is correct to argue that the basic bargain of 21st century trade agreements is 'foreign investment for domestic reforms' rather than 'exchange of market access', the point here is that for behind-the-border reforms, the sequence matters.[9]

Key to these countries winning the argument domestically against incumbents will be to understand the benefits of such reforms to other domestic producers up and down the production chain (as is often argued in the context of 'trade facilitation'), and to use these arguments to marshal domestic countervailing interests. It is certainly true that in the 21st century world of product (and service) fragmentation and global production networks, where domestic and foreign economic activities are complements rather than substitutes, there will be foreign goods and/or services suppliers who will also benefit from the domestic services reforms. However, though economic activity has been globalized, politics has not — the political economy pressures that will work are still primarily domestic.[10]

What are trade negotiating forums to do in the meantime? That critical question requires concerted leadership now, because otherwise the path of benign neglect is likely to lead to serious erosion of the most basic principle that has vouchsafed open markets — the most-favoured nation principle. That principle has already been seriously compromised by the proliferation of FTAs, and there is a danger that post-Doha developments will deliver a *coup de grâce*. There is general agreement that a 'single undertaking' approach is dead. This implies that in future, the WTO could oversee single-issue agreements at the multilateral level, although in all likelihood those agreements will also be plurilateral in the first instance. The WTO Agreement on Government Procurement is an existing example of such an agreement — it is both plurilateral and preferential. In the current discussions about a WTO plurilateral

---

[9] The sequencing issue is essentially the same as for the privatization of government-owned monopolies. In fact, Baldwin's statement of the 21st century bargain is 'foreign factories for domestic reforms' — his arguments are almost exclusively about merchandise trade. Yet the biggest requirements for foreign direct investment in much of East Asia and virtually all of South Asia are now in infrastructure.

[10] It is ultimately because politics has not been globalized that when services reform is negotiated, the negotiations are done on an 'us and them' basis.

agreement on services, there is again pressure in some circles for this to be preferential. A pattern is already being set.

Is the most-favoured nation principle worth preserving when it comes to behind-the-border issues? Its economic value arises when unequal treatment of different trading partners would lead to allocative efficiency losses. Such losses can arise when regulatory barriers create rents, but not when they create deadweight costs.[11] As noted by Mattoo and Sauvé (2010), among others, removing a deadweight cost is always beneficial, even when it is done on a preferential basis. Yet barriers to competition can and do create rents. And when reform is preferential, it is partial; when it is partial, there is scope for rents to remain.[12]

The most-favoured nation principle also carries political implications. Those countries that are not currently ready to negotiate on behind-the-border issues urgently need to consider what global trading rules they would like to see prevail by the time they are ready to return to the negotiating table. If the most-favoured nation principle has been substantially abandoned in the meantime, then their return to the negotiating table will essentially imply a negotiating task equivalent to a WTO accession, irrespective of what economic efficiency losses might have accrued in the meantime. Furthermore, they will be acceding to a mish-mash of regulatory outcomes they will have had no role in establishing. Conversely, those countries that are currently ready to negotiate on behind-the-border issues need to consider whether it is really in their own long-term interests to negotiate in a way that makes it difficult if not impossible for third parties to return to the table at all. These issues play right into the current global realignments of political as well as economic power.

The argument for forging ahead with preferential plurilaterals is that it is the only basis on which trade agreements can be concluded currently. But the question is whether it is better to make agreements at the expense of WTO principles, or to maintain the principles, even if this

---

[11] The economic losses from trade diversion essentially arise because economic rents (normally tariff revenue) are passed from the preference-granting country to its preferential partner.

[12] For example, recent evidence is that while rents might have been partly squeezed out of banking markets (Dinh 2013), they persist in insurance (Dee and Dinh 2013).

implies a temporary hiatus in agreement-making while unilateral reform temporarily carries the load.[13] And in the meantime, the WTO dispute settlement process can only continue its valuable enforcement role if the principles it is enforcing are upheld; if they are diluted, its role collapses.

If concerted leadership can be brought to bear to maintain the most-favoured nation principle as the basis for any future WTO-based single-issue trade negotiations, and no such negotiations therefore take place, this does not imply that the WTO has nothing else to do. It could explore the possibilities for developing new pro-competitive regulatory *principles* that would be relevant for behind-the-border issues.

In services, the regulatory issues fall into three broad categories — competition and access issues relevant for network infrastructure industries, prudential issues relevant for financial industries, and quality control and equity issues relevant for social infrastructure industries (eg health, education). Prudential issues are dealt with in other forums, but the WTO could develop additional regulatory principles in the other two areas. The WTO reference paper on telecommunications is an example of a set of regulatory principles that has already been developed in the WTO. This enshrines some broad basic principles of interconnectivity and access to essential facilities on cost-based and non-discriminatory terms. Such principles could be extended to other infrastructure industries with network characteristics (eg rail) or with high fixed costs (airports, maritime ports). Disciplines are also needed on quality control regimes in social infrastructure industries, along lines outlined in Dee (2013a).[14]

Both the WTO and regional forums could also explore how to contribute to regulatory transparency. Recent developments in the context of the EU Services Directive provide a model of what might be useful (McNaugton and Furlong 2008). The EU has recently undertaken a mutual evaluation process in which member states have had an

---

[13] As noted in Chapter 14, Pauwelyn (2005) argues cogently that the bicycle theory of trade negotiations does not apply to behind-the-border issues.

[14] Similarly Baldwin (2011) has identified four types of 21st century barriers that might be the subject of WTO rule-making — competition policy, movement of capital, intellectual property rights and investment assurances. Note that three of these, along with the movement of people, are already elements of the services agenda.

opportunity to evaluate their own and others' services regulations against the EU's core regulatory principles — non-discrimination, necessity and proportionality. The EU has then begun a series of performance checks, in which a single hypothetical cross-border services transaction is defined, and regulators in various countries are asked to examine how all the EU regulation relevant to that transaction would impinge on it. This is an exercise in checking regulatory coherence in a globalized world. These developments would be worth monitoring to assess the usefulness of adapting them elsewhere.

Looking ahead to the types of trade negotiations that might take place when developing countries are ready to return to the negotiating table, a final issue that needs reconsideration is the way in which WTO Members give credit for 'autonomous' (ie unilateral) liberalization. The non-solution arrived at for services as part of the Doha Round is that credit would be negotiated. Clearly once the sunk costs of unilateral reform are incurred, the scope for opportunism by trading partners is enormous. Especially if it is not possible to get agreement on preserving the most-favoured nation principle in any post-Doha trade negotiations, granting credit for unilateral reform *as it occurs* in a type of tally process, to be cashed in when negotiations occur, would make it substantially easier for the emerging countries undertaking the unilateral reforms to return to the negotiating table at a later stage. If the WTO had developed additional regulatory principles in the meantime, these could in turn define the types of unilateral reforms to which credit would accrue. The granting of credit would give *all* countries a stake in developing the principles, even if not all are ready to commit to them.

Part 1

Model Frameworks

Chapter 2

Issues in the Application of CGE Models to Services Trade Liberalization[1]

Philippa Dee, Alexis Hardin and Leanne Holmes

2.1 Introduction

One of the distinguishing features of the General Agreement on Trade in Services (GATS), the key forum for multilateral liberalization of services trade, is the inclusion of commercial presence as a mode of service delivery. The other modes — cross-border supply, consumption abroad and temporary movement of people — all result in trade transactions that are captured, albeit imperfectly, in balance of payments accounts, on which the services trade structures of existing computable general equilibrium (CGE) trade models are based. Commercial presence does not. It represents a mode of delivery that would need to be added explicitly to most existing model structures. This is the first challenge in the application of CGE models to services trade liberalization.

The second challenge, highlighted in Holmes and Hardin (2000), is how to characterize the non-discriminatory restrictions on market access and the discriminatory restrictions on national treatment that apply to services trade. What are the appropriate tax or tariff equivalents of these restrictions, on what production or trade flows should they apply, and

---

[1] First published as Chapter 16 in Christopher Findlay and Tony Warren (2000), *Impediments to Trade in Services: Measurement and Policy Implications*, London and New York: Routledge: 267–86.

who gets the rents? Only once these issues have been decided can CGE models be used to analyse the impact of services trade liberalization, via the reduction or elimination of these tax or tariff equivalents.

2.2   Past Modelling of Services Trade and Foreign Direct Investment

Model frameworks

Only a few attempts have been made to model the impacts of liberalizing investment in a general equilibrium framework. The approaches adopted in these studies can be divided broadly into three groups. The first group does not model foreign direct investment (FDI) explicitly but, when examining the impact of services trade liberalization, it implicitly includes the reduction of FDI barriers. The second group of studies does not explicitly model FDI or the reduction of investment barriers; it simulates the effects of investment liberalization by making assumptions about the variables that increased capital mobility may affect. The third group explicitly models FDI and captures many of the important characteristics of FDI that are not included in the other studies. While the approaches of the third group have some shortcomings, they provide a sound basis for examining the implications of investment liberalization for Australia.

The first group of studies includes those that use Hoekman's (1995) estimates of tariff equivalents to examine the impacts of services trade liberalization (see, for example, Brown *et al.* 1995, Brown, Deardorff, Fox and Stern 1996, Dee *et al.* 1996). These estimates include barriers to services traded cross-border, via the temporary movement of people and via FDI. Therefore, estimating the impacts of reducing these tariff equivalents necessarily includes the reduction of barriers to FDI. There are a number of problems with this approach, the most important being that the models do not capture the important economic characteristics of FDI. For example, foreign-owned firms typically benefit from their parents' firm-specific assets. Hence, the demand and production characteristics of foreign affiliates need to be modelled as distinct activities from other production activities in both the host and home economies.

A good example in the first group is Brown, Deardorff, Fox and Stern (1996) who model trade liberalization in services under various assumptions using a general equilibrium framework. The authors argue that the movement of factors from the exporting country to the importing country, as in FDI, to provide a service does not pose a problem within their model. Such factors are still part of the home country's factor markets, and the fact that they happen to be located abroad should not matter for the determination of the various market equilibria.

This approach to modelling FDI liberalization has some appeal as it does not require a restructuring of most general equilibrium models. Barriers to FDI are combined with barriers to services traded cross-border and removing them results in cheaper services and increased services trade for the liberalizing economy.

However, the possible benefits of FDI and its role in services trade are not modelled, so important effects such as the scope for foreign varieties of non-tradable services to be consumed in the host country via FDI are not captured. Furthermore, this approach requires that services traded via FDI are included in the initial database as exports and imports of services in each region. This is not usually the case in general equilibrium models. Brown, Deardorff, Fox and Stern (1996) use balance of payments data to assemble their services database. As noted, these data do not capture the value of services traded through FDI. This means that, although barriers to FDI are being removed as part of services trade liberalization, the original levels of services traded fail to include services traded through FDI.

The authors note that they do not take account of changes in FDI that might occur as a result of changes in the rate of return on capital. Therefore, removing impediments to FDI does not result in higher levels of FDI in the liberalization country as would be expected. An additional problem raised by Brown, Deardorff, Fox and Stern (1996) is their assumption that all factors of production are regarded as participating in the factor markets of their country of origin. Often services traded via FDI require factors to be employed from the importing country's factor markets. For example, most foreign subsidiaries are staffed, at least to some extent, with local labour. This will matter for the effects of trade on the economies involved.

In the second group of studies, FDI is not modelled explicitly and barriers to FDI are not incorporated explicitly. Investment liberalization is assumed to affect certain variables, such as the extent of capital mobility, and the effects of this are then simulated, For example, Bora and Guisinger (1997) use a general equilibrium model that incorporates international capital mobility. No distinction is made between portfolio investment and FDI. Investment liberalization is modelled as increasing capital inflows to liberalizing economies by varying degrees.

Donovan and Mai (1996) use the MEGABARE model to estimate the effects of trade liberalization under standard and high degrees of capital mobility. They assume that removing investment barriers will result in increased capital mobility. No distinction is made between portfolio investment and FDI. Investment in their model is a function of the differential between national and global rates of return. The parameter that determines the responsiveness of investment to changes in rates of return is initially set to achieve a plausible pattern of international capital flows. To represent a more liberal investment regime, the degree of capital mobility in the model is increased fourfold over the standard value.

McKibbin and Wilcoxen (1996) also allow international capital mobility in their general equilibrium model: G-Cubed. However, they do not attempt to model the impact of investment liberalization directly. Instead, they examine the impact of a rise in total factor productivity in the services sector, which they consider a plausible side effect of trade liberalization in services in the context of the GATS. While FDI is not included explicitly in the model, the economy-wide data presumably cover the activities of both domestic and foreign firms. Therefore, the productivity of both domestic and foreign firms operating in the domestic economy is assumed to increase as a result of services trade liberalization. The improved performance of services results in resources being channelled into that sector. These resources come from other sectors in the economy as well as from overseas. The increase in return to capital in the services sector leads to an inflow of foreign financial capital into physical investment in the liberalizing economy.

The third group of studies overcomes many of the problems discussed above by incorporating FDI into a general equilibrium model in a way consistent with theoretical work. The main feature of these models is that they recognize the links between parents and foreign affiliates, and they differentiate between foreign and domestic firms within a given region.

The first of these studies, Markusen *et al.* (1995), compares the impact of trade liberalization with and without multinational firms in an industry with increasing returns to scale and imperfect competition. The models are applied to the North American (Canada, Mexico and the United States) auto market, with the rest of the world supply explicitly modelled and endogenous. While the scope of this study is narrow and does not include investment liberalization, their methodology and results are useful when considering how to model the role of FDI and the effects of reducing barriers to it.

The principal difference between their model with multinational firms and that with only national firms is the response of a firm's market share to trade liberalization. In the multinational model, a firm's US market share includes imports from its branch plants in Canada and Mexico. Thus, additional cars imported from Mexico to the United States constitute an increase in the combined market share of US firms because the Mexican exporter is US-owned. Other general equilibrium models ignore multinationality (or FDI) and impose an assumption that a firm's domestic production equals its market share. In the national model, a car imported into the United States from Mexico constitutes an erosion of the US firm's market share.

Therefore, holding rest-of-world imports constant, an import from Mexico in the multinational model lowers the North American firm's perceived elasticity of demand and raises its markup. The same import in the national model raises the North American firm's perceived elasticity of demand and lowers its markup. Markusen *et al.* (1995) therefore hypothesize that the presence of multinational firms, or FDI, reduces the benefits of trade liberalization.

It is important to note that the results of this study are dependent on the assumption that multinational firms coordinate price and quantity decisions across markets to maximize global rather than regional profits. It is not clear whether this is generally the case in services markets or if some foreign affiliates make their own price and output decisions. Obviously, the extent of international coordination by multinationals will determine the relevance of the anti-competitive effects identified by Markusen and others and, therefore, the extent to which FDI affects trade liberalization.

The second study is more general in terms of incorporating FDI into a general equilibrium framework. Petri's (1997) model of FDI distinguishes between the activities of domestic and foreign-owned firms at the microeconomic level. Petri provides for production linkages between parents and subsidiaries. This is accomplished by identifying three types of requirements in the input structure — value-added inputs, inputs sourced from parents, and other intermediate inputs. Therefore, it overcomes the problem identified in Brown, Deardorff, Fox and Stern (1996) of assuming that all factors of production are from the country of origin.

The demand side of the model differs from the conventional approach. The Armington assumption that product varieties are differentiated by place of production is replaced with the assumption that they are differentiated by both country of ownership and place of production.[2] The resulting demand system means that foreign varieties are available not just as imports, but also as local purchases from the subsidiaries of foreign firms. Petri notes that an important economic implication is that FDI does not merely promote increased production of a commodity in the host country; it also changes how the products of that country enter world demand. The FDI mechanism has important implications for modelling services trade liberalization because it allows foreign varieties to be consumed in non-tradable sectors through the presence of foreign firms. This characteristic of FDI is not included in the first group of studies, which require all foreign products to be imported.

The allocation of capital across regions is modelled in an optimizing framework that allocates capital to the highest return activities, but also

---

[2] Petri's model does not capture product variety as a factor that affects consumer utility *per se*. However, increased choice is likely to be an important benefit of FDI liberalization.

takes into account investor preferences for a particular mix of investment instruments. The capital allocation function therefore relies not only on the investment's rate of return, but also on the investor's utility function, which minimizes risk. This is analogous to consumer choice among goods subject to a budget constraint and yields similar functions for relating investment allocations to asset prices. Thus, the allocation of capital between sectors and between domestic and foreign investments is not based on arbitrage conditions assuming perfect substitution, but on a constant elasticity of substitution (CES) formulation will less than perfect substitutability.

Treatment of services trade barriers

Petri models barriers to FDI as a tax on FDI profits. Therefore, such barriers affect the rate of return on FDI stocks and hence discourage FDI flows into the region imposing the barriers. Reducing or removing FDI barriers increases the returns to FDI stocks, which results in more foreign investment being allocated to the liberalizing country or region. As noted in Hardin and Holmes (1997), not all FDI restrictions are best treated as a tax on the returns to FDI. Nor does the search for high returns necessarily explain all of the motivations for undertaking FDI. Nevertheless, this approach to modelling barriers to FDI seems to be a reasonable place to start.

Many past studies (Brown *et al.* 1995, Brown, Deardorff, Fox and Stern 1996, Dee *et al.* 1996, Petri 1997) that attempt to estimate the impacts of services trade and/or investment liberalization have used tariff equivalents estimated by Hoekman (1995). These tariff equivalents were calculated on the basis of scheduled commitments under the GATS. Therefore, they include barriers that are applied on all four modes of supply identified by the GATS, including FDI. The limitations of these estimates are identified by Hoekman (1995) and are discussed in Holmes and Hardin (2000).

The implications of applying the estimated tariff equivalents to just services trade (as in Brown, Deardorff, Fox and Stern 1996), or just to FDI (as in Petri 1997), may not be important because the limitations of Hoekman's estimates mean that the results of the studies that use them provide only a very rough indication of the impacts of services and/or investment liberalization. Hoekman (1995) notes that care must be taken in allowing for a wide range of 'benchmark' tariff equivalents when the GATS-based tariff equivalents are used to model the impacts of liberalizing services trade. However, if modelling results are to provide insights into the role of FDI and the linkages between trade and investment liberalization, then FDI and barriers to it need to be modelled explicitly.

Studies that do not use Hoekman's tariff equivalent estimates have tended to use even more arbitrary measures of investment restrictions. For example, Bora and Guisinger (1997) model the impact of investment liberalization by varying the ratio of FDI flows to gross investment. Three cases are examined: high, medium and low. The high case involves doubling the 1995 ratio, the low case increases it by 30 per cent, while the middle case is between these two estimates. The authors do not distinguish between FDI and portfolio investment and do not allow for foreign firms in the domestic economy. Their results, therefore, reflect only the impact of a capital inflow on domestic firms. Donovan and Mai (1996) use a fourfold increase in the capital mobility parameter as a proxy for investment liberalization, because of the difficulties with quantifying investment barriers.

Data

Bilateral investment flows and stock data at a disaggregated industry level are available only for a few countries. Even data for services traded cross-border are weak compared with those on merchandise trade (see Box 2.1). The only study that attempts to incorporate FDI flows and stocks into a general equilibrium framework is Petri (1997). Other studies assume that services traded via FDI are incorporated in balance of payments data, or make use of more aggregated capital flow and stock data within the models.

Box 2.1   Services Data

The main source of data on trade in services is the balance of payments (BOP), which as many weaknesses. BOP statistics are often inconsistent between countries. For example, a user of BOP statistics cannot be certain that what is reported for exports of port services by country A consists of the same items reported as exports of port services by country B. Coverage of BOP statistics is also often incomplete. At virtually any level of aggregation, some nations may not report information on a certain item. This results in biased figures when data are added across countries to arrive at regional totals, and discrepancies when comparing world imports and exports for a category.

Information on trade by origin and destination is not available on a comparable and detailed basis. In general, the amount of detail or disaggregation for data on trade in services is very limited. Trade data on a volume basis are not available. This makes it very difficult to determine what proportion of growth in a category in a given year is due to inflation as opposed to improvements in quality.

Comparability of BOP statistics over time is difficult because methodologies and definitions employed by countries may vary between years. It is also difficult, if not impossible, to relate services trade statistics to domestic production and employment data. To some extent, this is because different countries include different items in various components of the current account. More important is that trade data are simply too aggregated, so that concordances have little meaning.

Finally, data on sales by foreign affiliates are excluded. BOP conventions imply that, if factors of production move to another country for a period longer than one year, a change of residency status is considered to have occurred. The output generated by such factors that is sold in the host market will no longer be registered as trade in the balance of payments.

Source: Hoekman (1995).

2.3   A Way Forward

The general equilibrium modelling framework developed by Petri (1997) captures some of the features of FDI identified in the theoretical literature that are important when examining the impacts of liberalization. Petri's framework recognizes that foreign-owned firms benefit from their parents' assets by modelling them as distinct from domestic-owned firms, both in terms of demand and production characteristics. Petri also allows foreign affiliates to be linked to parents through intermediate input flows. His model distinguishes between varieties produced by the foreign affiliate and those produced by domestic firms of the host economy or by subsidiaries of other parents.

As noted, reducing FDI barriers in Petri's model is equivalent to reducing taxes on the profits earned by foreign affiliates. As profits increase, foreign affiliates can offer lower prices to domestic consumers. Increased profits also attract FDI flows to the liberalizing economy, which increases competition and the demand for inputs from both the host and home economies. However, a more general treatment of barriers to services trade could be developed within his model framework. This is outlined in more detail below.

All of these links should be incorporated when modelling the impacts of FDI liberalization in the services sector. The inclusion of trans-border price and output coordination by multinationals, identified by Markusen *et al.* (1995), also needs to be considered. The relevance of multinational coordination will depend on the sectors and countries being analysed. It may be more likely to occur in the North American auto market (which Markusen *et al.* modelled) than for other types of FDI, such as that in services industries.

Petri notes a further interaction that is identified in the theory but not incorporated into his FDI model — the interaction between foreign affiliates and their host economy through various dynamic relationships, including externalities associated with scale or technological spillovers (see APEC 1996, and Blomström and Kokko 1997, for discussions of these effects). Also, Petri's model specification does not capture the benefits for consumers of increased product variety, which is likely to be an important outcome of FDI liberalization. The possibility of including these effects should also be examined.

Developing a global modelling framework similar to Petri's is a large task. Such a framework would nevertheless address many of the problems associated with earlier modelling of barriers to services trade. It would recognize the services traded by commercial presence as well as those traded via other modes of delivery. If the model recognized the different cost structures of foreign affiliates and allowed for economies of scale and product differentiation, it would capture at least some of the motivations for FDI stressed in the literature. And as outlined shortly, it would provide a framework within which there could be comprehensive coverage of the different types of barriers to services trade.

An alternative, smaller task may be to apply Petri's framework to a model of a single economy. This would allow the impact of FDI liberalization in that economy to be examined without requiring information for other individual regions. The microeconomic distinctions between domestic and foreign firms made by Petri would still have to be incorporated, although only for a single economy. A major drawback of this approach is the limitations a single economy model places on the liberalization scenarios that can be examined. Using a model of a single economy means that only unilateral FDI liberalization scenarios can be considered. While these scenarios will provide a starting point for examining FDI liberalization, useful policy results will require modelling multilateral FDI liberalization in the context of the GATS and other investment agreements.

Data

Limited FDI and services trade data continue to be major constraints on progress in modelling FDI liberalization. To model the gains from multilateral liberalization, data on bilateral investment stocks and flows are required, together with data on the value of services traded via FDI (as opposed to the other modes of supply, cross-border trade and the temporary movement of people), and data on the activities of foreign affiliates, so that their inputs and outputs can be distinguished from those of domestically-owned firms.

Petri has made some progress in addressing these data constraints by constructing a database showing the role of FDI in six broad regions and three sectors (agriculture, manufacturing and services), drawing on the 1992 Global Trade Analysis Project (GTAP) database (Hertel 1997) and detailed survey data for Japan and the United States. In addition, the GTAP project itself is undertaking a major upgrade of its conventional services trade data. However, considerable extensions to Petri's approach, involving further assumptions and estimates, would be required if the model were to be extended to more sectors and regions.

2.4   Incorporating Services Trade Barriers in Petri's Framework

A key characteristic of the Petri framework is that it expands the dimensionality of conventional multi-country, multi-sectoral CGE models. For example, in a conventional model such as GTAP, household demand would have a commodity–region–region dimension and capital stocks would have an industry–region dimension:

$x_h(i,s,d)$ demand by households in region d for commodity i from source region s

$k(j,d)$ capital stock in industry j in region d

By contrast, in the Petri framework, household demands would have a commodity–region–region–region dimension and capital stocks would have an industry–region–region dimension:

$x_h(i,s,h,d)$ demand by households in region d for commodity i from production facility located in host region s but owned by home country h[3]

$k(j,h,d)$ capital stock in production facility for industry j located in host region d but owned by home country h

Thus, capital located in a country might be domestic or foreign-owned, and would generate profit streams accruing to domestic and foreign owners. In principle, households in a country could purchase

---

[3] A complication to be grappled with at the level of both data and theory is that most foreign affiliates are not 100 per cent foreign-owned. In many countries, the minimum level of foreign control required for investment to be counted as direct rather than portfolio investment is as low as 10 per cent. However, incorporating this distinction at the theoretical level could involve modelling issues of corporate control, such as the trade-off between having a local partner with local knowledge, versus diluting foreign corporate control, which would be peripheral to issues of services trade liberalization.

from purely domestic firms, from foreign affiliates located at home or, via cross-border trade, from firms located offshore (including possibly the offshore affiliates of local firms). In practice, the nature of some services could make it hard to supply them via cross-border trade.

Household (as well as intermediate, investment and government) preferences among these different sources would be an important determinant of the ultimate mix of local provision, trade via commercial presence and trade via the other modes of supply. This would be captured through parameters specifying elasticities of substitution in demand between the various sources. The other key determinant would be the relative supply prices from these sources. These would be affected by the rates of return to capital required by investors in order to be willing to invest more in one location rather than another.

But each service flow, and each flow of profits, becomes a candidate for having a tax or tariff wedge attached to it to represent barriers to services trade.

The nature of barriers to services trade

How the barriers should be incorporated depends in part on how they have been estimated. The aim of many of the chapters in Findlay and Warren (2000) was to move beyond frequency-type measures of barriers to services trade, in order to obtain a price impact. Examples are the price estimates of the barriers to telecommunications trade in Trewin (2000), and the price estimates of the barriers to trade in banking services in Kalirajan *et al.* (2000). In the case of banking services, the estimated impact was on banks' net interest margins, a specific measure of the markup of 'price' over 'cost' for banks. Thus, at least for banking, the estimated price impact is precisely an estimate of the height of the 'rent rectangle'. But where should the rent rectangles be put?

The barriers to services trade can be subdivided in two dimensions. First, it is possible to distinguish barriers to establishment from barriers to ongoing operation (see, for example, Kang 2000 and Kalirajan *et al.* 2000). This is not quite the same as distinguishing barriers to commercial presence from barriers to other modes of services delivery since, as noted in Holmes and Hardin (2000), the barriers to commercial presence can themselves apply to establishment or to ongoing operation. But the distinction between barriers to setting up and barriers to ongoing operation is akin to Baldwin's (1999) distinction between barriers that raise the fixed costs of operating and those that raise the marginal costs. Barriers to establishment can be modelled as barriers to the movement of capital, and barriers to ongoing operation can be modelled as barriers on the services provided once the capital is established.[4]

Second, it is possible to distinguish barriers that discriminate against foreign suppliers (be they locally-based foreign affiliates or offshore suppliers) and those that affect domestic and foreign suppliers equally (eg Kang 2000 and Kalirajan *et al.* 2000). This is equivalent to the distinction between derogations from national treatment and restrictions on market access.

Now consider how this four-way classification of barriers can be incorporated into the Petri framework.

Restrictions on ongoing operation

Figures 2.1 and 2.2 show the restricted and unrestricted equilibriums in the market for a particular service in a particular region, indicating the impact of discriminatory and non-discriminatory barriers to ongoing operation. The panels distinguish the three sources of supply — from domestic firms, from locally-based offshore affiliates, and from offshore firms. Strictly speaking, in the Petri framework, these three sources of supply are imperfect substitutes in demand. However, the relevant elasticities of substitution are likely to be reasonable high, considering that they are capturing firm-level product differentiation (see Petri 1997 and also Francois and Shiells 1994). So, for the purpose of simplification, the diagram assumes perfect substitution on the demand side.

The left panel of Figure 2.1 shows total demand and the supply curve of domestic firms. The middle panel shows the resulting excess demand

---

[4] In common with some other frameworks (such as Dee *et al.* 1996), Petri's framework does not explicitly identify the fixed costs that might account for increasing returns to scale, even though it is broadly consistent with increasing returns and imperfect competition (see also Francois and Shiells 1994).

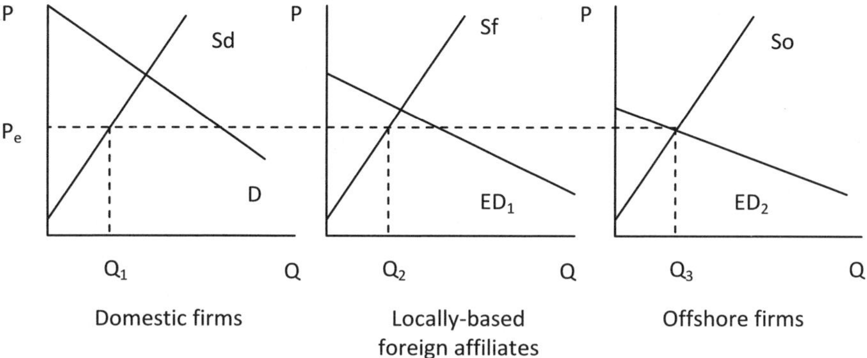

Figure 2.1.   Unrestricted Equilibrium for a Service

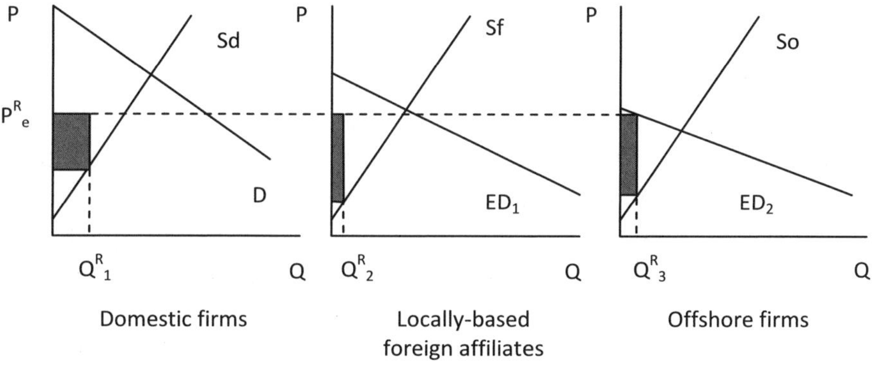

Figure 2.2.   Restricted Equilibrium for a Service

(the excess of total demand over the supply of domestic firms, taken from the left panel) and the supply curve of locally-based foreign affiliates. The right panel traces the excess demand taken from the middle panel, along with offshore supply. In the unrestricted equilibrium, the economy buys Q_1 from domestic firms, Q_2 from locally-based offshore affiliates, and Q_3 from offshore firms.

Figure 2.2 shows the corresponding restricted equilibrium, where discriminatory and non-discriminatory barriers to ongoing operation put a wedge between prices and costs of provision. Note that, because of the discriminatory restrictions, the wedge faced by locally-based foreign affiliates and offshore suppliers is higher than the wedge faced by domestic firms.

The restricted equilibrium price P^R_e is higher than the unrestricted equilibrium price P_e (compare the third panels of Figures 2.1 and 2.2), and both locally-based foreign affiliates and offshore firms unambiguously supply less in restricted than in unrestricted equilibrium. In the absence of any non-discriminatory restriction on domestic firms, they would unambiguously supply more under the restricted than the unrestricted equilibrium. But, if they face non-discriminatory restrictions of their own it depends whether the tax equivalent of these is sufficiently large to offset the advantage to domestic firms conferred by the discriminatory restrictions.

Thus, in a CGE context, the restrictions on ongoing operation faced by offshore firms selling in the local market can be modelled as a tariff equivalent. The restrictions faced by domestic firms and locally-based foreign affiliates can be modelled as a production tax equivalent on their operations. Both tariffs and production taxes put a wedge between the domestic price and the domestic or foreign cost of production. Note that using production taxes rather than consumption taxes assumes that any restrictions on ongoing operation would affect any exports made by domestic firms and by locally-based offshore affiliates, as well as their sales on the domestic market. Given the nature of the restrictions on ongoing operation in maritime, for example, this seems reasonable (see McGuire, Schuele and Smith 2000).

Restrictions on establishment

Figures 2.3 and 2.4 show the restricted and unrestricted equilibriums in the market for capital in a particular region, indicating the impact of discriminatory and non-discriminatory barriers to establishment. The left and right panels show, respectively, the supply and demand for local capital by domestic firms, and the supply and demand for foreign-owned capital by locally-based offshore affiliates. Since, in the Petri framework, these are two completely different types of firms, there is no necessary connection, at least in partial equilibrium, between demand for local and foreign capital. Similarly, domestic and foreign investors have preferences about the shares of their portfolios that they hold domestically and offshore, so there is no necessary connection, at least in partial equilibrium, between the supply of local and foreign capital (in contrast to perfect arbitrage models). Thus, in unrestricted equilibrium, there is no necessity for the rental prices of capital to equalize in the domestic firms and in the locally-based offshore affiliates (Figure 2.3).

Figure 2.4 shows the impact of discriminatory and non-discriminatory restrictions on establishment. Here the estimated impact of these restrictions on output prices has been converted (using capital–output ratios) to an equivalent impact on the rental price of capital. Because of

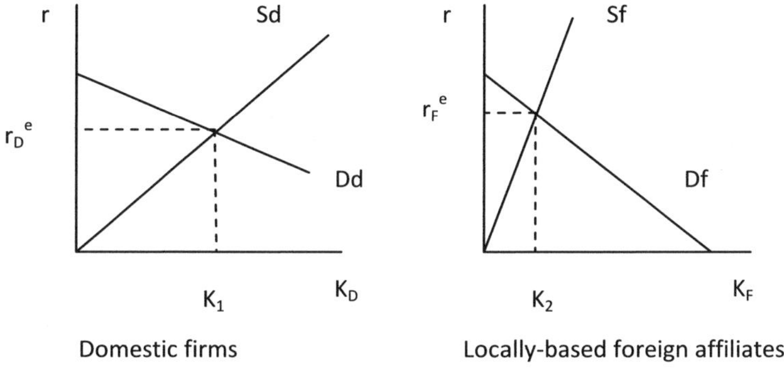

Figure 2.3.   Unrestricted Equilibrium for Capital

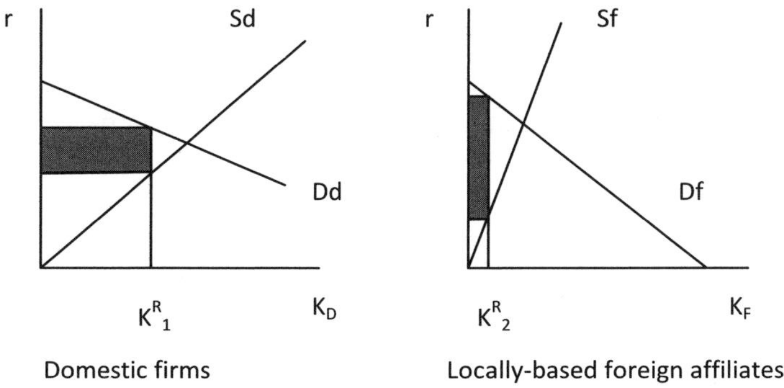

Figure 2.4.   Restricted Equilibrium for Capital

discriminatory restrictions, the wedge faced by locally-based offshore affiliates is larger than that faced by domestic firms.

It appears that the restrictions would lead unambiguously to less capital being used in both domestic firms and in locally-based offshore affiliates. However, this need not be the case once the effect on the 'output' market for the service is taken into account. If, because of discriminatory restrictions, locally-based offshore affiliates employ less capital and therefore offer fewer services, the demand faced by domestic firms would expand, moving their demand curve for capital to the right. Once these general equilibrium effects are taken into account, the story is likely to be the same as in Figure 2.2 — the impact on locally-based offshore affiliates is unambiguously negative, but the impact on local firms depends on whether the negative impact of non-discriminatory restrictions offsets the advantage conferred on them by discriminatory restrictions.

In a CGE context, the restrictions on establishment faced by domestic firms and locally-based foreign affiliates can be modelled as the equivalent of an income tax on capital.

Who gets the rents?

Who gets the rents depends on part on where they are generated. If the price impact of the restrictions to services trade has been estimated empirically by looking at the effects on some markup of price over cost (as in Kalirajan *et al.* 2000), the empirical work itself answers the question of where the rents are generated. This is the basis on which Figures 2.1 to 2.4 have been drawn, where the shaded areas in Figures 2.2 and 2.4 show the rents that are generated by the restrictions.[5]

---

[5] Note that, since in reality foreign affiliates are less than 100 per cent foreign-owned (and restrictions apply to the entire affiliate), a model that isolates FDI stocks into 'wholly foreign-owned' firms in its database and applies restrictions to those firms will understate the size of the rents generated by restrictions on foreign affiliates. Nevertheless, rescaling the size of the price wedge to generate the 'correct' levels of rents could overstate the allocative efficiency effects of the restrictions. Arguably, given the uncertainties associated with rent allocation in any event, the former treatment is preferable to the latter.

If the impact has been estimated by looking at prices alone, or costs alone, even the existence of rents is speculative — some restrictions may have raised prices by raising costs, with no clear impact on price–cost margins.

But rents can also be passed around, particularly by government mechanisms such as auctioning the rights to establish or operate, or by private mechanisms such as transfer pricing. The question of the ultimate beneficiary need not be the same as the question of where the rents are generated. Casual observation suggests that governments typically do not sell the rights to establish or operate in restricted service markets. By selling the rights, the rents from the restrictions would have been passed to governments. But this issue requires further research.

If governments do not acquire the rents by auction mechanisms, it seems natural to assume that they are retained by the firms in which they are generated and are then passed to their shareholders. But, to the extent that the rents show up in the taxable income of firms, governments may still acquire a portion. However, locally-based foreign affiliates may have the option of transferring the rents shown in the middle panel of Figure 2.2 and the right panel of Figure 2.4, along with other income, to their home country by transfer pricing — say, by inflating the price they pay their parent company for any intermediate inputs or headquarters services provided by the parent. A modelling decision would therefore still need to be made on which country, if any, the rents of foreign affiliates are taxed in. This question is also under-researched in a CGE context.

2.5   The Welfare Implications of Services Trade Liberalization

One of the truly great innovations introduced with the GTAP model framework was a mechanism for decomposing the welfare implications of trade liberalization scenarios, which can be highly complex, into a series of intuitive components (Huff and Hertel 1996, based on Keller 1980). So, even without having built a large Petri-style CGE model along the lines outlined, one can nevertheless anticipate what the welfare decomposition in such a model would look like, using the GTAP techniques, and try to anticipate the welfare effects of the sort of quantity responses to trade liberalization that were implicit in Figures 2.1 to 2.4.

GTAP welfare decomposition

The basic intuition of the GTAP decomposition is as follows. National income depends on real household consumption C, real government consumption G, and real national saving S. It is determined by the following maximization problem:

$$\text{Max } U(C,G,S) \text{ subject to } P_cC + P_gG + P_sS = \text{net national income} \quad (2.1)$$

If U takes a Cobb–Douglas form, then the equivalent variation (EV), which is a money measure of absolute changes in national utility, takes a particularly simple form:

$$EV = \text{scale term} * [nnp - p] \quad (2.2)$$

where nnp is the percentage change in net national income, and p is the percentage change in a price index that is itself a share weighted sum of percentage changes in P_c, P_g and P_s. In a model without FDI or other forms of international capital mobility, net national income is measured by factor income (net of depreciation) and total indirect tax receipts.

It turns out that a number of the standard zero pure profit and market clearing equations of a CGE model can be substituted into this expression for net national income, to yield a particularly useful decomposition of the EV measure:

$$\begin{aligned}
EV = \text{scale term}*[&TAX_1*q_1 + TAX_2*q_2 + \ldots + TAX_N*q_N \\
&+ \text{'terms of trade' effect} \\
&+ \text{'terms of saving and investment' effect} \\
&+ \text{contribution from endowment growth} \\
&+ \text{contribution from technical change} \\
&+ \text{terms from non-homotheticity of household preferences}] \quad (2.3)
\end{aligned}$$

The first terms, involving the product of an initial tax rate (TAX_i) and the percentage change in the quantity moving across that tax wedge (q_i), spell out the efficiency effects of trade liberalization. They measure the way in which the efficiency loss triangles, such as in Figures 2.2 and 2.4, would change as some or all of the trade taxes changed in a liberalization scenario.

Imagine a commodity or service that has a high production tax to start with, so that TAX_i is large and positive for that commodity. Economic theory would tell us that production of that commodity would be smaller than it would be in an undistorted equilibrium. Thus, any trade liberalization scenario that increased the quantity produced, so that q_i was positive, would move the economy closer to an undistorted equilibrium and contribute positively to national welfare (because $TAX_i{*}q_i$ would be positive). This could come about because this commodity was itself subject to liberalization, and the initial TAX_i was reduced as part of the scenario. But it could equally come about as an indirect result of liberalization elsewhere. If so, it would still contribute positively to overall welfare.

Now imagine a commodity or service that had a production subsidy to start with, so that TAX_i was negative. Production would be larger than in an undistorted equilibrium, and any liberalization scenario that reduced the quantity produced (so that q_i was negative) would also contribute positively to overall welfare (because $TAX_i{*}q_i$ would still be positive).

But the welfare decomposition also highlights the possibility of perverse welfare implications from trade liberalization scenarios. Suppose a commodity or service has a production tax in initial equilibrium, but that its quantity produced falls as a result of liberalization elsewhere in the economy. This might happen if taxes on close substitutes were eliminated as part of the liberalization scenario. This would contribute negatively to overall welfare (because $TAX_i{*}q_i$ would be negative). Thus, the welfare decomposition highlights quite explicitly possible dangers associated with partial liberalization, a topic that will be discussed further in the context of services trade liberalization below. It remains to explain briefly the remaining terms in the welfare decomposition, before explaining how it would change in the presence of FDI and other forms of international capital mobility.

The second term is a conventional 'terms of trade' effect, showing that when the price of something used to derive income (eg exports) rises relative to the price of something used to derive utility (eg imports), an economy enjoys a terms of trade improvement and this contributes positively to overall welfare. The 'terms of saving and investment' effect has a similar logic: when the price of something used to provide income (eg investment) rises relative to the price of something used to derive utility (eg saving), this also contributes positively to welfare.

The welfare decomposition also notes that, if capital stocks increase exogenously for some reason, this contributes directly to national utility. However, the normal non-static welfare decomposition for GTAP does not consider the question of how the increase in capital stocks comes about, or who finances it. This will be addressed shortly. The decomposition also notes that technical changes contribute directly to overall welfare. The final term in the decomposition arises because of the functional form of household preferences across commodities.

Incorporating FDI

Now consider how the welfare decomposition would change in the presence of FDI and other forms of international capital mobility. One way to view this would be to consider how the relevant definition of net national income would change. With international capital mobility, net national income would be the sum of total factor income (net of depreciation), total indirect tax receipts, net foreign dividend income from FDI, and net interest income from the issuing of bonds.

The last term would arise in a model that allowed each country to issue bonds internationally to finance its domestic investment and FDI. A model of international borrowing and lending was developed by McDougall (1993) and incorporated into the Salter (Jomini *et al.* 1994) and IC95 (Dee *et al.* 1996) models. A combined model of borrowing and FDI could have perfect international arbitrage on bond interest rates, while breaking the nexus between interest rates and rates of return on FDI, something that appears consistent with the empirical evidence (IC 1991).

With the definition of net national income altered in this way, the same derivations could be used to decompose the first two income terms. The amended definition would simply have the two additional income terms on the end:

$$EV = \text{scale term}*[TAX_1*q_1 + TAX_2*q_2 + \ldots + TAX_N*q_N$$
$$+ \text{ 'terms of trade' effect}$$
$$+ \text{ 'terms of saving and investment' effect}$$
$$+ \text{ contribution from endowment growth}$$
$$+ \text{ contribution from technical change}$$
$$+ \text{ terms from non-homotheticity of household preferences}$$
$$+ \text{ contribution from net income from FDI (including rents)}^6$$
$$+ \text{ contribution from net interest income]} \qquad (2.4)$$

Thus, the analysis of efficiency effects — the efficiency with which resources are deployed within an economy — would be the same as before. But there would be an additional consideration that the income generated within a country need not all accrue to the residents of that country. Experience with models such as Salter and IC95 suggests that the impact of net foreign income payments can alter the welfare implications of trade liberalization scenarios in important ways. This should not be surprising, since the rectangles in Figures 2.2 and 2.4 are typically larger than the triangles.

Principles of services trade liberalization

On the efficiency side, the results of services trade liberalization would depend again on the sizes and signs of the TAX_i*q_i terms. These terms suggest a number of possible principles of services trade liberalization.

In general terms, the greatest gains are to be had from liberalizing the most highly distorted sectors. These are the sectors where the TAX_i terms are the highest, and where the induced quantity responses q_i also tend to be the greatest.

---

[6] One complication for the welfare decomposition is that, while a dollar may be a dollar as far as net interest income is concerned, investors in the Petri framework have a preference for diversity in their FDI portfolios. This could be handled by modifying this net foreign dividend income term by a term reflecting investors' preference for diversity.

In the context of services trade liberalization, this suggests that the biggest gains would be achieved by removing discriminatory measures against foreign-based or foreign-owned suppliers. Because of the way distortions compound, a 10 per cent tax equivalent of a discriminatory barrier levied on top of a non-discriminatory barrier would yield higher welfare gains than eliminating a 10 per cent tax equivalent on its own. This is because, in the first case, the relevant TAX_i term would include the sum of the initial discriminatory and non-discriminatory barriers, and could be much higher than the 10 per cent.

In addition, reducing or eliminating the most highly distorted sectors usually helps to avoid the possibility of perverse second-best welfare effects. This has been explored by Dee *et al.* (1998) in the context of APEC's early voluntary sectoral liberalization initiatives.

Consider the liberalization of discriminatory barriers to services trade in the context of Figure 2.2. The 'tax' wedge on locally-based foreign affiliates and offshore firms would be reduced so as to equal the wedge on domestic firms. The equilibrium price P^R_e would fall slightly, and output of the locally-based foreign affiliates and offshore firms would expand, contributing positively to welfare. But output of domestic firms would contract slightly (because of the fall in P^R_e), contributing negatively to welfare. Thus, the removal of discriminatory restrictions could lead to a 'perverse' contribution from domestic firms. Because domestic firms face a smaller 'tax' wedge to start with, this perverse effect is unlikely to dominate. However, this possibility suggests that, for services, an across-the-board approach to liberalization may be better than a top-down approach.

The same principles can be used to consider which services sectors to liberalize first, as well as to consider the priority to be attached to services trade liberalization as a whole, relative to liberalization in other sectors.

The tax or tariff equivalents of barriers to trade in banking services appear to be as high as 60 per cent (Kalirajan *et al.* 2000). The tax or tariff equivalents of barriers to trade in telecommunications services are up to 50 per cent in developed countries (Warren 2000). These estimates are higher than most remaining tariffs in manufacturing, though lower than remaining protection in many areas of agriculture. This confirms the priority to be attached to the forthcoming GATS negotiations, along with further progress on agriculture. The relative sizes of the barriers among services sectors can also be used to prioritize negotiations within the GATS.

This discussion has been based primarily on efficiency effects. But there is still the question of the contributions to welfare of changes in the size of international income transfers, via the net returns to FDI and net interest income. This is difficult to assess without having built a CGE model of the type outlined in this chapter, to analyse empirically the impact of various services trade liberalization scenarios.

Chapter 3

Modelling the Policy Issues in Services Trade[1]

Philippa Dee

3.1 Why Worry?

Why should trade theorists and trade policy practitioners worry about services?

The answers are compelling:

- 60 per cent of the world's GDP is earned there (World Bank 2001);
- close to a third of world trade is generated there (Karsenty 2000);
- as will be shown, barriers to services trade are significant;[2] and
- services trade barriers are currently subject to negotiation in both multilateral and regional forums.

So it is incumbent on both trade theorists and trade policy practitioners to understand the nature of services, trade in services and services trade barriers. The aim should not just be to identify theoretical possibilities. It should also be to identify negotiating priorities, so as to maximize net benefits and reduce unintended consequences in a policy area that is still, sadly, largely unchartered territory empirically. With services sectors being large in most economies, the downside risk from

---

[1] First published in *Économie Internationale* (2003), 'Modelling the Policy Issues in Services Trade, 94–95: 283–300.

[2] Dee and Hanslow (2001) suggest that the global gains from eliminating barriers to trade in services, based on preliminary estimates of those barriers, could be about the same as those from eliminating all remaining barriers to trade in agriculture and industrials.

47

getting it wrong is significant, and the risk is certainly there (eg Dee, Hardin and Holmes 2000, Francois and Wooten 2001).

What follows is a discussion of these issues from the perspective of an empirical trade policy modeller who works in a policy advisory organization and who borrows (probably not enough) from trade theorists. The discussion may therefore miss some theoretical issues and contributions, but to compensate, will include data and parameter issues that could nevertheless use some input from trade theorists.

3.2   What is Special about Services?

These days, a trade theorist might say there is surprisingly little that is special about services. It is now commonplace to treat both manufactures and services as having increasing returns to scale, firm-level product differentiation and Dixit–Stiglitz preferences among firms (eg Francois, 1990, the survey by Markusen 1995, Markusen *et al.* 1999, Brown *et al.* 2000),[3] with only the interpretations sometimes differing about the source of the firm-level product differentiation and the nature of the fixed costs producing the economies of scale. Only the agricultural sector is routinely treated, in theoretical models at least, as being a constant returns to scale, homogeneous product industry. But perhaps this has as much to do with needing a simple mechanism to pin down returns to sectorally mobile factors as it has to do with reality in a world where agricultural policy issues now include genetic engineering, varietal property rights and geographical indications.

Ethier and Horn (1991) identified one characteristic that seemed to be special about services — many were customized to the needs of individual purchasers. This is one level of product differentiation below that now included in most trade models. Brown, Deardorff and Stern (1996, p. 21) stated

> We do view this as a potentially critical property of services for the effects of their international trade, although at the present time it does not seem possible to incorporate this property into any formal empirical analysis.

---

[3] Francois, McDonald and Nordstrom (1995) show how this treatment is close to the Armington preference structures in conventional computable general equilibrium models.

I am not aware of any subsequent analysis that has included this characteristic explicitly, but it seems to be implicit in the choice of nesting structure of demand for varieties in some more recent models of services trade. This issue is discussed below.

3.3   What is Special About Services Trade?

There is one characteristic of services trade policy that is special, and is starting to influence the way that services trade itself is modelled. That characteristic is the formal recognition within the World Trade Organization (WTO) of commercial presence as a method by which services are traded.

Although there has been little progress in achieving multilateral or plurilateral agreement on liberalizing barriers to foreign direct investment (FDI) generally, there has been progress in setting up a multilateral mechanism to liberalize FDI in services. That mechanism is the General Agreement on Trade in Services (GATS) under the WTO. The GATS is set up to liberalize trade in services, and it formally recognizes commercial presence, along with three other modes (cross-border trade, consumption abroad, and the movement of natural persons), as a method by which services are traded. Regional Trade Agreements are also increasingly including provisions to liberalize services and FDI.

So comprehensive modelling of services trade policy now needs to take into account liberalization of FDI in services as well as liberalization of other modes of services delivery.

At a theoretical level, this means that models need to distinguish the ownership of services activity from the location of that activity. The remainder of this section discusses some of the theoretical, data and parameter issues involved in modelling that distinction, while the next section looks at the issue of getting credible measures of the extent of barriers to FDI and conventional trade in services.

Theoretical issues in modelling ownership and location

By happy coincidence, many of the features required to model the location of economic activity were already being built into both analytical and empirical models of services trade via the recognition of increasing returns to scale and firm-level product differentiation, along with transport costs and the corresponding home market effect. Indeed, some of us who built increasing returns to scale into conventional computable general equilibrium (CGE) models that already had international capital mobility and an extensive treatment of tariffs and transport costs were unaware that we were adding 'economic geography' to our models until Paul Krugman (1991, 1998) told us so!

But in models that differentiate the ownership and location of economic activity, a number of seemingly innocuous modelling choices can sometimes have alarming effects on model results.

Are economies of scale regional?

One early choice is whether the economies of scale in services are regional or global.[4] In treatments that assume large group monopolistic competition, where the equilibrium mark-up of price over marginal cost is directly related to the extent of product differentiation, this boils down to the same thing (although Neary (2001) argues that perhaps it shouldn't) as whether domestic and foreign firms, although differentiated, are perfect substitutes at the margin. Equivalently, do all firms appear in a single nest in the preference functions, or are there multiple nests with different elasticities of substitution at each node? If economies of scale are global, they will obviously be much stronger than if they are regional.

Francois, McDonald and Nordstom (1995) argued that for manufactures, economies of scale should be seen as global. Although a Honda Civic may not be a perfect substitute for a Ford Fiesta, consumers the world over would feel equally better off whether it was a Fiesta or a Civic that was added to their choice set. And the extent to which economies of scale in production could be exploited would depend on

---

[4] The possibility of global economies of scale was first noted by Ethier (1982).

the global, not regional, sales of Civics or Fiestas. One way to rationalize this is to see the fixed costs of production, such as research and development and other 'headquarters' services, as being incurred at a single, global headquarters. Increased sales anywhere in the world could help to defray the centralized fixed costs.

As Ethier and Horn (1991) noted, services are often customized to the needs of individual purchasers. Although this appears never to have been modelled explicitly, it is easy to think of service firms who want to do this as needing to incur fixed costs to learn about either the regional characteristics of the individuals they are serving, or the regional regulatory frameworks in which they are operating. For example, accounting firms would need to invest in learning about the tax laws in the countries in which they were operating. In models where accounting firms could set up regional offices, and where those regional offices operated as separate profit centres, the fixed costs of acquiring regional knowledge would be offset against regional, not global sales. And from a customer's perspective, accounting firms that had not invested in regional knowledge would not be viewed as being perfect substitutes at the margin.

This was the thinking behind treating economies of scale as regional rather than global in Dee and Hanslow (2001).[5] Similar thinking seems to have been at play in Markusen, Rutherford and Tarr (1999). It would be interesting to see whether the relationship between regional economies of scale and Ethier and Horn's insight could be worked out formally, or whether the heuristic is a poor one and should be dispensed with. One question begged in the process, however, is whether regional service firms do indeed operate as separate profit centres. Markusen, Rutherford and Hunter (1995) offer a forceful example of how the welfare effects of trade liberalization can differ when firms instead coordinate their decision-making across regional locations.

---

[5] In fact, Dee and Hanslow (2001) treated economies of scale as regional in all sectors, based on the observation that even commodities such as Toyota Camrys and McDonalds hamburgers are often customized to meet regional tastes.

Is McDonalds the same the world over?

Since it would seem to make sense to allow the strength of substitution to vary by ownership and location, one way to do this is to 'nest' the preference structure, so that customers (either households, or firms purchasing the services as intermediate inputs, or both) choose across locations and then across places of ownership, or vice versa.

The key question here is which way round it should be. Unless the model builder wants to incorporate complementarity indirectly into their model, the nests should be ordered in increasing order of elasticity of substitution.

Petri (1997) had one of the pioneering empirical treatments of services traded both cross-border and via FDI. He modelled customers as first choosing among ownership categories, then among locations. This treatment assumes that in any given sector, individual US owned firms are closer substitutes for each other than for Australian firms, irrespective of location.

By contrast, Dee and Hanslow (2001) assumed that customers choose among locations and then among ownership categories. From an Australian perspective, a US multinational located in Australia is a closer substitute for an Australian owned firm than it is for a US firm located in the United States — McDonalds is not the same the world over.[6]

A key reason for their choice was that Petri's treatment produced a model in which multilateral liberalization of tariffs on manufactured goods produced large economic welfare losses, for most individual economies and for the world as a whole — an uncomfortable result at odds with conventional trade theory.

> Depending on relative shares, there is no guarantee that the price of the US aggregate would be dominated by the removal of the tariff on imports, rather than by endogenous changes in the cost structure of US multinationals in Australia. Simulations with a model of this structure showed that the price of the US aggregate rose relative to the price of the Australian aggregate in the face of a

---

[6] More than one international burger chain now offers its version of an 'Australian' burger in Australia — no pickle, but with a rasher of bacon, a fried egg, and above all, a slice of beetroot. Clearly, international transport costs also play a role in consumer choices, but need to be modelled explicity, and independently of the way preferences are characterized.

tariff cut, encouraging resources in Australia to move into the domestic protected sector as its protection was removed. This led to a deterioration in allocative efficiency and an overall economic welfare loss. The story was repeated in many other regions (Dee and Hanslow 2001, p. 119–20).

The treatment that assumes McDonalds is not the same the world over has subsequently been adopted by others, for example Brown, Deardorff and Stern (2000) and Lee and van der Mensbrugghe (2001).

Free entry?

In commenting on the recent book by Fujita, Krugman and Venables (1999) on new economic geography, Neary (2001) wondered whether the assumption of large group monopolistic competition, and the assumption of free entry that goes with it, was always appropriate. He suggested that models with restricted entry and scope for strategic behaviour might have more to say about the forces leading to the agglomeration of economic activity.

In the context of modelling services trade, many of the relevant trade barriers are regulatory barriers that protect the incumbents from new entry, be it from domestic or foreign firms. It would not make much policy sense to model complete liberalization of services trade without allowing for new entry to occur.

But as Low and Mattoo (2000) note, recent liberalization discussions have tended to focus on freeing up ownership restrictions rather than necessarily allowing new entry *per se*, with the danger that rents would simply be transferred to foreign multinationals. Francois and Wooten (2001) also show how, in the continuing presence of significant barriers to cross-border trade, freeing up entry restrictions could result in new foreign entrants being invited to join the domestic cartel. So issues of restricted entry and group size may be relevant for partial services trade liberalization scenarios.

Which factors of production move?

The above considerations deal with how to specify the output of FDI firms in various locations. But is it labour, capital or both that moves when FDI firms relocate?

Although it is at first sight natural to model FDI as the movement of capital, Markusen, Rutherford and Tarr (1999) build a model in which the distinguishing characteristic of services delivered via FDI is the intensity with which they use skilled labour from both home and host locations — capital does not appear in their model at all.

More generally, FDI firms can be modelled as using combinations of capital, local labour (of various skills), and local and imported goods and services, which could include imported 'headquarters' services intensive in the use of skilled labour in the supplying country. Examples (to varying degrees) of this general approach include Petri (1997), Brown, Deardorff and Stern (2000) and Dee and Hanslow (2001). The question of how to obtain data with which to calibrate the cost structures of FDI firms is discussed later.

A common feature of all these approaches is that labour is completely immobile regionally, and is traded only indirectly through trade in intermediate goods and services. This approach is nevertheless consistent with the temporary movement of people. If people move for less than a year, they do not officially change residence, their earnings are therefore recorded in balance of payments statistics as an international transaction (and in a model of the above sort could be lumped in with repatriation of profits), and if their movement is strictly short term, the chances are that most of the income so earned is spent back home, so from the expenditure side, it looks as if no movement has occurred.

Nevertheless, multinational operations often require the movement of people, particularly expatriate executives and specialists, for more than a year. Although this is a sensitive policy issue, none of the above modelling approaches handles such labour migration directly. Because of the complementarities involved, Dee and Hanslow (2001) lumped barriers to the permanent movement of people together with other barriers to FDI, and barriers to the temporary movement of people together with barriers to the other three modes of service delivery, but did not model either the temporary or permanent movement of people directly. This approach is adequate when the focus of attention is on barriers to FDI. But barriers to the temporary movement of people *per se* are of intense interest, especially to developing economies. If they are to be modelled directly, then the underlying flows of people will also need to be modelled. Winters *et al.* (2001) show how this can be done, taking into account differences in the productivity of temporary and permanent workers, and the importance of worker remittances to home country income.

Who owns the FDI capital and how is it financed?

Almost by definition of what distinguishes foreign direct investment from portfolio capital, it makes sense to model FDI capital as being wholly owned by asset holders in the 'home' country, rather than as being partially owned elsewhere. This nevertheless raises some theoretical and data issues associated with partial ownership in practice that are canvassed by Baldwin and Kimura (1998), Dee and Hanslow (2001), Karsenty (2000) and Kimura and Baldwin (1998).

The next question is why asset holders in the home country prefer to hold FDI capital in one location rather than another, or instead of other assets. The simplest way to deal with this is to assume perfect substitution between different types of capital and other financial assets, particularly bonds, so that global arbitrage ensures that FDI capital earns the going world real interest rate everywhere, and asset ownership does not need to be modelled explicitly (except if asset accumulation is to be allowed for — see McDougall (1993) for a very useful example of the latter approach).

However, if the source of firm-level product differentiation happens to be firm-specific assets in the form of human capital held in the head of the FDI capital owner back home, then the assumption of perfect arbitrage sits very uncomfortably with the notion of rents earned by firm-specific assets.

Petri (1997) realized this, and had asset holders in each home base allocate their (fixed) total wealth among capital in different locations according to a structure of preferences that did not assume perfect substitution, and hence did not impose perfect arbitrage or perfect capital mobility. Brown and Stern (2001) similarly allow for less than perfect capital mobility.

Dee and Hanslow (2001) combine Petri's (1997) treatment of less than perfect substitution across capital in different locations, with

McDougall's (1993) treatment of perfect arbitrage for bonds (which could also be seen to include portfolio capital) and his treatment of asset accumulation, to have a model in which the accumulation of FDI capital can be financed by international borrowing and lending. And the returns to FDI capital ultimately accrue to the region that finances it, which may not be the same as the region that nominally 'owns' it.

While not necessarily critical to model outcomes in terms of relative goods and factor price or quantity movements, these modelling 'frills' are critical to the way the gains from services trade liberalization are distributed regionally. Simple analytical models of services trade rightly tend to abstract from such issues, but probably need to acknowledge that their welfare results are qualified accordingly.

Nevertheless, the theoretical and empirical underpinnings for the rate of return to FDI capital remain weak. While it is tempting to assume that FDI capital earns a premium because of rents to firm-specific assets, there is still the question 'over what?' Domestically located capital? Or some other asset? There are alternative models that suggest that, because of a 'lemons' problem, FDI capital might instead earn a discount (Gordon and Bovenberg 1996). Does FDI capital have a role to play in explaining the equity premium puzzle (eg Kocherlakota 1996), the home equity bias (eg Lewis 1999), or any of the other 'six major puzzles in international macroeconomics' (eg Obstfeld and Rogoff 2000, McKibbin and Vines 2000)? Or have we 'missed the boat', and should we be assuming perfect arbitrage for FDI capital after all? These questions deserve a great deal more theoretical and empirical research.

Data and parameter issues in modelling ownership and location

Brown, Deardorff and Stern (2000) observe that:

> … although the New Trade Theory is perhaps best known for introducing new reasons why countries may lose from trade, in fact its greatest contribution is to expand the list of reasons for gains from trade.

The gestalt shift often comes from judicious choice of data and parameters. This is what can take analytical models beyond the realm of identifying theoretical possibilities, to identifying sensible (or at least weeding out non-sensible) economic policy options.[7]

There is a serious lack of data on the activities of offshore affiliates from which to obtain costs and sales shares for the activities of FDI firms, but the situation is improving. Karsenty (2000) documents the development of a new statistical framework, Foreign Affiliate Trade Statistics or FATS, to provide information on the activities of foreign affiliates. The OECD, in cooperation with Eurostat, initially provided data on this basis for 18 countries.[8] Provision of such data for further countries is to be encouraged, especially since Petri (1997) shows just how sensitive are imputed estimates to different imputation methods. But for what it is worth, the results from empirical models tend to be even more sensitive to estimates of the size of barriers to services trade than they are to estimates of the underlying services trade and FDI flows.

Another key issue (not unique to services) is the appropriate value of behavioural parameters, such as elasticities of substitution, that cannot be obtained from calibration to underlying data flows. Compared with Armington formulations, in models that assume firm-level product differentiation and Dixit–Stiglitz preferences, these parameters perform a double duty, so their values are in that sense doubly important — they not only determine the price-sensitivity of demand for particular varieties, but they also determine the extent to which customers (households and/or producers) benefit via a type of endogenous productivity improvement from having more varieties available. These productivity effects can contribute to violations of the Stopler–Samuelson effects from conventional trade theories — instead, all factors of production can gain in real terms from trade liberalization in a single sector (eg Brown *et al.* 2000).

---

[7] Neary (1999) gives a good example of where calibration to real world data rules out multiple solutions and hysteresis in models of new economic geography.

[8] These were Canada, the Czech Republic, Finland, France, Germany, Hungary, Ireland, Italy, Japan, Luxembourg, Mexico, the Netherlands, Norway, Poland, Sweden, Turkey, the United Kingdom and the United States.

Markusen, Rutherford and Tarr (1999) showed these anti-Stolper–Samuelson effects to be particularly strong, using a model with domestic/import substitution elasticities of 3 and elasticities of substitution among individual domestic or imported varieties of 5. But it could be argued that these values are unduly low. They are at the top end of econometric estimates of substitution, not among individual varieties, but among product groups (see the survey in Jomini *et al.* 1994, as well as Hertel 1997). Francois, McDonald and Nordstrom (1995) argued for using values larger than this when substitution among the products of individual firms was concerned. Recent work that chooses parameter values, not from conventional econometric estimation, but according to how they help the models to track historical trade trends, also argue for substantially higher values (Gehlhar 1997, Hillberry *et al.* 2001). Since in models with large group monopolistic competition, the elasticity of endogenous productivity with respect to industry output (proportional to the number of varieties) is just the inverse of the elasticity of substitution among individual varieties, one wonders whether Markusen, Rutherford and Tarr would have achieved the same spectacular results using an elasticity of, say, 15 (as in Dee and Hanslow 2001) instead of 5.

Clearly, parameter values matter, and conventional econometric techniques are unlikely to be of much help when the relevant concepts are substitution at or below the firm level. The methods pioneered by Gehlhar (1997) offer one way of getting more realistic estimates, but must deal convincingly with the problem that elasticities of substitution are not the only unobservable exogenous factors that can be selected to match history.[9]

3.4 What is Special about Services Trade Barriers?

Hoekman and Primo Braga (1997) noted that because service delivery often needs to take place 'face to face', tariffs are not a feasible means of trade protection because customs officials are unable to observe the transaction. Instead, services trade barriers are primarily regulatory, and like other non-tariff barriers, therefore difficult to quantify.

---

[9] See Chapter 7 of this volume for an update on these issues.

The GATS outlines the sorts of trade barriers that will be negotiated.

As noted, the GATS recognizes commercial presence as a mode of service delivery, so some of the important barriers to services trade are those that impede FDI by service firms.

The GATS also distinguishes barriers to market access and derogations from national treatment. Findlay and Warren (2000) argue that barriers to market access can be interpreted as being non-discriminatory barriers that affect the entry of any new firms, be they domestic or foreign, while derogations from national treatment are clearly those barriers that discriminate against foreign firms. Examples of market access barriers would be restrictions on the total number of bank licences, or restrictions on the total number of telecommunications carriers. Examples of derogations from national treatment would be restrictions on the number of foreign bank licences, or restrictions on foreign ownership of telecommunications carriers.

Thus modellers have to be prepared to recognize not only the activities of offshore affiliates and barriers to FDI flows, but also that barriers to services trade are not just discriminatory, but can also affect domestic new entrants. Dee, Hanslow and Phamduc (2003) discuss how these features of services trade barriers affect the applicability of conventional trade theorems such as the Stolper–Samuelson and Rybczynski theorems. Dee and Hanslow (2001) demonstrate just how important the additional components are empirically.

How to measure barriers to services trade?

The Productivity Commission and colleagues at Australian National University recently completed a three-year collaborative project designed to generate estimates of barriers to services trade. As with any research project, there are things we would now do differently, and issues we wish we had recognized earlier. Nevertheless, the project has generated the beginnings of a reasonably comprehensive (in terms of country and sectoral coverage) set of estimates of barriers to services trade. These estimates include barriers to services delivered via FDI, and non-discriminatory restrictions on market access.

The project has quantified regulations affecting trade in banking (McGuire 1998, McGuire and Schuele 2000, Kalirajan *et al.* 2000), telecommunications (Warren 2000), maritime (Kang 2000, McGuire, Schuele and Smith 2000), wholesale and retail distribution (Kalirajan 2000), education (Kemp 2000), professional services (Nguyen-Hong 2000) and foreign investment in services (Hardin and Holmes 1997) for selected economies. Wherever possible, this research has also measured the 'first round' impact of these barriers on economic outcomes — prices, costs, profits or quantities produced. The results of the research are summarized in Table 3.1. It shows, for example, that while Australia has reasonably liberal trade in banking and telecommunications services, it is less liberal in legal, accountancy and maritime services. The table also shows that developing countries often, but not always, have the least liberal services trade regimes. Finally, it confirms that the price impacts of services trade barriers in some key infrastructure industries are significant.

OECD (2000) gives an excellent summary of the 'state of the art' in the field of services trade barrier estimation, as it stood then. It compares our methodology with the few available alternatives (Hoekman 1995, Francois and Hoekman 1999), and identifies areas for further research. Some of these issues are discussed below.

The methodology used at the Productivity Commission and the Australian National University proceeds as follows.

First, qualitative information on barriers to services trade is converted into a quantitative 'restrictiveness index'. This involves identifying all relevant categories of restrictions, then for each country, (a) scoring their actual restrictions in each category according to their restrictiveness, and then (b) weighting together the different category scores according to an assessment of their relative economic significance. Note that in both steps, a judgement is required, although arguably, more in the second step than the first. For example, when the relevant category is restrictions on the proportion of foreign ownership, it makes sense to score 'no more than 25 per cent foreign ownership' as twice as restrictive as 'no more than 50 per cent foreign ownership'. What is more contentious is how to weight restrictions on foreign ownership together with other restrictions, such as licensing requirements or restrictions on lines of business.

Table 3.1.　Trade Restrictiveness Indexes and Their Price Effects for Selected Services

	Domestic[a]		*Foreign*		*Price effect*[b]	
	Maximum (country)	*Australia (rank*[c]*)*	*Maximum (country)*	*Australia (rank)*	*Maximum (country)*	*Australia (rank)*
Legal	0.33 (Austria, Japan)	0.27 (24/29)	0.58 (France, Turkey)	0.42 (10/29)	ne	ne
Accountancy	0.31 (India)	0.16 (12/34)	0.63 (Philippines)	0.41 (18/34)	ne	ne
Architectural	0.25 (Canada)	0.03 (12/34)	0.44 (Austria)	0.15 (12/34)	ne	ne
Engineering	0.2 (Austria, Germany)	0.04 (15/34)	0.39 (Austria)	0.08 (6/34)	14.5 (Austria)	2.8 (6/20)
Distribution	0.26 (Korea)	0.03 (5/38)	0.40 (Malaysia)	0.10 (7/38)	ne	ne
Banking	0.27 (Malaysia)	0.00 (1/38)	0.65 (Malaysia)	0.12 (22/38)	60.6 (Malaysia)	9.3 (21/38)
Telecoms	0.47 (Turkey)	0.04 (7/38)	0.80 (Turkey)	0.04 (7/38)	138.4 (Indonesia)	0.3 (8/37)
Maritime	0.28 (Korea)	0.13 (14/35)	0.64 (Philippines)	0.42 (21/35)	ne	ne

[a] The restrictiveness index scores range from 0 to 1. The higher the score, the greater are the restrictions for an economy.
[b] The price effect of restrictions is measured as a percentage.
[c] Rank refers to the position of Australia relative to other countries in the study, where 1 is the least restrictive economy. For example, 24/29 means Australia is the 24th least restrictive economy of the 29 economies included in the study — that is, there are five economies more restrictive than Australia.
ne Not estimated.
Sources: Kalirajan (2000), Nguyen-Hong (2000), Kalirajan et. al. (2000), McGuire and Schuele (2000), McGuire, Schuele and Smith (2000), Warren (2000).

McGuire (1998) shows how inadequate it is to restrict the information gathering at this stage to that listed by Member countries in their GATS schedules. He found that there were 165 separate restrictions on trade in financial services contained in Federal and State legislation in Australia, compared with 38 restrictions listed in Australia's GATS schedule. For this reason, the project's information gathering has extended to APEC, International Telecommunications Union, OECD, Tradeport, United States Trade Representative, and other sources.

The first step produces an index score for each country of the form:

$$R = R_1 + R_2 \tag{3.1}$$

where R_1 and R_2 are sub-indexes of individual services trade restrictions, scaled so that their maximum possible values reflect the relative economic significance of the individual restrictions, and where the maximum values sum to unity.

The second step is to enter the restrictiveness index into an econometric model of economic performance in the sector in question (where Y is some measure of performance, such as price, quantity, price/cost margin, or productivity), along with whatever other factors (X) economic theory suggests might be important determinants of performance (these can be industry-specific or economy-wide):

$$Y = \alpha + \beta R + \gamma X + \varepsilon \tag{3.2}$$

So far, the Productivity Commission's econometric work has been purely cross-sectional (cross-country), but panel estimation is also possible, although this involves collecting information about restrictions on services trade for more than one time period. In related work, the OECD has collected panel data on domestic regulatory regimes (a 'beyond the border' issue) in OECD countries, and has used panel estimation techniques to quantify their effects (Gonenc and Nicoletti 2000, Boylaud and Nicoletti 2000, Steiner 2000).

Finally, with an estimate of β in hand, the model can be used to predict the 'first round' effects of liberalization (equivalent to the extent of the vertical shift in the supply curve in partial equilibrium analysis). If total liberalization would yield a restrictiveness index score of zero, then βR itself gives an estimate of the effects of current restrictions on economic performance, relative to a free-trade benchmark (and holding other factors constant). Mathematical manipulation can convert this into a percentage 'tax equivalent' (the appropriate manipulation depending on the particular measure of performance and the particular functional form for the estimating equation). However, a 'free trade' benchmark need not always coincide with zero regulation. The method is flexible enough to allow that in a free trade situation, it would still be appropriate to have prudential regulation of financial services, safety regulation of air passenger transport services, and so on. Thus, free trade could be associated with an alternative value R' of the restrictiveness index, and the value of $\beta(R - R')$ would then be converted into a regulatory tax equivalent.[10]

Assessment

The first thing to note about the methodology is how it can be generalized to include additional countries. Once an estimate of β has been obtained from a particular sample, all that is required for additional countries is to produce an index score R to characterize their services trade restrictions, and their 'tax equivalents' can be calculated from βR or $\beta(R - R')$ without redoing the econometrics. Obviously, the original sample needs to be fairly representative for such 'out-of-sample forecasting' to be appropriate. In the Productivity Commission's estimation, we have tried to ensure that the samples include the individual APEC economies, the members of the European Union, and key economies from the rest of the world (preferably Switzerland, Turkey, India, and/or South Africa).[11]

A second advantage of the methodology is that it produces estimates of the effects of trade barriers that are explicitly linked to characterizations of the restrictions themselves, rather than being generated as an 'unexplained residual'.

---

[10] For example, if the performance measure is price P, then with the simple functional forms shown above, the price impact $(P - P')/P'$ can be calculated as $\beta(R - R')/[P - \beta(R - R')]$.

[11] An expanded version of the Productivity Commission's services trade barrier estimates is available in Dee (2005a).

The OECD (2000) survey paper highlights several issues associated with the methodology.[12]

The first is the judgemental nature of the weights used to create the initial restrictiveness index. This is certainly an issue if the overall restrictiveness index is used by itself as an indicator for policy purposes. But it is less of an issue when the index is used in econometric work to generate a 'tax equivalent'. This is because, wherever possible, the Productivity Commission has entered the components of the index separately into the econometrics:

$$Y = \alpha + \beta_1 R_1 + \beta_2 R_2 + \gamma X + \varepsilon \tag{3.3}$$

so that the econometric estimates β_1 and β_2 then provide non-judgemental, data-driven estimates of the weights to be attached to R_1 and R_2.

Often this approach is precluded by one of two econometric problems — multicollinearity, or lack of in-sample variation in one or more of the restrictiveness index components. However, the recent regulatory work by the OECD (Gonenc and Nicoletti 2000, Boylaud and Nicoletti 2000, Steiner 2000) is suggestive of how factor analysis (of which principal components is an application) could be used to overcome these problems. Prior to any econometric estimation, they used factor analysis to identify a set of orthogonal 'factors' that explained most of the variation in their original data on regulatory restrictions. But as Doove *et al.* (2001) point out, high cross-country variation in restrictions may have little or no relationship with the relative economic importance of particular restriction categories:[13]

> ... the use of factor analysis could lead to paradoxical results — in the sense that the more important restrictions, if they were applied widely and consistently across countries, could also have low cross-country variation and thus low factor analysis weights. (p. 17)

---

[12] More recent critiques are outlined in Dee (2013b). That volume also gives a set of 'second generation' estimates that deal with those concerns.

[13] Doove *et al.* (2001) extend the cited OECD examinations of regulatory regimes to non-OECD countries, and generate overall price impact measures for these regimes.

If, instead, principal components were used as the method of econometric estimation, then problems of multicollinearity would be overcome and orthogonal linear combinations of individual restrictions could be identified that explained most of the variation in economic outcomes — a truer measure of economic significance.

A final issue is how to interpret the 'tax equivalent' measures. There are two related issues:

- what is the appropriate measure of performance Y;
- what does each measure tell us about whether the restrictions are rent-creating or cost-escalating.

Take the second issue first. Restrictions could either create pure rents for incumbent firms, and should therefore be modelled as tax or tariff equivalents, in the same way as the MultiFibre Arrangement. Liberalization would be modelled as the elimination of those tax or tariff equivalents, yielding 'triangle gains' associated with improvements in allocative efficiency, along with redistributive effects associated with the elimination of rents to incumbents. As Dee and Hanslow (2001) demonstrate, the former effects would not be trivial, but the latter effects could also be significant. Alternatively, restrictions could increase the real resource cost of doing business. Liberalization would be modelled as a productivity improvement (saving in real resources), and yield 'rectangle gains' from freeing those resources for use elsewhere. Rectangle gains are likely to exceed triangle gains by a significant margin, given the importance of the services sectors in most economies.

To date, most modellers have made an *a priori* judgement about which treatment is appropriate (eg Hertel 2000, Brown *et al.* 2000, Dee and Hanslow 2001), but the truth is likely to lie in between, and to differ from sector to sector. Pure rents are relatively rare in practice, but it is easy to imagine them being a component of the returns to international finance and telecommunications companies, for example, given the artificial barriers to new entry in those sectors in many countries. On the other hand, it is easy to imagine how the trade restrictions built into the international system of bilateral air service agreements frustrate the ability of airlines to reap network economies, and thus increase their real costs of doing business.

Ideally, the empirical work involved in estimating the economic effects of the barriers should give insights as to whether they are rent-creating or cost-escalating. For example, if the restrictions are believed to create rents, then the relevant measure of performance to use in the econometric analysis would be price–cost margins. If the restrictions are believed to raise costs, then the relevant performance measure would be a measure of costs or productivity. Even more ideally, each study should use a range of performance measures to identify what type of effects are being created. In practice, only one or two measures of performance are used, and not always the most appropriate ones in hindsight.

Where restrictions are believed or shown to raise real resource costs, there is a subsidiary set of questions to answer. Do the restrictions raise fixed costs, sunk costs, or ongoing operating costs? And what is the commodity or primary factor composition of the real resource costs so created? In practice, little information is likely to be provided on these subsidiary questions in the process of estimating the barriers. But this will be a fruitful area for different modellers to take different theoretical approaches in their applications, and to test the implications accordingly.

Thus additional work on estimating barriers to services trade is warranted, not only to increase the sectoral and country coverage of the estimates, but also to give additional insights into the types of economic effects that are being created.

Part 2

Model Applications

Chapter 4

Multilateral Liberalization of Services Trade[1]

Philippa Dee and Kevin Hanslow

4.1 Introduction

This chapter uses comprehensive new measures of barriers to services trade in a multi-region, multi-sectoral CGE model of world trade and investment. The model is used to examine the impact of multilateral liberalization of services trade. Barriers to commercial presence are distinguished from those affecting other modes of service delivery (cross-border supply, consumption abroad, and the presence of natural persons), and barriers to national treatment are distinguished from barriers to market access. The effects of liberalization are examined using version 4.1 of the GTAP model of world trade, modified to handle services delivered via commercial presence through the inclusion of bilateral FDI flows. This treatment follows the work of Petri (1997). GTAP's welfare decomposition is also modified to allow for income earned from abroad. The model is used to demonstrate the importance of multilateral liberalization of services trade, relative to liberalization of trade in agriculture and manufactured products.

As the world faces a possible new round of multilateral trade negotiations, it is timely to examine what is at stake. This chapter provides preliminary estimates of the benefits to individual economies,

---

[1] This is an edited version of Chapter 5 in Robert M. Stern (2001), *Services in the International Economy,* Ann Arbor: The University of Michigan Press: 117–39. © 2001 by the University of Michigan. All rights reserved.

and to the world as a whole, from eliminating the barriers to trade that will remain after full implementation of the Uruguay Round.

The analysis compares estimates of the gains from eliminating remaining barriers in the traditional areas of agriculture and manufacturing, with those from eliminating barriers to trade in services. To do so, it uses a model that incorporates a treatment of foreign direct investment (FDI), one of the key vehicles by which services are traded internationally. This allows the chapter to examine the comprehensive removal of restrictions on all modes of service delivery, including restrictions on services delivered via FDI (though not on FDI more generally).

The structure of the chapter is as follows. It first describes the model used — a multi-sector, multi-regional computable general equilibrium model of world trade and investment. The theoretical structure of the model covers both FDI and portfolio investment. The model's database contains estimates of FDI stocks and the activities of FDI firms, each on a bilateral basis. These estimates allow a comparison of the extent to which both goods and services are delivered via FDI or via conventional trade. The chapter then looks at the size of the trade barriers that will remain after full implementation of the Uruguay Round. These estimates include comprehensive new measures of existing barriers to services trade. Next, the chapter looks at the implications of eliminating those trade barriers entirely. Since any new trade round is likely to lead to partial rather than full liberalization, the chapter then evaluates some options for partial liberalization of services trade. Finally, it outlines directions for further research.

4.2 The FTAP Model

The model is a version of GTAP (Hertel 1997) with foreign direct investment, known as FTAP. The treatment of FDI follows closely the pioneering work of Petri (1997). FTAP also incorporates increasing returns to scale and large-group monopolistic competition in all sectors. This follows Francois, McDonald and Nordstrom (1995), among others, who adopted this treatment for manufacturing and resource sectors, and

Brown *et al.* (1995) and Markusen, Rutherford and Tarr (1999), who used similar treatments for services. Finally, FTAP makes provision for capital accumulation and international borrowing and lending. This uses a treatment of international (portfolio) capital mobility developed by McDougall (1993), and recently incorporated into GTAP by Verikios and Hanslow (1999). FTAP is implemented using the GEMPACK software suite (Harrison and Pearson 1996). Its structure is documented fully in Hanslow, Phamduc and Verikios (1999). The most recent version of the model and its documentation are available at http://crawford.anu.edu.au/crawford_people/content/staff/pdee.php.

Theoretical structure

FTAP takes the standard GTAP framework as a description of the *location* of economic activity, and then disaggregates this by *ownership*. For example, each industry located in Australia comprises Australian-owned firms, along with US, European and Japanese multinationals. Each of these firm ownership *types* is modelled as making its own independent choice of inputs to production, according to standard GTAP theory. And each firm type has its own sales structure.

On the purchasing side, agents in each economy make choices among the products or services of each firm type, distinguished by both ownership and location, and then among the individual (and symmetric) firms of a given type. Thus, the model recognizes the firm-level product differentiation associated with monopolistic competition. Firms choose among intermediate inputs and investment goods, while households and governments choose among final goods and services.

Agents are assumed to choose first among products or services from domestic or foreign locations, with a CES elasticity of substitution of 5. They then choose among particular foreign locations, and among ownership categories in a particular location, both with a CES elasticity of substitution of 10. Finally, they choose among the individual firms of a particular ownership and location, with a CES elasticity of substitution of 15. With firm-level product differentiation, agents benefit from having more firms to choose among, because it is more likely that they can find a product or service suited to their particular needs. Capitalizing on this,

Francois, McDonald and Nordstrom (1995) show that the choice among individual firms can be modelled in a conventional model of firm types (not firms) by allowing a productivity improvement whenever the output of a particular firm type (and hence the number of individual firms in it) expands. But because the substitutability among individual firms is assumed here to be very high, the incremental gain from greater variety is not very great and this productivity enhancing effect is not particularly strong (the elasticity of productivity with respect to output[2] is 1/15 = 0.0667).

The first two choices, among domestic and foreign locations, are identical to the choices in the original GTAP model. They have been parameterized using values, 5 and 10, that are roughly twice the standard GTAP Armington elasticities. Two reasons can be given for doubling the standard elasticities. One is that only with such elasticities can GTAP successfully reproduce historical changes in trade patterns (Gehlhar 1997). The other is that higher elasticities accord better with notions of firm level product differentiation.

The order of the first three choices, among locations and then among ownership categories, is the opposite of the order adopted by Petri (1997). The current treatment assumes that from an Australian perspective, for example, a US multinational located in Australia is a closer substitute for an Australian-owned firm than it is for a US firm located in the United States. Petri's treatment assumes that US-owned firms are closer substitutes for each other than for Australian firms, irrespective of location.

There are two reasons for preferring the current treatment.

The first is that Petri's treatment produces a model in which multilateral liberalization of tariffs on manufactured goods produces large economic welfare losses, for most individual economies and for the world as a whole — an uncomfortable result at odds with conventional trade theory. The reason for the result can be seen by considering the

---

[2] The equivalent elasticity of productivity with respect to *inputs* is $0.0667/(1 - 0.0667) = 0.0714$, where this latter concept is used by Francois, McDonald and Nordstrom (1995). The elasticities of productivity with respect to output and inputs are not equal because of the assumption of increasing returns to scale. Another reason scale effects are not strong is that, with this nested structure, the economies of scale are regional rather than global.

choices that Australians would make at the top of Petri's decision tree in the face of a tariff cut. They would choose between an aggregate of the output of Australian firms (irrespective of location) and an aggregate of the output of US firms (irrespective of location). The first aggregate would be overwhelmingly dominated by the output of domestically located Australian firms, since 'boomerang' imports from Australian firms located offshore would be minimal. Thus the first aggregate would have a very small proportion of goods attracting a tariff. The second aggregate would include both goods produced by US multinationals located in Australia, and imports from US firms located in the United States. Only the latter would initially attract a tariff. Depending on relative shares, there is no guarantee that the price of the US aggregate would be dominated by the removal of the tariff on imports, rather than by endogenous changes in the cost structure of US multinationals in Australia. Simulations with a model of this structure showed that the price of the US aggregate *rose* relative to the price of the Australian aggregate in the face of a tariff cut, encouraging resources in Australia to move *into* the domestic protected sector as its protection was removed. This led to a deterioration in allocative efficiency and an overall economic welfare loss. The story was repeated in many other regions.

The second reason for preferring the current treatment is that, in many instances, it accords better with reality. Some Australian examples help to illustrate. Many Australian consumers prefer roomy cars with large capacity, 6 cylinder engines. Holden, originally locally-owned, was bought out by General Motors, and has since produced such cars. Ford Australia has invested in significant local design capacity in order to produce a close rival. Even Mitsubishi and Toyota in Australia now produce 6 cylinder versions for the local market. Similarly, Hungry Jacks, the local version of Burger King, has had some success with a hamburger reminiscent of those popular in Australia before the arrival of international franchises — one with no pickle, but with a rasher of bacon, a fried egg, and above all, a slice of beetroot. Recently McDonalds in Australia announced that it had delayed introducing a burger with beetroot because it had been unable to secure adequate supplies.

Thus US firms are often not the same, irrespective of location, even when their foreign direct investment is 'horizontal' rather than 'vertical'.

Indeed, one of the distinguishing characteristics of services is that they are tailored each time to meet the needs of the individual consumer. Another characteristic is that they are often delivered face to face, sometimes making commercial presence (through FDI) the only viable means of trade. These taken together mean that service firms in a given location, irrespective of ownership, will tailor their services to meet local tastes and requirements, and thus appear to be close substitutes, as in the current treatment.

While the demand for the output of firms distinguished by ownership and location is determined as above, the supply of FDI is determined by the same imperfect transformation among types of wealth as in Petri (1997). Investors in each economy first divide their wealth between 'bonds' (which can be thought of as any instrument of portfolio investment), real physical capital, and land and natural resources in their country of residence. This choice is governed by a constant elasticity of transformation (CET) semi-elasticity of 1, meaning that a one percentage point increase in the rate of return on real physical capital, for example, would increase the ratio of real physical capital to bond holdings by one per cent. A bond is a bond, irrespective of who issues it, implying perfect international arbitrage of rates of return on bonds. However, capital in different locations is seen as different things. Investors next choose the industry sector in which they invest (with a CET semi-elasticity of 1.2). They next choose whether to invest at home or overseas in their chosen sector (with a CET semi-elasticity of 1.3). Finally, they choose a particular overseas region in which to invest (with a CET semi-elasticity of 1.4).

The less than perfect transformation among different forms of wealth can be justified as reflecting some combination of risk aversion and less than perfect information. It is important to note, however, that while the measure of economic welfare in FTAP currently recognizes the positive income contribution that FDI can make, it does not discount that for any costs associated with risk taking, given risk aversion. This is an important qualification to the current results, and will be the subject of further research.

While the chosen CET parameters at each 'node' of the nesting structure may appear low, the number of nests means that choices at the final level (across destinations of FDI) are actually very flexible. For example, it can be shown that, holding total wealth fixed but allowing all other adjustments across asset types and locations to take place, the implied semi-elasticity of transformation between foreign destinations can easily reach 20, and be as high as 60. The variation across regions in these implied elasticities comes about because of the different initial shares of assets in various regional portfolios.

The choice of CET parameters at each 'node' was determined partly by this consideration of what they implied for the final elasticities, holding only total wealth constant. They were also chosen so that this version of FTAP gave results that were broadly comparable to an earlier version of GTAP with imperfect international (portfolio) capital mobility, for experiments involving the complete liberalization of agricultural and manufacturing protection. That earlier version of GTAP was developed by Verikios and Hanslow (1999). Imperfect capital mobility was also a feature of the GTAP-based examination of APEC liberalization by Dee, Geisler and Watts (1996) and Dee, Hardin and Schuele (1998). These parameters thus provide a familiar starting point, from which variations could be made in the future.[3]

In one respect, however, the current version of FTAP does differ from previous versions of GTAP with imperfect capital mobility. The GTAP variants assumed that capital was perfectly mobile across sectors, whereas FTAP has less than perfect sectoral mobility. Furthermore, the choice of sector is relatively early in the nesting structure, so that the implied elasticities guiding choice of sector, holding only total wealth constant, are relatively low (eg 1.2 in the United States). As a result, FTAP tends to exhibit behaviour where resources move less readily between sectors in a given region, but more readily across regions in a given sector, although the differences are not dramatic. The current treatment is consistent with the idea that the knowledge capital often required to succeed in foreign direct investment, despite the difficulties of language and distance, is likely to be sector-specific.

Petri's model assumed that total wealth in each region was fixed. In FTAP, while regional endowments of land and natural resources are

---

[3] More recent benchmarking of these parameters is described in Chapter 7 of this volume.

fixed (and held solely by each region's residents), regional capital stocks can accumulate over time, and net bond holdings of each region can adjust to help finance the accumulation of domestic and foreign capital by each region's investors. The treatment of capital accumulation follows the original treatment of McDougall (1993), and was also used by Verikios and Hanslow (1999), Dee, Geisler and Watts (1996) and Dee, Hardin and Schuele (1998).

With this treatment of capital accumulation, FTAP provides a long-run snapshot view of the impact of trade liberalization, ten years after it has occurred. To the extent that liberalization leads to changes in regional incomes and savings, this will be reflected in changes to the capital stocks that investors in each region will have been able to accumulate. As noted, investors in each region are not restricted to their own savings pool in order to finance capital investment. They may also issue bonds to help with that investment, but only according to their own preferences about capital versus bond holding, and only according to the willingness of others to accept the additional bonds.

Model database

The starting point for FTAP's database was not the standard GTAP database, since this includes measures of trade and investment barriers that are still to be eliminated under the Uruguay Round agreement. Instead, the starting point was an updated version of the GTAP database, following a simulation in which the barriers yet to be eliminated under the Uruguay Round had been removed. Such a database was provided by the work of Verikios and Hanslow (1999), under their assumption of less than perfect capital mobility.

The Petri treatment of FDI requires the addition of data on bilateral FDI stocks, and on the activity levels and cost and sales structures of FDI firms. The methods used to estimate such data were similar to those of Petri. APEC (1995) and United Nations (1994) provided limited data on FDI stocks by source, destination and sector. These data were fleshed out to provide a full bilateral matrix of FDI stocks by source, destination and sector, using RAS methods (Welsh and Strzelecki 2000). The results are summarized in Table 4.1. Unlike Petri, the FDI stocks have not been 'grossed up' to account for the contributions of local joint venture partners, for reasons to be explained shortly. Thus the estimates given here are lower than his, but the pattern is similar. Europe and the United States are the main sources of and destinations for FDI. Japan is much more important as a source than as a destination. The OECD provides 87 per cent of outward FDI and receives 73 per cent of inward FDI. The detailed data show that 80 per cent of FDI from Asia (excluding Japan) remains in Asia, and that there are strong bilateral, bi-directional ties between neighbouring countries (Australia–New Zealand, United States–Canada). Finally, about 20 per cent of FDI is in the primary sector, with about 40 per cent each in the secondary and tertiary sectors.

As shown in Table 4.1, the data were collected (and the model implemented) for 19 regions (where R. Cairns stands for the rest of the Cairns group — Brazil, Argentina, Colombia and Uruguay) and three

Table 4.1. FDI Stock Estimates (US$ billion)

	Inward FDI stocks				Outward FDI stocks			
	Pri	*Sec*	*Ter*	*Total*	*Pri*	*Sec*	*Ter*	*Total*
Australia	17.7	14.8	42.1	74.6	4.8	7.3	16.3	28.4
NZ	1.6	4.0	4.2	9.8	0.9	2.0	1.3	4.2
Japan	0.5	16.3	9.5	26.3	29.3	91.0	251.1	371.5
Korea	0.4	5.1	3.3	8.8	2.5	1.7	1.2	5.4
Indonesia	54.3	9.2	1.9	65.4	0.5	1.1	0.7	2.3
Malaysia	7.4	8.9	7.1	23.4	0.4	1.0	0.6	2.0
Philippines	1.6	1.6	1.0	4.2	0.0	0.2	0.7	0.8
Singapore	0.6	14.7	20.5	35.7	2.2	4.9	3.2	10.4
Thailand	1.7	5.1	6.2	12.9	0.0	0.1	0.6	0.7
China	7.3	15.6	16.7	39.6	0.4	0.2	0.4	1.0
Hong Kong	0.0	7.0	22.5	29.6	8.8	19.4	12.7	40.9
Taiwan	0.3	14.8	2.0	17.1	0.3	3.3	1.8	5.4
Canada	15.9	60.4	37.1	113.4	8.8	39.5	32.6	80.9
USA	36.7	185.4	219.5	441.6	57.3	196.0	228.3	481.6
Mexico	3.9	14.4	20.6	38.9	0.3	0.6	0.4	1.3
Chile	7.4	1.3	3.8	12.4	0.1	0.2	0.2	0.5
R. Cairns	10.1	47.1	20.5	77.8	1.0	2.2	1.5	4.7
EU	121.9	310.0	319.4	751.2	166.6	366.3	238.5	771.5
R. World	34.3	87.4	90.0	211.7	39.0	85.8	55.9	180.7
World	323.5	823.0	847.9	1,994.3	323.5	822.9	847.9	1,994.3

Source: Based on APEC (1995) and United Nations (1994).

broad sectors. The three sectors — primary (agriculture, resources and processed food), secondary (other manufacturing), and tertiary (services) — correspond broadly to the three areas of potential trade negotiation in a new trade round. The intention is to use similar methods to produce a model with greater sectoral detail in the future.[4]

The FDI stock data were used in turn to generate estimates of the output levels of FDI firms. Capital income flows were estimated by multiplying the FDI stocks by rates of return. The GTAP database does not contain rate of return estimates by sector, so these were calculated (using averages over five years where available) from the accounting information in the Worldscope Global Equity Database (Disclosure 1999).

Using the idea that there could be a premium earned on the firm-specific assets embodied in FDI, the rate of return taken to be relevant for a given FDI stock was the greater of the average rate in the home and host region. Thus the model allows rates of return to differ between locally-owned and foreign firms. For this reason, it was considered unwise to allow for some fixed proportion of local equity in joint ventures, as in Petri (1997), since welfare results would then be tainted by the relatively arbitrary reallocation of locally-owned capital between domestically-owned firms and joint ventures. Furthermore, many of the barriers to trade in services directly affect that proportion!

Capital rentals were then grossed up to get an output estimate for FDI firms, using capital rental to output ratios from the GTAP database. Thus FDI firms were assumed to have the same capital rental to output ratios as domestically-owned firms, although those rentals may imply a higher rate of return on the underlying capital stock. These output estimates for FDI firms were then compared with GTAP's output estimates, and adjusted downwards (along with the underlying FDI stock) in instances where they implied negative values for the residual output of locally-owned firms. The resulting output estimates are summarized in Tables 4.2 and 4.3, which compare the output of outward FDI firms with conventional exports (post-Uruguay), and the output of inward FDI firms

---

[4] See Chapters 6 and 7 in this volume for examples.

Table 4.2. FTAP's Exports and Outward FDI Output (US$ billion)

	Conventional exports			*Outward FDI output*		
	Pri	*Sec*	*Ter*	*Pri*	*Sec*	*Ter*
Australia	42.5	16.1	11.1	19.1	14.4	8.8
NZ	9.4	5.3	3.4	0.8	3.0	1.7
Japan	4.4	417.4	56.7	57.1	159.3	134.3
Korea	3.8	113.9	22.2	3.4	2.4	0.5
Indonesia	20.2	28.5	4.7	0.2	1.6	1.2
Malaysia	15.0	64.2	6.1	0.2	1.2	0.8
Philippines	3.7	15.2	8.1	0.0	0.4	0.6
Singapore	6.5	90.8	24.3	1.2	5.5	3.6
Thailand	16.5	38.2	12.2	0.0	0.2	0.6
China	18.5	189.3	16.4	0.9	0.2	0.3
Hong Kong	1.1	33.4	41.2	5.2	18.1	25.6
Taiwan	4.8	117.6	8.8	0.1	6.5	2.3
Canada	33.1	145.3	19.4	22.2	64.5	17.5
USA	84.9	472.8	179.5	167.2	417.5	126.9
Mexico	13.6	60.2	9.2	0.3	0.8	0.4
Chile	7.2	8.2	2.6	0.0	0.2	0.2
R. Cairns	43.4	40.9	11.2	1.1	2.8	1.7
EU	224.3	1577.6	422.7	299.1	538.2	196.3
R. World	296.9	379.6	152.3	108.9	213.9	75.8
World	849.7	3,814.7	1,012.2	686.8	1,450.8	599.3

Source: FTAP model database.

with conventional imports (post-Uruguay). The tables confirm the impression that, in many regions, goods and services delivered via FDI are as important as conventional trade.

The detailed cost and sales structures of FDI firms were assumed to be the same as for locally-owned firms, and were obtained by pro-rating the GTAP database. A subject for future research will be to make use of available information on the true cost and sales structures of FDI firms.

In a final step, estimates of existing barriers to services trade were injected into the model's database, using the techniques of Malcolm (1998). The process will be documented in Hanslow, Phamduc, Verikios and Welsh (2000). The GTAP model already contains estimates of the barriers to trade in agricultural and manufactured goods, and the updated version of this database obtained from Verikios and Hanslow (1999) has these at their post-Uruguay levels. However, GTAP does not contain

Table 4.3. FTAP's Imports and Inward FDI Output (US$ billion)

	Conventional Imports			**Inward FDI output**		
	Pri	*Sec*	*Ter*	*Pri*	*Sec*	*Ter*
Australia	7.0	54.8	18.1	19.9	25.9	28.2
NZ	1.7	11.3	4.4	3.2	5.2	3.2
Japan	122.0	201.7	108.5	0.0	27.6	6.6
Korea	30.9	98.2	24.7	0.0	6.9	1.5
Indonesia	7.0	34.8	8.1	85.7	4.9	2.1
Malaysia	6.1	64.6	9.0	7.7	9.3	5.1
Philippines	6.8	24.7	6.4	4.8	1.9	1.0
Singapore	15.0	101.1	15.7	0.0	20.2	18.7
Thailand	9.2	60.0	14.9	2.0	1.8	2.8
China	19.8	141.0	16.3	7.3	19.7	32.5
Hong Kong	12.8	82.1	18.9	11.3	9.8	9.6
Taiwan	11.3	81.6	17.0	0.0	28.1	1.5
Canada	16.3	136.7	26.0	9.0	115.4	21.4
USA	117.9	657.2	128.3	45.0	247.0	167.6
Mexico	6.5	55.8	7.8	5.5	12.5	5.5
Chile	2.7	12.7	3.1	15.0	1.1	2.0
R. Cairns	16.6	74.9	20.2	9.7	44.7	11.5
EU	348.6	1512.6	409.8	377.0	678.5	187.2
R. World	151.2	582.7	154.8	83.8	190.3	91.3
World	909.4	3,988.3	1,012.2	686.8	1,450.8	599.3

Source: FTAP model database.

estimates of barriers to services trade. Instead, estimates of barriers to trade in banking services were taken from Kalirajan *et al.* (2000), and estimates of barriers to trade in telecommunications services were taken from Warren (2000). These are the first of a comprehensive new set of estimates of barriers to services trade, to be documented in Findlay and Warren (2000). The rates can be taken as indicative of post-Uruguay rates, since while the Uruguay Round established the architecture for services trade negotiations, it did not achieve much in the way of services trade liberalization (Hoekman 1995).

A simple average of the estimates for banking and telecommunications was taken as being typical of most services — all of the GTAP service categories of trade and transport and finance, business and recreational services, and half of public administration and defence, education and health. The remainder of public administration and defence, education and health, along with electricity, water and gas, construction, and ownership of dwellings were assumed to be strictly non-traded (note that engineering services are part of business services, not construction). The resulting average estimates of barriers to trade in the tertiary sector would have been about 50 to 100 per cent bigger, had the banking and telecommunications estimates been taken as indicative of the whole of the services sector. A topic of future research is to use the next version of the GTAP database, which will have more services sector detail, to model barriers to each service separately, thus overcoming the arbitrariness of these assumptions.

The resulting structure of post-Uruguay barriers to trade in services is summarized in Table 4.4. Barriers to trade in agricultural and food products are represented via a combination of taxes on imports, and subsidies (shown in Table 4.4 as negative taxes) on exports and output.

Table 4.4. Tax Equivalents of Post-Uruguay Barriers to Trade and Investment (percent)

	Imports		*Exports*		*Domestic output*	*Foreign affiliates' output*	*Domestic capital*	*Foreign affiliates' capital*
	Pri	*Sec*	*Pri*	*Ter*	*Ter*	*Ter*	*Ter*	*Ter*
Australia	1.69	7.30	0.65	4.81	0.00	0.69	0.62	14.79
NZ	1.16	4.51	−3.25	3.78	0.00	0.67	0.41	4.18
Japan	16.19	1.81	−8.12	4.41	3.59	4.75	0.33	3.01
Korea	12.95	6.61	−1.22	4.57	5.11	6.78	1.91	22.01
Indonesia	4.40	6.71	0.00	4.68	13.23	28.11	22.69	68.06
Malaysia	21.18	5.97	6.68	4.50	3.58	10.20	15.35	37.58
Philippines	16.16	18.51	−0.10	4.80	8.38	22.65	7.40	54.28
Singapore	3.22	0.56	0.01	4.70	3.40	8.32	2.42	24.50
Thailand	12.12	14.81	−16.98	4.14	4.69	13.36	12.16	36.49
China	8.92	28.45	5.13	4.08	18.75	36.40	123.46	250.66
Hong Kong	0.00	0.00	0.00	9.91	1.39	2.36	1.35	5.41
Taiwan	27.31	5.63	−1.82	4.35	2.88	4.90	1.90	19.19
Canada	3.57	1.40	−0.43	3.54	0.25	1.67	0.53	6.11
USA	1.29	2.24	−0.02	4.26	0.07	1.08	0.00	3.83
Mexico	−1.50	2.99	1.89	5.23	2.17	5.59	0.68	12.99
Chile	6.76	10.26	0.02	4.36	2.97	4.11	14.15	20.36
R. Cairns	3.82	13.39	6.30	4.49	0.98	5.55	7.19	19.45
EU	3.17	1.13	−2.33	4.72	0.10	1.31	1.33	6.49
R. World	15.94	13.67	0.59	4.95	4.89	13.92	39.07	86.97

Source: FTAP model database.

Unfortunately, at FTAP's three sector level of aggregation, the actual taxes on primary exports and output are a combination of subsidies used for protective purposes, and taxes (eg excises on alcohol and tobacco) used for revenue raising. (While the average taxes on primary output are not shown in Table 4.4, they are all relatively small and mostly positive.) In modelling the liberalization of post-Uruguay trade barriers, the greater sectoral detail of Verikios and Hanslow's database was used to calculate what would happen to the average tax rates on primary exports and output, were the subsidies (where they occur) to be removed but the taxes (where they occur) to remain. In this way, the problem of averaging could be partially overcome when modelling liberalization. A remaining problem is that GTAP's database aggregation facility implicitly uses import weights to aggregate import taxes, and the work of Anderson and Neary (eg 1994, 1996) shows that these give insufficient weight to very high (and therefore very distortionary) import taxes, leading to incorrect welfare results from trade liberalization. In future, this 'aggregation bias' will be reduced by using a database with greater sectoral detail.

Once the Uruguay Round is fully implemented, the remaining trade barriers on manufacturing will comprise mainly tariffs on imports, since the export tax equivalents of the Multifibre Arrangement will have been eliminated. These average tariff levels are shown in the second column of Table 4.4.

The structure of barriers to services trade in the last five columns of Table 4.4 requires some explanation. The General Agreement on Trade in Services (GATS) framework distinguishes four modes of service delivery — via commercial presence, cross-border supply, consumption abroad, and the presence of natural persons. Accordingly, the FTAP model distinguishes barriers to establishment from barriers to ongoing operation. This is similar to the distinction between commercial presence and other modes of delivery, since barriers to establishment are a component of the barriers to commercial presence.

In Table 4.4, barriers to establishment have been modelled as taxes on capital. Barriers to ongoing operation may affect either FDI firms or those supplying via the other modes, and have been modelled as taxes on the output of locally-based firms (either domestic or foreign-owned), and taxes of the same size on the exports of firms supplying via the other modes, respectively. The estimates of export taxes on services in the fourth column of Table 4.4 are trade weighted averages of the taxes on exports to particular destinations, where these are equal in turn to the taxes on foreign affiliates' output in the destination region, shown in the sixth column. The reason for modelling these as taxes in the exporting region, rather than as tariffs in the importing region, is that it allows the rents created by the barriers to be retained in the exporting region. The issue of rents is addressed in more detail shortly.

The GATS framework also distinguishes restrictions on market access from restrictions on national treatment. The former are restrictions on entry, be it by locally-owned or foreign-owned firms. In this sense, they are non-discriminatory. Restrictions on national treatment mean that foreign-owned firms are treated less favourably than domestic firms. These restrictions are discriminatory. Thus the taxes on domestic capital and domestic output in Table 4.4 represent the effects of restrictions on market access (affecting establishment and ongoing operation, respectively). The taxes on the capital and output of foreign affiliates are higher than the corresponding taxes on domestic firms, because they represent the effects of restrictions on both market access and national treatment. The estimation of barriers to trade in banking and telecommunications services by Kalirajan *et al.* (2000) and Warren (2000) allowed the price effects to be split up according to this two-by-two classification.

The estimates in Table 4.4 indicate that barriers to trade in services are generally at least as large as those on agricultural and manufactured products. In addition, the *ad valorem* equivalents of barriers to establishment are generally much higher than those on ongoing operation. This is significant, since taxes on capital can distort input decisions in ways that taxes on output do not.

Most economies have at least some significant barriers to trade in services. The only regions where barriers are low across the board are New Zealand, Japan, Hong Kong, Canada, the United States and the European Union. But this statement should be heavily qualified, because it is based only on estimates of barriers to banking and tele-communications.

Barriers to trade in services have been modelled as tax equivalents that generate rents — a mark-up of price over cost — rather than as things that raise costs above what they might otherwise have been (eg Hertel 2000). This decision was based on the way in which the price impacts of barriers to trade in banking and telecommunications services were measured. Kalirajan *et al.* (2000) measured the effects of trade restrictions on the net interest margins of banks, a direct measure of banks' mark-up of price over cost. Warren (2000) measured the effects of trade restrictions on the quantities of telecommunications services delivered, and these were converted to price impacts using an estimate of the elasticity of demand for telecommunications services. Thus, Warren's estimates did not provide direct evidence of a mark-up of price over cost, but the relative profitability of telecommunications companies in many countries suggests that some element of rent may exist. By contrast, there is evidence that trade restrictions in sectors such as aviation raise costs (Johnson *et al.* 2000). As estimates of the effects of trade barriers in these sectors are incorporated into the model, it will be appropriate to treat some restrictions as cost-raising rather than as rent-creating.

One important implication of the current treatment is that welfare gains from liberalizing trade in services are likely to be understated, perhaps significantly. If trade restrictions create rents, then the allocative efficiency gains from trade liberalization are the 'triangle' gains associated with putting a given quantum of resources to more efficient use. By contrast, if trade restrictions raise costs, then the gains from trade liberalization include 'rectangle' gains (qualified by general equilibrium effects) from lower costs, equivalent to a larger effective quantum of resources for productive use.

Because barriers to services trade appear to be significant, and because they have been modelled as taxes, the rents they generate will be significant. A key issue is whether those rents should be modelled as being retained by incumbent firms, appropriated by governments via taxation, or passed from one country to another by transfer pricing or other mechanisms. In FTAP, the rents on output have been modelled as accruing to the selling region, and those on capital have been modelled as accruing to the region of ownership, once the government in the region of location has taxed them at its general property income tax rate. Despite this, the asset choices of investors are modelled as being driven by pre-tax rates of return. This is because many economies, in the developed world at least, have primarily destination-based tax systems. For example, if tax credits are granted for taxes paid overseas, investors are ultimately taxed on *all* income at the owning region's tax rate. Although such tax credits have not been modelled explicitly, their effect has been captured by having investors respond to relative pre-tax rates of return. Nevertheless, investor choices are also assumed to be determined by rates of return excluding any abnormal rent component. Investors would like to supply an amount of capital consistent with rates of return including abnormal rents, but are prevented from doing so by barriers to investment. The amount of capital actually supplied is, therefore, that amount that investors would like to supply at rates of return excluding abnormal rents.

Thus a portion of the rent associated with barriers to services trade is assumed to remain in the region of location in the form of property income tax revenue, while the remainder accrues to the region of ownership. Thus liberalization of services trade could have significant income effects in both home and host regions as these rents are gradually eliminated. The next section shows how significant these effects are, relative to the allocative efficiency effects and other effects normally associated with trade liberalization.

A final point to note is that the model's database does not contain estimates of barriers to investment in agriculture and manufacturing, even though they are likely to be significant. It is unlikely that a new trade round would include negotiations on them. Nevertheless, their omission will affect the model's estimates of the effects of liberalization elsewhere, and the results need to be qualified accordingly.

4.3 The Effects of Eliminating Post-Uruguay Barriers to Trade

The FTAP model has been used to examine the effects of eliminating the post-Uruguay barriers to trade summarized in Table 4.4. The results are comparative static, showing only the impact of trade liberalization. During the ten year adjustment period, many other changes will affect each economy, but they are not taken into account in the current analysis. For this reason, the results should not be interpreted as indicating the likely changes that would occur over time in each economy — such results would require *all* changes, not just changes in trade barriers, to be taken into account. The model results should instead be seen as providing an indication, at some point in time ten years after liberalization, of how different each economy would be, compared with the alternative situation at the same point in time, had the liberalization not taken place.

The distinction is important to keep in mind. Sometimes, to aid fluency, the results are couched as if key indicators 'rise' or 'fall'. This should not be interpreted to mean that the indicators would be higher or lower than they are now. It means that they would, at some future time, be higher or lower than they otherwise would have been had the liberalization not occurred. In both cases, in a growing economy, these indicators could be higher than they are now.

Table 4.5 shows first the projected effect on resource allocation, by showing the percentage changes in sectoral outputs.

As expected, liberalization of trade in agricultural and manufactured products is projected to encourage resources to shift out of the relatively highly protected agricultural sectors in Japan, Korea, Malaysia, Philippines, Thailand, China, Taiwan, the European Union and the rest of the world region. According to Table 4.4, the agricultural sector in the European Union does not look to be particularly highly protected post-Uruguay. However, this is an artefact of the averaging of subsidy assistance and revenue-raising taxes, mentioned earlier. As noted, liberalization has been modelled by eliminating the subsidies but keeping the revenue-raising taxes.

It is harder to generalize about the effects on manufacturing sectors of liberalizing trade in agricultural and manufactured products. Some of the Asian economies, such as the Philippines, Thailand and China, have the highest levels of manufacturing assistance post-Uruguay. But eliminating this protection also means they have much to gain by way of improvements in allocative efficiency. Thus, the manufacturing sectors

Table 4.5. Projected Effects on Sectoral Output of Eliminating Post-Uruguay Trade Barriers (per cent)

	Primary and secondary liberalization			*Tertiary liberalization*		
	Primary	*Secondary*	*Tertiary*	*Primary*	*Secondary*	*Tertiary*
Australia	3.6	−8.1	0.6	1.2	1.0	−0.3
NZ	27.4	−22.1	−1.2	1.8	1.0	−0.7
Japan	−9.3	2.0	0.1	−0.4	−0.3	0.1
Korea	−4.2	5.6	−0.8	−0.8	−1.6	1.1
Indonesia	1.0	2.0	−0.2	0.3	2.6	9.2
Malaysia	−0.4	3.6	−0.6	0.1	0.1	1.5
Philippines	−4.4	36.8	−2.4	−1.9	−3.6	2.5
Singapore	54.2	−0.1	−6.5	−3.9	−6.6	1.0
Thailand	−3.9	2.7	1.4	−0.1	−0.8	1.3
China	−0.8	3.1	1.1	−0.2	2.4	32.5
Hong Kong	26.5	27.2	−6.9	0.2	−2.2	0.6
Taiwan	−1.0	6.2	−1.5	0.1	1.0	−0.2
Canada	1.3	−3.6	0.8	0.7	1.0	−0.6
USA	6.0	−2.4	0.3	0.6	0.6	−0.4
Mexico	0.5	−2.2	0.7	−0.1	0.1	0.1
Chile	2.1	−2.7	0.6	0.1	−1.0	0.9
R. Cairns	3.7	−4.1	0.9	0.3	0.4	−0.1
EU	−5.5	−0.5	0.7	1.0	1.3	−0.6
R. World	−0.6	−0.7	0.8	−0.2	−0.4	1.5

Source: FTAP model projections.

in these economies are projected to expand, despite facing the biggest reductions in protection. On the other hand, the manufacturing sectors in the United States and Canada are projected to be smaller than otherwise, despite experiencing the loss of relatively modest protection. This is partly because resources are reallocated into the primary and tertiary sectors in those regions.

The sectoral effects of liberalizing barriers to trade in services are relatively straightforward. The services sectors in most Asian economies are projected to expand as their relatively large barriers to entry are removed. The services sector in China is projected to be fully 33 per cent bigger than otherwise, because its barriers to entry had been particularly high. Services sectors in economies with low barriers to entry, such as Australia, New Zealand, Canada, the United States, and the European Union are expected to be slightly smaller than otherwise. In part, this is because of increased competition via cross-border trade from the newly expanded Asian service sectors. But if the size of barriers to services trade in these economies has been underestimated, then the reductions in their service sector output will be overstated.

Table 4.6 shows the effects of these sectoral resource shifts on regional activity levels (as measured by changes in real GDP) and on economic wellbeing (as measured by the equivalent variation, a measure of the change in net national product, or real income accruing to the residents in each economy). It shows that all economies except Singapore are projected to be bigger than otherwise as a result of full trade liberalization. But the Singaporean economy being smaller than

Table 4.6. Projected Effects on Real GDP and Welfare of Eliminating Post-Uruguay Trade Barriers

	Real GDP (%)			Equivalent variation (US$ million)		
	Primary and secondary	Tertiary	Total	Primary and secondary	Tertiary	Total
Australia	0.2	0.0	0.2	1,994	2,098	4,092
NZ	1.2	−0.1	1.1	4,400	257	4,657
Japan	0.3	0.0	0.3	20,964	4,130	25,094
Korea	1.5	0.1	1.6	8,784	1,886	10,670
Indonesia	0.7	5.1	5.9	1,451	2,470	3,921
Malaysia	3.7	0.7	4.5	3,532	1,015	4,547
Philippines	5.1	0.4	5.5	1,601	1,236	2,837
Singapore	−0.3	−1.3	−1.5	7,421	−247	7,174
Thailand	2.6	0.2	2.8	4,063	1,698	5,762
China	3.4	14.6	18.0	14,088	90,869	104,957
Hong Kong	−0.2	1.0	0.9	916	5,896	6,812
Taiwan	2.7	0.2	3.0	11,659	−142	11,517
Canada	0.1	−0.1	0.0	−539	−499	−1,038
USA	0.2	−0.1	0.1	22,734	−1,809	20,925
Mexico	0.3	0.1	0.4	−83	357	274
Chile	0.7	0.4	1.1	45	330	375
R. Cairns	1.2	0.1	1.3	12,766	6,970	19,736
EU	0.1	0.0	0.1	6,394	−6,169	225
R. World	1.1	0.8	1.9	11,324	23,039	34,363
World				133,515	133,386	266,901

Source: FTAP model projections.

otherwise does not make Singaporeans poorer than otherwise. They may simply have substituted FDI for investment at home, and be earning significantly higher incomes from these foreign investments. This is examined in more detail shortly.

In terms of real income, the world as a whole is projected to be better off by more than US$ 260 billion as a result of eliminating all post-Uruguay trade barriers. About US$ 50 billion of this would come from agricultural liberalization, and a further US$ 80 billion from liberalization of manufactures. This shows that there are still considerable gains to be had in traditional areas, even if no progress is made in services.[5] But an additional US$ 130 billion would come from liberalizing services trade. And about US$ 100 billion of the gains from services liberalization would accrue in China alone.[6]

Australia is projected to gain as much from global liberalization of services trade as it would from global liberalization of trade in agriculture and manufacturing. Each would make Australia's real income about US$ 2 billion higher than otherwise, for an overall gain of about US$ 4 billion a year. This is the projected gain in annual income, about ten years after the liberalization has occurred and the associated resource adjustments have taken place.

---

[5] It might seem a possible source of second-best welfare problems to reduce trade barriers in agriculture and manufacturing, while leaving even higher restrictions in services untouched. But because services are a general equilibrium complement (rather than substitute) to agriculture and manufacturing, reducing trade restrictions in the traditional areas would mitigate the restrictions in services.

[6] In a recent similar exercise, Hertel's (2000) world welfare gains from eliminating barriers to services trade were smaller than those projected here. Although his income base was 2005 rather than 1995, and although he treated services trade barriers as being cost-raising rather than rent-creating, his exercise was limited to barriers in construction and business services (using estimated price impacts from Francois 1999), and did not include liberalization of FDI. Hertel's estimated gains from full liberalization of agriculture and manufacturing were larger than those presented here. But correcting for the difference in income base by applying FTAP's results to Hertel's income base (we are grateful to Tom Hertel for making this available), FTAP's gain from liberalizing manufactures is $120 billion, very close to Hertel's estimate of $129 billion. FTAP's gains from liberalizing agriculture are still about half of Hertel's estimate of $160 billion. This is largely because Hertel assumed no effective Uruguay liberalization post-1995, leaving much more to be done in a post-Uruguay environment. Reconciling FTAP's results with DFAT (1999) is more difficult because of a lack of detail in the DFAT study.

Most other economies are also projected to gain individually from these reforms. Only Canada is projected to be slightly poorer than otherwise as a result of complete trade liberalization.

For some economies — the European Union, the United States, Canada, Singapore and Taiwan — the contribution of multilateral services trade liberalization is projected to be negative. For the European Union, the projected loss of US$ 6 billion would almost completely outweigh its gains from multilateral liberalization of agriculture and manufacturing. The United States is projected to lose almost US$ 2 billion from services trade liberalization, though it would still gain significantly overall. The following discussion tries to uncover the reasons for these projected income losses.

The measure of real income used here is similar to that in the GTAP model — a measure of national income, deflated by an index of the prices of household consumption, government consumption, and national saving. But for FTAP, as noted, the relevant measure of national income is net national product — the income accruing to the residents of a region — rather than net domestic product — the income generated within the borders of a region. Thus, net domestic product must be adjusted for the income earned on outward FDI, net of the income repatriated overseas from inward FDI, plus the income from net bond holdings.

As in the GTAP model, the measure of welfare can be decomposed into a number of influences. For agricultural and manufacturing liberalization, the welfare results are dominated by two things — the contribution of improvements in allocative efficiency, and the contribution of changes in the terms of trade (which can be positive or negative). As shown above, the model's regions are projected to experience positive income gains, or in a few cases small losses, as a result of these effects.

For services liberalization, however, changes in foreign direct investment patterns contribute two additional effects. Firstly, FDI can lead to an expansion or contraction in the capital stock located within a region, leading to a positive or negative contribution to income from this change in national endowments. Secondly, the changes in rents earned on foreign direct investments can also affect national incomes.

The first column of Table 4.7 shows the contribution to real income from changes in real capital endowments. Generally, if capital endowments improve, real GDP is higher than otherwise. However, sometimes real GDP can rise, even if endowments fall, because those endowments are used more efficiently. The benefit of having additional varieties as output expands is another source of productivity improvement.

Some of the change in endowments comes from foreign direct investment, and some comes from investment by domestic residents. The second column of Table 4.7 shows the contribution to real income from

Table 4.7. Contributions to Real Income Changes from Liberalizing Services Trade
(US$ million)

	Contribution of endowment change to EV	*Contribution of change in real FDI stocks to EV*	*Contribution of change in real bond holding to EV*	*Contribution of change in rents on FDI capital*	*Contribution of change in rents on FDI output*
Australia	58	0	4	534	−39
NZ	−43	5	52	−10	6
Japan	−1,030	3,120	−2,978	−3,629	−5,101
Korea	438	−5	39	51	72
Indonesia	7,158	−541	−4,519	162	368
Malaysia	367	−103	−168	253	332
Philippines	164	−91	47	70	144
Singapore	−1,071	−198	−108	401	1,049
Thailand	305	−24	−393	227	259
China	52,164	−12,649	−5,776	4,163	8,686
Hong Kong	102	7,829	−621	−2,638	−5,573
Taiwan	312	378	−583	−137	−286
Canada	−747	34	1,086	27	−52
USA	−5,713	2,665	1,708	−3,057	−3,659
Mexico	131	−67	332	247	266
Chile	202	−39	−54	101	56
R. Cairns	401	−137	1,800	450	486
EU	−3,672	1,441	6,327	−2,265	−3,110
R. World	15,002	−2,337	3,285	5,427	6,581

Source: FTAP model projections.

changes in real FDI stocks. The third column shows the contribution to real income from changes in real bond holdings. Both help to indicate the way in which changes in capital endowments are financed.

For example, Japan's capital stock shrinks, partly because it has a big increase in outward FDI. In fact, it also borrows (a negative change on bond holding) in order to finance its outward FDI. By contrast, China's increase in capital endowments comes partly from a large increase in inward FDI, and partly from additional foreign borrowing. The United States is projected to have a smaller capital endowment than otherwise, offset by an increase in outward FDI and increased lending to other regions. The pattern for the European Union is the same as for the United States.

The last two columns of Table 4.7 show the income contributions to recipient countries of changes in the rents from barriers to services trade, as these barriers are eliminated. What is striking is the loss of rents to the main providers of outward FDI — Japan, Hong Kong, the United States and the European Union. In fact, the loss of rents to the United States is more than sufficient to explain its projected real income loss from services trade liberalization in Table 4.6, and the loss of rents in the European Union would explain most of its projected loss from services trade liberalization. Given the uncertainty about the allocation of existing rents, it is not at all clear that the true impact on the United States and European Union would be as great as shown in Table 4.7. And if barriers to services trade in these economies have been understated, then so too will their gains in allocative efficiency. Thus, their projected net income losses from services trade liberalization in Table 4.6 should be heavily qualified. Similarly, Canada's overall income loss, which comes primarily from adverse terms of trade effects, should also be qualified, given uncertainty about many key features of the model.

4.4 The Effects of Partial Liberalization of Services Trade

While the preceding section examined the effects of complete liberalization, a new trade round is likely to deliver only partial liberalization. Because the structure of trade barriers in the services area is relatively complex, there is a real question as to the best way to approach partial liberalization in that sector. It is well known that some approaches to partial liberalization can worsen disparities in protection, moving resources further away from their pattern in a world free of distortions, and worsening real income. Thus, it is important to determine paths of partial liberalization of services trade that avoid such outcomes.

It is hard to identify such paths *a priori*. In liberalization of goods trade, 'tops down' and 'across-the-board' strategies to lowering tariffs are known to generally avoid second-best economic welfare losses. A 'tops down' approach to services trade liberalization might suggest that restrictions on national treatment be tackled first, since these cause barriers to be higher for foreign than for domestic service providers. It might also suggest that barriers to commercial presence be tackled ahead of barriers to other modes of service delivery, since their *ad valorem* equivalents tend to be higher (see Table 4.4). Putting these two propositions together, does this mean that the best strategy is to remove restrictions on national treatment for firms seeking to deliver via commercial presence? The problem is that, given the pervasiveness of restrictions elsewhere, there is a real danger that resources will move in the 'wrong' direction, a result demonstrated in a partial equilibrium framework in Dee, Hardin and Holmes (2000).

Table 4.8 gives a breakdown of the effects on world real income of various partial approaches to services liberalization, comparing the removal of restrictions on market access and national treatment, as well as the removal of barriers on establishment versus ongoing operation.

Table 4.8. Effects of Partial Services Liberalization on World Real Income (US$ billion)

	Remove restrictions on market access	*Remove restrictions on national treatment*	*Both*
Remove barriers to establishment	56.8	3.7	64.2
Remove barriers to ongoing operation	25.6	12.9	39.3
Both	98.8	19.3	133.4

Source: FTAP model projections.

The first thing to note is that, because of interaction effects, the effects of various types of partial liberalization are not strictly additive. Instead, the effects of combining two types of liberalization generally exceed the sum of the effects of doing each separately. One reason is that the more widespread the liberalization, the less the chance of a second-best deterioration in allocative efficiency.

Table 4.8 shows that the best *single* type of liberalization for world economic welfare is the removal of those barriers to establishment that affect domestic and foreign firms equally (ie affect market access). Removing *all* barriers to establishment would be better than removing *all* barriers to ongoing operation. This reflects the particularly distortionary effects of taxes on capital. Removing *all* restrictions on market access would be much better than removing *all* restrictions on national treatment. This is more like an 'across-the-board' than a 'tops down' approach, and it avoids the second-best welfare losses identified in Dee, Hardin and Holmes (2000).

Of course, the pattern shown in Table 4.8 need not hold for individual economies. The results show, however, that the global removal of those barriers to establishment affecting domestic and foreign firms equally (ie affecting market access) remains a winning outcome for 14 of the 19 regions in the model (including Australia), leading to significant real income gains in those economies. The exceptions include Japan, Hong Kong and Canada, all significant sources of outward FDI. However, the United States and the European Union are not exceptions. Thus, the exceptions do not seem to arise because of a loss of rents — this tends to occur no matter what the type of liberalization. Instead, it seems to reflect differences in the pattern of allocative efficiency and terms of trade effects.

The detailed results therefore show that it is difficult of find a Pareto improvement (an outcome where at least some economies gain and none lose) from partial liberalization when it involves a particular *type* of barrier. This suggests that a better strategy may be to negotiate gradual reductions in *all* types of barriers simultaneously.

4.5 Agenda for Further Research

Much of the development agenda has been outlined already. It involves continuing to obtain estimates of the price impacts of barriers to services trade, along the lines outlined in Findlay and Warren (2000). Such methods could also be used to estimate the price impact of barriers to foreign direct investment in agriculture and manufacturing. More sectoral detail needs to be incorporated into FTAP, so as to be able to model the barriers to each service separately. More research is required to obtain more realistic cost and sales structures for FDI firms and, if possible, a realistic initial allocation of rents. And the welfare measure in FTAP needs to be amended to take account of the costs of risk taking, given risk aversion.

Chapter 5

Measuring the Cost of Barriers to Trade in Services[1]

Philippa Dee, Kevin Hanslow, and Tien Phamduc

To what extent can the traditional tools of trade policy analysis be used to analyse the economic costs of barriers to trade in services?

Traditional analysis of trade barriers has focused primarily on the effects of tariffs. These are discriminatory taxes levied on foreign-produced goods at the border of a country.

The Heckscher–Ohlin (HO) framework is a standard framework in which tariffs have been analysed (Heckscher [1919] 1949, Ohlin 1933). This framework assumes perfect substitutability between domestically-produced and foreign goods of the same type, fixed endowments of primary factors of production, and perfect mobility of those factors between sectors within an economy. The framework has been extended to consider more than two goods and factors (Jones and Scheinkman 1977), the presence of a sector-specific factor of production (Mayer 1974, Mussa 1974), imperfect competition (Markusen 1981), increasing returns to scale (Melvin 1969) and product differentiation (Krugman 1979, Helpman 1981).

However, barriers to trade in services are unlike tariffs. They are typically regulatory barriers, rather than explicit taxes. They need not

---

[1] This is an edited version of Chapter 1 in Takatoshi Ito and Anne O. Krueger (2003), *Trade in Services in the Asia–Pacific Region*, NBER–East Asia Seminar on Economics, Volume 11, Chicago and London: University of Chicago Press: 11–46. © 2003 by the National Bureau of Economic Research. All rights reserved.

discriminate against foreigners. Indeed, barriers to market access are often designed to protect incumbent firms from *any* new entry, be it by domestic or foreign firms. And barriers to services trade are not restricted to affecting the *output* of services firms. One particularly important category of barriers to services trade — restrictions on foreign direct investment by service firms — affects the use of primary factors. These restrictions are recognized in the General Agreement on Trade in Services (GATS) under the World Trade Organization (WTO), since this agreement recognizes commercial presence as one of the modes by which services are traded.

To date, few papers of either a theoretical or an empirical nature have reviewed all these aspects of barriers to services trade. Some early papers largely dismissed concerns that the determinants of comparative advantage in services might differ from those in goods (Hindley and Smith 1984, Deardorff 1985). A few theoretical papers in the late 1980s examined some of the important characteristics of services, including knowledge intensity (eg Markusen 1989, Melvin 1989). This characteristic also featured in subsequent analysis of goods trade under imperfect competition (eg Grossman and Helpman 1991). However, those early theoretical papers did not look at the nature of barriers to services trade. Recently, a few empirical papers have examined the effects of removing barriers to trade in services. Many of these have failed to take account of barriers to commercial presence as an important category of barriers to trade in services (Brown *et al.* 1995, Brown, Deardorff, and Stern 1996, Hertel 2000, Nagarajan 1999). One seminal paper by Petri (1997) introduced a treatment of barriers to foreign direct investment in the services sector, but it failed to take into account barriers on the other modes of service delivery. Moreover, all empirical papers have suffered from a dearth of convincing empirical estimates of the incidence and economic significance of barriers to services trade.

A recent empirical paper by Dee and Hanslow (2001) sought to analyse the effects of removing barriers to services trade in a more comprehensive fashion.[2] The barriers included non-discriminatory

---

[2] Brown and Stern (2001) contains a services model that was developed independently and shares a number of conceptual and data features with the model presented here.

barriers to market access as well as discriminatory restrictions on national treatment. They included barriers to commercial presence as well as barriers to the other modes of service delivery. The focus of that paper was to compare the gains from liberalizing services trade with the gains from removing all post-Uruguay barriers to trade in agriculture and manufacturing. The paper also compared the gains from the total removal of barriers to services trade with the gains from several alternative approaches to partial liberalization. It identified significant second-best problems with some approaches to partial liberalization.

The purpose of this chapter is to look more deeply at that analysis of services trade liberalization in order to assess the extent to which the traditional Stolper and Samuelson (1941) and Rybczynski (1955) results from the HO framework are still relevant in a more realistic model of services trade liberalization. In the process, the analysis examines whether and how the benefits of services trade liberalization are passed on to other sectors in the economy. Thus, the analysis tries to open up the 'black box' of what is a rather complex general equilibrium model of services trade in order to gain insights into the sectoral results from that model in terms of more simple textbook treatments of trade policy analysis.

The structure of the chapter is as follows. It first describes the model used — a multi-sector, multi-regional computable general equilibrium model of world trade and investment. The theoretical structure of the model covers both foreign direct investment (FDI) and portfolio investment. The model's database contains estimates of FDI stocks and the activities of FDI firms, each on a bilateral basis. Thus, the model recognizes that both goods and services can be delivered via FDI as well as by conventional trade. The chapter then looks at the size of the barriers to trade in services and the cost impost they impose on other sectors of the economy. This analysis uses the first of a comprehensive new set of estimates of barriers to services trade. To understand the general equilibrium effects of removing these barriers, the effects on each sector in selected economies are built up from a more restricted, partial equilibrium multi-country model. To this partial model are gradually added the resource constraints and income linkages associated with general equilibrium. It is as the resource constraints are added that the relevance of Stolper–Samuelson and Rybczynski effects can be analysed. The chapter then briefly summarizes the implications of services trade liberalization for regional incomes. Finally, the chapter identifies areas for further research.

5.1 The FTAP Model

The model is a version of the Global Trade Analysis Project model (GTAP, Hertel 1997) with foreign direct investment, known as FTAP. The treatment of FDI follows closely the pioneering work of Petri (1997). The FTAP model also incorporates increasing returns to scale and large-group monopolistic competition in all sectors. This follows Francois, McDonald, and Nordstrom (1995), among others, who adopted this treatment for manufacturing and resource sectors, and Brown *et al.* (1995) and Markusen, Rutherford, and Tarr (1999), who used similar treatments for services. Finally, FTAP makes provision for capital accumulation and international borrowing and lending. This uses a treatment of international (portfolio) capital mobility developed by McDougall (1993) and recently incorporated into GTAP by Verikios and Hanslow (1999). FTAP is implemented using the GEMPACK software suite (Harrison and Pearson 1996). Its structure is documented fully in Hanslow, Phamduc, and Verikios (1999). The most recent version of the model and its documentation are available at http://crawford.anu.edu.au/crawford_people/content/staff/pdee.php.

The theoretical structure and model database are described in detail in Dee and Hanslow (2001), reproduced as Chapter 4 in this volume.

Estimates of barriers to services trade

The estimates of barriers to services trade were the first of a comprehensive new set of estimates, documented in Findlay and Warren (2000). The general methodology of these studies is as follows.

- Qualitative information on barriers to services trade is converted to a quantitative index measure of trade restrictiveness, based on coverage and some initial judgements about the relative restrictiveness of the different sorts of restrictions.

- An econometric model is developed to measure the determinants of the economic performance (e.g., price, profit margin, cost, or quantity) of service firms in a given sector in different countries, taking account of all the factors that economic theory would suggest are relevant, including the index measure of trade restrictiveness.

- The economic model is used to estimate the determinants of economic performance. Wherever possible, the components of the trade restrictiveness index are entered separately so that the econometrics can reveal something about the relative weights attached to the separate components.[3]

- The results of the econometrics are used to calculate the effect of trade restrictions on performance. Where necessary, quantity or profit effects are converted to price or cost effects.

Estimates of barriers to trade in banking services along these lines were taken from Kalirajan *et al.* (2000), and estimates of barriers to trade in telecommunications services were taken from Warren (2000). The rates can be taken as indicative of post-Uruguay rates, because although the Uruguay Round established the architecture for services trade negotiations, it did not achieve much in the way of services trade liberalization (Hoekman 1995).

For modelling purposes, the barrier estimates were decomposed according to a two-by-two classification.

- The GATS framework distinguishes four modes of service delivery — via commercial presence, cross-border supply, consumption abroad, and the presence of natural persons. Accordingly, the FTAP model distinguishes barriers to establishment from barriers to ongoing operation. This is similar to the distinction between commercial presence and other modes of delivery, because barriers to establishment are a component of the barriers to commercial

---

[3] This is not possible where there is high multicollinearity between the various components, or where there is a lack of in-sample variation in some of the components.

presence. Barriers to establishment are modelled as taxes on the movement of capital. Barriers to ongoing operation are modelled as taxes on the output of the service providing firms.

- The GATS framework also distinguishes restrictions on market access from restrictions on national treatment. As noted above, the former are restrictions on entry, be it by locally-owned or foreign-owned firms. In the FTAP model, they are treated as non-discriminatory. Restrictions on national treatment mean that foreign-owned firms are treated less favourably than domestic firms. These restrictions are treated as discriminatory.

The decomposition of trade barriers into this two-by-two classification follows the classifications used by Kalirajan *et al.* (2000) and Warren (2000). Table 5.1 shows how they classify barriers to trade in banking and telecommunications services. Note that in the banking sector, prudential regulations were not counted as trade barriers or included in the restrictiveness index. This was based on the recognition that they are designed to address a genuine market failure and the judgement that they are generally implemented in an appropriate fashion to that end. It is also consistent with the so-called 'prudential carve-out' allowed for in the GATS.

Note also that in the banking study, horizontal (ie not sector-specific) restrictions on the permanent movement of people were counted as a barrier to establishment, and hence they were modelled as a barrier to the movement of capital. More properly, these restrictions should be modelled as a barrier to the movement of labour, but so far FTAP does not allow for international labour mobility. Similarly, horizontal restrictions on the temporary movement of people were counted as a barrier to ongoing operation, affecting both offshore affiliates and services delivered via 'cross-border' trade, where the latter is broadly defined to include services delivered via the temporary movement of the consumer or the producer. In reality, the barriers affecting true cross-border trade are sufficiently different from those affecting trade involving temporary movement to warrant modelling them separately. These are areas for further research.

Table 5.1.　Classifying Barriers to Trade in Banking and Telecommunications Services

	Non-discriminatory barriers to market access	***Discriminatory derogations from national treatment***
Barriers to Establishment		
Banking	Are there restrictions on the number of bank licenses?	Are there restrictions on the number of foreign bank licences? Are there restrictions on foreign equity investment or requirements for foreigners to enter through a joint venture with a domestic bank? Are there restrictions on the permanent movement of people?
Telecommunications	One measure of restriction is actual number of competitors in fixed and mobile markets. Is there an enforced monopoly, partial competition or full competition in various fixed line markets and mobile market? What percentage of the incumbent fixed or mobile operator is privatized?	What percentage of foreign investment is allowed in competitive carriers?
Barriers to Ongoing Operation		
Banking	Are there general restrictions on raising funds, lending, providing other lines of business, or expanding the number of banking outlets?	Are foreign banks restricted in raising funds, lending, providing other lines of business, or expanding the number of banking outlets? Are there restrictions on the proportion of foreigners on the board of directors? Are there restrictions on the temporary movement of people?
Telecommunications	Are there restrictions on leased lines or private networks? Are there restrictions on third party resale? Are there restrictions on connection of leased lines and private networks to the public switched telephone network?	Are there restrictions on callback services?

Source: McGuire and Schuele (2000) and Warren (2000).

A simple average of the estimated price effects of barriers to trade in banking and telecommunications was taken as being typical of most services — all of the GTAP service categories of trade and transport; finance, business, and recreational services; and half of public administration, defense, education, and health. The remainder of public administration, defense, education, and health, along with electricity, water and gas, construction, and ownership of dwellings were assumed to be strictly non-traded (note that engineering services are part of business services, not construction). The resulting average estimates of barriers to trade in the tertiary sector would have been about 50 to 100 percent bigger had the banking and telecommunications estimates been taken as indicative of the whole of the services sector. A procedure for future research is to use the next version of the GTAP database, which will have more services-sector detail, to model barriers to each service separately, thus overcoming the extreme arbitrariness of these assumptions. In the meantime, the computational results should be treated as preliminary and interpreted with appropriate caution.

The resulting structure of post-Uruguay barriers to trade in services was summarized in Table 4.4 in Chapter 4 of this volume. Barriers to trade in primary (agricultural, resource, and processed food) and secondary (manufacturing) products were also shown for comparison purposes. Barriers to primary products are represented via a combination of taxes on imports, and subsidies (shown in Table 4.4 as negative taxes) on exports and output. The way that services trade barriers are handled in the theoretical structure of the model was also explained in Chapter 4 of this volume.

5.2 The Cost Impact of Barriers to Trade in Services

The direct 'tax equivalents' of barriers to trade in services (shown in Table 4.4 of the previous chapter) are often significant, compared with the trade barriers expected to remain in agriculture and manufacturing after full implementation of the Uruguay Round. The estimates also show that barriers to services trade tend to be much higher in developing than in developed economies.

A priori, this does not mean that the services sectors in developing economies would suffer most from services trade liberalization. Because barriers to services trade are unlike tariffs, there are two key mechanisms by which the services sectors in developing countries could expand following services trade liberalization.

- Not all services trade barriers discriminate against foreign services suppliers, so the services sector could expand because of new domestic entry.
- Some services trade barriers restrict inward FDI, so the services sector could expand because of new foreign entry.

These mechanisms could be sufficient to offset the traditional mechanisms by which a protected sector can be harmed by removal of protection.

- Some services barriers discriminate against foreign services delivered cross-border, so the services sector could contract in the face of additional import competition.
- Services trade liberalization may benefit downstream using industries, and the services sector may lose out in the competition for domestic resources (eg labour).

Figure 5.1 examines the extent to which downstream using industries are likely to benefit from services trade liberalization. It shows the direct and indirect cost impost of domestic barriers to trade in services on all sectors in selected model regions, as calculated from the FTAP model database.

In general terms, the figure shows the direct and indirect input requirements needed to produce a unit of final demand in each sector. For example, a unit of processed food (a primary activity) sold to households might require inputs of unprocessed food (another primary activity), as well as packaging materials from the secondary sector. The packaging materials might again require inputs from forestry (a primary activity), along with electricity from the tertiary sector. Each of these

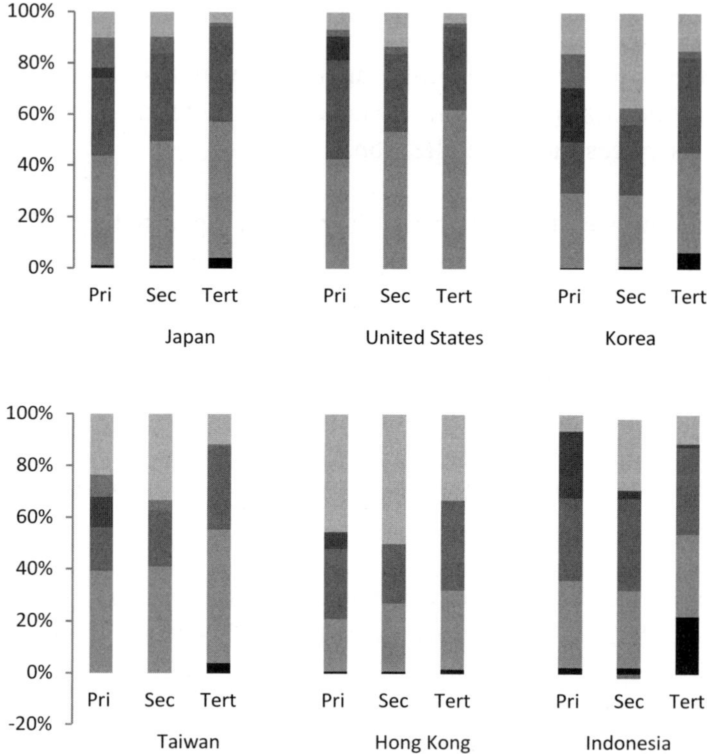

Figure 5.1. Direct and Indirect Requirements per Unit of Final Demand

direct and indirect inputs would have its own requirements for labour, capital, fixed factors (land and natural resources), and imported inputs, and these can be added up. Where the cost of the direct and indirect inputs is inflated by taxes, the direct and indirect tax contributions can also be calculated.

Thus, the direct and indirect cost impost of domestic barriers to services trade has been calculated by adding together the following:

- the output and capital taxes on direct and indirect services inputs, where those taxes represent the effects of domestic barriers to commercial presence (both establishment and ongoing operation); and

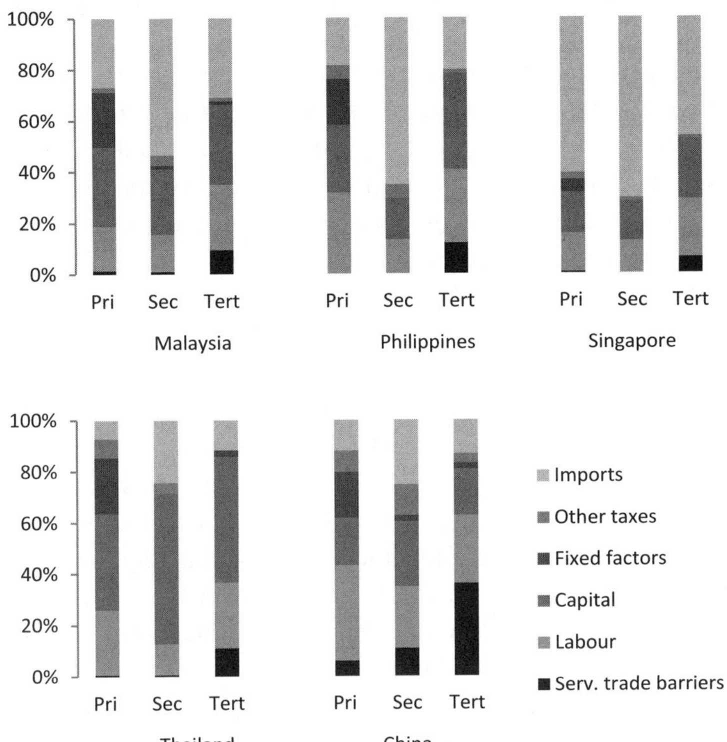

Figure 5.1. Direct and Indirect Requirements per Unit of Final Demand (continued)

- the export taxes in the source region falling on direct and indirect imported inputs, where these export taxes represent the effects of domestic barriers to cross-border services trade (where the term 'cross-border' is interpreted loosely to include services traded via the temporary movement of the producer or consumer).

All other domestic taxes are collected in the contribution of 'Other taxes', and all other taxes on imports (primarily tariffs) are included with the contribution of 'Imports'.

Figure 5.1 shows that, in every region shown, the greatest unit cost impost from services trade barriers falls on the services sector itself. This reflects two factors. First, the services sector experiences a direct taxing effect, whereas in other sectors the burden is indirect, through the higher cost of service inputs. Second, this effect is reinforced by the fact that in both developed and developing economies, the services sector itself tends to have a higher direct services input requirement than any other sector. Although other sectors may need service inputs, the greatest intensity of use of services is within the services sector itself. Thus, as will be seen, the benefits of services trade liberalization in many economies are concentrated within the services sector. This result is contrary to the normal effects of tariff removal, where the benefits are typically concentrated in other sectors.

Another feature of Figure 5.1 is that in the economies with the highest per capita incomes (Japan, the United States, Korea, Taiwan, and Hong Kong), the cost impost of domestic services trade barriers on other sectors is minimal. Although these economies tend to be more service dependent, in terms of having higher direct service input requirements, their domestic barriers to services trade are also relatively low.

Somewhat surprisingly, in the economies with the lowest per capita incomes (Indonesia, Malaysia, the Philippines, Singapore, Thailand, and China), the cost impost of domestic services trade barriers on other sectors is not much greater. Only in China, where services trade barriers are particularly high, does the cost impost on other sectors approach 10 percent.[4]

By showing the cost impost of only domestic barriers to trade in services, Figure 5.1 understates the potential first-round impact of multilateral liberalization of services trade. When barriers are removed globally, not only will domestic goods and services be cheaper, but so too will goods and services available in other economies. This benefit is likely to be significant in the highly import-intensive economies such as Korea, Taiwan, Hong Kong, Malaysia, the Philippines, and Singapore. Moreover, because the trade and transport services used to ship goods

---

[4] The cost impost is estimated to be particularly high in China because its telecommunications market is particularly restrictive. When estimates of services barriers are incorporated for a broader range of services than banking and telecommunications, the overall cost imposts could differ from those shown here. Not only could the overall impost in China be lower, but the impost in developed countries could also be higher (since banking and telecommunications happen to be sectors in which developed countries are particularly liberal).

internationally will also be cheaper, there will be an additional cost reduction effect not captured in Figure 5.1.[5]

5.3 The Sectoral Effects of Removing Barriers to Trade in Services

Partial equilibrium effects on sectoral output

A useful way to understand the sectoral effects of removing barriers to trade in services is to start with a partial equilibrium framework and to gradually add the economy-wide constraints that distinguish a general from a partial equilibrium approach. This is a very useful technique of analysis, developed by Hertel (1997).

An initial partial equilibrium model is obtained by 'turning off' the following parts of FTAP:

- *Factor supply constraints.* Each sector in each region can get all the labour and capital it needs at the going wage or rental price. Thus, the secondary and tertiary sectors in each region have horizontal supply curves (which nevertheless move downward as services barriers are removed). The primary sector continues to have an upward-sloping supply curve because fixed factors (land and natural resources) are still treated as being in fixed supply in each economy.
- *Income linkages.* Irrespective of what is projected to happen to factor prices and other variables, the model's measure of welfare is held fixed in each region. This 'equivalent variation' is essentially a measure of net national product, or the real income accruing to the residents of each economy. In general equilibrium, it is affected not just by the amount of activity generated within a region, but also by net foreign interest and dividend payments associated with foreign borrowing and lending and with FDI.
- *The endogenous productivity and taste changes* associated with a love of variety. (In the full FTAP model, firms benefit from a wider choice

---

[5] See Dee (2012b) for the importance of this effect in ASEAN countries.

of intermediate inputs in the same way that consumers benefit from a wider choice of final goods.)

In partial equilibrium, all the demand-side substitution possibilities of the full FTAP model are still in operation. Thus, for example, the demand for the output of the secondary sector in a region will depend on the following factors:

- how the cost (and hence price) of its output changes relative to the cost (and price) of output of secondary sectors in other economies, and how consumers and users in each region substitute between domestic and various imported sources of secondary output as a result of those relative price changes;
- how the cost (and hence price) of its output changes relative to the average price (across sources) of primary and tertiary output, and how domestic consumers and government substitute between the outputs of these different sectors as a result of these relative price changes;[6] and
- what the secondary input requirements are per unit of output in other sectors, and whether those other sectors are expanding or contracting.

Thus, even in the partial equilibrium model, the richness of substitution possibilities and inter-industry linkages on the demand side make for a rather complicated story.

Because real incomes in each economy are assumed to be fixed, it would be expected that unless substitution effects dominate, the demand for, and hence output of, a commodity or service should increase whenever services trade liberalization reduces its price. And the only sector in which services trade liberalization would conceivably *not* reduce the price is the primary sector, where the return to the fixed factor could conceivably be bid up. Thus, the presumption is that services trade

---

[6] In FTAP, as in GTAP, consumers and government are the only agents to substitute directly among different commodities. For intermediate and investment usage, different commodities (aggregated across sources) are used in fixed proportions.

liberalization should reduce prices and increase output. Where this does not occur, it must be as a result of substitution effects.

Within the services sector itself, prices fall and output rises in the ASEAN economies and China (Table 5.2). Note that although the prices of domestic services fall in these economies, the prices of imported services fall by significantly more. Thus, substitution toward imports in these economies might suggest that services output should fall. Offsetting this, however, is an increase in exports of services from these economies. In the services sector, the price of a service import in the destination country can fall by significantly more than its output price in the exporting country. This is primarily because services trade liberalization involves removing the 'export tax' equivalent of barriers to cross-border trade imposed by the destination country. Thus, although domestic services in the ASEAN region and China are disadvantaged relative to imports at home, when the same services are exported, their prices compare favourably with service exports from most other regions. (This is indicated indirectly by the fact that the domestic output price of services falls by more in ASEAN and China than in the other regions.) Thus, the services output expansion in ASEAN and China is primarily an export story.

Table 5.2.　Partial Equilibrium Effects on Selected Regions of Removing Global Barriers to Trade in Services, by Sector (per cent)

	Primary			*Secondary*			*Tertiary*		
	Q	Pd	Pm	Q	Pd	Pm	Q	Pd	Pm
Japan	−0.3	−2.4	−0.9	−1.4	−2.6	−3.9	−3.4	−2.1	−21.9
United States	−1.3	−0.7	−1.3	−7.3	−0.6	−3.3	−4.3	−0.4	−13.6
Korea	−0.1	−1.9	−1.0	2.3	−2.9	−3.1	−2.3	−3.5	−16.3
Taiwan	1.2	−1.2	−0.9	2.9	−2.3	−2.9	−4.5	−2.5	−14.7
Hong Kong	6.9	−1.1	0.1	15.2	−3.8	−3.9	−14.5	−5.2	−23.1
Indonesia	2.7	−0.5	−0.9	8.8	−3.6	−3.1	13.4	−12.1	−30.6
Malaysia	4.2	0.5	−0.9	6.9	−3.3	−2.9	0.3	−8.2	−21.3
Philippines	1.2	−1.1	−0.9	2.9	−2.9	−2.9	8.1	−7.5	−27.9
Singapore	18.2	−1.6	−0.9	8.9	−3.5	−3.0	1.9	−6.7	−19.6
Thailand	3.1	0.6	−1.3	−5.3	−1.9	−3.0	0.3	−7.6	−21.9
China	36.6	18.1	−1.2	132.0	−10.2	−2.6	245.2	−27.9	−31.9

Q = domestic output quantity, Pd = domestic price, Pm = import price.
Source: FTAP model projections, partial equilibrium closure.

In the higher per capita income economies, services output falls, despite a reduction in the domestic price, because of substitution toward imports. This is in accordance with the relative price movements shown in Table 5.2.

The declines in the output of the secondary sector in Japan and the United States are because of substitution toward imports, especially in intermediate usage. For the other higher-income economies (Korea, Taiwan, and Hong Kong), the prices of domestic secondary output do not change greatly relative to secondary import prices, so the secondary-output expansions in these economies are primarily an export story. In ASEAN and China, the secondary-output expansions are because of both increased exports and substitution away from imports.

Although in the secondary and tertiary sectors the results are driven primarily by substitution among different sources of each commodity, in the primary sector it is possible to see the effects of each region's households' substituting among different commodities. This explains the slight falls in the output of the primary sector in Japan and Korea. In these economies, the prices of imported services fall significantly more than the prices of any other final commodity. Households tend to substitute toward imported services and away from everything else. Thus, primary output in these economies falls, despite the fact that the price of domestic primary output falls by more than its import price.

In the United States, the effect on primary-sector output of households' switching away from the primary sector in general is reinforced by substitution (in relative terms) toward primary imports.

In Taiwan, Hong Kong, Singapore, and Thailand, the expansion of the primary sector is primarily an export story. (The landed cost plus insurance and freight [cif] price of Thai primary exports falls, despite a slight increase in the domestic output price, because of cheaper international trade and transport services.) This can be confirmed by looking at more detailed model results not shown in Table 5.2.

In Indonesia, Malaysia, the Philippines, and China, the switch by households away from the primary sector in general is offset by increased intermediate input demand, and some increase in export demand, for primary sector output. The increased intermediate demand occurs despite an adverse relative price movement against imports (in all but the Philippines), because of inter-industry linkages between the primary sector and the downstream secondary and tertiary sectors.

In summary, multilateral liberalization of services trade reduces domestic costs and prices across all economies, and the partial equilibrium sectoral effects are of three types.

- In economies such as those of Japan and the United States, where initial domestic services barriers are particularly low, domestic prices do not fall by much, and substitution toward cheaper imports leads to a reduction in output in all sectors of the economy. Real income can remain constant, however, because of the cheaper imports.
- At the other extreme, in the economies of the ASEAN region and China, where initial domestic services barriers are relatively high, domestic prices tend to fall significantly, and output in (almost) all sectors of these economies expands.
- In between are the economies of Korea, Taiwan, and Hong Kong, where initial domestic services barriers are moderate, but where all sectors are more trade exposed than in Japan and the United States. Thus, although the services sectors in these economies may not benefit from services trade liberalization, at least some of their other sectors benefit from cheaper domestic and imported inputs and thus gain an advantage on export markets.

General equilibrium effects on sectoral output

The partial equilibrium results of Table 5.2 assumed that each sector in each economy could get any additional labour and capital at the going wage or rental price. The results also ignored the income implications of services trade liberalization.

In Table 5.3, these effects are gradually reintroduced into the model. The first column reproduces the partial equilibrium results from Table 5.2. In the second column, primary factor supply constraints are imposed. As in textbook models, aggregate supplies of capital and labour are assumed to be fixed, and these factors are treated as being perfectly mobile within each sector of the economy. In the third column, sectoral

Table 5.3. Partial and General Equilibrium Effects on Sectoral Output in Selected Regions of Removing Global Barriers to Trade in Services (per cent)

		Full partial equilibrium	*Fixed factors*	*Capital as in general equilibrium*	*Full general equilibrium*
Japan	Primary	−0.3	0.2	−0.3	−0.4
	Secondary	−1.4	0.9	−0.5	−0.3
	Tertiary	−3.4	−0.3	0.2	0.1
United States	Primary	−1.3	2.4	0.4	0.6
	Secondary	−7.3	1.9	0.2	0.6
	Tertiary	−4.3	−0.7	−0.2	−0.4
Korea[a]	Primary	−0.1	−0.5	−0.7	−0.8
	Secondary	2.3	−0.4	−1.4	−1.6
	Tertiary	−2.3	0.3	1.0	1.1
Taiwan[a]	Primary	1.2	0.4	−0.1	0.1
	Secondary	2.9	2.5	0.2	1.0
	Tertiary	−4.5	−1.1	0.1	−0.2
Hong Kong[a]	Primary	6.9	3.7	0.0	0.2
	Secondary	15.2	9.0	−1.2	−2.2
	Tertiary	−14.5	−2.1	0.4	0.6
Indonesia[a]	Primary	2.7	−3.4	0.3	0.3
	Secondary	8.8	−9.7	2.5	2.6
	Tertiary	13.4	8.9	8.5	9.2
Malaysia[a]	Primary	4.2	−1.1	0.0	0.1
	Secondary	6.9	−1.8	0.2	0.1
	Tertiary	0.3	3.3	1.5	1.5
Philippines[a]	Primary	1.2	−3.0	−1.9	−1.9
	Secondary	2.9	−6.6	−2.6	−3.6
	Tertiary	8.1	5.6	2.3	2.5
Singapore	Primary	18.2	3.2	−4.0	−4.0
	Secondary	8.9	−4.2	−5.6	−6.6
	Tertiary	1.9	4.5	0.6	1.0
Thailand[a]	Primary	3.1	0.7	−0.2	−0.1
	Secondary	−5.3	−8.0	−0.7	−0.8
	Tertiary	0.3	8.1	1.3	1.3
China[a]	Primary	36.6	−6.5	−1.1	−0.2
	Secondary	132.0	−16.7	4.5	2.5
	Tertiary	245.2	43.7	28.7	32.5

[a] Aggregate capital stock projected to increase in general equilibrium closure.
Source: FTAP model projections, partial and general equilibrium closures.

capital stocks are assumed to take the values they would in the full general equilibrium model. Thus, not only do aggregate capital stocks change in each economy, but capital is no longer perfectly mobile across sectors. Finally, the full general equilibrium results are presented. These incorporate not only the primary factor behaviour of the full general equilibrium model, but also the associated income effects (including the net foreign income flows associated with FDI).

In broad terms, the imposition of factor supply constraints is the single most important step in taking the partial equilibrium sectoral results toward their general equilibrium values.

Even with factor supply constraints, the results for the tertiary sector in each region are qualitatively quite close to the partial equilibrium results:

- the services sectors in Japan and the United States are still smaller than in the absence of services trade liberalization;
- the services sectors in most other high-income economies are also projected to decline (Korea is the exception); and
- the services sectors in the ASEAN region and China still gain from services trade liberalization.

Now, however, the wage–rental ratios in each economy adjust to ensure that the induced output changes in other sectors do not lead to a violation of the overall primary factor supply constraints. Thus, the output of the primary and secondary sectors in Japan, the United States, Taiwan, and Hong Kong is now projected to rise to counteract the decline in their services sectors. In the ASEAN region, China, and Korea, output in many of the primary and secondary sectors is now projected to decline to offset the expansion of their services sectors.

One question is whether the changes in wage–rental ratios in the 'fixed factors' version of the model are consistent with those predicted by the Stolper–Samuelson theorem. That theorem would predict that in the face of a decline in the relative price of services (induced by services trade liberalization) there would be a decline in the real return to the factor of production used relatively intensively in the services sector. In most economies, that factor is labour (see Figure 5.1). Although the assumption of fixed factor supplies and perfect factor mobility is consistent with the assumptions of the Stolper–Samuelson theorem, there are many other assumptions in the 'fixed factors' model that do not match the textbook Stolper–Samuelson assumptions exactly. It is nevertheless useful to see if the 'fixed factors' model retains a Stolper–Samuelson flavour in the context of services trade liberalization.

Broadly speaking, the Stolper–Samuelson theorem would predict a decline in the wage–rental ratio in most economies; by contrast, the wage rental ratio faced by producers in all economies in the 'fixed factors' model is projected to rise. The reason is simple. Services trade liberalization includes liberalization of FDI in the services sector. The removal of taxes on service-sector capital leads to a direct and significant decline in capital rentals, relative to wages, because, with fixed capital supplies, the loss of rents from barriers to capital are borne directly by capital owners.[7]

Thus, the nature of barriers to services trade leads to a significant departure from one of the standard textbook trade theorems.[8]

The results in the third column hint at the complexity of the capital supply story in the full FTAP model. Even though services trade liberalization involves removing taxes on service-sector capital, it is not always the case that cautious investors would invest more in those service sectors than they would if they viewed investment in any sector as being equally desirable (consistent with perfect sectoral capital mobility). In Japan, the United States, Korea, Taiwan, and Hong Kong, service-sector capital stocks are larger than in the 'fixed factors' case, but in the other economies they are smaller. This demonstrates how the capital supply behaviour in the FTAP model plays an important role in relocating capital across regions within a sector, as opposed to the textbook treatment of capital allocation across sectors within a region.

One question is whether the sectoral output responses associated with a change in aggregate capital stocks are consistent with those predicted

---

[7] The implication of this for regional incomes is not yet incorporated.

[8] The particular result depends on the assumption that barriers to trade in services create rents rather than raising costs. If barriers to services trade raise costs and hence move the production possibility frontier toward the origin, then services trade liberalization could raise the real returns to all factors of production, although the effects on relative factor returns could still be unclear *a priori*. Brown, Deardorff, and Stern (2000) also show how real returns to both factors can be raised by the additional gains from trade arising from increasing returns to scale, competition, and product variety, even when barriers are treated as tariff equivalents.

by the Rybczynski theorem. That theorem states that if product prices are fixed (say, by 'world prices'), an expansion in capital would lead to an expansion in the output of the product that uses capital relatively intensively and a contraction of the other product. Leamer and Levinsohn (1994, p. 7) give an insightful reinterpretation of the Rybczynski theorem:

> What is really at stake here is not the Rybczynski Theorem but rather its travelling companion, the Factor Price Equalization Theorem. These results together imply that factor supply changes . . . do not have much affect [*sic*] on factor prices because the potential affect [*sic*] on factor prices is dissipated by product mix changes in favour of the products that use the accumulating factor intensively.

Clearly, critical assumptions of the Rybczynski Theorem do not hold in the FTAP model. Products are imperfect substitutes, so that product prices are not 'given' to any single region. As a result, relative factor prices can also change to absorb the impact of an increase in capital, so that it does not have to be absorbed by changes in product composition.

However, one would expect the FTAP model to display the same underlying economic forces that lead to the Rybczynski result under its special set of assumptions. This can be demonstrated in an intermediate simulation in which aggregate capital in each region moves as it does in general equilibrium but is still perfectly mobile between sectors (thus, each region still has a unique economy-wide wage–rental ratio). In this intermediate simulation, there is the expected relationship between the direction of movement of the capital stock and whether the wage–rental ratio is higher or lower than in the 'fixed factors' version of the model. When the capital stock rises, the wage–rental ratio is higher than in the 'fixed factors' case, and when the capital stock falls, the wage–rental ratio is lower.

The final column of Table 5.3 incorporates the FTAP model's income linkages: real income in each region is no longer constant but reflects the induced changes in factor prices and international capital movements. Dee and Hanslow (2001) demonstrate that such income effects are crucial to the welfare implications of liberalizing trade in services, as will be seen shortly. However, Table 5.3 shows that these income effects do not have strong additional effects on the sectoral distribution of gains from services trade liberalization.

General equilibrium models are often regarded as 'black boxes', offering little chance of understanding what is inside. The above analysis suggests that because the structure of barriers to services trade is complex, the hardest part about understanding the effects of multilateral liberalization of services trade is understanding what happens in partial equilibrium.

The partial equilibrium results help to demonstrate how liberalization of services trade can differ from tariff removal. Barriers to services trade affect domestic new entrants as well as foreign suppliers, and the sector to benefit most in output terms from liberalization can often be the services sector itself.

The transition from partial to general equilibrium analysis also demonstrates how some of the standard textbook results fail to hold in the context of services trade liberalization. In particular, because services trade barriers affect the price of service-sector capital as well as service-sector output, the Stolper–Samuelson theorem fails to hold: the movement of relative factor prices is dominated by the removal of the barriers to capital movement. The Rybczynski theorem also fails to hold in its textbook form, but the underlying economic forces that lead to its result are still relevant.

General equilibrium welfare effects

The first column of Table 5.4 summarizes the effects of full liberalization of services trade on economic well-being in selected model regions (Dee and Hanslow 2001 present results for all model regions). As in GTAP, the measure of economic well-being is the equivalent variation — essentially a measure of the change in real income in each region, where the deflator is an index of the prices of household consumption, government consumption, and national saving. For FTAP, however, the relevant measure of national income is net national product — the income accruing to the residents of a region — rather than net domestic product — the income generated within the borders of a region. Thus, net

Table 5.4. Welfare Effects of Full Multilateral Liberalization of Services Trade (absolute change in US$ millions)

	Equivalent variation	*Contribution of endowment change to equivalent variation*	*Contribution of change in real FDI stocks to equivalent variation*	*Contribution of change in real bond holdings to equivalent variation*	*Contribution of change in rents on FDI capital and output*
Japan	4,130	−1,030	3,120	−2,978	−8,730
United States	−1,809	−5,713	2,665	1,708	−6,716
Korea	1,886	438	−5	39	123
Taiwan	−142	312	378	−583	−423
Hong Kong	5,896	102	7,829	−621	−8,211
Indonesia	2,470	7,158	−541	−4,519	530
Malaysia	1,015	367	−103	−168	585
Philippines	1,236	164	−91	47	214
Singapore	−247	−1,071	−198	−108	1,049
Thailand	1,698	305	−24	−393	486
China	90,869	52,164	−12,649	−5,776	12,849

Source: FTAP model projections, general equilibrium closure.

domestic product is adjusted for the income earned on outward FDI, net of the income repatriated overseas from inward FDI, plus the income from net bond holdings.

Three of the selected economies are projected to have incomes lower than otherwise as a result of full multilateral liberalization of services trade — the United States, Taiwan, and Singapore. Dee and Hanslow (2001) show that in each case, the losses from multilateral liberalization of services trade would be more than offset by income gains accruing from multilateral liberalization of trade in agriculture and manufacturing. Nevertheless, the source of the income losses from multilateral liberalization of services trade warrants further investigation, especially for the United States, where the losses are projected to be significant.

Dee and Hanslow (2001) show that for agricultural and manufacturing liberalization, the welfare results are dominated by two things: the contribution of improvements in allocative efficiency, and the contribution of induced changes in the terms of trade. The model's regions are projected to experience positive income gains, or in a few cases small losses, as a result of these effects.

For services liberalization, changes in FDI patterns contribute several additional effects. First, FDI can lead to an expansion or contraction in the capital stock located within a region, leading to a positive or negative contribution to income generated within a region from this change in national endowments. Second, it can lead to changes in net FDI and net lending positions, with consequent changes in net foreign income flows accruing to residents. Third, it can induce changes in the returns earned on those net foreign asset holdings. An important example here is changes in the rents earned on FDI.

The second column of Table 5.4 shows the contribution to real income from changes in real capital endowments. Generally, if capital endowments are higher than otherwise, real GDP will be higher than otherwise, and vice versa.[9] A major reason that Singapore is projected to lose slightly from services trade liberalization is that its capital stock is projected to be lower than otherwise.

---

[9] For a few regions, real GDP can be higher than otherwise, even if endowments are lower than otherwise, because the endowments are used more efficiently.

However, a lower capital stock located domestically need not always lead to lower incomes for domestic residents. Earnings from higher outward FDI and higher lending abroad could offset it. The third column of Table 5.4 shows the contribution to residents' real income from changes in real FDI stocks. The fourth column shows the contribution from changes in real bond holdings. Both also help to indicate the way in which changes in capital endowments are financed.

For example, Japan's capital stock is lower than otherwise, but it has a big increase in outward FDI. In fact, it also borrows (a negative change in bond holding) in order to finance its outward FDI. By contrast, China's increase in capital endowments comes partly from a large increase in inward FDI and partly from additional foreign borrowing. Thus, the large projected increase in China's service-sector output and exports, noted above, comes as much from an expansion in foreign-owned service firms located in China as it does from an expansion in Chinese-owned service firms. The United States is projected to have a smaller capital endowment than otherwise, but this is offset to some extent by an increase in outward FDI and increased lending to other regions.

For a few regions, real incomes are affected not so much by changes in net asset positions, but by changes in returns on those assets. Although the details are not shown in Table 5.4, Taiwan is projected to lose slightly from services trade liberalization, primarily because in the FTAP database it is a net creditor economy and is adversely affected by a small induced fall in real interest rates.[10]

A further source of change in asset returns is the change in rents generated by barriers to services trade. The last column of Table 5.4 shows the income contribution to recipient countries of changes in the rents accruing to FDI, as barriers to services trade are eliminated. What is striking is the loss of rents to the main providers of outward FDI — Japan, Hong Kong, and the United States. In fact, the loss of rents to US incumbent multinationals is more than sufficient to explain its overall

---

[10] Interest rates fall primarily because of an assumption that government saving *rates* are held constant. Growing revenues and saving *levels*, therefore, allow some government debt retirement.

projected income loss from multilateral liberalization of services trade. Note, however, that this result is sensitive to the assumption that all barriers to services trade are rent-creating rather than cost-raising.[11]

Generally, although induced changes in capital stocks — both those located domestically and those owned abroad — do not appear to play a major role in explaining the effects of multilateral services trade liberalization on sectoral output, they play a major role in explaining the effects on real regional incomes. Barriers to services trade affect capital movements as well as the output of services firms, so services trade liberalization can have a significant effect on the regional location and ownership of capital. The flow-on effects to regional incomes demonstrate another way in which liberalization of services trade can differ from tariff removal.

5.4 Agenda for Further Research

Much of the research agenda for further development of the FTAP model has been outlined already. It involves continuing to obtain estimates of the price impacts of barriers to services trade along the lines outlined in Findlay and Warren (2000), both for additional sectors and for additional modes of service delivery within a sector. The methodologies should in the process reveal whether the barriers are rent-creating or cost-raising.[12] Such methods could also be used to estimate the price impact of barriers to FDI in agriculture and manufacturing. More sectoral detail needs to be incorporated into FTAP, to model the barriers to each service separately. More research is required to obtain more realistic output estimates and cost and sales structures for FDI firms and, if possible, a realistic initial allocation of rents. Additionally, the welfare measure in FTAP needs to be amended to take account of the costs of risk taking, given risk aversion.

---

[11] Brown, Deardorff, and Stern (2000) show that if barriers are cost-escalating, then welfare effects are dominated by the movement of real physical capital. However, they have a more simple treatment of profit repatriation and debt service payments than here.
[12] This is done in Dee (2013b).

In addition, some of the simplifying assumptions made during the original development of FTAP could now be relaxed, and the sensitivity of the results to these assumptions tested. One such assumption was the uniformity of behavioural parameters across sectors and regions. Although this reflected a deliberate research strategy, its importance could be tested using systematic sensitivity analysis (Arndt and Pearson 1996). The importance of data issues (eg the initial distribution of rents) and theoretical issues (eg investor behaviour) could also be explored.[13]

However, there is also scope for much more work using simple analytical models of services trade that better incorporate the features of services and the nature of the barriers to their trade. Insights of the sort available in Markusen, Rutherford, and Hunter (1995), for example, provide invaluable guidance to those attempting to build better empirical models of FDI and services trade.

---

[13] Investor behaviour is roughly calibrated in Chapter 7 of this volume.

Chapter 6

Economy-wide Effects of Further Trade Reforms in Tunisia's Services Sectors[1]

Philippa Dee and Ndiame Diop

6.1 Introduction

Tunisia has been one of the best performers in the Middle East and North Africa region since the mid-1990s, when it accelerated market-oriented reforms. Economic growth reached an average 5 per cent in 1996–2007, despite many external shocks. As a result, the poverty incidence dropped to about 7 percent in 2007 (World Bank Global Poverty numbers 2008). Nevertheless, because of its strong trade ties with Europe, Tunisia's real sector was affected by the global financial crisis through Europe's 2009 recession. As a result of a sharp decline in exports (–12 per cent in real terms), GDP growth was only half of what was predicted (3 per cent against an expected 6 per cent).

Tunisia's global integration policies can be traced back to 1971, when the country decided to create an offshore sector in order to reduce the anti-export bias inherent in the heavy protection of the economy. The offshore sector provided generous fiscal and financial incentives to exporters and triggered a rapid rise in foreign direct investment (FDI) and the birth of a large labour-intensive textile industry integrated vertically with the EU's production networks. This heterodox trade policy stance — similar

---

[1] This is an edited version of Chapter 4 in John Gilbert (2010), *New Developments in Computable General Equilibrium Analysis for Trade Policy*, Frontiers of Economics and Globalization 7, Bingley UK: Emerald Group Publishing: 61–101.

to the ones also applied at different points in time by Japan, Korea, Malaysia, and Mauritius — led to the first wave of diversification away from hydrocarbons. However, overall productivity growth was heavily constrained by the high level of protection of the economy.

A decisive step toward liberalizing trade occurred in the middle of the 1990s. As part of the Tunisia–EU Association Agreement, trade protection *vis-à-vis* the EU was scheduled for gradual and systematic dismantling, starting in 1996. As a result, tariffs on industrial goods imported from the EU (the source of 65 per cent of Tunisia's imports), went from about 100 per cent in 1996 to 0 per cent in January 2008. World Bank (2008) shows that Tunisia's industrial sectors that are highly integrated to the global market have been able to attract investment, converge to EU's labour productivity standards, and boost job creation. In sharp contrast, in the services sector where many entry and competition barriers remain, convergence to EU labour productivity standards is slow.

Tunisia is now preparing to embark on bolder services liberalization. The sector currently provides 59 per cent of GDP and absorbs 55 per cent of employment. So far, the country has no free trade agreement (FTA) that includes services. Its multilateral liberalization of services under WTO's General Agreement on Trade in Services (GATS) has been very limited. Tunisia included only three sectors (tourism, telecommunications and financial services) in its GATS Uruguay Round commitments. While some of its sectors not included are quite open (eg maritime transport), entry into many other services sectors is restricted. Under the Uruguay Round, Tunisia bound without limitation many cross-border (mode 1) transactions (eg in the financial sector), but in reality, those GATS measures overlap with strict foreign exchange controls, making them partly ineffective. Apart from the financing of current operations, opportunities for cross-border (mode 1) trade are sharply restricted, and foreign competition is mostly possible through commercial presence (mode 3) or through the presence of natural persons (mode 4). But the measures affecting the presence of natural persons (mode 4) remain unbound, with the exception of wholly exporting enterprises that can recruit up to four executives and managers of foreign nationality.

It is not clear whether Tunisia will significantly increase its commitments at the end of the ongoing Doha Round. In its *conditional* Doha offer of 2005,

Tunisia maintained some restrictive horizontal commitments. For instance, freedom of investment would be guaranteed only to 'wholly exporting' firms and a nationality condition would be attached to the exercise of commercial activities (whole and retail trade) in Tunisia. In terms of sectoral coverage, five sectors were included in the conditional offer (out of eleven possible): telecommunications, environmental services, financial services, health services and tourism and travel.[2] In a recent unilateral move, however, a new global telecom licence (fixed, mobile and VSAT) has been granted to a new operator that started operations in April 2010.

Tunisia started a process of negotiations for a services trade agreement with the EU in March 2006 in the Euro–Med context. Discussions on the general provisions of the agreements have started. These will be followed by bilateral negotiations on market access commitments. For Tunisia, mode 4 (temporary movement of professional services providers) and mode 2 in the area of health services represent two big areas of interest. These negotiations are crucial to secure better market access for its services providers to Europe, which would require a relaxing of restrictions in obtaining visas and mutual recognition agreements for diplomas and professional qualifications with some EU countries.

To our knowledge, the only quantitative analysis of the impact of services trade liberalization for Tunisia is Konan and Maskus (2006). An earlier quantitative analysis of potential impacts of Tunisia–EU Association Agreement by Brown *et al.* (1997) did not include services sectors. Konan and Maskus used a computable general equilibrium model with multiple products, services and trading partners and found that reducing services barriers would generate relatively large welfare gains and low adjustment costs. However, their benchmark data and Social Accounting Matrix are dated 1995, which no longer reflect the current situation. Moreover, a strong assumption made in their paper is that barriers to foreign direct investment were half rent-creating and half

---

[2] Environment services relate to the management of solid waste, dangerous waste and sanitation. Foreign firms can enter the market but face a majority holding restriction (they can own up to 49 per cent of the capital) and they should agree to transfer technologies, recruit local staff and train staff locally. In the health sector, establishment is free without limit imposed on the capital for a list of medical fields where Tunisia has an export potential.

cost-escalating. As is well-known, the results of reform simulations are very sensitive to those assumptions. In the current chapter, the treatment of barriers is based on empirical evidence, where available, rather than assumption.

The purpose of this paper is to: (i) benchmark Tunisia against other emerging economies in terms of the regulatory barriers affecting its services trade; (ii) assess the economy-wide effects of further liberalizing services trade restrictions in particular sectors, either regionally or unilaterally; (iii) compare this with the effects of further liberalizing Tunisia's agricultural and manufacturing trade in the context of its Association Agreement with the EU; and (iv) also contrast this with the effects of bringing its most-favoured nation (MFN) tariff rates on manufacturing goods closer to EU preferential rates. These comparisons give important insights into Tunisia's trade policy priorities over the next few years.

6.2   Methodological Approach to Measuring Services Trade Barriers

Barriers in services trade vary by sector and a sector-by-sector analysis is needed to identify policy restrictions to entry and competition in services. The analytical framework that has been used to measure services trade barriers comprises three stages.

The <u>first stage</u> is to collect qualitative information about regulatory restrictions affecting services delivery, and to convert it into a quantitative index (or indexes), using weights that reflect the relative severity of the different restrictions. Sometimes the weights are based on *a priori* judgements drawn from detailed knowledge of the industry concerned. Sometimes the weights are derived using statistical techniques, giving greatest weight to restrictions that have the greatest variability within the sample. Studies along these lines include the OECD studies of product market regulation (OECD 2005a, 2005b, Conway, Janod and Nicoletti 2005), Findlay and Warren (2000), Kalirajan (2000), Kalirajan *et al.* (2000), Nguyen-Hong (2000), Doove *et al.* (2001), Copenhagen Economics (2005) and OECD (2005c).

Since services trade barriers typically operate behind the border, the <u>second stage</u> is to quantify the effects of these indexes of services trade barriers on some behind-the-border measure of economic performance — often prices or price–cost margins, but sometimes quantities or costs — while controlling for all the other factors that affect economic performance in that market. These econometric results are used to construct the counterfactual — what economic performance would be in the absence of the services trade restrictions, holding all other factors constant.

This does not give a 'tariff equivalent', because the 'tariff equivalent' concept (a) assumes services are traded primarily cross-border, whereas most are traded behind the border via the movement of people or capital, and (b) assumes that domestic and foreign services are perfect substitutes, whereas most are highly differentiated to particular users. Instead, the counterfactual comparison gives a behind-the-border 'tax equivalent', if the restrictions have raised price–cost margins, or a behind-the-border 'productivity equivalent', if the restrictions have raised real resource costs. Econometric studies along these lines include Findlay and Warren (2000), Gonenc and Nicoletti (2000), Steiner (2000), Kalirajan (2000), Nguyen-Hong (2000), Barth, Caprio and Levine (2004), Clark, Dollar and Micco (2004) and OECD (2005c).

In the <u>third stage</u>, the 'tax equivalents' or 'productivity equivalents' are entered into a computable general equilibrium model, which is then used to project the direct and indirect effects of services trade liberalization for each sector and for the economy as a whole. Examples include Dee and Hanslow (2001), Dee, Hanslow and Phamduc (2003), OECD (2004) and Copenhagen Economics (2005).

This study benchmarks Tunisia against a range of other emerging countries using index measures of services trade barriers derived from the first stage. The index measures are somewhat arbitrary — it is the econometrics in the second stage that establishes the true economic significance of the barriers. However, the index measures bear a monotonic relationship to the tax or productivity equivalent measures, and there are more of the former available than the latter. So for benchmarking purposes, the arbitrariness of the index measures is not a drawback.

6.3 Benchmarking Tunisia on Services Restrictiveness

This section benchmarks Tunisia against emerging and high-income countries for which restrictiveness indices, calculated consistently, exist. We consider seven key services sectors — postal services, telecommunications, air passenger transport, the accounting, legal and engineering professions, and banking. Tourism and maritime services sectors, two important sectors in Tunisia, are not covered because they are traditionally open to trade and investment with no significant barriers. One important sector not included is distribution. Entry into the distribution sector is strictly regulated and trading activities, including wholesale distribution and retail trading services, are reserved for enterprises in which Tunisians hold a majority interest. Table 6.1 shows the importance of the different services sectors in Tunisia's economy (where the professional services are included in 'Other business services' and banking is included in 'Other financial services').

As noted, one rich source of index measures is the OECD studies of product market regulation (OECD 2005a, 2005b). Figures 6.1 to 6.6 show how Tunisia compares against the worst performing developed and

Table 6.1. Sectoral Value Added in Tunisia

	Millions of US dollars	*Percentage of total*
Agriculture, other primary and food	3,281	20.1
Other manufacturing	2,111	12.9
Electricity	344	2.1
Gas and water	126	0.8
Construction	975	6.0
Trade	2,744	16.8
Other transport	1,194	7.3
Air transport	382	2.3
Communications	778	4.8
Other financial services	557	3.4
Insurance	67	0.4
Other business services	680	4.2
Other services	3,098	19.0
Total	16,336	100.0

Source: FTAP model database, based on the GTAP version 6 database (Hertel 1997).

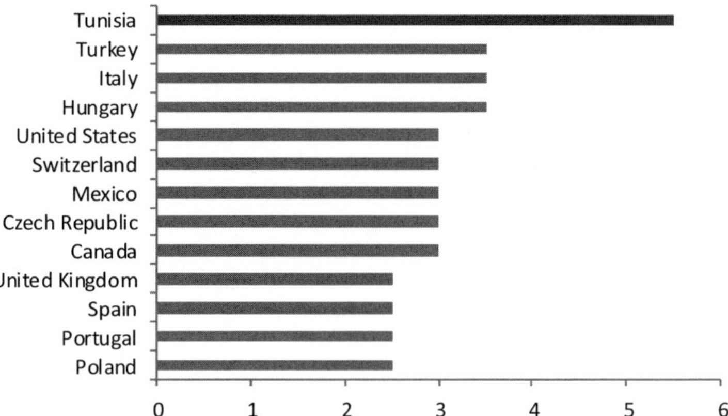

Figure 6.1.   OECD Index of Regulatory Restrictions in Postal Services
Data source: Based on OECD (2005b).

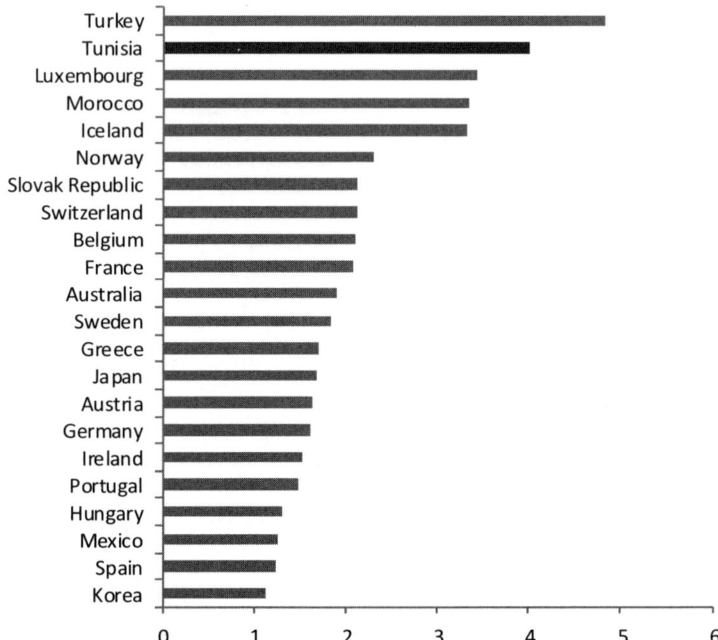

Figure 6.2.   OECD Index of Regulatory Restrictions in Telecommunications Services
Data source: Based on OECD (2005b).

                    Services Trade Reform: Making Sense of It

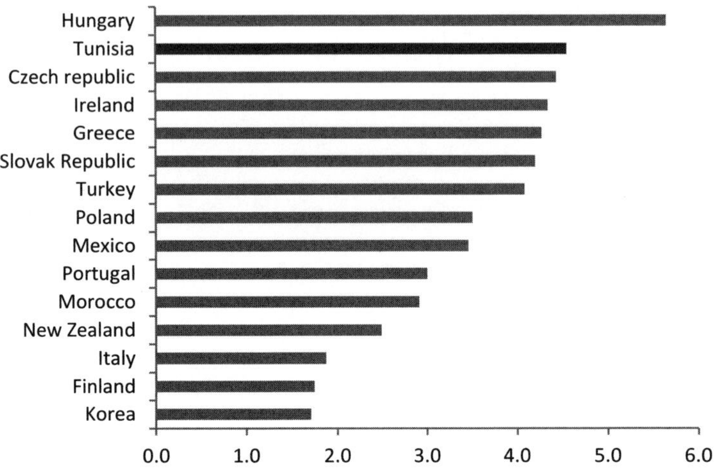

Figure 6.3.   OECD Index of Regulatory Restrictions in Air Passenger Transport
Data source: Based on OECD (2005b).

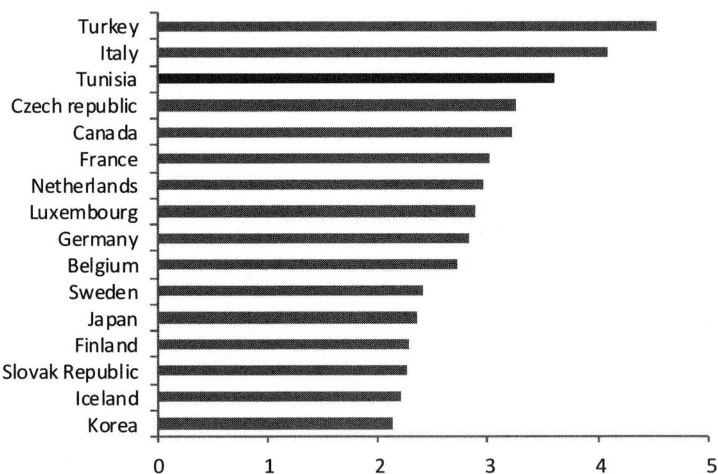

Figure 6.4.   OECD Index of Regulatory Restrictions in Accounting Services
Data source: Based on OECD (2005a).

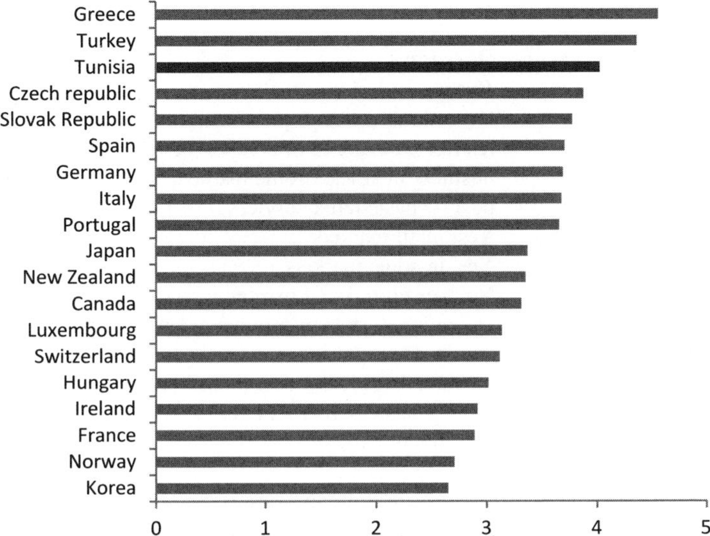

Figure 6.5. OECD Index of Regulatory Restrictions in Legal Services
Data source: Based on OECD (2005a).

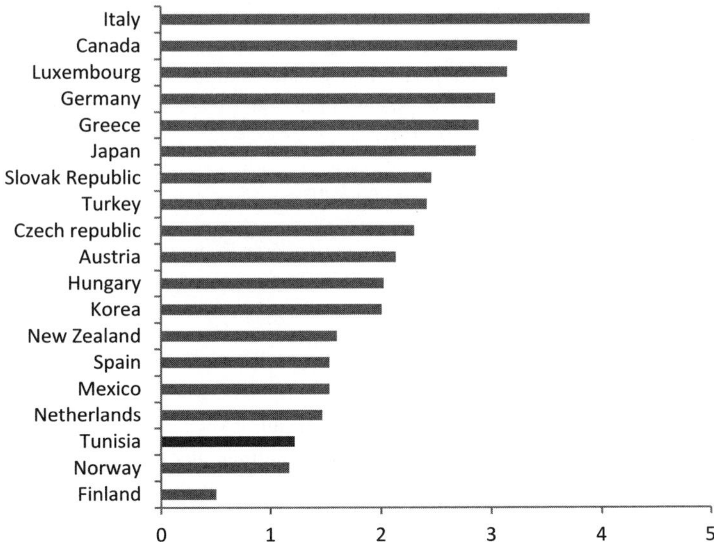

Figure 6.6. OECD Index of Regulatory Restrictions in Engineering Services
Data source: Based on OECD (2005a).

Table 6.2.   OECD Regulatory Questionnaire for Postal Services

Weights by theme	*Question weights*	*Score*	*Question*
1/2			***Entry regulation***
	1/3		Do national, state or provincial laws or other regulations restrict the number of competitors allowed to operate a business in at least some markets in the sector: national post — basic letter services?
		6	Yes, in all markets
		3	Yes, in some markets
		0	No, free entry in all markets
	1/3		Do national, state or provincial laws or other regulations restrict the number of competitors allowed to operate a business in at least some markets in the sector: national post — basic parcel services?
		6	Yes, in all markets
		3	Yes, in some markets
		0	No, free entry in all markets
	1/3		Do national, state or provincial laws or other regulations restrict the number of competitors allowed to operate a business in at least some markets in the sector: courier activities other than national post?
		6	Yes
		0	No
1/2			***Public ownership***
	1/3		What percentage of shares in the largest firm in the sector: national post — basic letter services are owned by the government?
		6	100%
		3	Between 0 and 100%
		0	None
	1/3		What percentage of shares in the largest firm in the sector: national post — basic parcel services are owned by the government?
		6	100%
		3	Between 0 and 100%
		0	None
	1/3		What is the extent of public ownership in the courier activities (other than national post) sector?
		6	Government controls all dominant firms in the sector
		3	Government controls at least 1 firm, but other firms operate as well
		0	No government involvement in the sector

Source: OECD (2005b).

Table 6.3. OECD Regulatory Questionnaire for Telecommunications Services

Weights by theme	*Question weights[a]*	*Score*	*Question*
1/3			***Entry regulation***
	$w^t(1-w^m)$		What are the legal conditions of entry into the trunk telephony market?
		6	Franchised to 1 firm
		3	Franchised to 2 or more firms
		0	Free entry
	$(1-w^t)(1-w^m)$		What are the legal conditions of entry into the international market?
		6	Franchised to 1 firm
		3	Franchised to 2 or more firms
		0	Free entry
	w^m		What are the legal conditions of entry into the mobile market?
		6	Franchised to 1 firm
		3	Franchised to 2 or more firms
		0	Free entry
1/3			***Public ownership***
	$(1-w^m)$		What percentage of shares in the public telecommunications operator is owned by the government?
		% government ownership/100*6	
	w^m		What percentage of shares in the largest firm in the mobile telecommunications market is owned by the government?
		% government ownership/100*6	
1/3			***Market structure***
	$w^t(1-w^m)$		What is the market share of new entrants in the trunk telephony market?
		6-normalized market share[b]	
	$(1-w^t)(1-w^m)$		What is the market share of new entrants in the international telephony market?
		6-normalized market share[b]	
	w^m		What is the market share of new entrants in the mobile telephony market?
		6-normalized market share[b]	

[a] The weight w^m is the OECD-wide revenue share from mobile telephony in total revenue from trunk, international and mobile. The weight w^t is the OECD-wide revenue share of trunk in total revenue from trunk and international telephony.

[b] The market share of new entrants has been normalized to be between 0 and 6 with 6 being the smallest market share over all countries and 0 being the largest.

Source: OECD (2005b).

Table 6.4. OECD Regulatory Questionnaire for Air Passenger Transport

Weights by theme	*Question weights[a]*	*Score*	*Question*
1/2			***Entry regulation***
	½*w		Does your country have an open skies agreement with the United States?
		6	No
		0	Yes
	½*w		Is your country participating in a regional agreement?
		6	No
		0	Yes
	(1–w)		Is the domestic aviation market in your country fully liberalized? That is, there are no restrictions on the number of (domestic) airlines that are allowed to operate on domestic routes?
		6	No
		0	Yes
1/2			***Public ownership***
	1		What percentage of shares in the largest carrier (domestic and international traffic combined) are owned by national, state or provincial authorities?
			% of shares owned by government/100*6

[a] The weight w is the average share of international traffic in total traffic (measured in thousands of revenue passenger kilometres) for each country.
Source: OECD (2005b).

emerging countries in the OECD sample in six key services sectors of interest. The scoring is based on answers to the questions shown in Tables 6.2 to 6.6. The OECD questionnaires collect and score information about a range of regulatory restrictions, but do not distinguish whether the restrictions only affect foreign operators, or also affect domestic players.

Tunisia scores particularly poorly in postal services because it is one of the few countries in the world to retain restrictions on courier services — private operators are required to operate in partnership with Rapid Poste. Tunisia's restrictions are second only to Turkey's in telecommunications, largely because it still has a monopoly in fixed line telecommunications and a duopoly in mobile telephony. Its restrictions in

Table 6.5. OECD Questionnaire for Entry Regulation in the Professions[a]

Weights by theme	Question weights	Score	Question
2/5			*Licensing*
	1		How many services does the profession have an exclusive or shared exclusive right to provide?
		6	More than 3
		4.5	3
		3	2
		1.5	1
		0	0
2/5			*Education requirements (only applies if licensing not 0)*
	1/3		What is the duration of special education/university/or other higher degree?
			Equals number of years of education (max of 6)
	1/3		What is the duration of compulsory practice necessary to become a full member of the profession?
			Equals number of years of compulsory practice (max of 6)
	1/3		Are there professional exams that must be passed to become a full member of the profession?
		6	Yes
		0	No
1/5			*Quotas and economic needs tests*
	1		Is the number of foreign professionals/firms permitted to practice restricted by quotas or economic needs tests?
		6	Yes
		0	No

[a] The indicator for each profession is calculated as the simple average of the indicators of entry (Table 6.5) and conduct (Table 6.6) regulation.
Source: OECD (2005a).

air passenger transport are second only to Hungary, because Tunisia has not entered into an open skies agreement with the United States or regionally, because the rates are regulated for domestic aviation, and because the government still retains majority ownership in the largest carrier.

Tunisia also scores relatively poorly in legal and accounting services. Here the OECD questionnaires are largely restricted to measures that are non-discriminatory — for example, exclusive licensing, and restrictions on fees, advertising and the legal form of business. Tunisia's range of

Table 6.6. OECD Questionnaire for Conduct Regulation in the Professions[a]

Weights by theme	Question weights	Score	Question
0.38			***Regulations on prices and fees***
	1		Are the fees or prices that a profession charges regulated in any way (by government or self-regulated)?
		6	Minimum prices on all services
		5	Minimum prices on some services
		4	Maximum prices on all services
		3	Maximum prices on some services
		2	Non-binding recommended prices on all services
		1	Non-binding recommended prices on some services
		0	No regulation
0.23			***Regulations on advertising***
	1		Is advertising and marketing by the profession regulated in any way?
		6	Advertising is prohibited
		3	Advertising is regulated
		0	No specific regulations
0.19			***Regulations on form of business***
	1		Is the legal form of business restricted to a particular type?
		6	Sole practitioner only
		5	Incorporation forbidden
		2	Partnership and some incorporation allowed
		0	No restrictions
0.19			***Quotas and economic needs tests***
	1		Is cooperation between professionals restricted?
		6	Generally forbidden
		4.5	Only allowed with comparable professions
		3	Generally allowed
		0	All forms allowed

[a] The indicator for each profession is calculated as the simple average of the indicators of entry (Table 6.5) and conduct (Table 6.6) regulation.
Source: OECD (2005a).

regulations, particularly on fees, make it second only to Turkey and Italy in restricting competition in accounting, and second only to Greece and Turkey in restricting competition in law. What the OECD index fails to indicate is the strength of Tunisia's discriminatory restrictions in these professions — foreign firms cannot practice law, but can only provide legal consulting services, and accounting firms must be 100 per cent locally owned.

Only in engineering services does Tunisia receive a relatively liberal score. Tunisia has been trying to encourage FDI, and accordingly provides a relatively unrestrictive regulatory regime for both the domestic and foreign engineers required for large projects.

The index measures of regulatory restrictions in banking services originate from one of a series of studies carried out by the Australian Productivity Commission (McGuire and Schuele 2000). Figure 6.7 shows how Tunisia compares against the worst performing developed and developing countries for which recent banking estimates are available. The scoring is based on the template shown in Table 6.7.

These index measures in banking explicitly distinguish between regulations that affect only foreign banks (the foreign index), and those

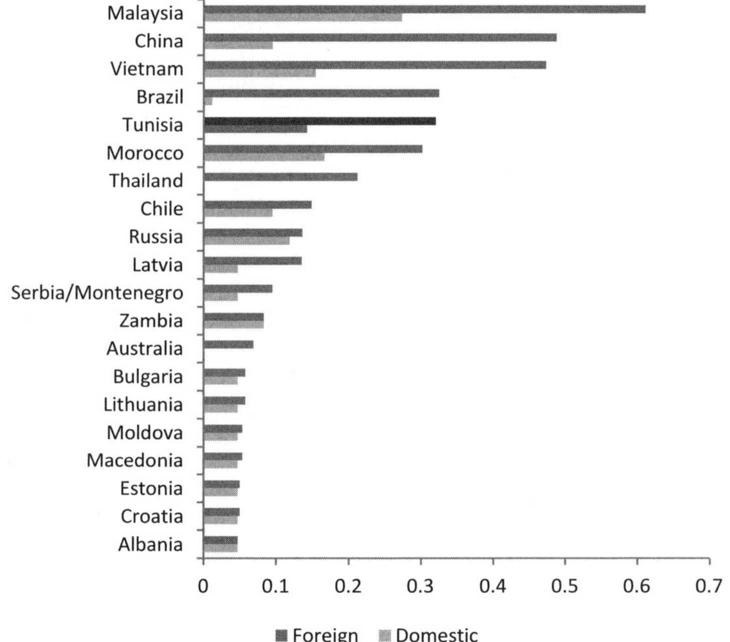

Figure 6.7.   Productivity Commission Index of Regulatory Restrictions in Banking Services
Data source: Based on Dee (2005a) and McGuire and Schuele (2000).

Table 6.7. Productivity Commission Template for Restrictions in Banking Services

Weight - foreign index	Weight - domestic index	Score	Restriction
			Restrictions on commercial presence
0.1900	0.1900		**Licensing**
		1.00	Issues no new banking licences
		0.75	Issues up to 3 new banking licences with only prudential restrictions
		0.50	Issues up to 6 new banking licences with only prudential restrictions
		0.25	Issues up to 10 new banking licences with only prudential restrictions
		0.00	Issues new banking licenses with only prudential restrictions
0.1900	0.1900		**Direct investment** The score will be inversely proportional to maximum equity participation permitted in an existing domestic bank. For example, ownership to a maximum of 49 per cent of a bank would receive a score of 0.51.
0.0950	0		No new licenses and JV arrangements
		1.00	Issues no new banking licences and no entry is allowed through a joint venture with a domestic bank
		0.50	Bank entry is only through a joint venture with a domestic bank
		0.00	No requirement for a bank to enter through a joint venture with a domestic bank
0.0190	0		Movement of People — permanent
		1.00	No entry of executives, senior managers or specialists
		0.80	Executives, specialists and/or senior managers can stay a period of up to 1 year
		0.60	Executives, specialists and/or senior managers can stay a period of up to 2 years
		0.40	Executives, specialists and/or senior managers can stay a period of up to 3 years
		0.20	Executives, specialists and/or senior managers can stay a period of up to 4 years
		0.00	Executives, specialists and/or senior managers can stay a period of more than 5 years

Table 6.7. Continued.

Other Restrictions

0.1425 0.1425   **Raising funds by banks**

    1.00   Banks are unable to raise funds from domestic sources

    0.75   Banks are restricted from raising funds from domestic capital markets

    0.50   Banks are restricted in accepting deposits from the public, or face interest rate controls

    0.00   Banks can raise funds from any source with only prudential restrictions

0.1425 0.1425   **Lending funds by banks**

    1.00   Banks are not permitted to lend to domestic clients

    0.75   Banks are restricted to specified lending size or lending to government projects

    0.5   Banks are restricted in providing certain lending services such as leasing, credit cards and consumer finance

    0.25   Banks are directed to lend to certain sectors such as housing and small business

    0.00   Banks can lend to any source with only prudential restrictions

0.0950 0.0950   **Other business of banks — insurance and securities services**

    1.00   Banks can only provide banking services

    0.50   Banks can provide banking services plus one other line of business - insurance or securities services

    0.00   Banks have no restrictions on conducting other lines of business

0.0475 0.0475   **Expanding operations — street branches, offices and ATMs**

    1.00   One banking outlet with no new banking outlets permitted

    0.75   Number of bank outlets is limited in number and location

    0.25   Expansion of banking outlets is subject to non-prudential regulatory approval

    0.00   No restrictions on banks expanding operations

0.0095 0   **Movement of people — temporary**

    1.00   No temporary entry of executives, senior managers and/or specialists

    0.75   Temporary entry of executives, senior managers and/or specialists up to 30 days

    0.50   Temporary entry of executives, senior managers and/or specialists up to 60 days

    0.25   Temporary entry of executives, senior managers and/or specialists up to 90 days

    0.00   Temporary entry of executives, senior managers and/or specialists over 90 days

Table 6.7.   Continued.

0[a]	0		**Movement of people — Board of Directors**
		1.00	Board cannot comprise foreigners
		0.00	No restrictions on the composition of the board of directors
			The score is inversely related to the percentage of the Board which can comprise foreigners. For example, if 20% of a BOD can comprise foreigners this would receive a score of 0.80.
0.9310	**0.8075**		**Total**

[a] Weight was 0.019 in McGuire and Schuele (2000).
Source: Dee (2005a) based on McGuire and Schuele (2000).

that affect domestic and foreign banks equally (the domestic index). Thus the difference between the domestic and foreign index measures the pure margin of discrimination against foreign banks.

Tunisia's banking restrictions against foreign banks are not as severe as those in Malaysia, China, Vietnam and Brazil. But they are marginally worse than those in Morocco, and significantly worse than those in South Eastern Europe. Tunisia's score reflects in part the restrictions on both lending and raising funds that are faced by foreign banks. Tunisia also maintains non-discriminatory restrictions, including the authorization process that is required of both domestic and foreign banks.

6.4 Reform Options

Reform strategies

It appears that the regulatory restrictions affecting Tunisia's services sector are generally relatively severe, compared with those in comparable emerging economies. Liberalizing these restrictions could help to harness the export potential of its emerging services, such as ICT-enabled services and the professions, allowing Tunisia to be better positioned as a location for the outsourcing of the back-office functions of European companies. Greater use of business-to-business (B2B) e-commerce within Tunisia could also improve the competitiveness of Tunisia's own manufacturing and services sectors. Finally, liberalizing the restrictions in key backbone services such as banking, telecommunications and air passenger transport could boost competition and investment in these sectors, for further gains to the economy as a whole.

Given Tunisia's relatively uncompetitive position in services relative to other emerging economies, there is little reason for Tunisia to wait for other countries to reciprocate in liberalizing their services. France, its key client economy within Europe, is already significantly more liberal than Tunisia. And Tunisia lags behind many of the emerging countries that would compete with it for outsourced services. For the professions, banking and telecommunications, it would make sense for Tunisia to liberalize unilaterally, although there is also scope for reform on a bilateral basis in the professions.

Air passenger transport is another matter. International air flights require international cooperation to provide the necessary infrastructure and air traffic rights. If Tunisia were to liberalize, while its partners continued to restrict entry, capacity and air fares, this could lead to adverse outcomes for Tunisia's aviation industry, without providing benefits to its consumers. A more sensible first step would be a bilateral 'open skies' agreement with the European Union. This would not provide the maximum opportunity for Tunisia to optimize its own international air services network, and hence achieve the full cost savings available from reaping network economies. This would likely require open skies agreements with Tunisia's Arab League partners as well. However, an open skies agreement with the European Union would open those bilateral routes up to low-cost carriers, putting competitive pressure on air fares on those routes.

First-round impacts on sectoral prices

In *telecommunications*, Tunisia could lift the numerical restrictions on the number of carriers in both fixed and mobile telephony, to increase the general contestability of the market. It could also lift the foreign ownership limits on competitive carriers, to attract further foreign direct investment. This would likely have two types of effects.

First, the greater market contestability and foreign competition would squeeze price–cost margins within telecommunications. This effect has been quantified in second-stage econometric work by Warren (2000), as summarized in Dee (2005a). The top portion of Table 6.8 shows that Tunisia's general restrictions on competition could currently be inflating the prices of domestically-owned telecommunications services by 6.8 per cent, while the additional restrictions on foreign ownership mean that the prices from foreign suppliers could be inflated by 15.5 per cent. Were Tunisia to remove these restrictions, price–cost margins would be squeezed, and prices would be lower accordingly (middle portion of Table 6.8).

A second possible effect of telecommunications reform is a productivity improvement in wholesale and retail trade, as a result of

Table 6.8. Direct Price Impacts of Tunisia's Regulatory Restrictions in Selected Services (per cent)

| | *Direct price impact* | | |
| | *Through markups on* | | *Through* |
Sector	*output*	*exports to Tunisia*	*costs*
Currently			
Telecommunications – domestic providers[a]	6.8		
– foreign providers[a]	15.5		
Banking – domestic providers	7.5		
– foreign providers	17.5		
Professional services – domestic providers[b]			6.0
– foreign providers[b]	19.1	19.1	
After unilateral reform			
Telecommunications – domestic providers[a]	0.0		
– foreign providers[a]	0.0		
Banking – domestic providers	4.9		
– foreign providers	6.8		
Professional services – domestic providers[b]			6.0
– foreign providers[b]	11.9	11.9	
After further bilateral reform			
Professional services – domestic providers[b]			6.0
– foreign providers[b]	6.4	6.4	

[a] Simple average of price impacts for fixed line and cellular services.
[b] Simple average of estimates for legal, accounting, and engineering services.
Source: Dee (2005a), based on Warren (2000), Kalirajan *et al.* (2000) and Nguyen-Hong (2000).

greater use of the internet for B2B e-commerce. Like many other countries, Tunisia has allowed limited competition in mobile telephony, and this has mitigated somewhat the adverse effects of the monopoly in fixed line telephony for telephony services as such. But the monopoly in fixed line telephony is one factor holding back internet penetration. Although Tunisia has more computers per head of population than Morocco (5.63 per 100 inhabitants in 2005, compared with 2.35 per 100 inhabitants in Morocco), its internet penetration is lower (9.46 users per 100 inhabitants in 2005, compared with 14.61 users per 100 inhabitants in Morocco) (ITU 2006).

A Japanese study reported in Hertel, Walmsley and Itakura (2001) finds that the use of e-commerce for B2B transactions could reduce wholesale–retail margins from 19.6 per cent to 4.9 per cent of prices — a 75 per cent reduction in wholesale–retail margins themselves, equivalent to a 300 per cent productivity improvement in wholesale and retail trade — when B2B commerce is in use. Even in Japan, internet penetration is by no means universal, so the sector-wide cost savings are diluted accordingly. The Hertel, Walmsley and Itakura (2001) study suggests an average 2 per cent penetration rate across Japanese agriculture, manufacturing and services, with up to 14 per cent penetration in autos, while ITU statistics give 50.2 internet users per 100 inhabitants in Japan. If Tunisia were to increase its internet penetration rate to that of Morocco, and to achieve cost savings comparable to that in Japan, it would be equivalent to a 0.6 per cent improvement in productivity across the entire wholesale and retail trade sector, with benefits spread throughout the economy, including in services and manufacturing.

In *banking*, Tunisia could remove the discretion associated with the granting of new bank licences (domestic and foreign). It could also lift the restrictions faced by foreign banks in lending and raising funds domestically. These moves would squeeze price–cost margins in banking, an effect that has been quantified in second stage econometrics by Kalirajan *et al.* (2000), as summarized in Dee (2005a). The results suggest that the removal of authorization could reduce the price impact of services trade restrictions on domestic banks from an estimated 7.5 per cent to 4.9 per cent (Table 6.8). This, together with the removal of the restrictions on foreign bank lending and raising funds, could reduce the price impact of services trade restrictions on foreign banks from 17.5 per cent to 6.8 per cent (Table 6.8).

In the *professions*, Tunisia could unilaterally get rid of the nationality requirement affecting law, accounting and engineering. The corresponding requirement in law and accounting for partners to be local could also be relaxed, with partners only required to be locally licensed. This reform would reduce the price impact of services trade restrictions from an estimated 19.1 per cent to 11.9 per cent for foreign services suppliers. And this would affect not just those wanting to establish a permanent commercial presence in Tunisia, but also those wanting to supply these services via e-commerce or via the temporary movement of individual professionals (Table 6.8, first and second columns, based on econometric work by Nguyen-Hong 2000).

A further potential reform would be for Tunisia to seek bilateral concessions in the context of its Association Agreement with the EU, in order to facilitate the outsourcing of back-office accounting and legal services to Tunisia, especially from France. Accordingly, Tunisia could allow up to 50 per cent EU ownership of local accounting or law firms, to allow those companies some management control over the local firms undertaking the outsourcing activities. And it could seek a mutual recognition agreement with France, allowing French recognition of local Tunisian professional qualifications for the purposes of undertaking the back office activities, in exchange for the recognition of French qualifications in Tunisia. This latter move could further reduce the price impact of remaining restrictions on the supply of foreign professional services in Tunisia to 6.4 per cent (bottom portion of Table 6.8), with a corresponding improvement in the competitiveness of Tunisian suppliers into the EU market.

It is assumed here that in return for these unilateral and bilateral reforms, the EU would agree to remove its discriminatory restrictions on a preferential basis — not just granting Tunisian professionals mutual recognition, but also relaxing the investment restrictions, nationality requirements, hiring and other restrictions that apply in at least some professions, as they affect Tunisian suppliers. This would reduce the average price impact of remaining restrictions on the supply of Tunisia professional services into Europe from 9.5 per cent to an estimated 5 per cent (not shown in Table 6.8).

Finally, the econometric work on which these estimates are based suggests that the unilateral and bilateral reductions in discrimination against foreign professionals would reduce prices by reducing price–cost margins. This is in contrast to the removal of non-discriminatory restrictions on both domestic and foreign professionals, which could reduce prices by reducing real resource costs.

As noted, in *air passenger transport*, Tunisia could seek an open skies agreement with the EU. The likely effects of this have been quantified in second-stage econometric work by Gonenc and Nicoletti (2000) and Doove *et al.* (2001). For the purposes of this paper, that work has been updated using more recent information about the content of air services agreements from ICAO (2004). The price impact of Tunisia's current air services agreements with the EU has been quantified at 15.4 per cent. This would drop to zero in a bilateral basis under an open skies agreement (Table 6.9). As noted above, this price reduction is likely to come about through a reduction in price–cost margins rather than through a reduction in resource costs. Cost savings from achieving

Table 6.9. Direct Price Impacts of Bilateral Air Service Agreements (per cent)

Destination countries	*Origin countries*			
	Tunisia	*EU*	*GAFTA*	*Rest of world*
Currently				
Tunisia	na	15.4	15.9	14.2
EU	15.4	0	12.3	16.9
GAFTA	15.5	12.3	15.9	14.9
Rest of world	14.2	18.2	14.9	18.3
After Tunisian open skies agreement with EU				
Tunisia	na	0	15.9	14.2
EU	0	0	12.3	16.9
GAFTA	15.5	12.3	15.9	14.9
Rest of world	14.2	18.2	14.9	18.3

Source: Updated from Dee (2005a), and based on Doove *et al.* (2001).

greater network economies would probably require a more extensive series of open skies agreements.

Furthermore, it is assumed that the open skies agreement extends to freight as well as passenger traffic. A freight agreement is likely to be less contentious, and could achieve similar benefits. Accordingly, the above estimated reduction in price–cost margins is applied to exports of the entire air transport industry, covering both freight and passengers.

6.5 Economy-wide Effects of Services Trade Liberalization in Tunisia

Modelling framework

The effects of these reform initiatives have been projected using the FTAP model of the world economy, which was developed by Dee and Hanslow (2001), is documented fully in Hanslow, Phamduc and Verikios (1999), and is available for download at http://crawford.anu.edu.au/crawford_people/content/staff/pdee.php. The FTAP model is a computable general equilibrium model incorporating services delivered via FDI. It differs in turn from GTAP (Hertel 1997), the 'plain vanilla' model from which it was derived, in three important respects.

First, because many services are delivered primarily via commercial presence, the modelling framework includes foreign direct investment as a mode of services trade delivery, and covers separately the production and trading activity of foreign multinationals. In other words, GTAP, the conventional multi-country model, is split out by ownership as well as location. In the current version of FTAP, the foreign ownership shares for Tunisia were obtained from survey data provided by Tunisia's *ONH* (INS). The relative size of the Tunisian communications industry was also adjusted upwards, compared with that in the original GTAP database (version 6), based on value added shares provided by INS.

Second, by virtue of foreign ownership, at least some of the profits of foreign multinationals will be repatriated back to the home countries. Thus the profit streams in the conventional multi-country model have to be reallocated from the host to the home country, after provision is made for them to be taxed in either the home or host country. This reallocation leads to a distinction between GDP — the income *generated* in a region — and GNP — the income *received by residents* of a region. The latter forms the basis of (although is not identical to) the welfare measure in FTAP. The information on profit repatriation comes from the Balance of Payments Statistics of the International Monetary Fund (IMF).

Finally, not all profits of foreign multinationals need be repatriated to the home country. Some may be reinvested in the host country. To account for this phenomenon, and to allow for the effect that regulatory reform may have on both domestic and foreign direct investment more generally, the model makes provision for savings and capital accumulation. This is particularly important, since some regulatory barriers are aimed directly at limiting foreign equity participation. It is therefore important to capture how regulatory reform will affect not just foreign ownership *shares*, but also the *total amount* of productivity capacity available to an economy. National savings rates are derived from the macroeconomic data in the International Financial Statistics and Balance of Payments Statistics of the IMF. Government savings rates are derived from the Government Finance Statistics of the IMF. Household savings rates are calculated as a residual.

The FTAP model also differs from GTAP in other respects. In particular, it allows for firm-level product differentiation, economies of scale and large-group monopolistic competition. This is also important, since services tend to be highly specialized, being tailored to the needs of individual customers. In the current version, economies of scale are assumed to be regional for services, and global for all other sectors (Dee 2003).

The version used here contains four regions — Tunisia, the EU, the GAFTA countries, and the rest of the world. It contains 30 sectors, including 11 in the services sector (Table 6.10). Note that tourism is included in the model as a sales activity rather than a separate productive industry. This means that sales to foreign tourists are recorded among the exports of the industries producing goods that foreign tourists buy (air

Table 6.10.   Sectoral Aggregation of the FTAP Model

Sectors in the FTAP model	*Corresponding GTAP sectors*
Live animals, products	Cattle, sheep goats, horses, animal products nec, meat, meat products nec
Dairy products	Raw milk, dairy products
Coffee, etc, sugar, cut flowers	Sugar cane, crops nec, sugar
Fruit and vegetables	Vegetables
Cereals	Paddy rice, wheat, cereal grains, processed rice
Oil seeds and fats	Oil seeds, vegetable oils
Beverages and tobacco	Beverages and tobacco
Other agricultural products	Plant-based fibres, wool, silk-worm cocoons, forestry, food products nec
Fish and products	Fishing
Mineral products	Coal, oil, gas, minerals nec
Metals, products	Ferrous metals, metals nec, metal products
Chemicals etc	Petroleum, coal products, chemical, rubber, plastic products, mineral products nec
Leather products	Leather products
Wood products, pulp, paper	Wood products, paper products, publishing
Textiles and apparel	Textiles, wearing apparel
Transport equipment	Motor vehicles and parts, transport equipment nec
Other machinery and equipment	Machinery and equipment nec
Electrical machinery	Electronic equipment
Other manufacturing	Manufactures nec
Electricity	Electricity
Gas and water	Gas manufacture, distribution, water
Construction	Construction
Trade	Trade
Other transport	Sea transport, transport nec
Air transport	Air transport
Communications	Communication
Other financial services	Financial services nec
Insurance	Insurance
Other business services	Business services nec
Other services	Recreation and other services, public admin, defence, health, education, ownership of dwellings

Source: Based on GTAP version 6 database.

passenger transport, and so on), while sales to domestic tourists are recorded among the sales to household consumption of those industries.

The model provides a long-run snapshot of how different each economy would look about ten years after the introduction of the reforms, compared to the situation at that same point in time if the reforms had not taken place. During the ten year adjustment period, many other changes would affect each economy, but they are not taken into account in the current analysis. For this reason, the results should not be interpreted as indicating the likely changes that would occur *over time* in each economy — this would require all changes, not just those in regulatory trade barriers, to be taken into account.

The distinction is important to keep in mind. Sometimes, to aid fluency, the results are couched as if key indicators 'rise' or 'fall'. This does not mean that the indicators would be higher or lower than they are now. It means that at some future time, they would be higher or lower than they would be otherwise. In both cases, in a growing economy, they could be higher than they are now.

Results

The effects of the above Tunisian services trade liberalization scenarios on economic well-being in each region are shown in Table 6.11. The effects on Tunisia are not large — gains in economic well-being of around US\$ 77 million per year after ten years (in an economy with GDP of about US\$ 20 billion per year in the model's initial database, which is mostly calibrated to 2001). The economy is also projected to be slightly larger, with real GDP being 0.29 percent larger than otherwise.

These projected macroeconomic effects are driven by the changes to consumer prices (from domestic and import sources), producer prices (of both Tunisian-owned and EU-owned firms), and real resource costs (for both Tunisian-owned and EU-owned firms) that are shown in Table 6.12. This pattern of projected price changes largely reflects the pattern of first-round effects shown in Tables 6.8 and 6.9.

The reason that the welfare gains are small is that most of the reforms are targeted at restrictions that have inflated price–cost margins, rather than real resource costs. The distinction is crucial for economic well-being. The prices of services have been inflated, not because the real resource cost of producing them has been inflated, but because incumbent firms have been able to earn economic rents — akin to a tax, but with the revenue flowing to the incumbents rather than to

Table 6.11. Welfare Implications of Tunisian Unilateral and Bilateral Services Trade Reform Initiatives (US$ million)

Reform scenario	*Welfare in*			
	Tunisia	*EU*	*GAFTA*	*Rest of world*
Unilateral telecommunications reforms	21	−13	0	−1
Increased B2B e-commerce	31	4	1	0
Unilateral banking reforms	3	−2	0	0
Unilateral and bilateral reforms in the professions	17	2	0	−5
Open skies agreement with the EU	4	14	−2	−37
Total[a]	77	4	−1	−42
Full reform in these sectors	175	−18	−2	−42

[a] Individual entries may not add to total because of interaction effects.
Source: FTAP model projections.

Table 6.12. Implications of Tunisian Unilateral and Bilateral Services Trade Reform Initiatives for Consumer and Producer Prices and Real Resource Costs in Tunisia (percentage deviation from baseline)

	Consumer prices		*Producer prices[a]*		*Real resource costs[a]*	
	Domestic goods	*Imports*	*Tunisian owned*	*EU-owned*	*Tunisian owned*	*EU-owned*
Electricity	0.4	0.0	0.4	0.0	0.4	0.0
Gas and water	0.3	0.0	0.3	0.0	0.3	0.0
Construction	0.3	0.0	0.3	0.3	0.3	0.3
Trade	−0.2	0.0	−0.2	−0.2	−0.2	−0.2
Other transport	0.4	0.0	0.4	0.4	0.4	0.4
Air transport	5.1	−8.1	5.1	5.0	5.1	5.0
Communications	−4.8	0.0	−4.5	−5.3	2.0	9.3
Other financial services	−1.2	0.0	−1.1	−1.7	1.3	8.1
Insurance	0.1	0.0	0.1	0.1	0.1	0.1
Other business services	−0.5	−8.4	−0.4	−1.8	−0.4	9.9
Other services	0.8	0.0	0.8	0.8	0.8	0.8

[a] Producer prices are inclusive of rents from services trade barriers, while real resource costs are not.
Source: FTAP model projections.

government. Liberalization of these barriers yields 'triangle gains' in producer and consumer surplus associated with improvements in allocative efficiency, but also has redistributive effects associated with the elimination of rents to incumbents. The net result is a large transfer from incumbent producers to consumers and other using industries, and a relatively small gain to the economy as a whole.

This is in contrast to the situation when services trade restrictions increase the real resource cost of doing business. Liberalization is then equivalent to a productivity improvement (saving in real resources), and yields 'roughly rectangle' gains associated with a downward shift in supply curves. This can increase returns for the incumbent service providers, as well as lowering costs for users elsewhere in the economy. The net result is a relatively large gain to the economy as a whole.

Whether barriers create rents or add to resource costs is under-researched currently. In some cases, the empirical evidence from the second stage econometrics is suggestive, but not conclusive. In other cases, a price impact is estimated, and then it is simply asserted whether the effect operates through price–cost margins or through real resource costs. For example, it was simply assumed in the Konan and Maskus (2006) study of Tunisia that barriers were half rent-creating and half cost-escalating.

However, theory can provide some guidance. Rents are likely to be created by quantitative and other barriers that limit entry (or exit, though this is far less common). Some red-tape measures may add to resource costs. There are also many ways in which rents can be dissipated or capitalized. So, regulatory barriers that may once have been rent-creating for the initial incumbent can become cost-escalating for subsequent incumbents. For example, Kalirajan (2000) provides indirect evidence that some of the zoning and other restrictions common in the wholesale and retail sector create rents that are subsequently capitalized into the price of commercial land.

The limited empirical evidence tends to accord with this intuition. In banking and telecommunications, where explicit barriers to entry are rife, barriers appear to create rents. In distribution services, where indirect trade restrictions also apply, barriers appear to increase costs. In air passenger transport and the professions, barriers can potentially have both effects (Gregan and Johnson 1999, Kalirajan *et al.* 2000, Kalirajan 2000, Nguyen-Hong 2000, OECD 2005c, Copenhagen Economics 2005). And theoretical arguments suggest that barriers in maritime and electricity generation primarily affect costs (Steiner 2000, Clark, Dollar and Micco 2004).

The above reform scenarios were concentrated in sectors where barriers appear to create rents. In addition, the reform measures were largely aimed at removing discrimination against foreign suppliers. This is no coincidence. When regulatory restrictions are targeted only at foreign suppliers, they tend to be explicit quantity controls, since this is the most feasible way of imposing discrimination.

The welfare gains modelled here are significantly smaller than those in the Konan and Maskus (2006) study of the impact of services liberalization in Tunisia. As noted, those authors simply assumed that barriers to foreign direct investment were half rent-creating and half cost-escalating. On the basis of this assumption, their projected gains in economic well-being from services trade liberalization were about 4 per cent. By contrast, when they assumed the barriers to be entirely rent-creating, their projected gains in economic well-being fell to 0.33 per cent, close to that projected here (see their Table 4). In the current study, the treatment of barriers is based on available empirical evidence, where available, rather than assumption.

Another reason for the gains in the Konan and Maskus (2006) to be slightly bigger is that they implicitly assumed that the services of domestic and foreign-owned firms in Tunisia were perfect substitutes (they did not explicitly identify the proportion of each industry that was foreign-owned, but assumed that the reduction in barriers to foreign investment would affect the prices of all firms in Tunisia, not just the foreign-owned firms). By contrast, the FTAP model assumes that the services of domestic and foreign-owned firms are close but imperfect substitutes. This also reduces the gains from reform slightly, but this is of second order importance, compared to the different treatment of the barriers themselves (as the Konan and Maskus sensitivity analysis shows).

If Tunisia were to also contemplate domestic regulatory reform initiatives aimed at the non-discriminatory restrictions in sectors such as ports, electricity generation and wholesale and retail trade, where the empirical evidence suggests that restrictions raise real resource costs, this could provide much larger gains to the economy as a whole.

This can be demonstrated in a small way by considering the gains to the Tunisian economy from full rather than partial reform in the four chosen sectors. Here, full reform is defined to mean that all the discriminatory *and* non-discriminatory restrictions in telecommunications, banking and professional services are eliminated entirely, while air passenger transport is liberalized on a bilateral basis with the EU. So importantly, full reform would include reform of the non-discriminatory restrictions in the professions that appear to raise real resource costs (see the last column of Table 6.8). The welfare gains to the Tunisian economy from full reform are projected to be US$ 175 million per year after ten years (last row of Table 6.11), compared to US$ 77 million per year from partial reform. And fully 80 per cent of the difference is accounted for by lower resource costs in the professions.

The point is also demonstrated by studies that have looked at the impact of more widespread reforms in services, including reform of the non-discriminatory restrictions in wholesale and retail trade, electricity generation and ports, where costs have been raised. These studies suggest that reform of the non-discriminatory restrictions can yield between 75 and 90 per cent of the total gains from reform (eg OECD 2004). These results suggest that if Tunisia were to contemplate broader domestic regulatory reform initiatives aimed at non-discriminatory restrictions in these other sectors, the gains could be several orders of magnitude greater than those projected here.

There are still some useful insights from the narrower set of reforms. Because the Tunisian reforms are mostly behind the border (with the main exception of the open skies agreement in air passenger transport, which is in any event bilateral), the gains to other regions from so-called 'free-riding' are minimal. This has been observed in other studies of services trade reform. In the current case, the EU is in fact projected to lose slightly in welfare terms from unilateral reform of Tunisia's telecommunications and banking sectors. The EU is an important source of Tunisia's foreign investment in these sectors, so is adversely affected to a small degree by the loss of rents of its foreign multinationals in Tunisia. In other studies, trading partner countries can be slightly adversely affected by unilateral reforms, especially those that reduce costs in the reforming country. This is because such reforms improve the international competitiveness of the reforming country, so partners suffer a small terms of trade loss.

But reversing the argument, it means that Tunisia also has little to gain from behind-the-border reform in other countries. This is an additional reason why Tunisia should not wait for services trade reform initiatives to be reciprocated, except in sectors like air passenger transport where unilateral action would clearly be unwise.

The reforms also have implications for the ownership structure of Tunisian industries. Surprisingly, even though many of the reforms remove discrimination against foreign suppliers, the projections do not suggest that domestically-owned services suppliers would be significantly smaller than otherwise (Table 6.13). Only in the professions (the model's 'Other business services' sector) are domestically owned firms projected to be smaller than otherwise — by less than 1 per cent, a result that could be easily absorbed by normal economic growth. In banking (the model's 'Other financial services' sector) and communications, the domestically-owned firms are projected to benefit from the removal of some of the discrimination against foreign firms.

One important reason for this is that domestically-owned and foreign firms in these sectors have been modelled as providing closely, but not perfectly, substitutable services. In many services sectors, local firms in fact have local advantages that allow them to thrive alongside foreign providers.

Another reason is that, as in most other countries, the most intensive users of services are other services sectors, not agriculture or manufacturing. For example, there are typically more telephones in office buildings than in factories. So the sectors to benefit most from services sector reform are the services sectors themselves — not just banking and telecommunications, but also construction, trade and insurance. Most sectors in agriculture and manufacturing are projected to be slightly smaller than otherwise as a result of the services sector reforms. This is because there is assumed to be the same amount of skilled and unskilled labour available to the economy, whether or not the reforms take place. So if the reforms encourage some sectors to be larger than otherwise, then at least some other sectors need to be smaller than

Table 6.13. Implications of Tunisian Unilateral and Bilateral Services Trade Reform Initiatives for Sectoral Output in Tunisia (percentage deviation from baseline)

	Tunisian firms owned by		
Sector	*Tunisia*	*EU*	*Rest of world*
Live animals, products	−0.4	0.0	0.0
Dairy products	0.2	0.0	0.0
Coffee, etc, sugar, cut flowers	−0.6	−0.5	−0.5
Fruit and veg	−0.5	−0.4	−0.4
Cereals	−1.3	−1.2	−1.2
Oil seeds and fats	−0.9	0.0	0.0
Beverages and tobacco	−0.3	−0.2	−0.2
Other agricultural products	−1.3	−1.2	−1.2
Fish and products	0.0	0.0	0.0
Mineral products	−0.1	−0.1	−0.1
Metals, products	−1.3	−1.2	−1.2
Chemicals etc	−0.9	−0.9	−0.9
Leather products	−0.8	−0.7	−0.7
Wood products, pulp, paper	−0.5	−0.4	−0.4
Textiles and apparel	−1.0	−0.9	−0.9
Transport equipment	−0.7	−0.6	−0.6
Other machinery and equipment	1.3	1.4	1.4
Electrical machinery	−0.8	−0.8	−0.8
Other manufacturing	−0.7	−0.6	−0.6
Electricity	−0.3	0.0	0.0
Gas and water	−0.5	0.0	0.0
Construction	0.1	0.2	0.2
Trade	0.3	0.4	0.5
Other transport	−1.1	−1.0	0.0
Air transport	16.1	16.6	16.6
Communications	1.2	10.4	10.4
Other financial services	0.5	7.0	7.0
Insurance	0.4	0.5	0.5
Other business services	−0.7	14.9	7.8
Other services	−1.4	−1.3	−1.3

Source: FTAP model projections.

otherwise. But overall, the services sector reforms are good for the Tunisian labour market — real wages are projected to be 1.4 per cent higher than otherwise as a result of the reforms.

Table 6.14 confirms a significant boost in exports from the services sectors undergoing reform — by about 30 per cent in air passenger transport (including increased exports to foreign tourists), 50–70 per cent

Table 6.14. Implications of Tunisian Unilateral and Bilateral Services Trade Reform Initiatives for Sectoral Export Volumes from Tunisia (percentage deviation from baseline)

	Exports from Tunisian firms owned by		
Sector	*Tunisia*	*EU*	*Rest of world*
Live animals, products	−5.6	0.0	0.0
Dairy products	−1.3	0.0	0.0
Coffee, etc, sugar, cut flowers	−1.5	−1.5	−1.5
Fruit and veg	−3.9	−3.8	−3.8
Cereals	−2.6	−2.5	−2.5
Oil seeds and fats	−0.9	0.0	0.0
Beverages and tobacco	−4.4	−4.3	−4.3
Other agricultural products	−1.7	−1.6	−1.6
Fish and products	−2.3	−2.2	−2.2
Mineral products	−0.1	0.0	0.0
Metals, products	−1.8	−1.7	−1.7
Chemicals etc	−1.2	−1.1	−1.1
Leather products	−1.0	−0.9	−0.9
Wood products, pulp, paper	−1.2	−1.1	−1.1
Textiles and apparel	−1.0	−0.9	−0.9
Transport equipment	−1.1	−1.0	−1.0
Other machinery and equipment	1.3	1.4	1.4
Electrical machinery	−1.2	−1.2	−1.2
Other manufacturing	−1.1	−1.0	−1.0
Electricity	−3.9	0.0	0.0
Gas and water	−3.4	0.0	0.0
Construction	−3.3	−3.2	−3.2
Trade	2.3	2.4	2.4
Other transport	−2.7	−2.6	0.0
Air transport	28.3	28.8	28.8
Communications	58.6	73.1	73.2
Other financial services	11.7	18.9	18.9
Insurance	−0.9	−0.8	−0.8
Other business services	29.1	49.4	40.1
Other services	−8.1	−8.0	−8.0

Source: FTAP model projections.

in communications, 10–20 per cent in banking and 30–50 per cent in professional services. Again, the export performance comes not just from the foreign-owned services suppliers in these industries, but also from Tunisian-owned firms, and contributes to a 0.9 per cent increase in total export volumes. The services exports shown in Table 6.14 are those recorded in traditional balance of payments statistics — predominantly exports delivered via cross-border trade and consumption abroad (eg sales of services to foreign tourists). The growth in the output of foreign-owned firms in Tunisia (Table 6.13), and the corresponding increases in their sales to other firms in Tunisia, represents an increase in Tunisian imports of services delivered via commercial presence. But Table 6.14 confirms that those same foreign-owned firms contribute significantly to increases in services exports delivered via other modes.

In summary, the services sector reforms examined here could provide small but useful benefits to the Tunisian economy (Table 6.15). The economy is projected to be slightly bigger than otherwise, slightly more services intensive than otherwise, with a slightly bigger proportion of foreign ownership than otherwise, and with a greater export intensity than otherwise, providing a projected slight improvement in economic well-being.

Table 6.15. Structure of the Tunisian Economy Before and After Unilateral and Bilateral Services Trade Reforms

	In benchmark equilibrium	*After reforms*
Output (US$ million)	37,758	37,811
Services share (%)	48.4	48.7
Value added at factor cost (US$ million)	16,335	16,600
Services share (%)	67.0	67.5
Intermediate usage (US$ million)	20,439	20,347
Services share (%)	34.0	33.9
Household consumption (US$ million)	11,611	11,693
Services share (%)	37.8	37.8
Investment (US$ million)	5,402	5,421
Services share (%)	59.0	59.0
Government consumption (US$ million)	3,006	3,027
Services share (%)	100.0	100.00
Imports cif (US$ million)	10,355	10,438
Services share	10.6	10.9
Exports fob (US$ million)	8,976	9,052
Services share (%)	25.0	26.2
Export share of output (%)	23.8	23.9
Foreign ownership share of output (%)	15.37	15.40

Source: FTAP model database and projections.

Note that the representation of the Tunisian economy in the benchmark equilibrium in Table 6.15 is after the injection into the FTAP model's database of the estimated initial barriers to services trade in each region (carried out using the GTAP model's 'altertax' procedure adapted to the FTAP model — see Malcolm 1998 for details), and after an increase in the relative size of the Tunisian communications industry, to better match national data (carried out via a taste shift in favour of communications). The benchmark equilibrium matches neither national data nor the GTAP model database exactly.

A further policy question is how the benefits from services sector reforms would compare to those from further reform of agriculture and manufacturing. This is the topic of the next section.

6.6   Economy-wide Effects of Further Liberalizing Agriculture and Manufacturing

In 2005, the tariff assistance provided to Tunisia's agricultural and manufacturing sectors was both high and variable. Detailed data for 2005 (summarized in WTO 2005) show that tariffs on agricultural products were in the 20–90 per cent range, while MFN tariffs on manufactures were mostly 20–30 per cent (Table 6.16). Thus the protection in agriculture was much higher than in manufacturing. Both were higher than the tax equivalents of the regulatory restrictions in the particular services sectors considered above. However, they would not necessarily be of less economic significance than cost-raising restrictions elsewhere in services.

Tunisia has been in the process of phasing out its tariffs on manufactured imports from the EU, so that in 2005 tariffs on manufactures from this source were less than 10 per cent (Table 6.16). This is an additional source of variability in Tunisia's protection structure.

Once account is taken of tariff rate quotas and the *ad valorem* equivalent of specific tariffs, Tunisia's protection structure may be even more variable. Such protection estimates are available from the GTAP

Table 6.16. Tunisia's Tariff Structure, 2005

Sector	*EU preferential tariff (%)*	*MFN tariff (%)*	*Imports 2004 (US$ million)*
Live animals, products	91.8	91.8	40.5
Dairy products	94.2	95.3	42.2
Coffee, etc, sugar, cut flowers	66.1	70.3	188.5
Fruit and veg	94.6	96.8	61.7
Cereals	45.1	45.3	342.3
Oil seeds and fats	38.0	42.6	309.9
Beverages and tobacco	23.9	31.3	70.7
Other agricultural products	21.8	28.0	126.8
Fish and products	40.0	40.1	28.7
Mineral products	5.3	25.6	584.8
Metals, products	4.0	20.4	1,051.1
Chemicals etc	2.1	15.5	1,371.4
Leather products	7.6	32.8	270.1
Wood products, pulp, paper	8.2	31.6	426.2
Textiles and apparel	9.1	31.1	2,464.8
Transport equipment	4.1	18.3	924.4
Other machinery and equipment	2.7	12.5	1,474.5
Electrical machinery	5.1	24.0	1,448.7
Other manufacturing	4.2	23.7	396.8

Source: WTO (2005).

model database for the year 2001, and are shown in Table 6.17. The estimates for manufactures from this source are very roughly the same as those for 2005 from the WTO (note that the GTAP version 6 database incorporates trade-weighted applied preferential tariff rates). The estimates for agriculture are more variable than from the WTO, reflecting in part the incidence of tariff rate quotas and specific tariffs in this sector.

Tunisia has also signed a trade agreement with GAFTA countries, and has been reducing its formal tariffs from this source. But reports are that any reduction in tariffs on imports from GAFTA has been countered by an increase in administrative barriers, with no real increase in market access. So the extent of true protection from GAFTA imports now is probably the same as that shown in Table 6.17 for 2001. It generally lies somewhere between that for the EU and that for other countries.

Table 6.17. Estimates of the Tariff Equivalents of *Ad Valorem* and Specific Tariffs and
		Tariff Rate Quotas on Tunisian Imports, 2001 (per cent)

Sector	*Imports from EU*	*Imports from GAFTA*	*Imports from Rest of World*
Live animals, products	87.9	18.8	75.4
Dairy products	60.7	9.2	108.3
Coffee, etc, sugar, cut flowers	78.6	20.9	21.2
Fruit and veg	74.0	67.0	85.1
Cereals	87.7	15.4	56.6
Oil seeds and fats	14.7	114.1	21.8
Beverages and tobacco	32.5	17.2	34.8
Other agricultural products	28.4	12.4	45.9
Fish and products	41.4	20.4	27.0
Mineral products	7.2	6.0	16.4
Metals, products	9.3	16.7	27.0
Chemicals etc	6.0	7.9	25.9
Leather products	14.5	21.0	38.1
Wood products, pulp, paper	16.8	14.6	25.6
Textiles and apparel	18.0	9.0	32.6
Transport equipment	7.5	13.4	19.5
Other machinery and equipment	7.9	7.4	18.2
Electrical machinery	4.8	12.4	20.3
Other manufacturing	21.7	19.3	34.0

Source: GTAP version 6 database.

The policy dilemma facing Tunisia is that the further reductions in its tariffs on imports from EU, while reducing the average level of protection, may greatly increase the dispersion in protection — both the dispersion between agriculture and manufacturing, and the dispersion between different country sources of manufactured goods. Since the welfare damage done by import protection comes from the dispersion and well as the average level, Tunisia's current policy course may not yield benefits unless the question of dispersion is also addressed.

The extent of this policy dilemma is now examined empirically. For this purpose, the structure of protection from the GTAP version 6 database is used, since although it slightly overstates the current tariffs on manufactures from the EU, it picks up the incidence of tariff rate quotas and specific tariffs in agriculture, as well as the likely real structure of protection against imports from GAFTA countries.

Reform scenarios

One way that Tunisia could address the issue of dispersion in protection is by including agriculture in its bilateral reductions in protection with the EU — currently agriculture is largely omitted by both sides. This forms the basis of one reform scenario — Tunisia eliminates its border protection (import barriers and export subsidies) on agricultural goods from the EU, and the EU reciprocates.

Tunisian agricultural producers could have difficulty taking full advantage of this market access, without improvements in the quality of the exportables they produce.

> The cases of citrus and olive oil illustrate how potential is not being realized. The key issue is quality. Supply chains must be responsive to consumers' specific demands. But to get premium oranges and oil onto the market, farmers need first-rate technical and marketing support from research, extension and producers' organizations. And Government interventions, in the form of fixed retail margins and the Office des Huiles' control over quotas and testing, are interposed between the producer and consumer. The result is that Tunisian oranges and olive oil command low prices and EU quota is left unused. Conversely, when Government has made partial reforms, such as the removal of the ONH's olive oil export monopoly, the private sector has responded. (World Bank 2006, pp. 6–7).

Improving the quality of agricultural exportables would require not just technical solutions (research, extension) but also domestic regulatory reforms to remove government controls over quality control and wholesale and retail distribution networks, allowing Tunisian producers' direct access to their customers in Europe. The benefits of a 10 per cent productivity improvement in Tunisia's agricultural exportables (Fruit and vegetables, Oil seeds and fats, Other agricultural products) is also examined here, although the broader benefits of reform in wholesale and retail distribution, which could help bring it about, are not included.

Another way in which Tunisia could address the issue of dispersion in protection is by accompanying the elimination of the remaining tariffs on manufactures from Europe with a concomitant reduction in applied tariffs on imports from other sources. Tariffs on imports from the EU have been eliminated in recent years — Tunisia could also consider reducing its tariffs on imports from all other sources by 25 per cent.

Results

The effects of these reform scenarios in Tunisian agriculture and manufacturing are shown in Table 6.18. As expected, the results confirm that there are significant gains from reforming border protection in Tunisian agriculture. Current protection levels are so high that any form of liberalization yields gains, even if it is on a preferential basis with the EU. This alone is projected to improve economic well-being in Tunisia by US$ 114 million per year after about ten years.

Unlike in services, there are also significant gains in other countries reciprocating. Tunisia would gain US$ 295 million per year after about ten years if the EU were to drop its border protection (import tariffs and quotas and export subsidies) against Tunisian agriculture. Productivity improvements in Tunisian agriculture are probably a precondition for these gains to be realized. But a 10 per cent productivity improvement in

Table 6.18. Welfare Implications of Tunisian Reform of Agricultural and Manufacturing Protection (US$ million)

Reform scenario	*Welfare in*			
	Tunisia	*EU*	*GAFTA*	*Rest of world*
Tunisia removes border protection on agriculture from the EU	114	63	13	−52
EU reciprocates	295	−70	−1	3
10 per cent productivity improvement in Tunisia's agricultural exportables	258	58	12	5
Subtotal[a]	*733*	*183*	*23*	*−61*
Tunisia eliminates remaining tariffs on manufactures from EU	−184	417	−3	−133
Tunisia lowers tariffs on manufactures from other sources by 25 per cent	74	−38	3	65
Subtotal[a]	*−104*	*388*	*−1*	*−93*
Total[a]	641	570	22	−153
Full unilateral liberalization in manufacturing	65	203	6	210

[a] Individual entries may not add to total because of interaction effects.
Source: FTAP model projections.

agricultural exportables would by itself provide US\$ 258 million per year in gains. The combined package of agricultural reforms would provide total gains of US\$ 733 million per year after about then years (equivalent to almost 4 per cent of GDP). Real GDP itself would be 4.6 per cent higher than otherwise.

The results confirm, however, that manufacturing tariffs against EU imports in 2005 were sufficiently low, relative to protection elsewhere, that the welfare cost of exacerbating the dispersion in protection would dominate — phasing out the remaining tariffs against EU manufactures would mean economic well-being was US\$ 184 million per year lower than otherwise, after about ten years. This adverse effect could be partially offset by reducing tariffs on imports from all other sources by 25 per cent. By itself, this would provide gains of US\$ 74 million per year. The combined package of reforms to manufacturing tariffs would yield a net loss of US\$ 104 million per year.

But the structure of protection in Tunisia in 2005 was so variable that perhaps the only strategy in manufacturing to guarantee an overall net gain would be an across-the-board-approach — full liberalization of protection on imports from all sources, both EU and otherwise. In the bottom line of Table 6.18, this is shown to produce net gains of US\$ 65 million per year, after about ten years.

So it appears that on the basis of a rather restricted sample of services sectors, partial regulatory reform in those sectors would yield gains roughly equivalent to full unilateral reform of manufacturing tariffs, but roughly one tenth the gains from full bilateral reform of border protection in agriculture with the EU.

Unlike in services, however, the gains in agriculture and manufacturing tend to come at the expense of domestic output in the reforming sectors — the gains are greater, but so too are the adjustment costs.

In agriculture, the biggest loser in output terms would be Tunisia's highly protected cereals industry, which is projected to be about 40 per cent smaller than otherwise after about ten years as a result of the agricultural reforms. This would be consistent with the economy as a whole growing by 5 per cent a year over that period, but the cereals industry remaining stagnant. Thus if the agricultural reforms took place in an environment where general economic growth was greater than 5 per cent a year, the cereals industry might have to contract in *relative* terms in response to the reforms, but it would not have to contract in *absolute* terms.

The adjustment pressures would not be as great in manufacturing as in agriculture, because the initial levels of assistance are not as great. The worst affected sectors — wood and paper products, metals and products, and transport equipment — would be smaller than otherwise by 10 per cent or less after about ten years as a result of eliminating the remaining tariffs on EU imports and cutting tariffs on imports from other sources by 25 per cent. Adjustment of this magnitude could be absorbed with underlying economic growth rates of just 1 per cent a year.

In summary, the protection afforded Tunisia's agricultural and manufacturing sectors is both high and variable. Expanding the scope of bilateral liberalization with the EU to include agricultural products would yield significant gains to Tunisia. In manufacturing, there is now an urgent need to address the increasing dispersion of assistance created by the gap between tariffs on imports from the EU and imports from other sources. Accompanying the elimination of the remaining tariffs on EU products with a reduction in tariff rates from other sources appears to be a precondition for further economic gains. These expanded reforms in agriculture and manufacturing will create adjustment pressures, but especially in manufacturing, they are of a scope to be easily absorbed with normal rates of underlying economic growth.

6.7 Concluding Comments

This paper has examined the possible effects of services trade initiatives that could improve Tunisia's competitiveness relative to comparable emerging economies, particularly in European markets. Tunisia's ongoing discussions with the EU in a Euro–Med context could provide a possible forum for these next steps. The paper considers seven key services sectors — postal services, telecommunications, air passenger transport, the accounting, legal and engineering professions, and banking. Tourism and maritime services, which are important to the

Tunisian economy, are not covered because they are traditionally open to trade and investment with no significant barriers.

The possible first-round impacts of services trade initiatives in these sectors have been determined using econometric work that has quantified the effects of regulatory restrictions on economic performance in the sectors, while controlling for all other factors that affect that economic performance. The economy-wide effects of the services trade initiatives have then been projected using a computable general equilibrium model that includes foreign direct investment as an important mode of services trade delivery, and covers separately the production and trading activity of foreign multinationals.

On the basis of this restricted sample of services sectors, partial regulatory reform would yield gains roughly equivalent to full unilateral reform of manufacturing tariffs, but roughly one tenth the gains from full bilateral reform in border protection in agriculture with the EU. The adjustment costs associated with these services trade reforms are minimal. Even though many of the reforms remove discrimination against foreign suppliers, the projections do not suggest that domestically-owned services suppliers would be significantly smaller than otherwise. In many services sectors, local firms in fact have local and/or niche market advantages that allow them to thrive alongside foreign providers. The model makes provision for this differentiation.

One reason that the projected gains from services trade reform are relatively small is that most of the reforms are targeted at restrictions that have inflated price–cost margins rather than real resource costs. Liberalization therefore induces a relatively large transfer from incumbent producers to consumers, and a relatively small net gain to the economy as a whole. Nevertheless, whether barriers create rents or add to resource costs is under-researched currently. In the past, the issue has tended to be resolved by assertion, and sensitivity analysis has merely confirmed the importance of the assertion. Ideally, the econometric work that quantifies the first-round effects of regulatory restrictions should use a sufficiently rich set of performance measures to shed empirical light on the issue (Dee 2005a).[3]

---

[3] Dee (2013b) provides new evidence on this issue.

Another reason that the projected gains from services trade reform are relatively small is that, as noted, the services trade reforms are largely aimed at removing discrimination against foreign suppliers. Dee (2007) provides a number of reasons why in practice, formal services trade negotiations tend to focus on this dimension of liberalization. But those regulatory restrictions that are targeted only at foreign suppliers tend to be explicit quantity controls, since this is the most feasible way of imposing discrimination. Quantity controls in turn are the restrictions most likely to inflate price–cost margins rather than raise real resource costs.

Studies that have looked at the impact of more widespread reforms in services, including reform of non-discriminatory restrictions that tend to raise real resource costs, suggest that these can yield more than three-quarters of the overall gain from services trade reform. If Tunisia were to contemplate wider reforms, including in areas such as wholesale and retail trade, electricity generation and ports, the gains could be several orders of magnitude greater than those projected here. To the extent that the wider reforms targeted non-discriminatory restrictions, they could further benefit locally-owned new entrants. To the extent that they targeted restrictions at raised real resource costs, they could even benefit incumbent suppliers. A wider set of reforms could therefore provide win-win outcomes and even fewer adjustment problems than projected here.

Relative to the selected services trade reforms considered here, reducing the dispersion in Tunisia's barriers to its merchandise trade would yield at least as big a gain. This could be achieved, either by including agriculture in the bilateral liberalization occurring with the EU, or by accompanying the current elimination of tariffs against EU manufactures with a reduction in tariffs against imports from other sources. Unlike in services, however, the gains in agriculture and manufacturing would tend to come at the expense of domestic output in the reforming sectors — the gains are greater, but so too are the adjustment costs.

Chapter 7

The Employment Implications of Liberalizing Foreign Direct Investment in Services[1]

Philippa Dee (with Appendix by Hildegunn Nordås)

7.1 Introduction

As the world emerges from the global financial crisis, unemployment remains high in some of the major economies of Europe and North America. Accordingly, there is considerable interest in whether further trade liberalization could contribute to job creation, in both these economies and their trading partners.

In the case of services trade, this proposition is by no means obvious. Services trade barriers occur behind the border, often in the form of restrictive regulations affecting the establishment and operations of domestic and foreign services suppliers. To the extent that the restrictive regulations induce services firms to use more inputs than otherwise, then trade liberalization will have the effect of lowering costs by reducing input requirements — equivalent to a productivity improvement. And productivity improvements cost jobs rather than creating them, all other things being equal.

---

[1] This chapter is an edited version of Chapter 3 in OECD (2011), 'The Impact of Trade Liberalization on Jobs and Growth: Technical Note', OECD Trade Policy Working Papers, No. 107, Paris: OECD Publishing: 51–93. Available at http://dx.doi.org/10.1787/5kgj4jfj1nq2-en. The appendix is a preliminary version of Appendix 3.A. in OECD (2011), but gives the estimates used in the CGE analysis.

However, not all things will be equal, even in the short run. Productivity improvements lead to lower prices, which can encourage the demand for services. A key empirical question is whether these 'scale' effects of increased demand are likely to dominate the initial reductions in unit labour requirements in services. Another key question is whether any employment gains will be balanced across domestic and foreign suppliers, or whether the growth will occur in foreign suppliers at the expense of domestic ones. Thus the key empirical questions are about the scale of total employment effects in each economy, and the extent of the structural adjustments required.

The purpose of this chapter is to examine these two issues. It examines the possible effects of liberalizing barriers to foreign direct investment (FDI) in a number of services sectors in both the short and long run. By assuming that the liberalization is targeted just at foreign-invested firms, the chapter maximizes the possibility of finding that structural adjustments are adverse to domestically-owned services suppliers. If liberalization were instead targeted at regulatory restrictions that also affected domestically-owned services suppliers, then the structural adjustments would likely be less severe than those projected here.

The chapter examines the possible effects of liberalizing barriers to foreign direct investment in both the short and long term. Over the longer term, wages in each economy can be expected to adjust in the face of services trade liberalization to bring total employment levels into equilibrium, with any remaining unemployment being only the frictional unemployment associated with job search. Thus the longer-term effect of services trade liberalization can be expected to be on the level of real wages rather than the level of aggregate employment. Liberalization that has beneficial impacts on labour markets will generate real wages that are higher than otherwise. If liberalization has adverse effects, real wages will be lower than otherwise.

In the current economic climate, however, trade liberalization is being contemplated in economies that already have significant levels of structural unemployment. In the short term, therefore, the labour market effects of services trade liberalization can be expected to be felt on aggregate levels of employment or unemployment, rather than on real wages. Furthermore, in the short run, the additional foreign direct investment spurred by liberalization may not yet flow through into additional productive capacity. This provides a brake on the ability of services trade liberalization to generate scale effects that might boost jobs. The short-run treatment of services trade liberalization in this chapter takes both of these factors into account.

Finally, the chapter examines the effects of investment liberalization in services jointly by a number of FDI-sending and receiving countries. The chapter first examines the effects of liberalization undertaken on a non-preferential or 'most-favoured nation' basis by the G20 countries. It also looks at the effects of global liberalization of investment in services.

To examine these issues, the chapter uses a multi-regional computable general equilibrium (CGE) model of the global economy that has an explicit treatment of foreign direct investment. The exercise makes use of information on regulatory barriers to foreign direct investment compiled by the OECD. It also makes use of econometric estimates from the OECD of the extent to which FDI stocks can be expected to respond to changes in foreign investment barriers. The sizes of the FDI responses to liberalization that are used in the general equilibrium model are therefore firmly based on historical patterns. The model then 'traces back' the impacts on the level and distribution of employment, using a fully-articulated theory of supply and demand for both labour and capital, calibrated to estimates of the price-responsiveness of FDI that are also based on real-world data. In addition to generating projections for labour market impacts, the model can also generate projections for activity levels, macroeconomic aggregates, and measures of overall economic well-being.

7.2 Barriers to Foreign Direct Investment in Services

One of the earliest systematic compilations of barriers to foreign direct investment designed for use in subsequent empirical work was the study by Hardin and Holmes (1997). The OECD has subsequently undertaken similar exercises (Golub 2003, Takeshi and Golub 2006), the most recent exercise being by Kalinova, Palerm and Thomsen (2010).

The latter paper compiles information on four key dimensions of regulatory restrictions affecting foreign direct investment — foreign equity limits as they apply to both start-ups and acquisitions, screening and approval processes for both start-ups and acquisitions, restrictions on the movement of intra-corporate transferees, and 'other' restrictions, a catch-all category covering restrictions on legal form, on profit/capital repatriation, on access to finance and land, and the presence of reciprocity requirements. The presence of each restriction is given a score measuring its relative perceived importance (see the original paper for details), and the scores are added together to give an overall restrictiveness index value lying somewhere between zero (no restrictions apply) and one (all restrictions apply).[2]

The resulting FDI restrictiveness indices for G20 countries and the rest of the world are shown in Table 7.1.[3] The sectoral coverage has been adjusted to match that used in the CGE model.

The table shows first that in many countries, FDI restrictions are either more prevalent or more severe in services than in other sectors of the economy. In part, this is because services sectors include key 'backbone' services (transport, communications, finance) that have often been legislated government monopolies, and are still viewed as being strategically important for a variety of reasons. Nevertheless, there is ample evidence of the benefits of making these sectors more contestable (eg Findlay 2008).

FDI restrictions are particularly severe in air and water transport. These are sectors where there are also significant barriers to services trade other than barriers to FDI. In maritime transport, cabotage restrictions can reserve coastal shipping services to vessels that are flagged, crewed and/or built locally. International air transport services are governed by a system of bilateral air services agreements that often incorporate both cabotage restrictions and restrictions on ownership, over

---

[2] However, if foreign equity limits are zero, then the overall index is zero, irrespective of the other measures.

[3] Throughout this chapter, information on the G20 economies excludes information on Saudi Arabia, because it has not been possible to include a separate representation of Saudi Arabia in the CGE model used for this exercise.

and above the foreign equity limits written into general investment legislation.

FDI restrictions are also shown as being relatively high in communications. This is because the barriers are particularly high in broadcasting, where local ownership and local content requirements are both widespread. And foreign equity restrictions are still surprisingly prevalent in telecommunications, even though a combination of technology and regulatory reforms has made telecommunications markets highly contestable in other respects (see also Dee 2010b).

FDI restrictions are also severe in some countries in 'other business services,' a category that includes the professions. Some countries have relatively restrictive requirements for entry of any new professionals, foreign or otherwise. Others are highly discriminatory against foreign services suppliers, maintaining restrictions on foreign equity in, and the legal form of, professional firms, as well as restrictions on the movement of individual professionals.

Finally, Table 7.1 indicates that FDI restrictions are spread across both the developed and the developing world. They are particularly severe in developing countries such as China and Indonesia and in some emerging countries such as Russia. But they also feature in at least some services sectors in developed countries such as Australia, Canada, Japan and the United States.

Thus FDI restrictions are relatively widespread through the G20 economies. A threshold question, however, is whether these are the only, or even the most important, restrictions affecting trade in services.

One way to answer this question is to look at the extent to which services are actually traded via FDI. Commercial presence is recognized in the General Agreement on Trade in Services (GATS) under the World Trade Organization (WTO) as one of the means by which services are traded. It involves the service provider moving to establish a permanent commercial presence in the consumer's country, and is an important mode of delivery for services such as finance, telecommunications and land transport. Services can also be traded via the temporary movement of individual services suppliers. This is an important means by which many professional and other business services are traded. Services can be

Table 7.1. OECD FDI Restrictiveness Index (0 = no restriction, 1 = full restriction)

	ARG	AUS	BRA	CAN	CHN	REU	FRA	GER	IND	IDN	ITA	JPN	MEX	RUS	ZAF	KOR	TUR	GBR	USA	ROW
Agric. etc	0.000	0.075	0.397	0.200	0.697	0.084	0.153	0.092	0.300	0.417	0.333	1.000	0.517	0.317	0.060	0.333	0.000	0.206	0.183	0.217
Proc. food	0.000	0.075	0.025	0.100	0.248	0.006	0.000	0.000	0.120	0.060	0.000	0.050	0.100	0.183	0.060	0.000	0.000	0.023	0.000	0.071
Other primary	0.000	0.088	0.025	0.150	0.390	0.018	0.009	0.000	0.525	0.085	0.020	1.000	0.100	0.943	0.060	0.000	0.050	0.023	0.100	0.191
Textiles etc	0.000	0.075	0.025	0.100	0.248	0.006	0.000	0.000	0.120	0.060	0.000	0.050	0.100	0.183	0.060	0.000	0.000	0.023	0.000	0.071
Wood etc	0.000	0.075	0.025	0.100	0.248	0.006	0.000	0.000	0.120	0.060	0.000	0.050	0.100	0.183	0.060	0.000	0.000	0.023	0.000	0.071
Chemicals	0.000	0.075	0.025	0.100	0.280	0.006	0.000	0.000	0.010	0.135	0.000	0.333	0.100	0.183	0.060	0.000	0.000	0.023	0.000	0.071
Metals	0.000	0.075	0.025	0.100	0.243	0.006	0.000	0.000	0.000	0.060	0.000	0.000	0.100	0.183	0.060	0.000	0.000	0.023	0.000	0.071
Vehicles	0.000	0.075	0.025	0.100	0.265	0.006	0.000	0.000	0.000	0.060	0.000	0.000	0.113	0.250	0.060	0.000	0.000	0.023	0.000	0.071
Elect. mach.	0.000	0.075	0.025	0.100	0.225	0.006	0.000	0.000	0.000	0.060	0.000	0.000	0.100	0.183	0.060	0.000	0.000	0.023	0.000	0.071
Other mach.	0.000	0.075	0.025	0.100	0.243	0.006	0.000	0.000	0.000	0.060	0.000	0.000	0.100	0.183	0.060	0.000	0.000	0.023	0.000	0.071
Electricity	0.000	0.075	0.025	0.100	0.608	0.060	0.000	0.000	0.000	0.110	0.000	0.000	0.100	0.250	0.060	0.417	0.000	0.023	0.222	0.282
Gas, water	0.000	0.075	0.025	0.100	0.608	0.060	0.000	0.000	0.000	0.110	0.000	0.000	0.100	0.250	0.060	0.417	0.000	0.023	0.222	0.282
Construction	0.000	0.075	0.025	0.100	0.265	0.006	0.000	0.000	0.000	0.310	0.000	0.000	0.100	0.183	0.060	0.000	0.000	0.023	0.000	0.132
Trade	0.000	0.075	0.025	0.100	0.242	0.007	0.000	0.000	0.280	0.539	0.005	0.000	0.133	0.238	0.060	0.000	0.000	0.023	0.000	0.071
Other transp.	0.125	0.075	0.275	0.100	0.415	0.018	0.000	0.000	0.000	0.129	0.000	0.000	0.475	0.183	0.060	0.000	0.000	0.023	0.000	0.078
Water transp.	0.000	0.125	0.025	0.100	0.850	0.105	0.225	0.275	0.000	0.560	0.225	1.000	0.550	0.183	0.060	0.950	0.125	0.073	1.000	0.469
Air transp.	0.000	0.475	0.575	0.600	0.730	0.276	0.225	0.325	0.523	0.560	0.225	1.000	0.600	0.758	0.560	0.550	0.500	0.248	0.650	0.532
Communications	0.250	0.300	0.350	0.650	0.900	0.034	0.024	0.013	0.513	0.563	0.181	0.250	0.488	0.333	0.060	0.450	0.125	0.135	0.155	0.185

Table 7.1.   Continued.

Other finance	0.000	0.138	0.025	0.100	0.515	0.016	0.047	0.008	0.160	0.135	0.027	0.000	0.150	0.471	0.085	0.030	0.000	0.025	0.063	0.127
Insurance	0.000	0.125	0.025	0.000	0.800	0.008	0.068	0.000	0.500	0.160	0.000	0.000	0.100	0.658	0.110	0.000	0.000	0.023	0.000	0.094
Other bus. serv.	0.000	0.103	0.025	0.100	0.138	0.064	0.003	0.000	0.500	0.560	0.000	0.000	0.103	0.308	0.385	0.000	0.125	0.023	0.000	0.141
Other serv.	0.000	0.400	0.000	0.000	0.275	0.304	0.000	0.000	0.000	1.000	0.000	0.100	0.167	0.733	0.010	0.000	1.000	0.000	0.000	0.311
Overall Index	0.025	0.127	0.116	0.164	0.457	0.045	0.038	0.023	0.223	0.331	0.073	0.257	0.225	0.350	0.085	0.131	0.074	0.061	0.084	0.152

ARG=Argentina, AUS=Australia, BRA=Brazil, CAN=Canada, REU=Rest of EU, FRA=France, GER=Germany, IND=India, IDN=Indonesia, ITA=Italy, JPN=Japan, MEX=Mexico, RUS=Russia, ZAF=South Africa, KOR=Republic of Korea, TUR=Turkey, GBR=Great Britain, USA=United States, ROW=Rest of world.
Source: Kalinova, Palerm and Thomsen (2010).

traded via the temporary movement of the consumer to the producer's country, as when students or medical patients travel overseas to be educated or treated. Finally, services can be traded while neither the producer nor consumer moves. This is the main method of trade in air and maritime services, as well as for services traded primarily over the internet.[4]

Estimates of the extent of services traded via FDI are hard to come by, because while many countries collect statistics on FDI itself, few collect statistics on the subsequent production and sales activities of foreign affiliates, and it is the latter that constitutes the traded service. Nevertheless, ballpark estimates suggest that services traded via commercial presence account for about 56 per cent of global services trade, while trade involving the temporary movement of suppliers accounts for 2 per cent, the movement of consumers accounts for 14 per cent, and 'pure' cross-border trade accounts for 28 per cent (Karsenty 2002).

Thus trade via FDI is the single most important mode of services trade. The FDI restrictiveness indices capture barriers to this trade, as well as some of the barriers affecting the movement of individual services suppliers (via restrictions on the movement of intra-corporate transferees). Furthermore, the evidence is that trade occurring cross-border and via the movement of consumers is relatively unimpeded in most countries currently (Mattoo and Wunsch-Vincent 2004). Thus it would appear that barriers to commercial presence are probably the most important services trade barriers by mode.

A second question is whether barriers to FDI capture all of the important barriers to trade via commercial presence. In this respect, the WTO recognizes two types of barriers. Restrictions on 'national treatment' are restrictions that discriminate against foreign suppliers, *vis-à-vis* domestic ones, such as restrictions on the repatriation of profits. But the GATS also recognizes restrictions on 'market access'. These are six specific types of regulatory restrictions, most of which are

---

[4] About a quarter of cross-border services trade is intra-firm trade and thus driven by FDI, whereas about half of cross-border trade in services is transport and travel, probably driven by trade in goods and FDI in all sectors.

quantitative in nature (eg restrictions on the total number of services suppliers, or the total value of services transactions), and most of which do not necessarily discriminate against foreign suppliers — they could also affect potential domestic new entrants. Furthermore, the GATS also recognizes that there can be a raft of other domestic regulation that may be designed to meet legitimate domestic economic objectives (such as quality or safety), but may be 'more burdensome than necessary' to meet those objectives. To date, however, the GATS agreement itself imposes only very weak disciplines on this latter type of regulation.

How important are these various types of trade restrictions in practice? A recent assessment of services regulation in East Asian economies showed that non-discriminatory trade restrictions in services not only occur, but are of considerable economic significance (Dee 2007). Their significance arises because they tend to be the type that affects operations and creates pure waste by raising the real resource costs of services producers. This is in contrast to artificial barriers to entry that create artificial scarcity, and allow incumbent producers to raise prices above production costs. The latter kinds of barriers create large transfers from consumers to producers, but relatively small costs to the economy as a whole (relative to barriers that create pure waste). However, artificial barriers to entry are often used to discriminate against foreign suppliers, because they are often the most feasible way to impose discrimination.

These reasons help to explain the finding that a preferential trade agreement among East Asian economies would generate gains that were less than a fifth of those available were those economies to tackle the non-discriminatory regulations that affect both domestic and foreign new entrants equally. In a similar context, the gains from removing restrictions on market access could account for 75 per cent of the total gains from liberalizing services trade globally (Dee and Hanslow 2001).

Thus barriers to FDI in services are not necessarily the most important barriers to commercial presence, in terms of impact on overall economic well-being. So the impacts on economic well-being projected in the main part of this chapter are probably under-estimates of the total impact of liberalizing commercial presence in services. Nevertheless, because FDI restrictions are discriminatory, their removal in isolation will give an upper estimate of the structural adjustments produced by liberalizing commercial presence in services. Overall, therefore, the main analysis may underestimate the gains and overestimate the costs from FDI liberalization. Both these qualifications should be kept in mind in what follows.

In an alternative treatment, however, the liberalization of barriers to FDI is combined with an indicative easing of regulatory restrictions that affect domestic and foreign services suppliers equally. This gives an indication of the extent to which the main welfare and labour market results of this study are underestimated.

7.3   Modelling the First-round Effects of Liberalizing FDI in Services

Modelling the liberalization of barriers to services trade normally takes place as a two-step process (Dee 2005a). In the first step, econometric analysis is used to identify the 'first-round' impact of services trade barriers on various measures of sectoral economic performance, while controlling for all the other factors that might affect that performance. These first-round impacts are then fed into a CGE model to get a picture of the flow-on effects to other aspects of sectoral performance, to other sectors, and to the economy as a whole.

In the current exercise, the OECD has undertaken econometric analysis of the effects of FDI restrictions on FDI stocks — themselves the outcomes of FDI supply responses interacting with changes in the demand for FDI capital. Thus the econometric analysis is not structural, in the sense of identifying just the changes in the demand for FDI capital arising from vertical shifts in the supply curves of foreign-invested firms. This does not preclude use of a CGE model. The required 'market outcome' changes in FDI stocks can be fed into the CGE model as targets, and the supply curves of foreign-invested firms in the model can be shifted vertically by the (then model-determined) amounts required to guarantee the desired market outcomes.[5] The CGE model then yields

---

[5] Technically, this requires a closure switch so that the normally endogenous FDI stocks become a policy target and vertical supply curve shifters become endogenous 'enablers'.

insights into the effects along the supply chain and across sectors of increasing FDI stocks in services.

Ideally, however, the econometric analysis would be structural — that is, it would identify the impacts on services industry supply responses, rather than the impacts on overall services market outcomes after industry supply responses had interacted with market demand characteristics. When industry supply responses are identified at the econometric stage, they can be fed into the CGE model as vertical shifts in the CGE model's supply curves, and the CGE model can project how the supply responses would interact with demand characteristics to generate overall market outcomes.

The standard way of ensuring that the econometric analysis is structural is to estimate properly specified industry cost and profit functions. The key advantage of this approach is that it can identify directly and empirically whether the first-round impact of the restrictions has been to create pure waste (which would show up in the cost function estimation) or has allowed inflated price–cost margins for incumbent producers (which would show up in the profit function estimation). As noted, this plays a major role in determining the subsequent projected impact of liberalization on economic well-being. Recent examples of econometric analysis along these lines are in Dee and Dinh (2013) and Dinh (2013).

The difficulty with the current approach is that is does not resolve the question of whether the FDI restrictions have operated by raising the price–cost margins of foreign-invested firms, or have created pure waste. The arguments above suggest that *a priori*, we might expect at least some of the FDI restrictions to have generated rents for incumbents rather than pure waste. Nevertheless, in the base-case projections presented here, it is assumed that the FDI restrictions create pure waste. As suggested in the introduction, this is a 'conservative' treatment in the current context because it biases the model towards finding negative employment outcomes from the liberalization of foreign direct investment.

With FDI restrictions treated as creating pure waste, the required FDI responses to liberalization can be modelled as coming about through 'enabling' improvements in the productivity of foreign-invested firms.

These model-determined productivity changes correspond to the vertical shifts in the supply curves of foreign-invested firms required to elicit the required increases in FDI stocks from foreign investors.[6]

In an alternative treatment, FDI restrictions are treated as inflating the price–cost margins of foreign-invested firms, rather than creating pure waste. Price–cost margins are assumed to be inflated by the same amount as the productivity changes in the default treatment.[7] This alternative treatment is used as a sensitivity test on outcomes for employment and economic well-being.

The econometric analysis that is used by the OECD to determine the first-round impact of FDI liberalization on FDI stocks in services is described in the Appendix. It draws on a particular application of the 'knowledge capital' model of FDI by Baltagi, Egger and Pfaffermayr (2007), although data limitations have precluded the full implementation of their approach.

The results suggest that across the sample of OECD countries, the semi-elasticity of inward FDI stocks with respect to the FDI restrictiveness index is –0.24, meaning that a policy change from full restrictiveness to full liberalization would increase inward FDI stocks by 24 per cent. As Table 7.1 shows, however, no country in the study is fully restricted currently. Nor is it likely that, in response to the currently difficult employment climate, all countries would immediately move to full liberalization. Instead, this chapter examines the employment implications if countries were to remove half of their current FDI restrictions.

Using the econometric estimates from the Appendix, 50 per cent liberalization of FDI restrictions could be expected to increase inward

---

[6] There is an additional, more subtle reason for the current treatment. The model's database does not include a measure of inflated price–cost margins, if they exist. In order to get accurate welfare projections, the inflated price–cost margins would have to be injected into the model's database as tax equivalents first, before policy simulations could be undertaken. But with the intended closure switch, the size of the initial 'tax' wedge would not be revealed until a policy simulation was undertaken.

[7] Technically, the 'tax'-equivalents of the FDI restrictions in the alternative treatment are assumed to be the same size as the productivity shifters from the default treatment. These are first injected into the model's database as 'taxes' whose revenue accrues to incumbent firms as excess profits, and are then eliminated via policy experiment.

FDI stocks by the amounts shown in Table 7.2. Because of the relative simplicity of the econometric specification, there is a direct proportional relationship between the sizes of the initial FDI restrictions in Table 7.1 and the liberalization-induced increases in inward FDI stocks in Table 7.2.

Table 7.3 shows the model-generated estimates for the sizes of productivity improvements in foreign-invested firms required to induce the increases in FDI stocks shown in Table 7.2, in those sectors where FDI stocks are non-trivial to begin with (greater than US$ 1 million in 2004 dollars). Table 7.3 shows that the required productivity improvements are non-trivial — for example, a 5.9 per cent increase in FDI stocks in the communications sector in Mexico would require a 12.2 per cent increase in the productivity of foreign-invested firms in that sector, while a 7.2 per cent increase in FDI stocks in Mexico's air transport sector would require a 27.8 per cent increase in productivity of foreign-invested firms in that sector. These productivity improvements are the first round effects on foreign-invested firms. They bring about the necessary changes in FDI stocks. But they also have spillover effects to domestic firms in the same industry, to other industries, and to the economy as a whole. These spillover effects are discussed in a later section.

The projected increases in productivity required to bring about the econometrically estimated increases in FDI stocks are a function of three things — the model's assumed price responsiveness of demand for FDI capital, its assumed price responsiveness of the supply of FDI capital, and the estimated sizes of FDI stocks to begin with. Some of the largest changes in Tables 7.2 and 7.3 are associated with sectors in which FDI stocks are small to begin with. The foreign ownership shares that are implicit in the model's database are derived from data on FDI stocks, and are presented in the next section. The model's assumed price responsiveness of FDI capital supply and demand have also been roughly calibrated to real world responses, in a way that is explained further in the next section.

Table 7.2. Econometric Estimates of Increases in FDI Stocks from Removing 50% of all FDI Restrictions in Services (per cent)

	ARG	AUS	BRA	CAN	CHN	REU	FRA	GER	IND	IDN	ITA	JPN	MEX	RUS	ZAF	KOR	TUR	GBR	USA	ROW
Construction	0.0	0.9	0.3	1.2	3.2	0.1	0.0	0.0	0.0	3.7	0.0	0.0	1.2	2.2	0.7	0.0	0.0	0.3	0.0	1.6
Trade	0.0	0.9	0.3	1.2	2.9	0.1	0.0	0.0	3.4	6.5	0.1	0.0	1.6	2.9	0.7	0.0	0.0	0.3	0.0	0.9
Other transp.	1.5	0.9	3.3	1.2	5.0	0.2	0.0	0.0	0.0	1.6	0.0	0.0	5.7	2.2	0.7	0.0	0.0	0.3	0.0	0.9
Water transp.	0.0	1.5	0.3	1.2	10.2	1.3	2.7	3.3	0.0	6.7	2.7	12.0	6.6	2.2	0.7	11.4	1.5	0.9	12.0	5.6
Air transp.	0.0	5.7	6.9	7.2	8.8	3.3	2.7	3.9	6.3	6.7	2.7	12.0	7.2	9.1	6.7	6.6	6.0	3.0	7.8	6.4
Communications	3.0	3.6	4.2	7.8	10.8	0.4	0.3	0.2	6.2	6.8	2.2	3.0	5.9	4.0	0.7	5.4	1.5	1.6	1.9	2.2
Other finance	0.0	1.7	0.3	1.2	6.2	0.2	0.6	0.1	1.9	1.6	0.3	0.0	1.8	5.7	1.0	0.4	0.0	0.3	0.8	1.5
Insurance	0.0	1.5	0.3	0.0	9.6	0.1	0.8	0.0	6.0	1.9	0.0	0.0	1.2	7.9	1.3	0.0	0.0	0.3	0.0	1.1
Other bus. serv.	0.0	1.2	0.3	1.2	1.7	0.8	0.0	0.0	6.0	6.7	0.0	0.0	1.2	3.7	4.6	0.0	1.5	0.3	0.0	1.7

ARG=Argentina, AUS=Australia, BRA=Brazil, CAN=Canada, REU=Rest of EU, FRA=France, GER=Germany, IND=India,

IDN=Indonesia, ITA=Italy, JPN=Japan, MEX=Mexico, RUS=Russia, ZAF=South Africa, KOR=Republic of Korea, TUR=Turkey,

GBR=Great Britain, USA=United States, ROW=Rest of world.

Source: Author's calculations — see text.

Table 7.3. Projected Productivity Improvements in Foreign-invested Firms Required to Increase FDI Stocks by Estimated Amounts in Long Term (per cent)

	ARG	AUS	BRA	CAN	CHN	REU	FRA	GER	IND	IDN	ITA	JPN	MEX	RUS	ZAF	KOR	TUR	GBR	USA	ROW
Construction	0.1	1.3	1.1	0	0	0.4	0.1	0	0	0	0	0	8.6	4.4	0.8	0	0.1	0.6	0.1	2.5
Trade	0.3	1.7	0.5	3.1	8.6	0.6	0.1	0.2	9.8	9.7	0.1	0.2	14.6	11.7	1.9	0.3	0.4	1.0	0.1	2.7
Other transp.	3.8	0	0	0	14.9	0.9	0.1	0.1	0	0	0	0	3.4	5.2	2.0	0.3	0.3	0.9	0.1	2.8
Water transp.	0	5.9	0	4.2	0	4.9	0	0	0	0	0	28.3	15.3	7.4	3.2	23.3	8.1	0	23.8	13.9
Air transp.	0	12.0	0	9.3	0	6.0	0	6.8	0	0	0	17.0	27.8	0	0	0	0	0	13	13
Communications	7.6	0	12.9	0	33.5	1.6	0.7	0.8	0	0	0	0	12.2	6.4	2.4	0	8.8	4.3	4.3	6.7
Other finance	0.4	6.0	0.5	0	23.3	1.1	1.2	0.4	7.8	6.2	1.1	0	3.5	8.8	3.9	1.7	0.5	0.7	1.0	4.6
Insurance	0	3.9	0.5	0.6	0	0.4	1.0	0	0	0	0.1	0.1	2.0	19.3	3.5	0.2	0.4	0.3	0.1	2.3
Other bus. serv.	0.4	2.2	1.1	2.6	3.6	2.8	0.5	0.5	7.9	9.4	0.5	0	6.6	11.6	10.9	0	0	1.3	0.1	5.3

ARG=Argentina, AUS=Australia, BRA=Brazil, CAN=Canada, REU=Rest of EU, FRA=France, GER=Germany, IND=India, IDN=Indonesia, ITA=Italy, JPN=Japan, MEX=Mexico, RUS=Russia, ZAF=South Africa, KOR=Republic of Korea, TUR=Turkey, GBR=Great Britain, USA=United States, ROW=Rest of world.
Source: FTAP model projections.

7.4 Modeling the Economy-wide Effects of Liberalizing FDI in Services

As noted in the introduction, modelling the liberalization of FDI requires a model in which FDI is represented explicitly. The effects have been projected here using the FTAP model of the world economy, which was developed by Dee and Hanslow (2001), is documented fully in Hanslow, Phamduc and Verikios (1999), and is available for download at http://crawford.anu.edu.au/crawford_people/content/staff/pdee.php. The FTAP model is a computable general equilibrium model incorporating services delivered via FDI. It differs in turn from GTAP (Hertel 1997), the 'plain vanilla' model from which it was derived, in three important respects.

First, because many services are delivered primarily via commercial presence, the modelling framework includes foreign direct investment as a mode of services trade delivery, and covers separately the production and trading activity of foreign multinationals (in all sectors, not just in services). In other words, GTAP, the conventional multi-country model, is split out by ownership as well as location.

It is not advisable to impute foreign ownership shares simply by comparing sectoral estimates of FDI stocks with sectoral estimates of total capital stocks. This is because foreign-invested firms are likely to use a range of financing methods to finance their investments. In addition to using FDI capital from their parent company, they may also borrow, and accept equity injections from other minority stakeholders. As noted, however, few countries collect systematic Foreign Affiliate Trade Statistics (FATS) on the activities of foreign affiliates. But one that does is the United States.

The default way of deriving foreign ownership shares in the FTAP model is to make use of several ratios derived from US FATS statistics. Ratios of FDI capital to total assets, and total assets to total sales, were extracted by sector and by host country by researchers at the United States International Trade Commission. The ratios show less variation across host countries than across sectors. So sector-specific ratios of FDI capital to total sales are used to 'gross up' sectoral and bilateral estimates of FDI stocks, in order to generate sectoral and bilateral estimates of the output of foreign-invested firms. In the current version of the model, the sectoral and bilateral estimates of FDI stocks were provided by CEPII (Boumellassa, Gouel and Laborde 2007), and are derived from UNCTAD, Eurostat, and other sources.

The resulting estimates of the output of foreign-invested firms are compared with the data on total sectoral output from the GTAP model's database (version 7.1 is used for the current exercise), and the resulting implicit foreign ownership shares are used to derive full costs and sales structures for foreign-invested firms on a strictly *pro rata* basis. The *pro rata* treatment is not ideal, especially since the theoretical literature highlights that the cost and sales structures of foreign-invested firms are likely to feature significant amounts of intra-firm trade. Nevertheless, even where FATS data are collected, they rarely extend to a full treatment of cost and sales structures, so the current treatment is perhaps not much less sophisticated than would be feasible, even if FATS data were more widely available.

In any given application of the FTAP model, the default foreign ownership shares are typically overwritten with any application-specific information that might be available. The current application is no exception. FATS statistics for OECD countries are being compiled, where they exist, under the OECD's globalization project. This data provides estimates of the value added of foreign-invested firms, which can be compared with sectoral value added from national accounts sources, to provide alternative estimates of foreign ownership shares, albeit not broken down by host country. These scanty data have been used to very roughly calibrate the overall size of foreign ownership shares, although the sectoral and host country breakdown still comes from the default treatment. Interestingly, the calibration resulted in a downward adjustment to the overall size of foreign ownership shares.

The resulting foreign ownership shares used in the current application are shown in Table 7.4. They show many of the same problems as the underlying FDI stock data. Apart from the inevitable idiosyncrasies, a few more general qualifications that are pertinent to the current application are as follows. Firstly, foreign ownership shares in 'other

Table 7.4. Foreign Ownership Shares (per cent)

	ARG	AUS	BRA	CAN	CHN	REU	FRA	GER	IND	IDN	ITA	JPN	MEX	RUS	ZAF	KOR	TUR	GBR	USA	ROW
Agric. etc	0	0	0	0	0	0	0	0	0	0	0	0	0	0	0	0	0	0	0	0
Proc. food	1	19	4	33	0	26	9	3	7	0	11	1	3	5	2	8	4	17	8	10
Other primary	1	17	2	29	0	20	8	5	0	0	4	5	2	0	1	1	5	41	9	3
Textiles etc	1	10	2	8	0	10	13	10	1	0	5	2	1	2	1	7	1	31	5	3
Wood etc	1	9	1	16	0	14	9	4	0	0	7	1	2	2	1	7	4	38	3	11
Chemicals	3	37	7	45	0	36	33	14	2	0	10	4	5	4	3	11	7	46	24	16
Metals	0	4	1	14	0	6	7	3	0	0	3	1	1	0	0	1	1	12	4	5
Vehicles	2	31	8	15	0	27	16	12	5	0	31	10	2	4	1	8	4	32	22	51
Elect. mach.	7	80	1	100	0	20	34	15	1	0	24	2	2	16	9	2	8	43	13	6
Other mach.	4	39	2	57	0	31	16	13	1	0	7	3	4	3	2	18	7	39	23	16
Electricity	0	9	0	3	0	6	5	1	0	0	2	0	2	0	0	1	1	22	4	2
Gas, water	0	9	1	3	0	6	4	1	0	0	1	0	2	0	0	1	1	21	4	1
Construction	0	7	0	4	0	3	2	1	0	0	0	1	5	0	1	1	1	5	2	2
Trade	2	16	2	26	0	27	19	14	0	3	9	1	22	1	3	11	5	20	8	10
Other transp.	0	2	0	2	0	4	3	1	0	0	2	0	1	0	0	2	0	9	2	2
Water transp.	1	8	1	35	0	7	13	6	0	0	5	0	13	0	1	3	1	1	2	6
Air transp.	0	1	0	3	0	10	1	0	0	0	2	2	1	0	0	0	0	1	0	6
Communications	1	2	1	2	0	8	5	8	0	0	4	0	4	2	1	3	3	23	3	4

Table 7.4. Continued.

Other finance	11	26	3	5	0	28	12	2	0	0	5	0	37	11	20	6	5	29	5	18
Insurance	2	7	0	34	0	11	2	1	0	0	10	1	29	4	0	2	11	8	4	7
Other bus. serv.	7	11	2	2	0	8	9	9	0	1	1	0	100	5	5	1	3	2	8	11
Other serv.	0	0	0	0	0	0	0	0	0	0	0	0	0	0	0	0	0	0	0	0

ARG=Argentina, AUS=Australia, BRA=Brazil, CAN=Canada, REU=Rest of EU, FRA=France, GER=Germany, IND=India, IDN=Indonesia, ITA=Italy, JPN=Japan, MEX=Mexico, RUS=Russia, ZAF=South Africa, KOR=Republic of Korea, TUR=Turkey, GBR=Great Britain, USA=United States, ROW=Rest of world.

Source: FTAP model database.

finance' are probably overstated, because this sector is very often an intermediary, rather than the ultimate destination of the FDI. Secondly, foreign ownership shares are likely underestimated, and probably severely so, in countries such as China and Indonesia.[8] This is because OECD countries dominate the reporting of FDI data. Nevertheless, other aspects of the data are probably accurate. In particular, foreign ownership shares are likely very low in maritime and air transport, because of the raft of regulations preventing foreign penetration, over and above the restrictions written into investment legislation. And these shares are likely to remain low, even after FDI liberalization, for this very reason.

A second way in which FTAP differs from GTAP is that it recognizes, by virtue of foreign ownership, that at least some of the profits of foreign-invested firms will be repatriated back to the home countries. Thus the profit streams in the conventional multi-country model have to be reallocated from the host to the home country, after provision is made for them to be taxed in either the home or host country. This reallocation leads to a distinction between GDP — the income *generated* in a region — and GNP — the income *received by residents* of a region. The latter forms the basis of the welfare measure in FTAP. The information on profit repatriation comes from the Balance of Payments Statistics of the International Monetary Fund (IMF).

Thirdly, not all profits of foreign multinationals need be repatriated to the home country. Some may be reinvested in the host country. To account for this phenomenon, and to allow for the effect that regulatory reform may have on both domestic and foreign direct investment more generally, the model makes provision for savings and capital accumulation. This is particularly important, since some regulatory barriers are aimed directly at limiting foreign equity participation. It is therefore important to capture how regulatory reform will affect not just foreign ownership *shares*, but also the *total amount* of productive capacity available to an economy. National savings rates are derived from the macroeconomic data in the International Financial Statistics and Balance of Payments Statistics of the IMF. Government savings rates are

---

[8] Many of the foreign ownership shares in these economies appear to be zero, but this is because of rounding.

derived from the Government Finance Statistics of the IMF. Household savings rates are calculated as a residual.

The FTAP model also differs from GTAP in its assumptions about industry organization. In particular, it allows for firm-level product differentiation, economies of scale and large-group monopolistic competition. This is also important, since services tend to be highly specialized, being tailored to the needs of individual customers.

In practice, large-group monopolistic competition can be modelled using much the same theory as is used to specify the default Armington treatment in the GTAP model (eg Francois, McDonald and Nordstrom 1995). The main difference is in the parameterization. Where competition is monopolistic, and economies of scale are global, then the double-nested Armington treatment collapses to a single nest,[9] and the single demand parameter reflects the extent of product differentiation — in turn a function of the extent of economies of scale. Consumers and users globally also benefit from greater variety when industry output expands, a feature that is captured by having an endogenous productivity improvement tied to expansions in industry output. The size of this productivity boost from greater variety is also a function of the extent of product differentiation (see also Neary 2001).

In the current version, the parameterization is adapted from Berden *et al.* (2009), and shown in Table 7.5. The parameters used in Berden *et al.* (2009) were obtained by estimating a gravity equation explaining bilateral trade, which included an index of barriers to trade. If the elasticity of prices with respect to the index of trade barriers can be assumed to be unity, then the estimated coefficients on the index in the gravity equation can also be taken as estimates of demand elasticities. This was the approach taken in Berden *et al.* (2009) to parameterize export demands all sectors. It is used in this application to parameterize agriculture and manufacturing.

---

[9] This is achieved by having the same values for the elasticities of substitution in both nests — the one between domestic and imported goods, and the one between different sources of imports.

Table 7.5.   Demand Parameters

	Treatment of competition	*Treatment of economies of scale*	*Elasticity of substitution between domestic and foreign goods (ESUBD)*	*Elasticity of substitution between foreign goods from different sources (ESUBM)*	*Productivity parameter determining gains from variety[a]*
Agric. etc	Armington		4.8	4.8	0
Proc. food	Monopolistic competition	Global	5.0	5.0	0.2
Other primary	Armington		9.8	9.8	0
Textiles etc	Monopolistic competition	Global	7.2	7.2	0.14
Wood etc	Monopolistic competition	Global	7.9	7.9	0.13
Chemicals	Monopolistic competition	Global	5.1	5.1	0.20
Metals	Monopolistic competition	Global	13.0	13.0	0.08
Vehicles	Monopolistic competition	Global	7.1	7.1	0.14
Elect. mach.	Monopolistic competition	Global	12.2	12.2	0.08
Other mach.	Monopolistic competition	Global	7.1	7.1	0.14
Electricity	Armington		10	10	0
Gas, water	Armington		10	10	0
Construction	Monopolistic competition	Regional	5	10	0.1
Trade	Monopolistic competition	Regional	5	10	0.1

Table 7.5. Continued.

Other transp.	Armington		10	10	0
Water transp.	Armington		10	10	0
Air transp.	Armington		10	10	0
Communications	Monopolistic competition	Regional	5	10	0.1
Other finance	Monopolistic competition	Regional	5	10	0.1
Insurance	Monopolistic competition	Regional	5	10	0.1
Other bus. serv.	Monopolistic competition	Regional	5	10	0.1
Other serv.	Armington		10	10	0

[a] Given the way that productivity shifts are modelled in FTAP, the productivity parameter is just the inverse of ESUBM.
Source: FTAP model database.

For services, however, direct estimates are available for the elasticities of prices or costs with respect to indexes of trade barriers. Sourdin (2013) looks at how indexes of barriers to trade in air and maritime services have affected the cif/fob margins on goods shipped by air or sea, respectively. While Sourdin estimated semi-elasticities, the corresponding elasticities of these measures of air and maritime shipping costs with respect to the corresponding trade indexes, evaluated at the APEC average values of trade restrictions, are 0.14 for air transport and 0.30 for sea transport. These estimates can be used to adjust the demand parameters for services from Berden *et al.* (2009). The resulting adjusted trade parameters range from 7 to 14 but are centred on 10 if Sourdin's maritime estimate is used. They range from 14 to 30 but are centred on 22 if her air estimate is used. In Table 7.5, a representative value of 10 has been chosen.

A final feature of Table 7.5 is whether monopolistic competition is assumed to be global or regional. As argued in Dee (2003), many services are sold into markets that have very region-specific languages, cultures and regulatory structures (for example, local legal and accounting standards). This means that the services sold into those markets will tend to be tailored to meet the particular regulatory and market needs of those markets, and will not therefore be appropriate for delivery elsewhere. Accordingly, any economies of scale will be local rather than global. This explains the choices made on this score in Table 7.5. With regional economies of scale, the elasticity of substitution between domestic and imported services is less than the elasticity of substitution between different sources of imports, instead of being the same. However, some services, such as air and maritime transport, are recognized as being relatively homogeneous (in the sense of having generic rather than regional product differentiation) across different markets.

Finally, the FTAP model not only has a treatment of savings and capital accumulation, it also has an explicit treatment of how savings is used to finance investment — by building the investment portfolios of investors around the world. The model therefore includes an explanation of the portfolio allocation choices of investors in each country. They prefer to hold a mixed portfolio of debt and equity, and a mix of equities across different industries and host countries, albeit with some home country bias to the equity portfolio choice. Because they do not treat equities from different sectors and host countries as perfect substitutes (although they do treat debt as perfectly mobile), they therefore require non-trivial changes in the relative returns to equity from different countries in order to be induced to hold more in their overall portfolio. This is relevant to the current application, because FDI stocks can only be built up if investors are willing to hold them.

As noted earlier, however, the capital supply elasticities in the model can also be roughly calibrated to various pieces of econometric evidence. The evidence of Sourdin (2013) for maritime is that the semi-elasticity of services prices (or costs) with respect to an index of trade barriers (scaled between zero and one) is –0.487. The evidence in the Appendix is that the semi-elasticity of FDI stocks supplied by investors with respect to an index of trade and investment barriers (also scaled between zero and one) is –0.24. These together imply that the elasticity of FDI stocks with respect to costs is 0.24/0.487 = 0.5. This is the same order of magnitude as the relationship between the changes in FDI stocks in Table 7.2 and the changes in productivity required to generate them in Table 7.3. These were produced using the default capital supply elasticities in the FTAP model (Hanslow, Phamduc and Verikios 1999).

In the long-run treatment, the model provides a snapshot of how different each economy would look about ten years after the introduction of the investment liberalization, compared to the situation at that same point in time if the reforms had not taken place. During the ten year adjustment period, many other changes would affect each economy, but they are not taken into account in the current analysis. For this reason, the results should not be interpreted as indicating the likely changes that would occur *over time* in each economy — this would require all changes, not just those in regulatory trade barriers, to be taken into account. Instead, they should be interpreted as deviations from some future 'business-as-usual' control.

The distinction is important to keep in mind. Sometimes, to aid fluency, the results are couched as if key indicators 'rise' or 'fall'. This does not mean that the indicators would be higher or lower than they are now. It means that at some future time, they would be higher or lower than they would be otherwise. In both cases, in a growing economy, they could be higher than they are now.

In the long-run treatment, each economy is assumed to be able to adjust in various ways. Both the total sizes of capital stocks, and their allocation across sectors and countries, is assumed to adjust to the FDI liberalization. Employment of skilled and unskilled labour is also assumed to be able to move between sectors, but not between countries. Crucially, however, the sizes of the skilled and unskilled labour forces are assumed to be the same in the long run, whether or not the FDI liberalization takes place. In this long-run, equilibrium view of labour markets, FDI liberalization will not create jobs because it will not create new members of the labour force. To the extent that FDI liberalization increases the demand for labour, however, this will drive wages to be higher than otherwise. To the extent that it reduces the demand for labour, it will drive wages lower than otherwise. Thus, in the long run, labour markets clear.

In the short-run treatment, by contrast, the productivity improvements that follow from FDI liberalization flow through to higher returns to investors, but there is insufficient time for capital stocks to adjust to the changes in returns. Accordingly, capital stocks are assumed to be the same (by sector, host country and ownership category) with the reforms as without them. To capture the idea of FDI liberalization being undertaken in a situation of excess unemployment in some countries, the total levels of employment of skilled and unskilled labour in those economies are assumed to adjust to the liberalization, while real wages are kept fixed. This treatment is applied to North America (Canada, Mexico, United States), Europe (France, Germany, Italy, Great Britain, the rest of the EU) and South Africa.

7.5   Long-run Economy-wide Effects of the G20 Liberalizing FDI in Services

The projected long-run effects of liberalizing FDI in the G20 provide a benchmark for understanding the flow-on effects to labour markets, even though the short-run scenario may be of more immediate policy interest.

The long-run effects of FDI liberalization on labour markets begin with the effects on foreign-invested firms. These can be understood by reference to Figures 7.1 to 7.3. One of the immediate results of relaxing restrictions on FDI is productivity improvements in foreign-invested firms. This is shown by the downward shift in the supply curve in Figure 7.1. All other things being equal, the downward shift would imply that fewer inputs were required per unit of output. But with monopolistic competition, the productivity improvements should flow through to lower prices, and this in turn can stimulate demand for the services of foreign-invested firms. This is shown via the move outwards along the demand curve in Figure 7.1.

The first-round impact of the productivity improvements on unit input requirements would imply inward shifts in the demand curves for both capital and labour in Figures 7.2 and 7.3.[10] This would imply both lower employment and lower stocks of FDI capital. However, the econometric estimation in the Appendix suggests instead that FDI stocks can be expected to rise in response to FDI liberalization. This implies that the scale effects of the increased demand in Figure 7.1 outweigh the resource-saving effects of the productivity changes. So the demand curves for capital and labour move outwards, even beyond their original position. This is also consistent with the relatively high demand elasticities in services shown in Table 7.5.

If FDI liberalization implies an increase in FDI stocks, as the econometrics suggests, and if there is no substitution between capital and labour as output expands, then the demand for labour should also increase proportionately in foreign-invested firms. However, there is also likely to be some substitution (in relative terms) away from capital and towards labour in foreign-invested firms. This is because the supply of labour to foreign-invested firms is likely to be reasonably price-responsive, as indicated by the relatively flat supply curve in Figure 7.3. Labour is assumed to be perfectly mobile between sectors, and foreign-

---

[10] FDI liberalization implies fewer regulatory restrictions on the operations of foreign-invested firms. This is likely to affect all inputs, so the productivity improvements are modelled as being output-augmenting, rather than as being biased towards saving labour, capital or material inputs.

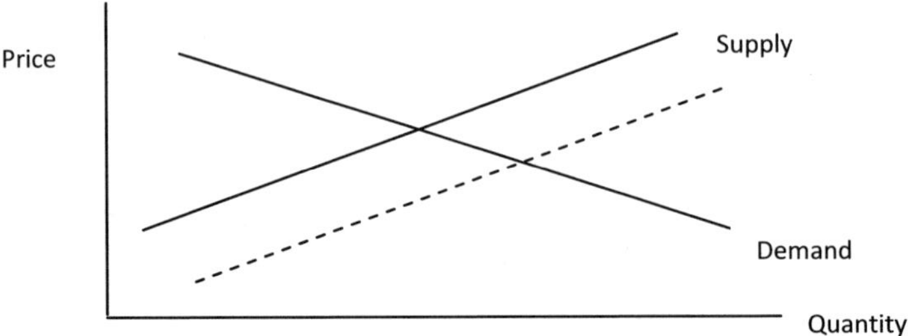

Figure 7.1. Foreign-invested Firms — Product Market

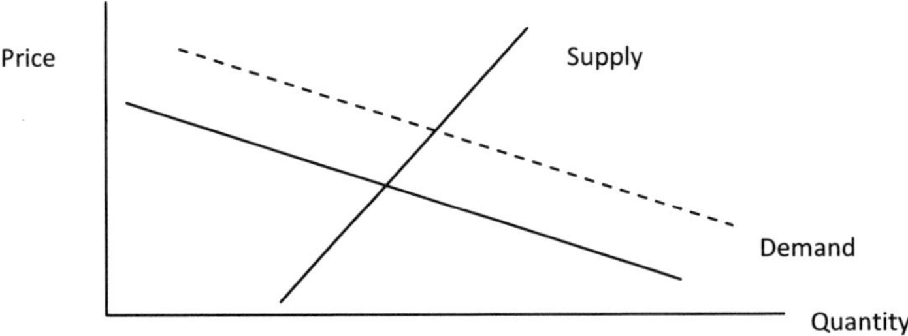

Figure 7.2. Foreign-invested Firms — Market for FDI Capital Input

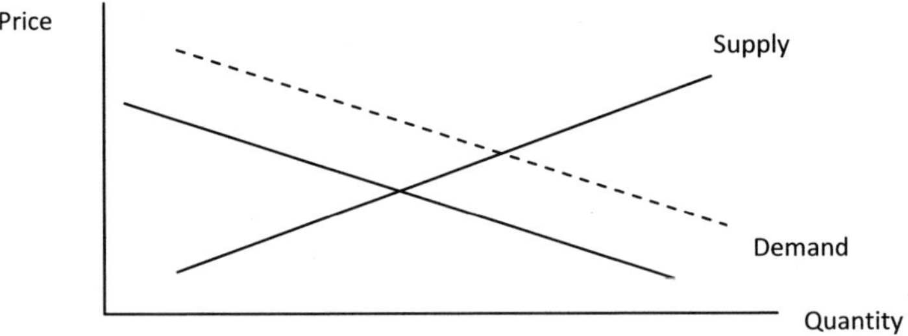

Figure 7.3. Foreign-invested Firms — Market for Labour Input

invested firms are a relatively small proportion of the economy in most countries, so foreign-invested firms should find it reasonably easy to attract labour away from domestically-owned firms in their own sector, and away from firms in other sectors. By contrast, the supply of FDI capital is likely to be less price-responsive, as shown by the relatively steep supply curve in Figure 7.2. This is because, having already made their preferred portfolio allocation choices, foreign investors are likely to require non-trivial increases in (sector- and ownership-specific) returns before they are willing to provide the additional FDI capital. As a consequence, there is likely to be an increase in the returns to that FDI capital, relative to wages, and further substitution towards labour in foreign-invested firms. This is shown by the greater outward move in the equilibrium quantity of labour in Figure 7.3 than of capital in Figure 7.2.

This story is shown numerically in Tables 7.6, 7.7 and 7.8 for the United States. The results for all other G20 countries are similar. Table 7.6 shows significant projected increases in the output of the foreign-invested firms undergoing the productivity improvements, particularly in those sectors (such as air and water transport) that have the highest demand elasticities. Table 7.7 shows even greater expansions in the employment of unskilled labour in those firms, despite the productivity improvements (the results for skilled labour are very similar). This is consistent with significant substitution towards labour. It is confirmed by Table 7.8, which shows FDI capital stocks growing less than proportionately with output in foreign-invested firms.

The overall story thus far is that although productivity gains in foreign-invested firms might imply job shedding, all other things being equal, there are also significant scale effects that serve to increase the demand for the services of these firms. There are also substitution effects that serve to increase their employment even more than their output.

The next key question is whether this is at the expense of employment in domestically-owned firms. Table 7.9 shows that in many cases, it is. In many cases, the change in overall employment (across both foreign-invested and domestic firms) of unskilled labour is negative in the sectors undergoing the FDI liberalization (once again, the results for skilled labour are similar). In other sectors, outside of services, the employment changes are often positive. This shows that the spillover effects of FDI liberalization can be mixed. Firms that compete directly with the foreign-invested firms, especially domestic firms in the same sector, suffer from lower priced competition (because of substitution in

Table 7.6. Projected Long-run Changes in Output of Domestic and Foreign-owned Firms in the United States, by Ownership Category, after 50% Liberalization of Investment in Services by all G20 Countries (percentage deviation from control)[a]

	ARG	AUS	BRA	CAN	CHN	REU	FRA	GER	IND	IDN	ITA	JPN	MEX	RUS	ZAF	KOR	TUR	GBR	USA	ROW
Elect. mach.	0	0.1	0	0.1	0	0.1	0	0	0	0	0	0	0.1	0	0.1	0	0	0	0	0
Construction	0	−0.1	0	0	0	0.2	0.3	0.3	0	0	0	0	0	0	0	0.1	0.1	0.3	0	0.3
Trade	0.2	−0.1	0.2	−0.1	0.1	0.2	0.6	0.4	0.3	0	0.3	0.2	−0.4	0.2	0.1	0.2	0.1	0.3	0	0.4
Other transp.	0	0	0	0	0	0.2	0.4	0.4	0	0	0	0.2	0.1	0	0	0.2	0	0.3	0	0.4
Water transp.	−2.3	0	−2.4	0	−2.3	123.0	121.8	0	−2.3	0	0	0	−2.3	−2.3	−2.3	126.5	−2.3	0	−2.3	122.8
Air transp.	−0.3	0	−0.3	0	−0.3	72.2	−0.4	72.5	−0.3	0	0	0	−0.3	−0.3	−0.3	−0.3	−0.3	0	−0.3	73.5
Communications	13.1	12.8	12.9	0	−0.3	12.8	13.3	13.4	−0.4	0	0	0	12.9	12.8	12.6	13.1	13	12.9	−0.3	13.3
Other finance	6.7	6.1	6.7	0	6.5	6.6	6.8	6.8	6.6	0	0	6.8	6.1	6.2	6.3	0	0	6.8	−0.3	6.9
Insurance	0	−0.1	0	0.1	0	0.2	0.4	0.4	0	0	0.3	0.2	−0.1	0	0	0.2	0	0.4	0	0.4
Other bus. serv.	0.3	0	0.3	0	0.2	0.1	0.5	0.4	0.2	0	0	0.3	0.3	0.2	0	0	0	0.5	−0.1	0.4

ARG=Argentina, AUS=Australia, BRA=Brazil, CAN=Canada, REU=Rest of EU, FRA=France, GER=Germany, IND=India, IDN=Indonesia, ITA=Italy, JPN=Japan, MEX=Mexico, RUS=Russia, ZAF=South Africa, KOR=Republic of Korea, TUR=Turkey, GBR=Great Britain, USA=United States, ROW=Rest of world.

[a] For sectors that are not reported, the results round to zero.

Source: FTAP model projections.

Table 7.7. Projected Long-run Changes in Employment of Unskilled Labour in Domestic and Foreign-owned Firms in the United States, by Ownership Category, after 50% Liberalization of Investment in Services by all G20 Countries (percentage deviation from control)[a]

	ARG	AUS	BRA	CAN	CHN	REU	FRA	GER	IND	IDN	ITA	JPN	MEX	RUS	ZAF	KOR	TUR	GBR	USA	ROW
Agric. etc	0	0.1	0	0	0	0	0	0	0	0	0	0	0	0	0	0	0	0	0	0
Eiect. mach.	0.1	0.1	0.1	0.1	0.1	0.1	0.1	0.1	0.1	0	0.1	0.1	0.1	0.1	0.1	0.1	0	0	0.1	0.1
Electricity	0	0.1	0	0	0	0.1	0	0	0	0	0	0	0.1	0	0.1	0	0	0	0	0
Construction	0	−0.1	0	0	0	0.2	0.3	0.3	0	0	0	0	0	0	0	0.1	0.1	0.3	0	0.3
Trade	0.2	−0.1	0.2	−0.1	0.1	0.2	0.6	0.4	0.3	0	0.3	0.2	−0.4	0.1	0.1	0.2	0.1	0.3	0	0.3
Other transp.	0	0	0	0	0	0.2	0.4	0.4	0	0	0	0.2	0	0	0	0.2	0	0.3	0	0.4
Water transp.	−3.3	0	−3.3	0	−3.3	122.7	121.4	0	−3.3	0	0	0	−3.3	−3.3	−3.3	126.2	−3.3	0	−3.3	122.5
Air transp.	−0.4	0	−0.4	0	−0.4	76.2	−0.5	76.5	−0.4	0	0	0	−0.4	−0.4	−0.4	−0.4	−0.4	0	−0.4	77.6
Communications	14.2	13.9	14	0	−0.6	13.9	14.6	14.6	−0.6	0	0	0	14.1	13.9	13.6	14.3	14.1	14.1	−0.6	14.5
Other finance	5.8	5.3	5.7	0	5.6	5.7	5.9	5.8	5.7	0	0	5.9	5.2	5.3	5.4	0	0	5.8	−0.4	5.9
Insurance	0	−0.1	0	0.1	0	0.2	0.3	0.4	0	0	0.2	0.2	−0.1	0	0	0.2	0	0.3	0	0.3
Other bus. serv.	0.2	0	0.2	0	0.2	0	0.4	0.3	0.1	0	0	0.2	0.3	0.1	0	0	0	0.4	−0.1	0.3
Other serv.	0	0.1	0	0	0	0	0	0	0	0	0	0	0	0	0	0	0	0	0	0

ARG=Argentina, AUS=Australia, BRA=Brazil, CAN=Canada, REU=Rest of EU, FRA=France, GER=Germany, IND=India, IDN=Indonesia, ITA=Italy, JPN=Japan, MEX=Mexico, RUS=Russia, ZAF=South Africa, KOR=Republic of Korea, TUR=Turkey, GBR=Great Britain, USA=United States, ROW=Rest of world.

[a] For sectors that are not reported, the results round to zero.

Source: FTAP model projections.

Table 7.8. Projected Long-run Changes in Capital Stocks in Domestic and Foreign-owned Firms in the United States, by Ownership Category, after 50% Liberalization of Investment in Services by all G20 Countries (percentage deviation from control)[a]

	ARG	AUS	BRA	CAN	CHN	REU	FRA	GER	IND	IDN	ITA	JPN	MEX	RUS	ZAF	KOR	TUR	GBR	USA	ROW
Water transp.	−0.4	0	−0.5	−0.1	−0.4	12.1	12.1	−0.1	−0.4	0	−0.1	−0.1	−0.3	−0.4	−0.3	12.1	−0.4	0	−0.3	12.1
Air transp.	0	0	0	0	0	7.8	−0.2	7.8	0	0	−0.2	0	0	0	0	0	0	−0.2	0	7.8
Communications	1.9	1.9	1.9	−0.1	−0.1	1.9	1.9	1.9	−0.1	0	0	−0.1	1.9	1.9	1.9	1.9	1.9	1.9	−0.1	1.9
Other finance	0.8	0.8	0.8	0	0.8	0.8	0.8	0.8	0.8	0	0	0.8	0.8	0.8	0.8	0	0	0.8	−0.1	0.8

ARG=Argentina, AUS=Australia, BRA=Brazil, CAN=Canada, REU=Rest of EU, FRA=France, GER=Germany, IND=India, IDN=Indonesia, ITA=Italy, JPN=Japan, MEX=Mexico, RUS=Russia, ZAF=South Africa, KOR=Republic of Korea, TUR=Turkey, GBR=Great Britain, USA=United States, ROW=Rest of world.

[a] For sectors that are not reported, the results round to zero.

Source: FTAP model projections.

Table 7.9. Projected Long-run Changes in Sectoral Employment of Unskilled Labour in each G20 Country after 50% Liberalization of Investment in Services by all G20 Countries (percentage deviation from control)

	ARG	AUS	BRA	CAN	CHN	REU	FRA	GER	IND	IDN	ITA	JPN	MEX	RUS	ZAF	KOR	TUR	GBR	USA	ROW
Agric. etc	0.1	0.1	0	0.1	0	0	0	0	0	0	0	0	0	0	0.1	0	0	0	0	0
Proc. food	0	0.2	0	0.1	0	0	0.1	0.1	0	0.1	0	0	0	0	0.1	0	0	0.1	0	0
Other primary	0	0	0	0	0	0	0	0	0	0	0	0	0.3	0	0	0	0	0	0	0
Textiles etc	0	0.4	0	0.2	0.1	−0.1	0	0	0.1	0.1	0	0	−0.2	0	0.3	0.1	0.1	0	0	0.1
Wood etc	0	0.1	0.1	0.2	0.1	0	0	0	0	0.2	0.1	0	−0.3	0.1	0.2	0	0	0	0	0.1
Chemicals	0	0.1	0	0.2	0	0	0	0	0	0.1	0	0	0	0.1	0.3	0.1	0.1	0	0	0.1
Metals	0.1	0.1	0.1	0.2	0	−0.1	−0.1	0	0.1	0.1	0	0	−0.3	0.2	0.1	0	0.1	−0.1	0	0.1
Vehicles	0.1	0.2	0.1	0.2	0	0	0	0.1	0	0	0.1	0	−0.3	0.9	0.3	0	0.1	0	0	0.1
Elect. mach.	0.1	0	0	0.3	0.1	0.1	−0.1	0	0.1	0.9	0	0	−0.4	0.4	0.7	0	0	−0.1	0.1	0.1
Other mach.	0	0.1	0	0.2	0	−0.1	0	0	0.1	0.1	0	0	0	0.1	0.3	0	0.1	0	0	0.2
Electricity	0	0.1	0	0	0	0	0	0.1	0	0.1	0	0	0.1	0.1	0	0	0	0	0	0.1
Gas, water	0	0.1	0	0.1	0	0	0.1	0	0	0	0	0	0.1	0	0	0	0	0.1	0	0.1
Construction	0	0	0	0	0	0	0	0	0	0.1	0	0	−0.4	0.1	0	0	0.1	0	0	0
Trade	0	0	0	−0.2	−0.1	0.1	0.1	0	0	−0.2	0	0	−1.6	−0.3	0.1	0	0	0	0	−0.1
Other transp.	0	0.1	0	0.1	0	0.1	0	0	0	0.1	0	0	0.3	0	0	0	0	0	0	0
Water transp.	−1.5	−0.2	−1.5	3.4	−0.4	−0.6	2.2	0.8	−0.4	−0.4	−0.4	−0.3	2.4	−1	−1.2	1.8	−0.4	−0.7	0	−1.1
Air transp.	−0.7	0	−0.5	0.8	−0.7	2.2	−0.9	−0.9	−0.1	−0.5	−0.6	0.7	−0.4	−0.5	−0.7	−0.6	−0.4	−0.5	−0.4	−0.7
Communications	−0.2	−0.3	−0.2	−0.2	−0.2	−0.3	−0.2	−0.3	−0.3	−0.5	−0.2	0	−0.2	−0.3	−0.3	−0.4	−0.2	0.1	−0.2	−0.4

202   *Services Trade Reform: Making Sense of It*

Table 7.9. Continued.

Other finance	−0.1	−0.7	−0.1	−0.1	−0.2	0	−0.2	−0.2	−0.2	−0.2	−0.1	−0.1	0.4	−0.5	−0.3	−0.2	−0.2	0.3	−0.1	−0.3
Insurance	0	0.1	0	0.4	−0.1	0.1	0.1	0	−0.1	−0.1	0	0	0.3	0.9	−0.1	0	−0.1	0.3	0	−0.1
Other bus. serv.	−0.1	−0.2	−0.1	−0.1	−0.1	0	−0.1	−0.1	−0.3	−0.1	−0.1	0	7.6	0.2	−0.6	−0.1	−0.1	−0.1	−0.1	−0.2
Other serv.	0	0	0	0	0	0	0.1	0	0	0	0	0	0	0	0	0	0	0.1	0	0.1

ARG=Argentina, AUS=Australia, BRA=Brazil, CAN=Canada, REU=Rest of EU, FRA=France, GER=Germany, IND=India, IDN=Indonesia, ITA=Italy, JPN=Japan, MEX=Mexico, RUS=Russia, ZAF=South Africa, KOR=Republic of Korea, TUR=Turkey, GBR=Great Britain, USA=United States, ROW=Rest of world.
Source: FTAP model projections.

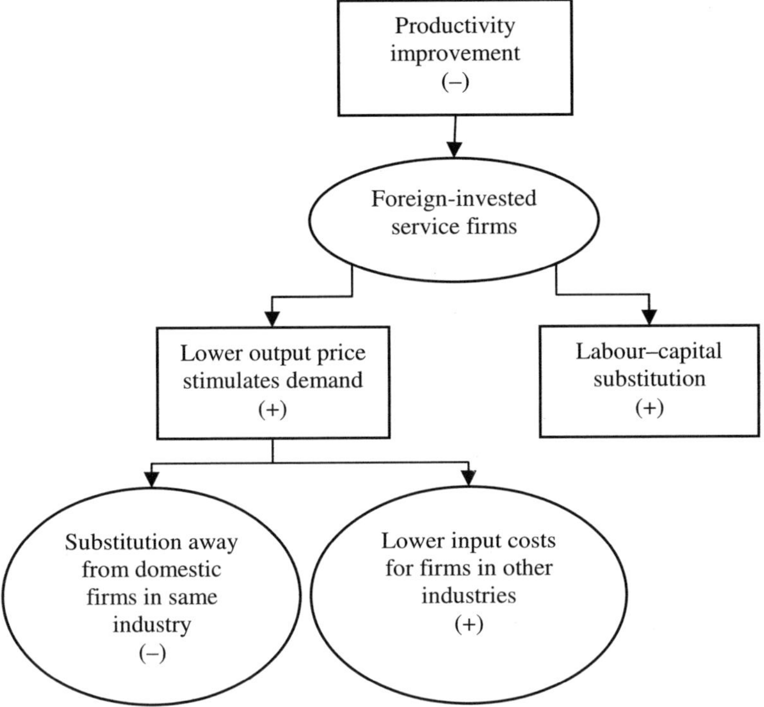

Figure 7.4. Labour Market Effects of FDI Liberalization

demand). But sectors that use the services of foreign-invested firms as inputs benefit from lower-priced inputs (see Figure 7.4).

The sum total of these mixed long-run effects on labour markets is shown in Table 7.10. This indicates that real wages for both skilled and unskilled labour are projected to be higher than otherwise in almost all G20 economies.

Thus in almost all cases, the long-run labour market implications of FDI liberalization in G20 countries are positive. To the extent that there are adjustment costs in the form of labour reallocation across sectors, Tables 7.7 and 7.9 show that most of the reallocation is within sectors — from domestic to foreign-invested firms. This is likely to be far less

Table 7.10. Projected Long-run Changes in Real Wages in each G20 Country after 50% Liberalization of Investment in Services by all G20 Countries (percentage deviation from control)

	ARG	AUS	BRA	CAN	CHN	REU	FRA	GER	IND	IDN	ITA	JPN	MEX	RUS	ZAF	KOR	TUR	GBR	USA	ROW
Unskilled labour	0.02	0.38	0.01	0.35	0.04	0.20	0.05	0.05	0.01	0.11	0.05	0.01	0.60	0.25	0.28	0.08	0.03	0.18	0.02	0.00
Skilled labour	0.01	0.36	0.00	0.36	0.03	0.19	0.05	0.04	−0.01	0.14	0.04	0.01	0.66	0.23	0.23	0.07	0.02	0.19	0.01	0.00
Overall	0.01	0.37	0.01	0.35	0.03	0.20	0.05	0.05	0.00	0.12	0.04	0.01	0.62	0.24	0.26	0.07	0.03	0.18	0.02	0.00

ARG=Argentina, AUS=Australia, BRA=Brazil, CAN=Canada, REU=Rest of EU, FRA=France, GER=Germany, IND=India, IDN=Indonesia, ITA=Italy, JPN=Japan, MEX=Mexico, RUS=Russia, ZAF=South Africa, KOR=Republic of Korea, TUR=Turkey, GBR=Great Britain, USA=United States, ROW=Rest of world.
Source: FTAP model projections.

costly for workers, in terms of retraining and job search costs, than reallocation across sectors.[11]

Tables 7.11 and 7.12 show the relative effects on sectoral output of a country's own FDI liberalization, relative to the effects of FDI liberalization in all G20 countries. The comparison gives an indication of the strength of spillover effects between countries. Sectors outside of services tend to gain from a country's own FDI liberalization. Those same sectors tend to gain more, or lose by less, when the liberalization occurs across the G20 as a group. This indicates that the spillover effects of lower services prices are positive both within and between countries. This positive spillover is not a foregone conclusion. If the price reductions across G20 countries were unbalanced, there could be some substitution in demand towards the goods and services from countries with lower prices. But with liberalization being relatively widespread, this substitution is kept to a minimum.

Finally, Table 7.13 shows the projected impacts of FDI liberalization on macroeconomic aggregates and overall economic well-being. The effects on overall levels of economic activity (as measured by real GDP) are positive, and tend to be larger in those economies that undergo more extensive reforms (Table 7.1), or where foreign-ownership shares are larger to begin with (Table 7.4).

Real income changes need not match changes in real GDP, however, in part because the increases in FDI stocks have to be financed, and this in turn implies higher debt service payments or profit repatriation in the long run. The bottom part of Table 7.13 shows the overall sizes and sources of gains in economic well-being in each economy. Some of the countries that are important sources of FDI (France, Germany, Japan, Great Britain and the United States) enjoy gains in the form of repatriated profits from the higher FDI stocks elsewhere in the world. But some of the biggest sources of FDI are also some of the biggest

---

[11] To the extent that foreign-invested firms are less labour-intensive than domestic firms in the same sector to start with, this reallocation of labour towards foreign-invested firms could also imply a negative influence on overall labour demand through compositional effects. The theoretical literature stresses that foreign-invested firms are likely to be more *skilled*-labour intensive, but the implication for overall labour intensity is unclear. And as noted, FATS data are insufficiently detailed to shed empirical light on this issue.

Table 7.11. Projected Long-run Changes in Sectoral Output in each G20 Country after *own* 50% Liberalization of Investment in Services (percentage deviation from control)

	ARG	AUS	BRA	CAN	CHN	REU	FRA	GER	IND	IDN	ITA	JPN	MEX	RUS	ZAF	KOR	TUR	GBR	USA	ROW
Agric. etc	0	0	0	0	0	0	0	0	0	0	0	0	0	0	0	0	0	0	0	na
Proc. food	0	0.1	0	0.1	0	0	0	0	0	0	0	0	0.1	0	0.1	0	0	0	0	na
Other primary	0	0	0	0	0	0	0	0	0	0	0	0	0.1	0	0	0	0	0	0	na
Textiles etc	0	0.3	0	0.1	0	−0.1	0	0	0	0.1	0	0	0	−0.1	0.2	0	0	−0.1	0	na
Wood etc	0	0.1	0	0.1	0	0	0	0	0	0	0	0	−0.1	0	0.1	0	0	0	0	na
Chemicals	0	0.1	0	0.1	0	0	0	0	0	0	0	0	0	0.1	0.2	0	0	−0.1	0	na
Metals	0	0.1	0	0.1	0	−0.1	0	0	0	0.1	0	0	−0.1	0.1	0.1	0	0	−0.1	0	na
Vehicles	0	0.1	0	0.1	0	0	0	0	0	0	0	0	0	0.7	0.2	0	0	−0.1	0	na
Elect. mach.	0	0	0	0.1	0	0	0	0	0	0.3	0	0	−0.1	0.2	0.4	0	0	−0.1	0.1	na
Other mach.	0	0.1	0	0.1	0	−0.1	0	0	0	0.1	0	0	0	0	0.2	0	0	−0.1	0	na
Electricity	0	0.1	0	0	0	0	0	0	0	0	0	0	0.1	0	0	0	0	0	0	na
Gas, water	0	0.1	0	0.1	0	0	0	0	0	0	0	0	0.1	0	0	0	0	0	0	na
Construction	0	0.1	0	0	0	0	0	0	0	0	0	0	0.5	0	0	0	0	0	0	na
Trade	0	0.3	0	0.7	0	0.2	0	0	0	0.2	0	0	3.3	0.1	0.1	0	0	0.2	0	na
Other transp.	0	0.1	0	0.2	0	0.1	0	0	0	0.1	0	0	0.2	0	0.1	0	0	0.1	0	na
Water transp.	0	0.6	0	4.2	0	0.5	2.7	1.3	0	0.1	0.9	0.2	3.4	0.1	0.1	1.8	0	0.1	0.8	na
Air transp.	0	0.5	0	1.4	0	2.3	0.1	0	0	0.1	0.3	1.1	0.2	0	0.1	0	0	0.3	0	na
Communications	0	0.2	0	0.5	0	0.1	0	0	0	0	0.1	0	0.5	0.2	0	0.3	0.3	1.2	0.1	na

Table 7.11. Continued.

Other finance	0	1.3	0	0.1	0	0.3	0.1	0	0	0	0	0	1.6	0.9	0.8	0.1	0	0.7	0	na
Insurance	0	0.5	0	0.4	0	0.2	0.1	0	0	0	0.1	0	1.1	1.4	0	0	0	0.3	0	na
Other bus. serv.	0	0.2	0	0.1	0	0.3	0	0	0	0.1	0	0	14.6	0.8	0.3	0	0.1	0	0	na
Other serv.	0	0	0	0	0	0	0	0	0	0	0	0	0	0	0	0	0	0	0	na

ARG=Argentina, AUS=Australia, BRA=Brazil, CAN=Canada, REU=Rest of EU, FRA=France, GER=Germany, IND=India, IDN=Indonesia, ITA=Italy, JPN=Japan, MEX=Mexico, RUS=Russia, ZAF=South Africa, KOR=Republic of Korea, TUR=Turkey, GBR=Great Britain, USA=United States, ROW=Rest of world.
na = not applicable.
Source: FTAP model projections.

Table 7.12. Projected Long-run Changes in Sectoral Output in each G20 Country after 50% Liberalization of Investment in Services by all G20 Countries (percentage deviation from control)

	ARG	AUS	BRA	CAN	CHN	REU	FRA	GER	IND	IDN	ITA	JPN	MEX	RUS	ZAF	KOR	TUR	GBR	USA	ROW
Agric. etc	0	0.1	0	0.1	0	0	0	0	0	0	0	0	0	0	0.1	0	0	0	0	0
Proc. food	0	0.2	0	0.1	0	0	0	0.1	0	0.1	0	0	0.1	0	0.1	0	0	0.1	0	0
Other primary	0	0	0	0	0	0	0	0	0	0	0	0	0.1	0	0	0	0	0	0	0
Textiles etc	0	0.4	0	0.1	0	0	0	0	0.1	0.1	0	0	0	0	0.3	0.1	0	0	0	0.1
Wood etc	0	0.1	0.1	0.1	0	0	0	0	0	0.1	0	0	−0.1	0.1	0.2	0	0	0	0	0.1
Chemicals	0	0.1	0	0.1	0	0	0	0	0	0.1	0	0	0	0.1	0.2	0	0	0	0	0.1
Metals	0.1	0.1	0.1	0.2	0	−0.1	0	0	0	0.1	0	0	−0.1	0.1	0.1	0	0	−0.1	0	0.1
Vehicles	0.1	0.2	0	0.2	0	0	0	0.1	0	0	0	0	0	0.7	0.2	0	0	0	0	0
Elect. mach.	0.1	0	0	0.2	0	0	−0.1	0	0	0.4	0	0	−0.1	0.3	0.5	0	0	−0.1	0	0.1
Other mach.	0	0.1	0	0.2	0	0	0	0	0	0.1	0	0	0	0.1	0.2	0	0	0	0	0.1
Electricity	0	0.1	0	0	0	0	0	0	0	0	0	0	0.1	0.1	0	0	0	0	0	0
Gas, water	0	0.1	0	0.1	0	0	0.1	0	0	0	0	0	0.1	0	0.1	0	0	0	0	0
Construction	0	0.1	0	0.1	0	0	0	0	0	0.1	0	0	0.5	0.1	0	0	0	0	0	0
Trade	0	0.3	0	0.7	0	0.2	0	0	0	0.2	0	0	3.4	0.1	0.1	0	0	0.2	0	0
Other transp.	0	0.1	0	0.2	0	0.1	0	0	0	0	0	0	0.2	0	0	0	0	0.1	0	0
Water transp.	−0.9	0.4	−1.3	3.9	−0.1	0	2.0	1.1	−0.3	−0.2	0	−0.1	2.7	−0.5	−0.5	1.5	−0.1	−0.5	0.6	−0.6
Air transp.	−0.4	0.2	−0.4	1	−0.2	2.2	−0.8	−0.5	−0.1	−0.2	−0.4	0.8	0.1	−0.3	−0.3	−0.3	−0.1	−0.3	−0.3	−0.4
Communications	−0.1	0.1	0	0.3	0	0	−0.1	−0.1	−0.1	−0.2	0	0	0.4	−0.1	−0.1	0.3	0.2	1.2	0.1	−0.2

Table 7.12. Continued.

Other finance	0	1.3	0	0.1	0	0.3	0	−0.1	−0.1	−0.1	0	0	1.6	0.8	0.7	0	−0.1	0.4	0	−0.2
Insurance	0	0.5	0	0.5	−0.1	0.2	0.1	0	0	0	0	0	0.8	1.3	0	0	0	0.3	0	−0.1
Other bus. serv.	0	0.2	0	0	0	0.3	0	0	−0.2	0	0	0	15.1	0.8	0.3	0	0.1	0	−0.1	−0.1
Other serv.	0	0.1	0	0.1	0	0	0	0	0	0	0	0	0	0	0.1	0	0	0	0	0

ARG=Argentina, AUS=Australia, BRA=Brazil, CAN=Canada, REU=Rest of EU, FRA=France, GER=Germany, IND=India, IDN=Indonesia, ITA=Italy, JPN=Japan, MEX=Mexico, RUS=Russia, ZAF=South Africa, KOR=Republic of Korea, TUR=Turkey, GBR=Great Britain, USA=United States, ROW=Rest of world.

Source: FTAP model projections.

Table 7.13. Projected Long-run Changes in Macroeconomic Aggregates after 50% Liberalization of Investment in Services by all G20 Countries (deviation from control in US$ million unless otherwise stated)

	ARG	AUS	BRA	CAN	CHN	REU	FRA	GER	IND	IDN	ITA	JPN	MEX	RUS	ZAF	KOR	TUR	GBR	USA	ROW
Real GDP (%)	0.00	0.33	0.01	0.28	0.01	0.16	0.03	0.02	0.01	0.10	0.02	0.01	0.37	0.17	0.20	0.06	0.02	0.13	0.02	0.00
Real national income (%)	0.00	0.21	0.01	0.19	0.02	0.10	0.11	0.07	0.01	0.07	0.04	0.02	0.29	0.07	0.10	0.02	0.01	0.15	0.04	0.03
Real GNE (%)	0.01	0.19	0.01	0.17	0.02	0.09	0.09	0.06	0.01	0.07	0.04	0.02	0.25	0.08	0.09	0.03	0.02	0.13	0.03	0.03
Trade balance	−3	820	−2	996	−11	2639	−1188	−991	−11	99	−299	−485	752	529	211	121	17	−185	−1928	−1083
Welfare gains	3	1227	41	1631	182	3636	1984	1578	79	134	571	640	1754	281	172	120	42	3008	4452	1121
Sources of gain:																				
Allocative efficiency	−3	135	8	196	54	546	189	124	13	16	48	73	1053	39	26	22	6	249	112	84
Endowments	−3	86	−4	80	4	261	−36	−44	−2	15	−21	9	41	44	23	6	1	20	−57	−80
Productivity	6	1805	48	2405	159	5859	441	521	31	217	259	182	1395	876	361	345	51	2510	1743	114
Terms of trade	7	−48	20	−123	64	−339	64	−67	38	11	39	17	−63	−42	−13	−85	16	−24	475	52
Int. interest and profit	−4	−751	−31	−927	−99	−2691	1327	1043	−1	−125	246	359	−672	−637	−225	−167	−32	253	2179	951

ARG=Argentina, AUS=Australia, BRA=Brazil, CAN=Canada, REU=Rest of EU, FRA=France, GER=Germany, IND=India, IDN=Indonesia, ITA=Italy, JPN=Japan, MEX=Mexico, RUS=Russia, ZAF=South Africa, KOR=Republic of Korea, TUR=Turkey, GBR=Great Britain, USA=United States, ROW=Rest of world.
Source: FTAP model projections.

destinations for FDI, so others (Canada, the rest of the EU) lose because of higher outward profit payments. Countries that are predominantly FDI recipients (eg Indonesia, Mexico, Russia, South Africa, Korea) also lose on this score.

Other important sources of real income gains are the productivity improvements themselves. Those measured in Table 7.13 include those generated by the FDI liberalization itself, as well as the endogenous gains from greater variety in monopolistically competitive industries. A further source of gain is via improvements in allocative efficiency. In the current context, this is a second-best welfare result, but it is almost invariably positive. Finally, note that terms of trade effects are minor — FDI liberalization is behind-the-border liberalization.

Overall, FDI liberalization by the G20 is projected to provide higher economic well-being than would otherwise be the case, about ten years after the reforms. Globally, the real income gains are about US\$ 23 billion a year (in 2004 dollars). The labour market effects are also projected to be positive, with real wage gains of up to 0.7 per cent in the G20 group.

Recall from the introduction that both these results are 'conservative'. Gains in economic well-being are likely to be very much higher if the liberalization were to include all the barriers to commercial presence in services (such as those canvassed in Dee 2007), not just the FDI barriers that discriminate against foreign providers. And the adjustment costs would also be lower, because local firms in the same industry would also gain from the liberalization (although the retraining and job search costs associated with the current reallocation of labour from domestic to foreign-invested firms are in any event likely to be relatively low). Further, the labour market outcomes here are biased downwards by the assumption that all of the gains from FDI liberalization accrue as productivity improvements rather than as reductions in the price–cost margins of foreign-invested firms.

7.6 The Short Run

The way in which foreign-invested firms respond to FDI liberalization in the short run is qualitatively similar to their response in the long run, although the magnitudes differ. Lower prices for their services encourage more demand, although the size of these scale effects is smaller than in the long run because FDI capital stocks cannot respond. In terms of Figure 7.1, the supply curve is steeper in the short run than in the long run, but it still moves downward by the same amount.

There is also substitution towards labour in the short run. In surplus-labour economies, FDI firms can get all the additional labour they want without bidding up wages. And without yet being able to increase their FDI capital stocks, they will expand entirely by hiring more labour. In terms of Figures 7.2 and 7.3, in the short run the supply curve of capital is vertical in all economies, while the supply curve of labour is perfectly flat in surplus-labour economies. On both counts, the substitution effect toward labour in all economies is likely to be stronger than in the long run. With a smaller scale effect but a larger substitution effect, it is hard to know *a priori* whether the overall short-run effect on labour markets is likely to be larger or smaller than the long-run effect. But it is still likely to be positive.

Tables 7.14 and 7.15 confirm that the scale effect is slightly smaller in the United States, a surplus-labour economy, in the short run than in the long run. And despite stronger substitution effects, the overall increases in employment in foreign-invested firms are smaller than in the long run, but only slightly.

There are now some noticeable differences in the overall outcomes between surplus-labour and other economies. Table 7.16 shows that in some of the economies projected to gain in the long term, such as Russia, there are now predominantly negative impacts on industry output throughout the economy. This reflects negative spillover effects from the surplus-labour to the other economies. The surplus-labour economies can expand without bidding up wages, and so gain a competitive advantage on others (in terms of Figure 7.1, they have flatter supply curves). But this result needs to be kept in perspective. At current levels of underlying growth, both types of economies will probably continue to experience positive growth *over time*. It is just that the surplus-labour economies will be able to catch up to their full-employment neighbours.

Table 7.14. Projected Short-run Changes in Output of Domestic and Foreign-owned Firms in the United States, by Ownership Category, after 50% Liberalization of Investment in Services by all G20 Countries (percentage deviation from control)[a]

	ARG	AUS	BRA	CAN	CHN	REU	FRA	GER	IND	IDN	ITA	JPN	MEX	RUS	ZAF	KOR	TUR	GBR	USA	ROW
Elect. mach.	0.1	0.1	0.1	0.1	0.1	0.1	0.1	0.1	0.1	0	0.1	0.1	0.1	0.1	0.1	0.1	0	0	0.1	0.1
Construction	0	−0.1	0	0	0	0.2	0.4	0.3	0	0	0	0	0	0	0	0.2	0.1	0.4	0	0.3
Trade	0.2	−0.1	0.2	−0.1	0.2	0.2	0.7	0.4	0.4	0	0.4	0.3	−0.4	0.2	0.1	0.2	0.2	0.3	0	0.4
Other transp.	0	0	0	0	0	0.2	0.4	0.4	0	0	0	0.2	0.1	0	0	0.2	0	0.3	0	0.4
Water transp.	−2.1	0	−2.1	0	−2.1	112.6	111.4	0	−2.1	0	0	0	−2.1	−2.1	−2.1	116	−2.1	0	−2.1	112.4
Air transp.	−0.3	0	−0.3	0	−0.3	67.2	−0.3	67.5	−0.3	0	0	0	−0.3	−0.3	−0.3	−0.3	−0.3	0	−0.3	68.5
Communications	11.0	10.7	10.9	0	−0.2	10.7	11.3	11.3	−0.2	0	0	0	10.9	10.8	10.5	11.0	10.9	10.9	−0.2	11.2
Other finance	6.3	5.7	6.2	0	6.1	6.1	6.4	6.3	6.2	0	0	6.4	5.6	5.7	5.8	0	0	6.3	−0.3	6.4
Insurance	0	−0.1	0	0.1	0	0.3	0.4	0.4	0	0	0.3	0.2	−0.1	0	0	0.2	0	0.4	0	0.4
Other bus. serv.	0.3	0	0.3	0	0.3	0.1	0.5	0.4	0.2	0	0	0.3	0.3	0.2	0	0	0	0.5	0	0.4
Other serv.	0.1	0.1	0.1	0.1	0.1	0.1	0.1	0.1	0.1	0	0.1	0.1	0.1	0.1	0.1	0.1	0.1	0.1	0.1	0.1

ARG=Argentina, AUS=Australia, BRA=Brazil, CAN=Canada, REU=Rest of EU, FRA=France, GER=Germany, IND=India, IDN=Indonesia, ITA=Italy, JPN=Japan, MEX=Mexico, RUS=Russia, ZAF=South Africa, KOR=Republic of Korea, TUR=Turkey, GBR=Great Britain, USA=United States, ROW=Rest of world.

[a] For sectors that are not reported, the results round to zero.

Source: FTAP model projections.

Table 7.15. Projected Short-run Changes in Employment of Unskilled Labour in Domestic and Foreign-owned Firms in the United States, by Ownership Category, after 50% Liberalization of Investment in Services by all G20 Countries (percentage deviation from control)

	ARG	AUS	BRA	CAN	CHN	REU	FRA	GER	IND	IDN	ITA	JPN	MEX	RUS	ZAF	KOR	TUR	GBR	USA	ROW
Agric. etc	0.1	0.1	0.1	0.1	0.1	0.1	0.1	0.1	0.1	0	0.1	0.1	0.1	0.1	0.1	0.1	0.1	0.1	0.1	0.1
Proc. food	0	0	0	0	0	0	0	0	0	0.1	0	0	0	0	0	0	0.1	0	0	0
Other primary	0.2	0.2	0.2	0.2	0.2	0.2	0.2	0.2	0.2	0	0.2	0.2	0.2	0.2	0.2	0.2	0	0.2	0.2	0.2
Textiles etc	0	0	0	0	0	0	0	0	0	0.1	0	0	0	0	0	0	0	0	0	0
Wood etc	0	0	0	0	0	0	0	0	0	0.1	0.1	0.1	0	0	0	0	0.1	0	0	0
Chemicals	0	0	0	0	0	0	0	0	0	0.1	0	0	0	0	0	0	0	0	0	0
Metals	0	0	0	0	0	0	0	0	0	0.1	0	0	0	0	0	0	0	0	0	0
Vehicles	0	0	0	0	0	0	0	0	0	0.1	0	0	0	0	0	0	0.1	0	0	0
Elect. mach.	0.2	0.2	0.2	0.2	0.2	0.2	0.2	0.2	0.2	0.1	0.2	0.2	0.2	0.2	0.2	0.2	0.1	0.1	0.2	0.2
Other mach.	0	0	0	0	0	0	0	0	0	0.1	0	0	0	0	0	0	0	0	0	0
Electricity	0.2	0.2	0.2	0.2	0.2	0.2	0.2	0.2	0.2	0.1	0.2	0.2	0.2	0.2	0.2	0.2	0.2	0.2	0.2	0.2
Gas, water	0.1	0.1	0.1	0.1	0.1	0.1	0.1	0.1	0.1	0.1	0.1	0.1	0.1	0.1	0.1	0.1	0.1	0.1	0.1	0.1
Construction	0	−0.1	0	0.1	0	0.2	0.3	0.3	0	0.1	0.1	0.1	0	0	0	0.2	0.1	0.3	0	0.3
Trade	0.2	−0.1	0.2	−0.1	0.2	0.2	0.6	0.4	0.3	0.1	0.3	0.3	−0.4	0.2	0.1	0.2	0.2	0.3	0	0.4
Other transp.	0	0	0	0.1	0	0.2	0.4	0.4	0	0.1	0.1	0.3	0.1	0	0	0.2	0	0.3	0	0.4
Water transp.	−3.1	0.1	−3.1	0.1	−3.1	117.5	116.2	0.1	−3.1	0.1	0.1	0.1	−3.1	−3.1	−3.1	121	−3.1	0.1	−3.1	117.3
Air transp.	−0.5	0.1	−0.5	0.1	−0.5	73.9	−0.5	74.2	−0.5	0.1	0.1	0.1	−0.5	−0.5	−0.5	−0.5	−0.5	0.1	−0.5	75.3
Communications	12.7	12.4	12.5	0.1	−0.5	12.3	13	13	−0.5	0.1	0.1	0.1	12.5	12.4	12.1	12.7	12.6	12.5	−0.5	12.9

Table 7.15. Continued.

Other finance	5.5	4.9	5.4	0.1	5.3	5.3	5.5	5.5	5.4	0.1	0.1	5.5	4.9	5	5.1	0.1	0.1	5.5	–0.3	5.6
Insurance	0	–0.1	0	0.1	0	0.2	0.3	0.4	0	0.1	0.3	0.2	0	0	0	0.2	0.1	0.4	0	0.3
Other bus. serv.	0.2	0	0.3	0.1	0.2	0.1	0.5	0.4	0.2	0.1	0.1	0.2	0.3	0.2	0	0.1	0.1	0.4	0	0.4
Other serv.	0.1	0.1	0.1	0.1	0.1	0.1	0.1	0.1	0.1	0.1	0.1	0.1	0.1	0.1	0.1	0.1	0.1	0.1	0.1	0.1

ARG=Argentina, AUS=Australia, BRA=Brazil, CAN=Canada, REU=Rest of EU, FRA=France, GER=Germany, IND=India, IDN=Indonesia, ITA=Italy, JPN=Japan, MEX=Mexico, RUS=Russia, ZAF=South Africa, KOR=Republic of Korea, TUR=Turkey, GBR=Great Britain, USA=United States, ROW=Rest of world.
Source: FTAP model projections.

Table 7.16. Projected Short-run Changes in Sectoral Output in each G20 Country after 50% Liberalization of Investment in Services by all G20 Countries (percentage deviation from control)

	ARG	AUS	BRA	CAN	CHN	REU	FRA	GER	IND	IDN	ITA	JPN	MEX	RUS	ZAF	KOR	TUR	GBR	USA	ROW
Agric. etc	0	0.1	0	0.2	0	0.1	0.1	0.1	0	0	0.1	0	0.2	0	0.1	0	0	0.2	0	0
Proc. food	−0.1	0.1	0	0.9	0	0.3	0.1	0.1	0	0	0	0	0.5	0	0.4	0	0	0.7	0	0
Other primary	0.1	0	0.1	0.1	0	0.1	0.1	0.1	0	0	0.1	0.1	0.1	0	0.1	0	0	0	0	0
Textiles etc	0	0.3	0	1.8	0	0.5	0.1	0.1	0	0.1	0	0	0.4	−0.1	0.9	0	0	1.1	0	0
Wood etc	0	0	0.1	1	0	0.3	0	0	0	0.1	0	0	0.3	−0.1	0.6	0	0	0.7	0	0
Chemicals	−0.1	0.1	0	1	0	0.3	0.1	0.1	0	0	0.1	0	0.4	−0.2	0.6	0	0	0.8	0	0
Metals	0	0	0	1.2	0	0.3	0	0.1	0	−0.1	0	0	0.3	−0.1	0.2	0	0	0.9	0	−0.1
Vehicles	0	0.1	0	1	0	0.3	0	0.1	0	0	0	−0.1	0.2	0.5	0.7	0	0	1.5	0	0
Elect. mach.	−0.1	0	0	2.5	0	0.3	0	0.1	0	0.2	0	0	0.2	−0.1	0.9	0	0	0.6	0.1	0
Other mach.	0	0	0	1.5	0	0.4	0	0	0	0	0	0	0.6	−0.1	0.5	0	0	0.8	0	0
Electricity	0	0	0	0.4	0	0.2	0.1	0.1	0	0	0	0	0.4	0	0.2	0	0	0.5	0	0
Gas, water	0	0	0	0.5	0	0.3	0.2	0.1	0	0	0.1	0	0.4	0	0.4	0	0	0.4	0	0
Construction	0	0.1	0.1	0.3	0	0.2	0.1	0.1	0	0.1	0.1	0.1	0.6	0.1	0.2	0	0.1	0.2	0	0.1
Trade	0	0.3	0	1.6	0	0.5	0.1	0.1	0	0.2	0	0	3.5	0.1	0.4	0	0	0.9	0	0
Other transp.	0	0.1	−0.1	0.9	0	0.3	0.1	0	0	0	0	0	0.5	0	0.3	0	0	0.6	0	0
Water transp.	−0.9	0.3	−1.5	4.5	−0.1	0.2	1.8	1	−0.3	−0.2	0	−0.1	2.9	−0.4	−0.3	1.3	0	−0.2	0.6	−0.6
Air transp.	−0.4	0.2	−0.6	2.1	−0.2	2.4	−0.7	−0.4	−0.1	−0.3	−0.4	0.9	0.4	−0.3	−0.1	−0.3	−0.1	0.1	−0.3	−0.3
Communications	0	0.1	0	1.1	0	0.2	0	0	−0.1	−0.1	0	0	1.3	−0.1	0.2	0.3	0.3	1.7	0.1	−0.2

Table 7.16. Continued.

Other finance	0	1.3	0	1	0	0.5	0.1	−0.1	0	−0.1	0	0	2.1	0.7	1	0	−0.1	0.9	0	−0.2
Insurance	0	0.4	0	1.3	−0.1	0.4	0.2	0	0	−0.1	0	0	6.4	1.1	0.3	0	0	0.9	0	−0.1
Other bus. serv.	0	0.2	0	0.9	0	0.5	0.1	0	−0.1	0	0	0	18.2	0.7	0.6	0	0.1	0.4	0	0
Other serv.	0	0	0	0.9	0	0.4	0.2	0.1	0	0	0	0	0.8	0	0.5	0	0	0.7	0.1	0.1

ARG=Argentina, AUS=Australia, BRA=Brazil, CAN=Canada, REU=Rest of EU, FRA=France, GER=Germany, IND=India, IDN=Indonesia, ITA=Italy, JPN=Japan, MEX=Mexico, RUS=Russia, ZAF=South Africa, KOR=Republic of Korea, TUR=Turkey, GBR=Great Britain, USA=United States, ROW=Rest of world.

Source: FTAP model projections.

These negative spillovers are also reflected in the overall results for real wages (in full employment economies) or aggregate employment levels (in surplus-labour economies) — see OECD (2011) for details. They are also evident in the results for macroeconomic aggregates and measures of overall economic well-being. The global gains in real income are larger in the short run than in the long run, at US\$ 68 billion per year (in 2004 dollars). This is because the short-run results incorporate the surplus-labour economies catching up to their current economic potential (helped by the FDI liberalization), as well as all economies expanding their potential, as in the long run.

7.7 Global Liberalization

There is very little to say about the effects when FDI liberalization is extended to the world as a whole, other than the global gains are bigger — see OECD (2011) for details. In the short run, they are US\$ 89 billion per year (in 2004 dollars), while in the long run they are US\$ 37 billion a year (in 2004 dollars). As before, the short-run gains include 'catch-up' in surplus-labour economies, an effect that is absent in the long-run results. The labour market outcomes for G20 economies when liberalization is global are quite similar to those when only the G20 liberalize. But as noted earlier, the more widespread the reforms, the less likely it is that any particular sector or economy will suffer adversely from substitution effects. Particularly when liberalization yields productivity improvements, there are distinct dangers that laggards will lose out.

7.8 Sensitivity Analysis

One of the key assumptions in the above analysis is that FDI liberalization will manifest as productivity improvements in foreign-invested firms, rather than as reductions in the price–cost margins of those firms. On this score, the global gains in economic well-being are probably over-stated. A key question, though, is whether this assumption has any significant effect on labour market outcomes.

Table 7.17 confirms that when FDI restrictions allow price–cost margins to be inflated, then liberalization causes significant redistribution of income between FDI-sending countries (who have been receiving the economic rents) and FDI-receiving countries (who have been paying them). The net long-run gains from global liberalization are considerably smaller than before, at US\$ 2.6 billion per year (in 2004 dollars). These results are similar to those by Dee and Hanslow (2001), who also treated services trade barriers as being rent-creating.

The difference that this alternative treatment makes to labour market outcomes, however, is much less dramatic — see OECD (2011) for details. In terms of Figure 7.1, the downward shift in the supply curve for services is the same as before. However, the smaller income gains mean that the 'general equilibrium' demand curve is steeper than before, so the scale effect is smaller. There is also less scope for positive spillover effects to other sectors. Nevertheless, the long-run labour market outcomes are remarkable similar.

Another key aspect of the above analysis is that it focuses on liberalizing barriers to FDI — it does not also consider the effects of easing of non-discriminatory regulatory barriers that affect domestic and foreign services providers equally. Dee and Findlay (2008) review the evidence available at that time on whether services trade barriers discriminate against foreign providers, or also affect domestic players. One generalization is that

> when there are significant barriers to foreign supply, there are typically also non-trivial barriers to domestic supply. It is very rare to have a significant barrier to foreign entry and/or operations with no barrier affecting domestic new entrants. (p. 54)

In an alternative treatment, it is assumed that in addition to the productivity improvements in foreign-invested firms that accrue from liberalizing barriers to FDI (Table 7.3), there are comparable productivity improvements available in both domestic and foreign-invested firms from easing non-discriminatory regulatory barriers. Thus the total productivity improvements in foreign-invested firms are twice those shown in Table 7.3, while the productivity improvements in domestic firms are the same as those in Table 7.3.

Table 7.17. Projected Long-run Changes in Macroeconomic Aggregates after 50% Liberalization of Investment in Services Globally, when Restrictions Treated as Affecting Price–cost Margins (deviation from control in US$ million unless otherwise stated)

	ARG	AUS	BRA	CAN	CHN	REU	FRA	GER	IND	IDN	ITA	JPN	MEX	RUS	ZAF	KOR	TUR	GBR	USA	ROW
Real GDP (%)	0.01	0.05	0.01	0.03	0.01	0.01	−0.02	−0.01	0.01	0.03	0	0	0.06	0.04	0.04	0.01	0.01	−0.01	0	0.04
Real national income (%)	0.09	0.15	0.05	0.15	0.02	0.04	−0.05	−0.04	0.02	0.11	0.01	−0.02	0.13	0.06	0.05	0.01	0.03	−0.02	−0.02	0.06
Real GNE (%)	0.07	0.13	0.04	0.13	0.01	0.03	−0.05	−0.03	0.02	0.09	0.01	−0.02	0.11	0.07	0.05	0.01	0.03	−0.02	−0.02	0.06
Trade balance	−72	−487	−166	−837	−30	−1171	527	419	−17	−118	−111	629	−298	−181	−10	−72	−25	303	2673	−956
Welfare gains	109	866	274	1270	209	1528	−874	−979	129	216	192	−944	769	259	88	39	86	−412	−2190	1965
Sources of gain:																				
Allocative efficiency	7	184	30	261	45	327	−84	−58	11	51	7	30	289	107	31	50	8	−42	−134	1050
Endowments	5	80	10	71	14	67	−178	−181	7	16	−23	−81	64	51	23	3	9	−92	−419	588
Productivity	−4	14	3	−59	67	−115	31	100	13	1	37	137	13	21	20	13	4	29	222	−151
Terms of trade	16	62	38	78	56	12	−87	−232	59	35	37	−98	33	−35	8	−66	30	−6	309	−251
Int. interest and profit	85	526	193	919	27	1237	−556	−608	39	113	134	−932	370	115	6	39	35	−301	−2168	729

ARG=Argentina, AUS=Australia, BRA=Brazil, CAN=Canada, REU=Rest of EU, FRA=France, GER=Germany, IND=India, IDN=Indonesia, ITA=Italy, JPN=Japan, MEX=Mexico, RUS=Russia, ZAF=South Africa, KOR=Republic of Korea, TUR=Turkey, GBR=Great Britain, USA=United States, ROW=Rest of world.
Source: FTAP model projections.

Clearly, this treatment is indicative in several respects. While the evidence surveyed in Dee and Findlay (2008) indicates that non-discriminatory regulatory barriers often tended to roughly double the total (discriminatory plus non-discriminatory) burden, there were notable variations across both sectors and countries. For example, in developed economies the relative importance of discriminatory barriers was higher in legal than in accounting services. In developing countries, the relative importance of discriminatory barriers was often, but not always, higher in banking than in telecommunications. Furthermore, the productivity gains in Table 7.3 came from empirical evidence on the extent to which FDI barriers affect FDI levels. There is no guarantee that non-discriminatory barriers would affect either domestic or foreign firms to the same extent. And ideally, the first-round impact on domestic firms should be estimated using direct measures of the performance of those domestic firms.

Nevertheless, Table 7.18 confirms that when the liberalization extends to measures that also affect domestic services providers, the long-run gains from global liberalization can be an order of magnitude larger than before, at around US\$ 620 billion per year (in 2004 dollars). The overall labour market benefits are also significantly greater.[12] The detailed employment results show that when the liberalization extends to domestic services providers, there is less relative movement of labour between domestic and foreign-invested firms within sectors.

7.9 Conclusion

This chapter has addressed the empirical question of whether liberalization of FDI in services can produce beneficial labour market outcomes. The answer is in the affirmative under a wide variety of circumstances — even if the first-round effect of that liberalization is to generate productivity improvements in foreign-invested firms that would, in the first instance, reduce their unit labour requirements.

---

[12] Details are available in OECD (2011).

Table 7.18. Projected Long-run Changes in Macroeconomic Aggregates after 50% Liberalization of Investment in Services and Indicative Liberalization of Domestic Regulation Globally (deviation from control in US$ million unless otherwise stated)

	ARG	*AUS*	*BRA*	*CAN*	*CHN*	*REU*	*FRA*	*GER*	*IND*	*IDN*	*ITA*	*JPN*	*MEX*	*RUS*	*ZAF*	*KOR*	*TUR*	*GBR*	*USA*	*ROW*
Real GDP (%)	−0.05	3.29	0.91	3.1	5.49	1.84	0.41	0.44	0.13	0.42	0.42	0.74	2.22	6.71	3.64	1.47	0.67	1.43	0.64	3.73
Real national income (%)	1.17	4	1.73	3.51	6.81	2.32	0.6	0.43	0.49	1.35	0.81	0.52	2.53	8.22	4.19	1.44	1.06	1.37	0.74	3.85
Real GNE (%)	1.09	3.32	1.57	2.99	4.99	2.05	0.65	0.55	0.58	1.39	0.88	0.61	2.2	7.33	3.8	1.32	1.22	1.31	0.74	3.27
Trade balance	−970	90	−2008	1200	14612	−10755	−3961	−5310	−1015	−1405	−5674	366	253	315	176	34	−1004	1255	−3420	17220
Welfare gains	1444	22566	8845	30276	90723	87868	10968	8597	3068	2744	11969	19260	15473	36690	7565	7955	3080	27956	87091	136300
Sources of gain:																				
Allocative efficiency	6	1682	1196	2842	2731	8524	354	1022	497	276	675	2913	5700	2845	652	725	192	2171	4126	14285
Endowments	0	686	370	954	5732	2311	−185	−353	79	101	−14	915	179	1154	268	55	116	422	1626	7680
Productivity	−73	18221	3857	25993	80947	67144	8288	11473	232	640	6358	29957	9177	33670	6746	9163	1656	27528	67811	136119
Terms of trade	598	760	1466	−291	1519	−938	1104	−2971	2015	922	2244	−6435	79	−1776	292	−1697	791	45	13198	−10936
Int. interest and profit	913	1217	1956	778	−206	10827	1407	−574	245	805	2706	−8090	338	797	−393	−291	325	−2210	330	−10848

ARG=Argentina, AUS=Australia, BRA=Brazil, CAN=Canada, REU=Rest of EU, FRA=France, GER=Germany, IND=India, IDN=Indonesia, ITA=Italy, JPN=Japan, MEX=Mexico, RUS=Russia, ZAF=South Africa, KOR=Republic of Korea, TUR=Turkey, GBR=Great Britain, USA=United States, ROW=Rest of world.
Source: FTAP model projections.

There are two key mechanisms leading to the positive labour market outcomes. The first is that a loosening of investment restrictions will lower the costs of foreign-invested firms, competition will ensure this is passed on in lower prices, and those lower prices will encourage greater demand by consumers and using industries, both locally and overseas. Econometric evidence suggests that this scale effect is likely to be substantial, because demands for services appear to be reasonably price responsive.

A second mechanism is that as foreign-invested firms expand, their labour intensity is likely to increase. This reflects their ability to attract additional labour, relative to additional FDI capital. Labour tends to be fairly mobile within and between sectors, and foreign-invested firms account for a relatively small proportion of total employment in most economies. So foreign-invested firms should have little trouble attracting labour away from domestic firms in their own sector, and from other sectors. By contrast, FDI capital is subject to the portfolio allocation choices of international investors, and FDI capital is far less mobile than debt and other financial instruments. Econometric evidence suggests that, having made their preferred choices, investors would require non-trivial increases in returns in order to be persuaded to invest more FDI capital in overseas locations. As a result, FDI liberalization is likely to require an increase in capital returns relative to wages, and this will encourage an increase in labour intensity in foreign-invested firms.

Nevertheless, overall labour market outcomes depend on the spillover effects to other firms and industries. The results suggest that these spillover effects of FDI liberalization can be mixed. Firms that compete directly with the foreign-invested firms, especially domestic firms in the same sector, suffer from lower priced competition. But sectors that use the services of foreign-invested firms as inputs benefit from lower-priced inputs. So long as the liberalization is reasonably widespread across economies, the positive spillovers dominate, both within and between economies. There could well be some significant structural adjustments as labour shifts from domestic to foreign-invested firms within each economy. But the adjustment costs from this type of reallocation, in terms of retraining and job search, are likely to be relatively small (compared with other types of structural adjustments). Furthermore, the structural adjustments projected here are probably overstated. The chapter considers only the liberalization of measures that discriminate against foreign services suppliers. In practice, there are also significant barriers in most economies to market entry by any new supplier, domestic or foreign. Were liberalization to extend to such measures, the structural adjustment costs would be smaller. And sensitivity analysis confirms that the overall economic and labour market gains would be an order of magnitude larger.

The positive labour market outcomes do not just accrue in the long term. The same two mechanisms that drive those outcomes also apply in the short run. Foreign-invested firms may have less time to put additional FDI capital in place in the short run, so the scale effects may be smaller. But particularly in surplus-labour economies, additional labour can be hired with no upward pressure on wages, so the substitution towards labour in foreign-invested firms should be greater. The net short-run effect on labour market outcomes is remarkably similar to the long-run effect.

Nor are the positive labour-market effects dependent on the assumption that the benefits of FDI liberalization accrue as productivity gains to foreign-invested firms, rather than as reductions in their price–cost margins. Both mechanisms lead to lower prices that can be passed on to consumers and using industries. Although the global gains in overall economic well-being are very much smaller when price–cost margins are squeezed than when productivity gains accrue, the labour market outcomes are again similar.

Overall, therefore, the liberalization of services trade can not only make a valuable contribution to overall economic well-being, particularly if it extends beyond the removal of discrimination against foreign suppliers. It can also contribute significantly and positively to labour market outcomes, in terms of employment gains in the short term, and real wages gains in the long term.

A.1. The Effects of FDI Restrictions on Bilateral FDI

Hildegunn Nordås, Directorate for Trade and Agriculture, OECD

The empirical analysis is based on Baltagi, Egger and Pfaffermayr (2007), hereafter BEP. They propose a 'knowledge capital' model of FDI extended by third country effects. The knowledge capital model features three factors of production; physical capital and skilled and unskilled labour. Horizontal as well as vertical investment is possible depending on relative factor endowments and market sizes. Further, national and multinational companies may coexist. Finally, the extension to include third country effects captures the fact that bilateral stocks and flows of FDI depend not only on market conditions in the home and host country of the multinational company, but also on market conditions and transaction costs in third countries, which obviously are alternative sources/hosts of FDI for any country pair considered.

This model is particularly useful for estimating inputs to the FTAP general equilibrium model featuring bilateral investment stocks and flows. The regression equation for BEP model 1 is without spatial effects and reads (sector subscripts are omitted):

$$
\begin{aligned}
F_{ijt} = {} & \beta_0 + \beta_1 G_{ijt} + \beta_2 S_{ijt} + \beta_3 k_{ijt} + \beta_4 h_{ijt} + \beta_5 l_{ijt} \\
& + \beta_6 \Gamma_{ijt} + \beta_7 \Theta_{ijt} + \beta_8 FDIri_{ijt}
\end{aligned}
\tag{A.1}
$$

The variables are defined as follows (all variables are sector-specific):
G_{ijt} : the log of combined output of country i and j
S_{ijt} : index of country pair similarity in output value $S_{ijt} = 1 - s_i^2 - s_j^2$ where lower case s is the share of country i in country pair output
k_{ijt} : the log of the relative capital stock invested in the sector in question
h_{ijt} : the relative share of hours worked performed by workers with tertiary education
l_{ijt} : the relative share of hours worked performed by unskilled workers
Γ_{ijt} : interaction term between G_{ijt} and k_{ijt}
Θ_{ijt} : interaction term between the log of distance and ($k_{ijt} - l_{ijt}$)
$FDIri_{ijt}$: is the OECD FDI restrictiveness index.

Data

Bilateral FDI data are available OECD databases for 22 countries for the period 1995–2005.[13] Data on output by sector and capital endowments are from OECD STAN, hours worked are from EU KLEMS and the FDI restrictiveness index is from OECD (Golub 2003, Takeshi and Golub 2006, Kalinova, Palerm and Thomsen 2010).

Regression results

The regression was first run as specified above in equation (A.1). Due to gaps in the data and the fact that the FDI restrictiveness index is only available for two years during the period 1995–2005, the number of observations is limited and the regression was run for pooled data (and sector dummies) for the seven major services sectors included in OECD FDI statistics and the FDI restrictiveness index (business services, telecommunications, construction, distribution, finance, hotels and restaurants, transport).

The result is reported in Table 7.19.

It is noted that over the ten year period with 7 sectors and 22 countries there are 33,880 possible observations, but information on all the variables included in regression equation (A.1) is available for only 640 of these. Selection bias and other problems related to a limited sample are therefore a concern. Nevertheless, the coefficients on combined output and output similarity have the same sign but are much smaller in magnitude than in BEP (who estimated the regression on outward US FDI and FATS). The host country's relative unskilled labour share of employment appears to have a positive effect on inward investment. Although we consider this model as the ideal approach to estimate parameter values for the FTAP simulations of FDI liberalization in services, further data gathering is necessary before reliable estimates can be made using this approach.

---

[13] Total bilateral stocks and flows of FDI and stocks and flows by country and sector are available from OECD.Stat. Based on this information, bilateral FDI stocks and flows have been estimated by OECD staff using an optimization technique.

Table 7.19. Regression Results, Equation A.1
(Dependent variable: ln inward FDI stock)

	Model (a)		Model (b)	
	coeff.	*s.d.*	*coeff.*	*s.d.*
Ln combined output	0.968	0.141***	1.539	0.213***
Similarity output index	1.393	0.759*	3.638	0.845***
Ln relative capital stock	−1.716	1.425	−1.468	1.332
Interaction output relative capital	0.1	0.114	0.037	0.107
Relative skilled labour share of employment	0.084	0.062	−0.062	0.064
Relative unskilled labour share of employment	0.301	0.15**	0.292	0.135**
Interaction ln distance and the difference between relative capital and unskilled labour	0.042	0.021	0.034	0.019*
FDI restrictiveness	0.089	1.35	−0.298	1.21
N	640		640	
Adjusted R^2	0.31		0.477	
Sector fixed effects	yes		yes	
Host country fixed effects	no		no	
Source country fixed effects	no		yes	

*** significant at the 1 per cent level, ** significant at the 5 per cent level, * significant at the 10 per cent level.
Source: Author's calculations.

We therefore turn to a simpler, gravity-based regression introducing bilateral distance and an interaction term between distance and FDI restrictiveness. The rationale for the interaction term is that FDI liberalization is likely to trigger more inward flows from source countries closer to home at the margin. For instance the marginal supply response to FDI liberalization in Canada is likely to be larger in the United States than in Japan, for example.

$$F_{ijt} = \beta_0 + \beta_1 G_{ijt} + \beta_2 S_{ijt} + \beta_3 dist_{ij} + \beta_4 FDIri_{ijt}$$
$$+ \beta_5 dist * FDIri_{ijt} + \varepsilon_{ijt} \tag{A.2}$$

Clearly, with this simpler specification the number of observations increases to an acceptable sample. The fact that the variable of interest, FDI restrictiveness, is only available for two years makes the total possible number of observations 6,776. The results in Table 7.20 suggest that the marginal effect of FDI liberalization in a host country declines

Table 7.20. Regression Results, Equation A.2
(Dependent variable: ln inward FDI stock)

	coeff	*s.d.*
Ln combined output	0.467	0.029***
Similarity index	0.002	0.272
Ln distance	−0.609	0.06***
FDI restrictiveness	−1.004	0.488**
FDI restrictiveness*distance (unlogged, in Km)	0.0001353	0.000***
N	5,162	
Adjusted R^2	0.309	
Sector fixed effects	yes	
Host country fixed effects	no	
Source country fixed effects	yes	

*** significant at the 1 per cent level, ** significant at the 5 per cent level, * significant at the 10 per cent level.
Source: Author's calculations.

with the distance to the source country, as expected. The value used in the FTAP simulation is the direct effect of FDI liberalization plus the indirect effect through trade costs related to distance evaluated at the mean distance, which is 5639.526 Km, which is −0.24 = (−1.004 + 5639.5*0.0001353).

Part 3

Policy Insights

Chapter 8

The Rise of Services Trade: Regional Initiatives and Challenges for the WTO[1]

Philippa Dee and Alexandra Sidorenko

8.1 The Rise of Services

Services are a significant part of every economy in output and employment terms. Services trade is also significant, although it is severely understated in conventional balance of payments statistics.

The share of services in GDP is high, even in developing economies, and rises further with the level of economic development. Based on the World Bank World Development Indicators, the share of services in total value added of the least developed countries was 42 per cent in 2000, compared with 55 per cent in the middle income countries and 69 per cent in the high income countries.

The share of employment in services follows a similar tendency. Table 8.1 shows that in all the selected economies but China, the share of employment in services exceeds that in industry by a significant margin. The share of employment in services is probably understated in some of the developing economies, where many of the services activities are informal.

Services are often delivered face to face. This means that trade in services often takes place via the movement of primary factors of

---

[1] First published as Chapter 10 in Christopher Findlay and Hadi Soesastro (2006), *Reshaping the Asia Pacific Economic Order*, London and New York: Routledge: 200–26.

Table 8.1. Disposition of Employment in Selected APEC Economies (per cent)

	Share of labour force in industry	*Share of labour force in services*
Australia	21	74
Canada	23	74
Chile	26	60
China	22	13
Indonesia	16	39
Japan	31	63
Malaysia	32	50
Mexico	25	53
New Zealand	23	68
Peru	19	76
Philippines	16	45
Russia	29	59
Singapore	29	71
Thailand	18	33
United States	23	75

Source: UNCTAD Handbook of Statistics Online, www.unctad.org/statistics/handbook, accessed 20 November 2003.

production — people or capital. Firstly, the consumer may move to the producer's economy. This happens most clearly with tourism services, but it also happens with services such as education and health, when the student or patient moves to another economy for education or treatment. In the language of the General Agreement on Trade in Services (GATS) under the WTO, this mode of services trade is called 'consumption abroad'.

Alternatively, the producer may move to the consumer's economy. This also happens in education, where teachers move to another economy to teach short courses. It is also very common for professionals to travel temporarily to the economy into which they are delivering professional services. In the language of the GATS, this mode of service delivery is called the 'movement of natural persons' (to distinguish it from the movement of corporate or other legal entities).

Many other services are delivered to other economies via 'commercial presence'. In banking and telecommunications, for example, it is common for companies to set up a permanent corporate presence in another economy and to make their sales from their foreign affiliate. The GATS also recognizes commercial presence as a mode of services delivery. This has policy significance, because it means that the GATS is a vehicle for negotiating foreign direct investment issues in the services area.

Another characteristic of services is that they are intangible. This means that where services are traded in the traditional 'cross-border' fashion, e-commerce is an important vehicle for that cross-border trade.

Three of these modes of services delivery are captured, to a greater or lesser degree of accuracy, in conventional balance of payments statistics. Commercial presence is not. There have been recent initiatives, especially by the OECD, to compile statistics on the activities of foreign affiliates (so-called FATS statistics). On the basis of these and other statistics, Table 8.2 gives a very crude estimate of the extent of global services trade. It shows that reliance on balance of payments statistics alone can lead to an underestimate of services trade by more than 50 per cent.

Nevertheless, conventional balance of payments measures of cross-border trade are the most prevalent indicator of growth rates of services trade. Table 8.3 shows that some of these growth rates have been significant, at up to 20 per cent per year.

Table 8.3 shows that the United States is the biggest importer and exporter of services via cross border trade. It is also one of the few countries to publish cross-border services trade data on a bilateral basis, as well as publishing FATS data. Table 8.4 summarizes this bilateral data for 1996, the latest year for which imports via the sales of foreign affiliates are available.

Table 8.2.   Trade in Services by Mode of Supply (US$ billion)

Mode of supply	Proxy measure	Estimate
Cross border supply	BOP: commercial services exports (excluding travel)	1,000
Consumption abroad	BOP: travel exports	500
Commercial presence	FATS statistics: turnover	2,000
Movement of natural persons	BOP: compensation of employees	50
Total		3,550

Source: Karsenty (2002).

Table 8.3. Leading Exporters and Importers of Commercial Services in the Asia Pacific Region

	Value in 2002 (US$ billion)	Annual change in 2002 (per cent)
Exporters		
United States	272.6	1
Japan	64.9	2
Hong Kong, China	45.2	9
China	39.4	20
Canada	36.3	–2
Korea	27.1	–4
Singapore	26.9	3
Chinese Taipei	21.1	9
Australia	16.7	5
Thailand	15.2	18
Importers		
United States	205.6	2
Japan	106.6	0
China	46.1	18
Canada	41.9	–2
Korea	35.1	8
Chinese Taipei	24.3	3
Hong Kong, China	24.2	0
Russia	21.5	16
Singapore	20.6	1
Australia	17.5	7

Source: UNCTAD Handbook of Statistics Online, www.unctad.org/statistics/handbook, accessed 20 November 2003.

Table 8.4 shows that while in aggregate, trade via foreign affiliates equals or exceeds cross border trade, this does not necessarily hold country by country. Not surprisingly, the countries that have been major destinations for FDI worldwide tend to be the major sources of US services imports delivered via the sales of foreign affiliates. This includes Canada, Europe and Japan. To date, the 'Other countries' that include most APEC member economies are much less important in US imports via commercial presence than they are in US imports via cross-border trade.

Conversely, the Unites States, as a major source of FDI worldwide, is also a major exporter of services delivered via FDI. And these exports go

Table 8.4.   US Trade in Services by Partner Region, 1996 (US$ billion)

	Cross order trade		*Sales of foreign affiliates*	
	Imports	*Exports*	*Imports*	*Exports*
Canada	12,239	19,331	27,282	21,160
Europe	55,078	80,959	101,296	128,655
Latin America and other Western Hemisphere	25,589	35,486	5,474	17,457
Australia	2,553	4,491	5,886	8,821
Japan	12,940	33,274	21,398	21,921
Other countries	26,245	42,056	6,211	22,594
China	1,937	3,166	na	na
Hong Kong	3,042	3,323	na	na
Korea	4,123	7,432	na	na
Malaysia	458	1,277	na	na
Singapore	1,823	3,849	na	na
Taiwan	2,709	4,046	na	na
International organizations and unallocated	2,246	5,792	898	2,567
All countries	136,885	221,390	168,444	223,175

na Not available.
Source: US Bureau of Economic Analysis,
www.bea.doc.gov/bea/di/1001serv/intlserv.htm (accessed 13 January 2004).

where US FDI has gone. So Europe features disproportionately as a destination of US services exports delivered via commercial presence. To date, the 'Other countries' are similarly less important in US exports via commercial presence that they are in US exports via cross-border trade.

The purpose of this chapter is to review some of the policy issues in services trade, and to review the progress that has been made in services trade liberalization in various forums — multilateral, plurilateral, bilateral and unilateral. Cooper (1988) stated that remarkably little homework had been done on what the objectives of services trade negotiations should be. Substantial progress has been made since then on defining the issues, if not achieving negotiated outcomes. The chapter concludes with some observations about the most promising forums for services trade liberalization, and the most appropriate form of support to help economies achieve the best outcomes in those forums.

8.2 Services Trade Liberalization

With services traded via the movement of people or capital, the transaction typically occurs behind the border. Even when cross-border trade takes place via e-commerce, it is not easily observed by customs officials.

So services transactions are not amenable to tariff protection. Instead, services trade barriers are typically behind-the-border, non-price regulatory measures. Table 8.5 gives examples of the key trade barriers affecting trade in two different services — banking, and legal services. Quantitative measures of the height of these trade barriers in Pacific and other economies can be found in Findlay and Warren (2000), Kalirajan (2000), Nguyen-Hong (2000), Doove *et al.* (2001), Clark, Dollar and Micco (2004), Barth Caprio and Levine (2004) and Fink, Mattoo and Rathindran (2002).

The key thing to note about the measures in Table 8.5 is that they do not always discriminate against foreigners.

In banking, the measures that affect only foreign participants are those that restrict equity participation, require it to take the form of a joint venture with a local partner, or restrict the temporary or permanent movement of executives. All other measures can be equally applied to domestic new entrants. These include restrictions on the number of banking licences or number of branches, restrictions on where and how

Table 8.5. Description of Barriers to Trade in Banking and Legal Services

Banking	*Legal services*
Restrictions on:	Restrictions on:
– number of bank licences	– form of establishment (eg partnership)
– equity participation	– equity participation
– joint ventures	– nationality or citizenship
– raising funds	– licensing and accreditation
– lending funds	– quotas or needs tests
– other lines of business	– advertising and fee setting
– number of branches	– multidisciplinary practices
– temporary or permanent movement of executives	– activities reserved by law to the profession

Source: McGuire and Schuele (2000), Nguyen-Hong (2000).

banks can raise funds or lend, and on whether banks can undertake other lines of business (eg insurance or securities).[2]

Similarly, for legal services, a few measures affect only foreign practitioners — requirements for nationality or citizenship, and whether quotas or needs tests are applied in order to practice. Other measures can affect domestic practitioners as well. These include restrictions on equity participation, since some economies place restrictions on whether non-lawyers can have an equity stake in a law practice. They also include restrictions on the form of establishment (eg whether corporate structures are allowed), licensing and accreditation requirements, restrictions on advertising or fee setting, restrictions on whether other disciplines (eg accountancy) can be practiced out of a law firm, and the reservation of certain activities (eg conveyancing) to the legal profession.

The GATS agreement similarly recognizes that services trade barriers need not be discriminatory against foreigners. It recognizes a specific list of (mostly quantitative) restrictions on 'market access' that are not discriminatory. Many analysts have extended the definition of 'market access' to cover all measures that are non-discriminatory. The GATS also recognizes 'derogations from national treatment', which is GATS-speak for discriminatory restrictions.

Thus a key feature of services trade barriers is that they often protect incumbent service suppliers from any competition, be it from domestic or foreign new entrants. This is the single most important feature distinguishing services trade barriers. It has implications both for the economic effects of services trade liberalization, and for the political economy of services trade reform. These implications are draw out later in the chapter.

Services are also an area where market failures can occur. Natural monopoly is a characteristic of some network industries such as telecommunications and air passenger transport — it may be economically inefficient to have key bottleneck facilities provided by more than one service provider, so regulation is required to prevent the abuse of this monopoly power. Information asymmetry is almost by definition a feature of professional services — the client is not in a

---

[2] Dinh (2013) gives a recent update of barriers to trade in banking services.

position to judge whether the service being delivered is of reasonable quality, so licensing or accreditation requirements can help to bridge the information gap. Similarly, there is a legitimate role for prudential regulation of financial services to ensure systemic stability, and for safety regulation in air passenger transport.

In these circumstances, services trade liberalization may not deliver the anticipated benefits if it is not supported by the appropriate domestic regulatory regimes. For example, liberalizing market access in financial services may not generate benefits if prudential regulation is either too heavy- or too light-handed. Similarly, allowing market entry in telecommunications may not reap benefits if new entrants cannot get access to the incumbent's bottleneck facilities — the local loop — on reasonable terms.

The GATS recognizes the right of individual governments to regulate, but requires that domestic regulatory regimes be the 'least burdensome' necessary to achieve their objectives. A counterexample would be a requirement for foreign health professionals to retrain in a new economy. Here the legitimate domestic objective of ensuring quality could be achieved by the less burdensome requirement to resit a qualifying examination.

While services are typically not protected by tariffs, services trade barriers may or may not be tariff-like, in the following sense. Some regulatory trade restrictions, particularly quantitative restrictions, create artificial scarcity. The prices of services are inflated, not because the real resource cost of producing them has gone up, but because incumbent firms are able to earn economic rents. Liberalization of these barriers would yield 'triangle gains' in producer and consumer surplus associated with improvements in allocative efficiency, but also have redistributive effects associated with the elimination of rents to incumbents. As Dee and Hanslow (2001) demonstrate, the former effects would not be trivial, but the latter effects could also be significant. Such rent-creating restrictions are tariff-like, with the redistribution of rent having effects similar to the redistribution of tariff revenue.

Alternatively, services trade restrictions could increase the real resource cost of doing business. An example would be the above requirement for foreign services professionals to retrain in a new economy. Liberalization would be equivalent to a productivity improvement (saving in real resources), and yield 'roughly rectangle' gains associated with a downward shift in supply curves. This could increase returns for the incumbent service providers, as well as lowering costs for users elsewhere in the economy.

The distinction is critical, for two reasons. First, in a unilateral or multilateral setting, rectangle gains are likely to exceed triangle gains by a significant margin, especially given the importance of the services sectors in most economies. Secondly, in the context of preferential trade agreements, the danger of net welfare losses from net trade diversion arises only if the relevant barriers are rent-creating. This second argument is elaborated further below.

8.3 Rationale for Reciprocity

Services trade liberalization can take place unilaterally, or in multilateral or plurilateral fora. Before examining recent developments and prospects in each forum, it is worthwhile reviewing the case for reciprocity — that is, the case for using plurilateral or multilateral fora — in light of the special features of services trade liberalization mentioned above.

There are two rationales in the literature. One is the mercantilist rationale in either its naïve or more sophisticated forms, both parodied by Krugman (1997), and another is the economic rationale outlined by Bagwell and Staiger (1999).

The naïve mercantilist view is 'exports good, imports bad'. Thus liberalizing import restrictions is seen as imposing a cost, which must be compensated for by receiving a similar concession from a trading partner. Of course, economic theory suggests that, in a world of perfect substitution, a small open economy will in fact gain from unilaterally lowering its import restrictions — what it loses in tariff revenue is more than made up for by access to lower priced imports for use at home. However, this comes at the cost of some disruption in production in the domestic import-competing industry. So the more sophisticated version of the mercantilist view is that reciprocity is required for political economy reasons, to buy off the sectional interests in the import-competing industry.[3] This presupposes that these sectional interests can be bought off by the prospect of gains to some other export sector, even though they cannot be bought off by gains to consumers.

Clearly, when services trade barriers are tariff-like and discriminatory, the logic applies in the same way. But if services trade barriers are non-discriminatory, or are cost-escalating, the need for reciprocity is less clear.

If trade barriers are primarily market access barriers affecting any new entrant, then the domestic import-competing industry can be too small, not too big. Liberalization can encourage additional entry by either wholly domestic firms or foreign multinationals into domestic production, and this can offset additional competition from cross-border trade, to the extent that this is also a feature of the market. Where heavily impeded cross-border trade is relatively unimportant (as is the case for many services), the size of the domestic industry can be bigger after liberalization than before.

The sophisticated mercantilist argument for the need to buy off adjustment pressures would still apply if it was the incumbent that needed to be bought off. But again, this presupposes that the incumbent could be bought off by the prospect of gains to some other export sector, even though they could not be bought off by gains to consumers *and* to other domestic new entrants.

It is the concern of some developing countries that liberalization of non-discriminatory market access barriers would encourage entry by foreign multinationals instead of domestic firms, and that given this first mover advantage, this could prevent successful domestic firms from ever emerging. If the output of domestic firms and foreign multinationals were perfectly substitutable, this argument might have force. But services are highly differentiated products.

- Services are commonly differentiated by economy. A domestic telephone call in the United States is not the same as a domestic telephone call in Australia, because the former is between

---

[3] The political economy dimensions of behind-the-border domestic reforms are considered in Chapter 14 of this volume.

Washington and Los Angeles whereas the latter is between Sydney and Melbourne. Similarly, the practice of law differs in the two economies, because the legal systems and legal traditions differ. What is more, some of the relevant trade restrictions in legal services are precisely to do with whether foreign legal professionals are able to practice host-economy law, home-economy law or international law in the host economy.

- Services are also commonly differentiated by firm. This is because the production of services often involves firm-specific human capital. Microsoft is not the same as any other software firm because Bill Gates is not the same as any other software proprietor. And the development and maintenance of Microsoft required considerable fixed and sunk expenditure on research and other 'headquarters services'. Thus the relevant industrial organization model for services is the same model of firm-level product differentiation and economies of scale that has been used to characterize the multinational manufacturing enterprise (eg Markusen 1995).

- Not only are services differentiated by economy and firm, they are also differentiated to the needs of individual customers. The legal services that my solicitor provides to me are not precisely the same as the services she provides to any of her other clients, because I have a unique individual situation. This characteristic was noted by Ethier and Horn (1991), and is one level of product differentiation below that now included in most trade models. This characteristic seems to be implicit in the choice of nesting structure of demand for varieties in some more recent models of services trade. This issue is discussed in more detail in Dee (2003).

With services being highly differentiated, and with local service firms having a comparative advantage in tailoring services to meet local needs, it is not clear that foreign multinationals would always have the edge.

But it is equally clear that in some key infrastructure sectors, such as banking and fixed line telecommunications, they could. However, empirical research also shows that in these sectors, contestability of the market by foreign multinationals, if not actual entry, does add significantly to economic performance, in terms of lower prices to downstream users (Warren 2000, Kalirajan *et al.* 2000). In these circumstances, protecting the market for local players could impose a significant cost on the rest of the economy.

A similar argument holds if trade barriers are primarily cost-escalating. In this case, trade liberalization can benefit everyone, even the incumbent. If there are sectional interests that need to be bought off, they are the people whose livelihoods depend on feeding the bureaucratic and red-tape processes associated with administering the cost-escalating barriers. They typically do not feature at the top of lists of political influence.

The economic argument for reciprocity, as outlined by Bagwell and Staiger (1999), is a terms of trade argument. Many commentators are willing to dismiss such arguments as being irrelevant for small open economies. Such dismissal may be warranted in a world of perfect substitution. But as noted, services are highly differentiated products, so even small open economies may have some market power in the services they provide.

In goods trade, the rationale is that, while tariff liberalization will yield an unambiguous triangle gain in allocative efficiency, it can also yield a terms of trade loss. So reciprocity creates a countervailing terms of trade effect in the other direction and can guarantee a Pareto improvement without the need for compensation.

In services trade, the argument will hold force *if* liberalization yields a terms of trade loss. To the extent that services are delivered via commercial presence, the relevant prices are local prices and terms of trade effects are not relevant. If the barriers are cost-escalating, it is much more likely that the rectangle gains from liberalization would dominate any terms of trade losses. So again, the case for reciprocity is missing.

Mattoo and Fink (2002, p. 2) have used these arguments to show that preferential liberalization of services trade on a bilateral or plurilateral basis is likely to provide gains to an economy, relative to the *status quo*:

> Compared to the *status quo*, a country is likely to gain from preferential liberalization of services trade at a particular point in time — as distinct from the more ambiguous conclusions emerging for goods trade. The main reason is that barriers are often prohibitive and not revenue generating, so there are few costs of trade diversion.

However, they note that non-preferential liberalization is likely to produce larger gains than preferential liberalization. Further, the sequence of liberalization matters more in services trade than it does in the case of goods trade (more on this later).

The arguments of this section have shown that if a country is likely to gain from preferential liberalization of services trade, relative to the *status quo*, it is primarily because the case for reciprocity is less strong than for goods trade — a country is more likely to gain, and arguably have fewer adjustment costs, if it liberalizes its services on a unilateral basis, compared with the more ambiguous conclusions emerging from goods trade.

8.4   Challenges for the WTO

The challenge for the WTO is clear. The GATS agreement was a monumental achievement in terms of recognizing what really mattered for services trade. It looked beyond conventional cross-border trade, and in recognizing other modes of delivery put the contentious issues of investment and immigration directly on the negotiating table. It looked beyond discriminatory measures, and so put the issues of domestic regulatory regimes directly on the negotiating table. Yet these are issues that trade negotiators are not well-equipped to deal with. And this is leaving aside questions of the limitations of the GATS architecture, which also contribute to a lack of reform momentum.

How have services negotiations fared in a WTO context? Not surprisingly, most offers to date are standstill offers, even from the OECD economies, doing no more than offering to bind what has been achieved by unilateral liberalization since the Uruguay Round.[4]

While the services negotiations are currently held hostage to other negotiating agenda items in the WTO, they have been advancing along two major paths. The mainstream negotiations on specific commitments have been conducted using bilateral requests and offers. In parallel, outstanding rule making issues are being discussed. The Working Party

---

[4] Evidence surveyed in Chapter 14 of this volume suggests that as of 2012, this is still the case.

on Domestic Regulations has been given the mandate to develop horizontal disciplines under GATS Article VI:4. Emergency safeguards, government procurement and subsidies in services are being dealt with by the Working Party on GATS Rules. Recognition of autonomous liberalization and special treatment of the Least Developed Countries (LDCs) have also been on the agenda of the Council for Trade in Services, with some significant breakthroughs achieved in the run-up to the Cancun Ministerial. Negotiations on the outstanding rule making issues, except for the safeguards, are scheduled to be completed by 1 January 2005, prior to the conclusion of the negotiations on market access. The deadline for emergency safeguards has been extended until 15 March 2004.[5]

Domestic regulation

The major challenge for GATS rule making on domestic regulation has been to agree on the design of domestic regulation so that legitimate regulatory objectives are fulfilled without creating unnecessary barriers to trade in services. The work program on GATS Article VI:4 has evolved around developing horizontal disciplines for technical standards, qualification and licensing requirements and procedures. Several instruments have been tested as a model for developing such horizontal disciplines.

In the current GATS architecture, the article on domestic regulation concerns only non-discriminatory measures, that is, if no national treatment commitment is undertaken in the country schedule of specific commitments, there is little recourse to Article VI. If a domestic regulatory measure impedes market access, it can be protected by being listed as a limitation under Article XVI. If it impacts discriminatorily on foreign service providers, then it can be protected by being scheduled under the negative list of exemptions to national treatment under Article XVII. If the regulation is not listed as a limitation on market access or national treatment, then Article VI provides general disciplines requiring that it not be an unnecessary barrier to trade. There is a divide among the

---

[5] Further progress is summarized in the next chapter of this volume.

Members on whether any horizontal disciplines for domestic regulation of services should be applicable across all sectors, or limited to committed sectors only, as Article VI:1 implies.

Apart from the debate about the coverage of Article VI, there is also an issue of whether regulatory disciplines should be horizontal or sectoral. Sidorenko and Findlay (2002) discuss the issue in more detail. In summary, major benefits of horizontal disciplines include the reduction in the probability of regulatory capture, disentangling unnecessary policy linkages, potentially greater degree of liberalization, and automatic inclusion of new services. Systematic approaches to building horizontal disciplines at the multilateral level that maintain the national right to regulate involve:

- an open international dialogue of domestic regulators and competition authorities to explore whether meaningful horizontal disciplines can be developed;
- building a judicial system in which the key principles/disciplines are bound in an international agreement (such as the GATS), voluntary guidelines established as a benchmark for domestic policymaking, and other private and public bodies and associations left to develop sector specific standards; and
- developing horizontal disciplines along the lines of safeguarding the contestability of markets while recognizing the national regulatory sovereignty in the areas pertinent to health, safety and prudential objectives.

To strengthen GATS Article VI, proposals have been made to require explicit statement of the policy objectives achieved by a regulation, to clarify the concept of 'quality of service', to ensure that regulation is limited to the minimum necessary. Performance-based regulations, market-based regulations and self-regulation by the industry are to be encouraged.

Several instruments could be used to provide a starting point on developing horizontal disciplines for domestic regulation of services. The GATS reference paper on telecommunications formulates regulatory disciplines for basic telecommunications that can be extended to other network services. These include competitive safeguards (access to essential facilities), transparency of the administration of any social objectives such as universal service obligations, transparency of licensing requirements and criteria for allocation of scarce resources, and an independent regulator.

Regulations that are formulated in order to prevent other instances of market failure can be disciplined by a generalized necessity test. The Disciplines on Domestic Regulation in the Accountancy Sector adopted by the Council for Trade in Services on 14 December 1998 provide an example of a necessity test, as well as other principles that can be extended on a horizontal basis, such as transparency, including the provision for a Member to request information from another Member on the rationale behind the domestic regulatory measure, and for a prior information and an opportunity to comment on a proposed measure. The disciplines for accountancy state that licensing and qualification requirements and procedures should not be impediments in themselves, and should serve legitimate objectives. Technical standards should also be designed only to fulfil legitimate objectives.

Emergency safeguards

The emergency safeguards agenda has been pushed by the ASEAN economies, arguing that such safeguards would lure more developing countries into making market access commitments that they otherwise would be reticent to schedule. The European Union and the United States are opposed to the concept of emergency safeguards in services, arguing that such measures applied to commercial presence would undermine investor confidence in the country and hence would impede the flow of foreign direct investment. The US Coalition of Service Industries (CSI 2002) argues that that safeguards do not work in the services sector as it is hard to demonstrate a surge in imports due to data collection problems, especially for cross-border trade. The deadline for negotiation on emergency safeguards has been extended to 15 March 2004, but there has been little progress so far in attaining common ground within the Working Party on GATS Rules.

Subsidies

Very little progress has been made to date in respect to subsidies in services. Yet to be clarified is the definition of subsidies in services, as well as the applicability of any multilateral disciplines to those services supplied partially by the government. Some argue that the extent of trade distortion arising from the presence of subsidies in services sector should be weighted against the developmental objectives of developing countries, especially in the areas where domestic support programs are aimed at achieving social policy objectives.

Government procurement

The in-built agenda on government procurement in services has been interpreted differently by developed and developing countries. Developed countries aim at pursuing multilateral disciplines on the general principles of non-discrimination (most-favoured nation and national treatment) and market access applied to government procurement in services, while developing countries perceive that those issues are explicitly outside the mandate, and that transparency in government procurement of services should be handled as part of the Singapore issues negotiations.

Autonomous liberalization

The GATS requires a method to be established by which Members would obtain recognition for liberalization undertaken autonomously. In March 2003, the Council on Trade in Services approved a method to be applied in the current round of negotiations. Credits for unilateral liberalizing efforts would be granted through bilateral negotiations. Unilateral liberalization measures would be assessed based on both qualitative and quantitative approaches. Criteria for evaluation of the autonomous liberalization include the extent of sectoral coverage, the liberalizing nature of the measure (its impact on market access, elimination of measures inconsistent with most-favoured nation and national treatment), its duration and economic significance. Credits granted for unilateral liberalizing effort can take several forms, including a liberalizing measure taken by a trading partner of the Member, or refraining from pursuing a request to the liberalizing Member, or any other measure agreed upon in bilateral negotiations.

Special treatment for LDCs

Methods for ensuring special and differential treatment of LDCs in services liberalization were adopted by the Council on Trade in Services on 3 September 2003. Examples include flexibility to open fewer sectors and liberalize fewer types of transactions. LDCs are not expected to make full national treatment commitments or to respond to the requests for 'additional commitments' that would stretch their administrative and institutional capacity. Other Members are encouraged to engage in capacity building and technical assistance activities in order to facilitate LDCs' engagement in international trade in services and to strengthen their domestic services capacity, both in terms of capital, infrastructure and human resources. Members are also requested to extend commitments to market access in mode 4 — the movement of natural persons — as requested by LDCs.

Movement of natural persons

Lack of commitments by developed countries to liberalize mode 4 has become a matter of frustration for developing countries. Proposals on domestic regulation by Japan and the European Union received criticism from several developing countries for avoiding discussion of mode 4 and relevant domestic regulation concerning visa procedures and requirements. Mode 4 liberalization sought by developing countries covers not only professional services providers but also less skilled services persons. Developing countries perceive that there are enormous economic benefits from freeing the movement of labour between developed and developing countries.

Analysis of the effects of liberalizing the temporary movement of natural persons is provided in Chanda (2001), Winters *et al.* (2003) and

OECD (2003). Using the GTAP model, Winters *et al.* (2003) estimate that an increase in inflow of temporary skilled and unskilled foreign workers from developing countries, equivalent to three per cent of total labour force of the developed countries, would generate an increase in the world welfare of US$ 156 billion a year, shared between developed and developing countries. Notably, the largest gains to both developed and developing countries are attributed to the liberalization of restrictions on unskilled rather than skilled labour.

Chanda (2001) and Winters *et al.* (2003) discuss the major impediments to mode 4 trade in services. They are:

- lack of transparency in regulation, licensing and work permits/visa arrangements for foreign service providers;
- recognition of qualifications, work experience and training;
- differential treatment of foreign service providers; and
- Economic Needs Test applied to foreign workers/service providers.

Current GATS commitments in mode 4 are horizontal, mostly restricted to intra-company transferees, managers and specialists employed by a foreign service provider operating through commercial presence. Developing countries would like to see the issue delinked from commercial presence and with less of a bias towards high-skilled occupations. They proposed to introduce a model schedule for mode 4 commitments that would include new categories of service providers such as contractual services suppliers and independent professionals. It is proposed that existing horizontal commitments on mode 4 be strengthened with sector-specific commitments in the modes where trade in mode 4 is predominant and further liberalization is sought (eg professional and business services).

Administrative impediments to mode 4 trade include lack of transparency and procedural hurdles in obtaining visas and working permits. It has been proposed by the developing countries that a special 'GATS visa' should be introduced to streamline temporary movement of services providers. Economic Needs Tests have been criticized as artificial barriers preventing free movement of labour. Lack of recognition of qualifications and prior experience affects movement of skilled labour significantly. Progress in domestic regulation may be helpful in addressing this issue in relation to mode 4.

In summary, negotiations on market access and rule-making in services have yet to fulfil the mandate of the Doha Development Agenda. Given apparent lack of consensus within the WTO currently on other major items such as agriculture, cotton and the Singapore issues, opinions were voiced that perhaps there should be a departure from a Single Undertaking approach and a move towards creating substructure within the WTO, to allow those prepared to take extra steps towards liberalization to bind them in a plurilateral agreement, creating a 'WTO I' and 'WTO II' structure (EC 2003). Whether such a structure would be consistent with the Doha Development Agenda remains open to debate. In particular, moving services out of the Single Undertaking could set an unfortunate precedent, while the benefits would be minor so long as negotiations yielded only standstill offers.

8.5 Regional Initiatives — Preferential Trading Arrangements

Since the stalling of WTO negotiations in Cancun, major players including the United States have stated their intention to pursue trade liberalization through formal Preferential Trading Arrangements (PTAs) on either a bilateral or plurilateral basis.

The economic analysis of PTAs in goods trade challenges the presumption that they are a step in the right direction.[6] It concludes that although PTAs ease one economic distortion, namely, the average tariff on imports in general, they exacerbate another, namely, the geographical disparity in import tariffs. This is a classic situation of 'second best', with no clear presumption in favour of gains to either PTA members or the world as a whole.

---

[6] The seminal work is Viner (1950). Other early contributions came from Gehrels, (1957), Lipsey (1957), (1958), Johnson (1960), Mundell (1964), Corden (1972) and Riezman (1979). Comprehensive surveys of the literature are available in Baldwin and Venables (1995), Pomfret (1997), Bhagwati, Krishna and Panagariya (1999) and Panagariya (2000), among others. Two recent policy-oriented reviews are by the WTO (1995) and the World Bank (2000).

As noted earlier, Fink and Mattoo (2002) have argued that the PTA route is more likely to lead to economic gains for services trade than for goods trade. But there is still the possibility of second best welfare losses under the following combination of circumstances:

- *Preferential liberalization.* Note that not all services trade barriers are amenable to liberalization on a preferential basis. For example, undertakings to more strongly enforce intellectual property rights, or to establish competition policy law, cannot be made on a preferential basis.
- *A trading partner who is not world's best producer of the particular service.*
- *Liberalization of measures that are tariff-like.* As noted above, not all services trade barriers fall into this category. And as Baldwin (1994) has shown, liberalization of cost-escalating trade barriers is always welfare enhancing, even if the trade partner is not the least cost supplier.

Preferential liberalization of tariff-like measures with a trade partner who is not the world's most efficient producer is problematic because a country can lose all the rents from the trade barriers, without receiving adequate compensation in the form of lower prices to consumers. This is the essence of the trade diversion problem in services. This loss could be offset if there was a sufficiently higher volume of trade with the new trade partner than with the old, so that the triangle gains in producer and consumer surplus from the higher trade volume offset the uncompensated loss of rents — trade creation could outweigh trade diversion. But the outcome is ambiguous.

Adams *et al.* (2003) have examined the effects of the trade and non-trade provisions of 18 extant PTAs on bilateral trade and foreign direct investment flows of a number of countries over the period 1970–97 (for trade) and 1988–97 (for investment). It was not possible to examine the effects of services trade provisions on services trade flows directly, because no comprehensive bilateral services trade data exist. But the effects on investment flows are suggestive because as Karsenty (2000) notes, a significant proportion of foreign direct investment is in services industries, supporting trade via commercial presence.

Adams *et al.* confirm that the traditional merchandise trade provisions governing agricultural and industrial goods have tended to cause net trade diversion. Of the 18 agreements studied in detail, 12 had diverted more trade from non-members than they had created among members. What is more, some of the apparently quite liberal PTAs — including EU, NAFTA and Mercosur — had failed to create significant additional trade among members (relative to the average trade changes registered among countries in the sample).

Part of the reason for the more negative finding than in previous studies was the more rigorous statistical test that was applied to ascertain whether intra-bloc trade was significantly greater after bloc formation (or expansion) than before. In the past, this was assessed, at best, only by reference to point estimates from various cross sections. But the finding is also consistent with the observation that many of the provisions needed in preferential arrangements to underpin and enforce their preferential nature — such as rules of origin — are in practice quite trade restricting.

The paper also examined the scant theoretical literature on the possible effects of non-merchandise trade provisions, including those on services, investment, competition policy, government procurement, intellectual property rights, and the temporary and permanent movement of people. While the paper noted some of the above reasons why conventional concerns about trade diversion may be less important for services than for goods trade, it also noted circumstances where concerns remained.

First, in an increasingly integrated world economy, even minor *trade* concessions could have a significant impact on *investment* flows. And if investment was attracted into one PTA partner in order to serve the markets of the others, then the trade from such 'beachhead' positions could constitute traditional trade diversion.

Second, the *non-trade* provisions of PTAs, particularly those related to investment and services, could also have a significant impact on *investment* flows. But the preferential nature of the PTA provisions could mean that investment was diverted from a low-cost to a higher-cost host country, and such investment diversion could also be harmful.[7]

The analysis in Adams *et al.* (2003) is among the first to check these propositions empirically. It found little evidence of beachhead investment, or an unwinding of 'tariff-jumping' investment, in response to the trade provisions of PTAs. In an update by Dee and Gali (2005), only for SPARTECA and the Andean Pact was there (weak) evidence of foreign direct investment responding in beachhead fashion to trade provisions. And only for EFTA and CER was there some evidence of an unwinding of tariff jumping investment.

There was evidence that foreign direct investment responded significantly to the non-trade provisions of PTAs. And in five of the nine PTAs examined by Dee and Gali for investment effects, the non-trade provisions led to net investment creation.

Although it was a weak test, this suggested that on balance, the non-trade provisions of these PTAs had created an efficient geographic distribution of FDI. This was consistent with the fact that at least some of the non-trade provisions were not strongly preferential in their nature. And if the non-trade barriers were cost-escalating rather than rent-creating, then preferential liberalization would be beneficial, even in the absence of net investment creation.

However, the trade that may have been generated from the new FDI positions may still have been diverted in the 'wrong' direction in response to the trade provisions of PTAs, and may therefore have contributed to the net trade diversion found in the paper.

There are additional cautions about the finding that the services and other non-trade provisions of PTAs are more likely to be beneficial than the merchandise trade provisions.

The first is the objection by Fink and Mattoo (2002, p. 3) that the sequence of liberalization matters more in services trade than it does in the case of goods trade:

> In particular, the benefits of eventual non-preferential liberalization may be different if it is preceded by preferential liberalization. This is because location-specific sunk costs of production are important in many services, so even

---

[7] This issue is examined empirically in Dee (2008b).

temporary privileged access for an inferior supplier can translate into a long-term advantage in the market. Thus, while the elimination of preferences may lead to a relatively painless switch to more efficient sources of goods supply, the entry of more efficient service providers may be durably deterred if their competitive advantage does not offset the advantages conferred by incumbency.

A second objection comes from several recent papers on the game theoretic nature of trade reform, which examine whether preferential liberalization is indeed likely to be followed by non-preferential liberalization.

Some partial answers to these questions were provided by Krugman (1993), Deardorff and Stern (1994), Baldwin, (1996), Levy (1997) and Krishna (1998). The most recent, comprehensive analyses by Zissimos and Vines (2000) and Andriamananjara (2002) acknowledge that joining a PTA may be the best safe-haven strategy when other countries are doing so. But they find that since PTA membership confers a terms of trade gain to members at the expense of non-members, at least some members will be better off limiting PTA membership than allowing expansion to cover the world as a whole. These are further developments of the arguments about the negative externalities from terms of trade changes developed by Bond and Syropoulos (1996) and Bagwell and Staiger (1998, 1999), among others.

In a sense, the situation is worse than a true prisoners' dilemma. In a prisoners' dilemma, every country would be made worse off by non-cooperative behaviour, so every country would have an incentive to agree in the WTO to instead act cooperatively. The findings of Zissimos and Vines (2000) and Andriamananjara (2002) suggest that at least some countries are better off acting non-cooperatively towards third parties in preferential arrangements than they are acting cooperatively in seeking multilateral free trade. The finding casts doubt on the likelihood of successful redesign of the WTO rules disciplining the formation of PTAs.

A final caution is that the theoretical literature on PTAs assumes that the preferential liberalization removes all trade barriers against PTA partners. The WTO rules do contain a requirement that in PTAs among developed countries, 'duties and other restrictive regulations of commerce' should be eliminated on 'substantially all trade' in goods.

The vagueness of this provision imposes little discipline, with PTAs as long-standing as the EU agreement containing significant exclusions for significant periods of time.

The GATS agreement contains a similar article V for services requiring 'substantial sectoral coverage', and the 'absence or elimination of substantially all discrimination'. However, the article contains no requirements with respect to non-discriminatory market access restrictions nor domestic regulatory regimes. In effect, this sanctions services provisions in PTAs that are explicitly about the redistribution of rents, rather than the introduction of additional competition to a sector. Under these circumstances, it is not surprising that PTA forums have been no more successful that the WTO in achieving significant services trade liberalization, as Sauvé (2002) finds. But what is more, conceding to PTA provisions of this nature is unlikely to be the best safe-haven strategy under any circumstance.

A concrete example is provided by the requests made by the United States in audio-visual services in recent PTAs. These have focused on freeing up local content requirements. But the broadcasting sectors in many countries are typically the subject of a much broader range of anti-competitive regulation than that. Further, some argue that there is a legitimate market failure rationale for local content regulation, at least in culturally sensitive sectors such as drama, documentaries and children's broadcasting. A Productivity Commission study of the Australian broadcasting industry (PC 2000) identified a number of additional entry barriers, including:

- the profligate allocation of spectrum to incumbents, limiting that available to new entrants;
- a regulatory ban on the entry of new television stations until 2006;
- controls on foreign ownership;
- cross-media rules preventing mergers between traditional media businesses of newspapers and free to air commercial radio and television, which prevented undue concentration in old media businesses, but did nothing about the new; and
- 'anti-siphoning' rules, designed to ensure free to air coverage of major sporting events and preventing their migration to pay

television, but having the perverse effect of reducing rather than increasing total customer access to broadcast sport.

In the absence of measures to liberalize some of these more fundamental restrictions on competition, Australia's relaxation of its local content restrictions would risk handing rents to foreign media producers without offsetting benefits to the Australian viewing public. And if Australians are ever to be persuaded to dismantle the additional barriers to competition in broadcasting, with the disruption to incumbents that this would cause, it is likely to be because they are persuaded of significant benefits to the Australian viewing public in terms of lower costs and greater diversity, not because of a relaxation of beef quotas into the United States.

8.6 Other Regional Initiatives

Not all regional initiatives are preferential — Asia Pacific Economic Cooperation (APEC) is an example of a non-preferential trade arrangement. APEC members are to liberalize on a most-favoured nation basis so that non-APEC members will also receive equal access to APEC markets. This is in sharp contrast to a traditional Free Trade Agreement or customs union, which are preferential in nature.

In principle, APEC goes beyond WTO commitments, but is non-binding to members. Its major principle is unilateral reforms. Members have endorsed the common liberalization targets, and have full autonomy over the reform path pursued to meet these common goals (the 'concerted unilateralism' effort). Much of the APEC agenda focuses on encouraging members to voluntarily enhance their WTO commitments in both goods and services.

Several APEC initiatives illustrate how voluntary cooperation in the area of professional standards and recognition of qualifications and experience may contribute to liberalization of movement of professionals within the region. These programs include the APEC Business Travel Card and APEC Engineer.

The APEC Business Travel Card program has been developed to facilitate movement of business persons travelling frequently to conduct trade and investment activities in APEC economies by providing pre-cleared entry to participating economies as well as streamlined immigration control on arrival. Currently there are fourteen APEC economies participating in the scheme,[8] although the eligibility criteria are sufficiently tight and advantages offered sufficiently few that there are few individual card holders.

The APEC Engineer program has been established in eleven APEC member economies[9] to facilitate cross-border mobility of professional engineers. Effectively there is an international standard established for accreditation of the engineering teaching programs and recognition of degrees and experience. An agreement on mutual recognition of engineering qualifications was signed in 1989 (the Washington Accord). The Washington Accord and the Engineering Mobility Forum are distinct from the APEC Engineer initiative but closely involved in coordination and mutual harmonization of professional standards. Each participating economy maintains its own APEC Engineer Register. In August 2003, there were 467 members on the Australian Engineer Register, representing less than 5 per cent of those registered with the National Professional Engineers Register (NPER) but, according to NPER, there is a keen interest among the export-oriented engineering professionals to join the APEC Engineer Register.

Several APEC member economies have recently expressed interest in liberalizing trade in health services, including mode 4 — movement of health services providers. Major impediments to the movement of professional health services providers (medical practitioners, dentists and nurses) are:

- registration and licensing requirements and procedures for foreign-trained medical practitioners, including fees;
- lack of agreement on mutual recognition of medical degrees;

---

[8] Australia, Brunei, Chile, China, Hong Kong, Indonesia, Japan, Korea, Malaysia, New Zealand, Peru, Philippines, Chinese Taipei, and Thailand.

[9] Australia, Canada, Hong Kong, Indonesia, Japan, Korea, Malaysia, New Zealand, Peru, Thailand and the United States.

- limitations on the ability of foreign-trained practitioners to attract public/private insurance benefits;
- limitations on the mobility of locally trained medical practitioners (eg requirement to serve a certain time after graduation in certain areas, quotas); and
- limitations on the mobility of foreign trained practitioners (eg economic needs test in granting work permits to foreign doctors, dentists and nurses, quotas).

Many developing countries are looking at health tourism as a major export growth area. Singapore has announced its ambition to become a healthcare hub in Asia, planning to secure 2 per cent of the Asian healthcare market by 2007, increasing to 3 per cent by 2012 (Sidorenko and Findlay 2003). In Malaysia, another exporter of health tourism, foreign fee-paying patients represented 4.5 per cent of total patients in 2001. Other countries such as the Philippines and Indonesia have abundant human resources and are becoming the major source countries for trained nurses, recruited not only within the region but also in Europe and North America.

The APEC Group on Services is discussing a proposal by Indonesia to develop APEC professional standards for nursing, in order to facilitate the movement of professional nurses within APEC. Harmonization of nursing standards has been implemented in Caribbean, and in East, Central and Southern Africa. The International Council of Nurses has been involved in developing Competencies for the Generalist Nurse, and is planning to develop further standards for the Family Nurse. Internationally accepted standards provide a useful benchmark for the local professional nursing bodies and contribute to the process of harmonization. An alternative route to harmonization of standards (which is often criticized for yielding the 'lowest common denominator' level of standard) is through Mutual Recognition Agreements concluded between like countries, such as those existing in the European Union and the Trans-Tasman Mutual Recognition Arrangement between Australia and New Zealand. It is worth noting that even in like economies such as

Australia and New Zealand, complete harmonization of standards has not been achieved, not even at a national level.[10]

In summary, there is a scope for non-preferential regional trade arrangements to provide useful testing grounds for exploring liberalizing steps that can be further extended on a most favoured nation basis and bound in the WTO. As discussed earlier, the proposal for the 'GATS visa' matches the existing APEC Business Travel Card program, although the eligibility criteria for the proposed GATS visa are less demanding than those in the APEC program. Similarly, development of common APEC standards for professional training and core competencies (such as for engineers and perhaps nurses) creates opportunities for internationalization of standards and hence, for removing one of the significant barriers to the mobility of professional services providers.

8.7 Back to Basics — Services Trade Liberalization as Domestic Microeconomic Reform

The above review of achievements in various forums suggests that progress on services trade liberalization in multilateral and plurilateral forums has been disappointing, except where the plurilateral initiatives have been voluntary and non-preferential. To some commentators, this has spelt disenchantment with either WTO or PTA forums, as they are currently constructed, as means of achieving liberalization. And they have looked to reforms of the rules governing those forums as a possible solution.

But as this chapter has argued, the fundamental problem is not with the architecture of the GATS or the nature of the WTO rules disciplining the formation of PTAs. The fundamental problem is that the logic for reciprocity in services trade liberalization is absent — or is at least substantially weaker than for goods trade.

A recent paper by Dee and Nguyen-Hong (2003) reviewed the Australian experience with domestic microeconomic reform in four key

---

[10] An update on the regulations affecting trade in health services in ASEAN countries is given in Dee (2013a).

infrastructure sectors — financial services, communications, air transport and maritime. It catalogued the policy reforms of the 1980s and 1990s under three headings now familiar from the GATS — market access measures, national treatment measures, and domestic regulatory reforms. The breakdown in terms of numbers of pages was instructive — just over half the measures were domestic regulatory reforms, involving overhauls of prudential regulation, establishment of access regimes for essential infrastructure, and so on. One third were market access measures increasing the contestability of markets. And only one sixth were the national treatment measures that are the 'bread and butter' of the current generation of trade negotiators, whose training has typically been in the field of goods trade.

And what is significant, these Australian reforms were achieved unilaterally, under the rubric of domestic microeconomic reform. The Australian political process delivered these reforms because Australians were persuaded that they were in the best interests of the majority of Australians, and that the adjustment costs on those harmed by the reforms could be accommodated by existing social safety nets, by phasing, or occasionally by special adjustment assistance arrangements.

In part, Australia had no choice but to take the unilateral route, because until recently its main trade negotiating interest — agriculture — was off the negotiating table at the WTO. But it is doubtful that Australia would have achieved the same microeconomic reforms just because of the arm-twisting of trade partners.

And it is hard to imagine how it could have been in Australia's trading partners' interests to sequence the reforms in the best way for Australians. In some industries, such as telecommunications, the reform sequence has been particularly long and complex. The establishment of an access regime for essential infrastructure has required the dismantling of retail price regulation in telecommunications, so as to allow for reasonable subscriber access charges, in addition to use-based call charges. This is because only when incumbents are covering the cost of the essential facility — the local loop — from subscribers in this way will they be willing to make it available to competitors on reasonable terms. But dismantling retail price regulation has required the establishment of alternative means to achieve the policy objective it was designed to deliver — universal service to all Australians at the same price, regardless of cost. Universal service is now funded via a financial contribution from all carriers, rather than from cross-subsidies built into the incumbent's retail price regime. The WTO reference paper on telecommunications recognizes the need for cost-based access regimes for essential infrastructure. But it is silent on these sequencing issues, which need to be worked out within each economy.

This chapter is not arguing to take services trade liberalization out of the WTO. But it is arguing that the slow progress in that forum is simply to be expected. Some economies have a long way to go in implementing the appropriate domestic regulatory regimes and increasing the general contestability of the market. It is critical that they do this before offering up their national treatment restrictions to negotiation — otherwise, they are risking handing economic rents to foreigners for no return.

It is also critical that they win the regulatory reform debate internally, rather than via arm-twisting from trade partners.[11] For while trade partners may have a common view about outcomes, they need not always have a common view about sequencing and the need for collateral reforms elsewhere. So what is required in the short term is capacity building to help economies win the internal debate. Only then should these economies be expected to come to the negotiating table to offer up their national treatment barriers in a multilateral forum. And in the meantime, they need to recognize many PTA proposals for what they are — proposals to redistribute rents, rather than to assist in genuine services trade liberalization.

---

[11] Chapters 12 and 13 of this volume survey some of the domestic reform debates in East and South Asia, and consider the institutional mechanisms that have helped to ensure that those domestic reforms have occurred.

Chapter 9

Services: A 'Deal-maker' in the Doha Round?[1]

Philippa Dee and Christopher Findlay

9.1 Introduction

Progress in the Doha Round of trade negotiations requires leadership — not just from the negotiators at the World Trade Organization (WTO) but also from the national capitals where trade policy strategy is constructed. This chapter focuses on the weight that policy strategists might put on services and the manner in which services negotiations should be treated.

There have been reports that 'services *demandeurs* [the countries making requests] such as the US, the EU, and Japan... emphasise in Davos that services trade is a critical component of the overall market access negotiations' and that they have called on other WTO members to put more effort into 'fleshing out commitments in services trade'.[2] This reinforces the value of an examination of how services might be treated.

To date, trade negotiators have been stuck on the more familiar territory of issues concerning goods markets. As a result, they have let services negotiations become a hostage to negotiations in agriculture. The lack of progress in the latter may be an excuse, but it has also probably come as a relief to services negotiators. They would, in any

---

[1] This is an edited version of Chapter 3 in Bruce Blonigen (2008), *Monitoring International Trade Policy: A New Agenda for Reviving the Doha Round*, Kiel: Kiel Institute for the World Economy and London: Centre for Economic Policy Research: 49–63.
[2] *Bridges Weekly Trade News Digest* 11:2 (24 January 2007) and 11:4 (7 February 2007).

case, be constrained by other concerns about the potential effects of freeing up services trade and investment.

To some extent, these concerns relate to the non-economic implications of services reform and the 'rules' applying in services transactions. These were among the topics of a 'mini cluster' of services meetings held in the last week of February 2007.

But while disciplines on domestic regulation, subsidies and government procurement are important, they are not a fundamental issue. Nor is the concern with how to preserve non-economic objectives in policy-making, given that a continuing 'right to regulate' and a 'carve-out' or exemption of public sector services have been acknowledged.

It is more likely that the main issue of substance — at least for the developing countries — is the lack of capacity to respond to domestic political concerns about foreign penetration and establishment of operations in local services markets. These also contribute to demands for 'safeguard' mechanisms.

There has been a lack of progress in services despite the demonstrable gains that would arise from services reform. In that sense, negotiators have cut themselves loose from their national interests. A reorientation is now critical.

At the same time, with the slow progress being made in the WTO, negotiators have embarked on a series of bilateral and preferential trade agreements (PTAs). Through these channels, they have been able to offer their political masters a new portfolio of their services. Since these preferential negotiations have proliferated, they also demand attention, and their interaction with the WTO process has to be explored, particularly with respect to services.

This chapter offers a framework for dealing with the main sticking point: the concern about foreign participation in local services markets. It argues the case for taking a wider view of reform, rather than simply focusing on the conditions of foreign entry, a perspective that has blocked progress to date.

This perspective leads to specific recommendations for the application of WTO processes to services reform, and to a strategy for the treatment of services in the negotiations, including their relationship to negotiations in other sectors.

The next two sections examine the nature of services trade barriers and the empirical evidence on their impact. The main interest is in services traded across borders or via the establishment of an operation in another country.[3] The following section examines the prospects for services negotiations in the Doha Round, concluding that:

- Services is not likely to be a 'deal-maker' in the WTO — but nor is it a good idea for services to break away from the 'single undertaking' principle (currently understood to require all WTO members to sign up to all new agreements) and 'go it alone', despite the superficial appeal of this option.
- It is important to recognize that the big gains from services reform are in market access and especially domestic regulation, *not* in national treatment.
- The main value of using the WTO framework is to further the domestic reform agenda of each country.

The chapter therefore ends with the observation that 'the question is not what services can do for the WTO and its negotiations, but what the WTO and its principles can do for services reform.'

9.2 The Nature of Services Trade Barriers

When services are traded, the transaction typically occurs 'behind the border', through a foreign establishment or a transaction with a visiting consumer. Even when cross-border trade takes place via e-commerce, it is not easily observed by customs officials.

So how does protection work in the services sector? Such transactions are not amenable to border protection. Instead, services trade barriers are typically behind-the-border, non-price regulatory measures. These may be of two types:

---

[3] There are many important issues associated with the movement of people, but these issues impinge on immigration policy as much as on services trade policy, and should probably be addressed as such.

- They may specifically discriminate against *foreign* suppliers — either against their entry or against the nature and scope of their operations once they have entered the market.
- They may protect incumbent service providers by discriminating against *all* new suppliers, be they domestic or foreign — either by restricting entry or by restricting the nature and scope of new entrants' operations.

The General Agreement on Trade in Services (GATS) under the WTO recognizes that services trade barriers need not be discriminatory against foreigners. It recognizes a specific list of (mostly quantitative) restrictions on market access that are not discriminatory, and are to be the subject of negotiation.

Many research studies on the effects of services trade barriers have extended the definition of market access to cover all measures that are non-discriminatory (for example, Findlay and Warren 2000). The GATS also recognizes 'derogations from national treatment', meaning discriminatory restrictions.

Thus, a key feature of services trade barriers is that they often protect incumbent service suppliers from any competition, be it domestic or foreign new entrants. This has implications both for the economic effects of services trade liberalization, and for the political economy of services trade reform.

Services are also an area where market failures can occur. For example:

- 'Natural monopoly' is a characteristic of some network industries: it may be economically inefficient to have key 'bottleneck' facilities provided by more than one service provider, so regulation is required to prevent the abuse of this monopoly power.
- 'Information asymmetry' is almost by definition a feature of professional services: the client is not in a position to judge whether the service being delivered is of reasonable quality, so licensing or accreditation requirements can help to bridge the information gap.

- Similarly, there is a legitimate role for prudential regulation of financial services to ensure systemic stability, and for safety regulation in air passenger transport.

The GATS recognizes the right of individual governments to regulate: non-economic objectives can be pursued, for example, through universal service obligations; and services provided by governments can be quarantined.

But the GATS also requires that domestic regulatory regimes be the 'least burdensome' necessary to achieve their objectives. This provides a further WTO discipline on non-discriminatory measures that fall outside the narrow scope of GATS market access commitments, although the discipline is rather loose, especially since the definition of 'least burdensome' has yet to be decided by WTO members.[4]

While services are typically not protected by tariffs, services trade barriers may or may not be tariff-like, in the following sense. Some regulatory trade restrictions, particularly quantitative restrictions, create artificial scarcity. The prices of services are inflated, not because the real resource cost of producing them has gone up, but because incumbent firms are able to earn economic 'rents'. These are akin to a tax, but with the revenue flowing to the incumbent rather than to government.

Liberalization of these barriers would yield relatively small gains associated with better resource allocation, but they would also have redistributive effects associated with the elimination of rents to incumbents. Such rent-creating restrictions are tariff-like, with the redistribution of rent having effects similar to the redistribution of tariff revenue.

Alternatively, services trade restrictions could increase the real resource cost of doing business. An example would be a requirement for foreign services professionals to retrain rather than pass an accreditation process when they have relocated to a new country.

In this case, liberalization would be equivalent to a productivity improvement (saving in real resources), and yield relatively large gains.

---

[4] See the previous chapter of this volume.

This could increase returns for the incumbent service providers, as well as lowering costs for users elsewhere in the economy.

To understand the economic effects of services trade barriers, and to work out policy priorities, it is therefore critical to know three things:

- The 'height' of the trade barrier — the equivalent of the tariff rate in goods trade.
- The 'incidence' of the barrier — whether it applies only to foreign suppliers or also applies to domestic operators.
- The 'impact' of the barrier — whether the barrier has created rents or raised real resource costs.

There is a growing body of research devoted to the first two aspects, but less clarity on the third.[5]

9.3 The Empirical Evidence on Services Trade Barriers

Tariffs come with ready numbers attached — the tariff rate *is* the height of the trade barrier. For services, things are not as simple. Measurement methodologies have needed to take account of the nature of services themselves.

Services are highly differentiated. Not only do they differ from one firm to the next, they also differ from one customer to the next. As Ethier and Horn (1991) note, what makes services special is that they are customized to meet the needs of individual purchasers.

This has meant that the measurement of services trade barriers cannot assume services are homogeneous. Nor is it appropriate to use the price comparisons methodology often used to measure non-tariff barriers in goods trade, since this assumes homogeneity across borders. Strictly speaking, it is not even appropriate to talk about a 'tariff equivalent', since this concept first assumes that services are primarily traded cross-border, and second, it often also assumes that the domestic and foreign service are perfect substitutes.

---

[5] Dee (2013b) gives the most recent comprehensive evidence on these three issues.

Because services trade barriers operate behind the border, research has typically quantified the effects of services trade barriers on some behind-the-border measure of economic performance. And because the counterfactual is unobservable, econometric techniques have been used to construct the counterfactual — what domestic prices or costs would have been in the absence of the services trade restrictions. This chapter draws on the evidence in Dee (2005a).

The height of the barrier

In some services sectors, particularly banking and telecommunications, services trade barriers are typically much higher in developing than in developed countries. In most cases, the remaining barriers in the developed world are low or negligible.

In other services sectors, particularly the professions, the distribution sector (wholesale and retail trade) and electricity generation, the barriers still tend to be higher in developing countries than in developed countries, but the barriers in the latter are often non-trivial:

- Particular developed countries have maintained high barriers to entry and operations in the professions, particularly the accounting and legal professions.
- Some have maintained significant restrictions on the operations of large wholesale and retail chains, either directly or through restrictions on zoning and hours of operation, to protect local 'Mom and Pop' stores.
- Trade barriers are also non-trivial in those developed countries that have yet to open their electricity generation sectors fully to competition.

In some sectors, barriers are as high in the developed world as in the developing world. For more than 50 years, air passenger transport has been governed by a system of bilateral air services arrangements, largely outside the multilateral framework of trading rules. The bilateral system developed because international air flights require international cooperation to provide the necessary infrastructure and air traffic rights.

But the bilateral system has also created various limits on competition and trade in aviation services.

Some economies have recognized the costs of these restrictions in terms of higher costs and prices, and substantially liberalized air service arrangements, or made commitments to do so. There is now an 'open skies' arrangement within Europe, between the United States and a number of partner countries, and increasingly elsewhere. But on bilateral routes still governed by traditional air services agreements, the restrictions are as high for developed as for developing countries.

For a few services sectors, the barriers are higher in at least some developed countries than in some developing countries. Maritime is a prime example. The United States maintains stringent cabotage restrictions, exempts liner shipping conferences from the normal disciplines of competition policy, and maintains a range of other restrictions, including on hiring foreign crews and on shipping non-commercial cargoes. Its trade barriers in maritime are estimated to be higher than in Latin America and most of Asia (McGuire, Schuele and Smith 2000).

Given these services trade barriers in developed countries, it is perhaps no coincidence that air passenger transport is carved out of the GATS, while maritime is an area where negotiations have tried and failed.

The incidence of the barrier

There is more variability among both developed and developing countries in whether barriers discriminate against foreign services providers or also affect domestic operators:

- In particular sectors, some developing countries maintain high barriers that are also strongly discriminatory against foreign operators, for example, banking in Malaysia and telecommunications in Thailand.
- In other sectors, barriers are lower but also strongly discriminatory, for example, banking in Thailand.

- In other countries, barriers tend to be both lower and less discriminatory, for example, the banking and telecommunications sectors in Russia, the Baltic states and much of south-eastern Europe.

- In the developed world, trade barriers in banking and telecommunications are sufficiently low on average that any margin of discrimination is also trivial. At the other extreme, barriers in maritime are both high and discriminatory (see Figures 9.1 and 9.2 — Dee 2005a has more results).

- In Europe, the trade barriers in engineering services tend to be non-discriminatory, while those in legal services can be highly discriminatory.

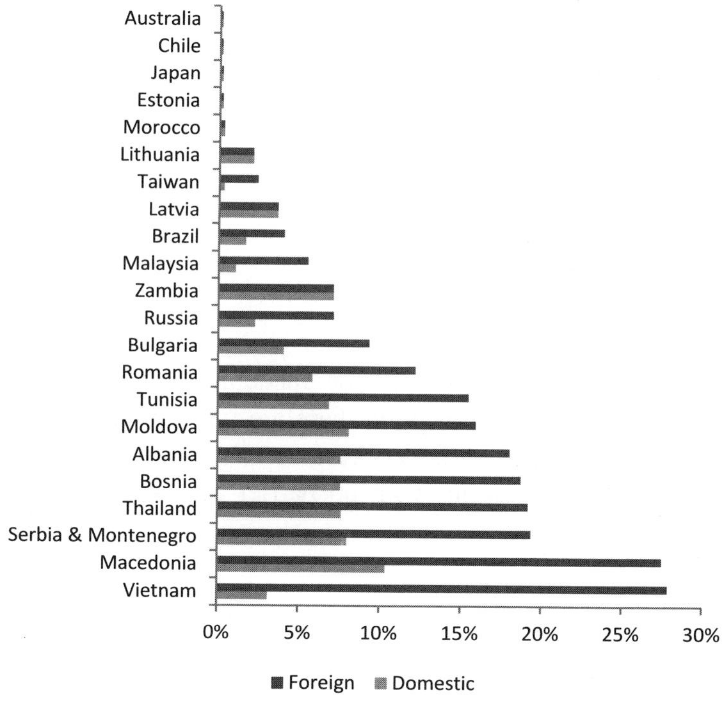

Figure 9.1. The Price Impact of Trade Restrictions for Domestic and Foreign Players in Telecommunications
Source: Dee (2005a).

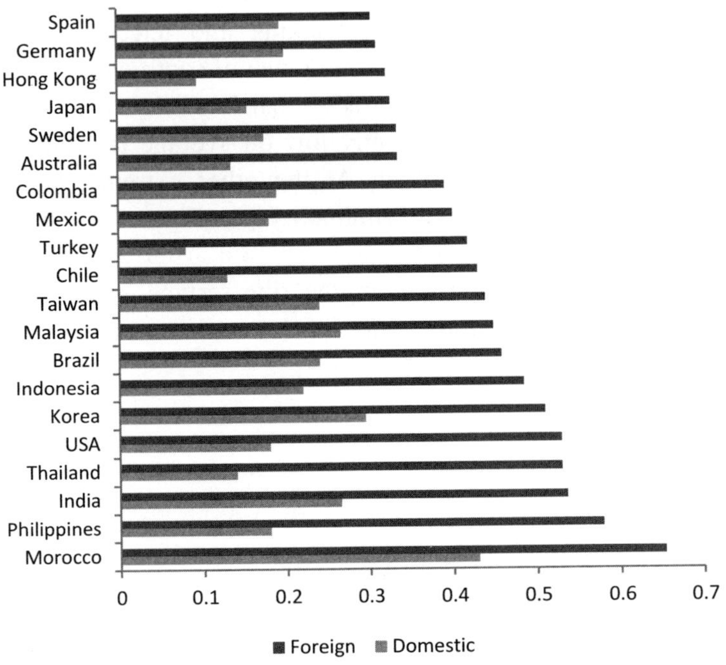

Figure 9.2. Index of Trade Restrictions for Domestic and Foreign Players in Maritime
Source: McGuire, Schuele and Smith (2000).

The one generalization that can be made is that when there are significant barriers to foreign supply, there are typically also non-trivial barriers to domestic supply. It is very rare to have a significant barrier to foreign entry and/or operations with no barrier affecting domestic new entrants.

The impact of the barrier

A critical determinant of the projected gains from services trade liberalization (and the policy priorities that flow from that) is whether the trade barriers are seen as affecting mark-ups or real resource costs. In modelling applications (for example, Dee and Hanslow 2001, Dee *et al.*

2003, Dee 2007 and Copenhagen Economics 2005), this 'treatment effect' can dominate the estimated height of the trade barrier.

Whether barriers create rents or add to resource costs is severely under-researched. In some cases, the empirical evidence is suggestive, but not conclusive, because only one performance measure has been used. In other cases, a price impact is estimated, and then it is simply asserted whether the effect operates through price–cost margins or through real resource costs.

Theory can provide some guidance. Rents are likely to be created by quantitative and other barriers that limit entry (or exit, though this is far less common). Some 'red-tape' measures may add to resource costs. There are also many ways in which rents can be dissipated or capitalized. So non-tariff barriers that may once have been rent-creating for the initial incumbent become cost-escalating for subsequent incumbents.[6]

The limited empirical evidence tends to accord with this intuition.[7] In banking and telecommunications, where explicit barriers to entry are rife, barriers appear to create rents. In distribution services, where indirect trade restrictions also apply, barriers appear to increase costs. In air passenger transport and the professions, barriers appear to have both effects. And theoretical arguments suggest that barriers in maritime and electricity generation primarily affect costs.[8]

9.4 Prospects for Services Negotiations in the WTO

Before turning to specific aspects of the WTO services negotiating processes, it is worth reviewing the rationale for a multilateral approach. One economic reason for negotiating services trade barriers multilaterally rather than liberalizing them on a unilateral basis is if there are benefits from reciprocity *within* the services sector — a country gains

---

[6] For example, Kalirajan (2000) provides indirect evidence that some of the zoning and other restrictions in the wholesale and retail sector have created rents that are subsequently capitalized into the price of commercial land.
[7] Gregan and Johnson (1999), Kalirajan *et al.* (2000), Kalirajan (2000), Nguyen-Hong (2000), OECD (2005c), Copenhagen Economics (2005).
[8] Steiner (2000), Clark *et al.* (2004).

more if other countries also liberalize their services sectors than if it 'goes it alone'.

One reason for there to be benefits from reciprocity within a sector is to offset adverse terms of trade effects (Bagwell and Staiger 1999). In goods trade, while tariff liberalization will provide gains in allocative efficiency, it can also generate a terms of trade loss. So while the world as a whole would be better off, individual countries may not be. Reciprocity creates a countervailing terms of trade effect in the other direction, making it more likely that all countries unambiguously gain. This is the economics underlying the 'mercantilist' approach to goods trade negotiations in the WTO.

But since services trade barriers operate behind the border, services trade reform has its first round effect primarily on domestic prices and costs. If at least some of the barriers are cost-escalating, the resource savings from liberalization are likely to dominate any direct terms of trade effects. And research suggests that services trade reform can often yield an indirect terms of trade gain, rather than a loss (for example, OECD 2004). So the case for reciprocity *within* the services sector is far less strong than it is for goods trade.

This is not to deny that there might be important political economy benefits from proceeding multilaterally. A key benefit from undertaking reform under the multilateral disciplines of the WTO is that the formal bindings provide protection against the risk of policy reversal. So even the current *status quo* offers have value. Furthermore, it is argued that the additional pressure from abroad can help countries to overcome domestic political constraints on reform. But in the area of services, other countries may make demands that are not in the reforming country's best interests.

Are there benefits from reciprocity across sectors?

Although the economic case for taking a multilateral approach to services trade negotiations in the first place is weak, services could still be a deal-maker in the Doha Round. This would require there to be benefits from reciprocity *across* sectors — countries gain more (or lose less) from liberalizing their agriculture and/or manufacturing sectors if services sectors are also liberalized.

One economic reason for there to be benefits from reciprocity across sectors is that by spreading reforms widely, the resulting pressures for structural adjustment can offset each other. The expectation is that services trade reform will lower input costs for agricultural producers in the European Union, cushioning their adjustment costs associated with reductions in agricultural support.

This argument presupposes that if services trade barriers were reduced, then resources would be released from the services sector to be used elsewhere, including in agriculture. This is the basis on which agriculture's own structural adjustment problems would be eased.

If services trade barriers were tariff-like and discriminatory, then a domestic services sector could be expected to shrink as its trade barriers were removed. But if trade barriers also include non-discriminatory barriers affecting any new entrant, then the domestic import-competing industry can be too small, not too big.

Liberalization can encourage additional entry by either wholly domestic firms or foreign multinationals into domestic production, and this can offset additional competition from cross-border trade, to the extent that this is also a feature of the market. Where heavily impeded cross-border trade is relatively unimportant, as Mattoo and Wunsch-Vincent (2004) argue is the case for many services, the size of the domestic industry can be bigger after liberalization than before.

A second reason why a services sector may grow in size when services trade barriers are liberalized is that, according to most input-output tables, the most intensive users of services are other services sectors, not agriculture or manufacturing (Dee *et al.* 2003, OECD 2004). For example, there are typically more telephones in office buildings than in factories.

Modelling results tend to show that the biggest output gains from services trade reform are within the services sector. Anecdotal evidence is also beginning to support this proposition. Members of the Australian Services Roundtable, a newly-formed services industry lobby group, have observed that their biggest customers are also Roundtable members, and they are increasingly seeking liberalization of services sectors overseas to lower their own input costs, rather than to gain market access.

In summary:

- Comprehensive services trade liberalization is unlikely to ease the adjustment pressures associated with agricultural or manufacturing trade liberalization.
- Hence the economic case for services to be a deal-maker in the Doha Round is weak.

Does this mean that services should break away from the single undertaking and 'go it alone' in the WTO? This is the inclination of some services trade negotiators who are frustrated at being held hostage to the negotiations on agriculture.

Some commentators have argued that this approach is not likely to yield much, since the 'ongoing' services negotiations that took place prior to the launch of the Doha Round (an earlier example of a stand-alone approach) yielded little. This comparison is probably unfair. It is likely that services industry groups in many countries are now much further up the learning curve, with a better appreciation of where their negotiating interests lie, and are now better able to articulate their interests through the trade negotiations than they were before.

But more recent experiences with services trade negotiations hint at something more fundamentally wrong. Following the 2005 ministerial conference in Hong Kong, there was a flurry of activity in the first part of 2006, as services trade negotiators convened for 'plurilateral' market access negotiations, a break from the more traditional bilateral request-and-offer approach. The talks were described as 'extremely positive' by Hamid Abdel-Mamdouh, the director of the WTO's services division.

Yet the reasons for the positive assessment were telling. The *demandeur* countries were pleased that the negotiations on the collective requests were not as contentious as many had feared. And some of the members that received requests felt they had been able to take advantage of the plurilateral approach to strengthen 'defensive' stances in areas where they were reluctant to increase their commitments to liberalization. This prompted one observer to call the plurilateral approach a 'toothless process'.[9]

Such reactions suggest that members see the services negotiations as a 'zero-sum game' — where what is a gain for one side must be a loss for the other — rather than a positive-sum game with the potential for a 'win-win' outcome. So long as this is a common view, then questions about whether services should go it alone or whether negotiations should be bilateral or plurilateral within the WTO framework are second-order questions.

The perception of the negotiations as a zero-sum game arises from a preoccupation with national treatment in services trade negotiations, rather than market access or domestic regulatory reform. But until this fundamental imbalance is addressed, there would be little use in services breaking away from the single undertaking and going it alone, despite the superficial appeal of this option.

Are services negotiations a zero-sum or positive-sum game?[10]

It is worth examining the evidence from services trade negotiations in PTAs since, in the absence of progress in the WTO, this is where services trade negotiators have been plying their trade. While many PTAs go further than the GATS, they have tended to be selective in two important ways:

- They have tended to be preferential, even in the provisions that go beyond goods trade.
- They have tended to target only those provisions that explicitly discriminate against foreigners.

There are strong political economy explanations for both of these outcomes.

With some exceptions, recent PTAs have tended to do one of two things in new areas like services — either bind the *status quo* or make

---

[9] *Bridges Weekly Trade News Digest* 10:13 (12 April 2006).
[10] Parts of this section are taken from Dee (2007).

concessions on a preferential basis, even when logic suggests they could sensibly be made non-preferentially.[11]

One very clear reason for this outcome is that countries with strong 'offensive' interests in the Doha Round are unlikely to give away negotiating power by making defensive concessions on a non-preferential basis within a PTA, prior to a Doha Round settlement. This reason for selectivity need not apply in the WTO itself. But other reasons for selectivity apply in both forums.[12]

Partly because they have been preferential, recent PTAs have tended to target only those provisions that explicitly discriminate against foreigners. This is because, in many cases, the only provisions that can feasibly be liberalized on a preferential basis are those that discriminate against foreigners.[13]

But even without this feasibility constraint, there are economic and political economy forces that tend to limit concessions within PTAs to those that explicitly discriminate against foreigners. The central one is the threat to sovereignty that is felt most strongly by countries when contemplating making reforms to non-discriminatory domestic regulatory regimes as part of a trade agreement. To many countries, both developed and developing, this may be viewed as too much of a threat to the 'right to regulate'.

Negotiating 'modalities' have also contributed a focus on provisions that explicitly discriminate against foreigners, not just in PTAs but also

---

[11] For example, two of Australia's concessions in the Australia–United States free trade agreement were the lifting of Foreign Investment Review Board screening on inward foreign direct investment in non-sensitive sectors, and a commitment to provisions similar to those in the WTO agreement on government procurement. Both measures were made preferentially, even though the arguments advanced by the Australian government would have applied *a fortiori* to non-preferential liberalization.

[12] Two statements often heard from trade negotiators are that they 'do not want to give away negotiating coin' and that 'they are not in the business of negotiating on behalf of other countries'. This latter sentiment in particular places the imperative on ensuring that trade concessions in PTAs are restricted to being preferential, even when economic arguments suggest that a country could gain more from making them on a non-preferential basis.

[13] The converse does not hold. Because some provisions do discriminate against foreigners, it does not mean that they can be liberalized on a preferential basis. For example, when countries liberalize restrictions on foreign ownership, it may be very difficult to ensure that the new foreign owners are only from selected partner countries.

in the WTO. The request-and-offer modality is currently being used in the Doha negotiations on services, and is the means by which many PTAs are negotiated.

Under this modality, countries are asked to contemplate, not just reforms that are in their own best interests, but reforms that are in their trading partners' best interests. It will tend to be in a trading partner's best interests to target only those provisions that explicitly discriminate against foreigners — in this way, the foreign market share is maximized. Foreign producers would generally have little interest in unleashing competition from promising domestic new entrants. They would rather join a cartel on a far more selective basis! And in these circumstances, the liberalizing countries risk simply handing monopoly rents to foreigners. Indeed, this is the basis of the East Asian desire to have safeguard provisions in services negotiations.

A further consideration is one of visibility. Regulatory regimes are always complex, and often not very transparent to insiders, let alone outsiders. The regulations that will tend to be visible to potential foreign entrants are those that discriminate against foreigners.

A final consideration is the requirements for WTO consistency. These require PTAs to have 'substantial sectoral coverage', and provide for the absence or elimination of 'substantially all discrimination'. Thus WTO disciplines only require PTAs to remove limitations on national treatment. They do not require them to address issues of market access or domestic regulation.

But this focus on measures that discriminate against foreigners means that PTAs are not concentrating on the trade barriers that matter most in an economic sense. Dee (2007) shows that the gains from such PTAs are small compared with a moderately successful completion of the Doha Round. And they are trivial compared with a comprehensive program of unilateral regulatory reform, one that targets non-discriminatory behind-the-border restrictions on competition.

What then is the source of the interest in PTAs? A major motivation by *demandeur* countries is to capture 'first mover' advantage. Given the nature of services production, with its large sunk costs, first movers have a significant advantage. Mattoo and Fink (2002) compare the effects of 'sequential entry' to 'simultaneous entry'. A PTA negotiation might give a first mover advantage to a supplier who is not competitive in world terms. The country giving the preference risks landing itself with a second-class supplier that is difficult to budge. No wonder service negotiations are seen as zero-sum.

So what should happen with services?

The big gains in services are from reforming the non-discriminatory restrictions on competition that affect foreign and domestic new entrants equally. This is best done domestically, where a debate can be held about how any losses to incumbents can be managed politically. The important political economy considerations are about incumbents versus new entrants, not domestic versus foreign.

Negotiators' fundamental concerns may be the impact of rapid foreign entry into their markets. Such concerns are understandable if rapid entry occurs as a result of the removal of impediments to foreign firms while domestic incumbents remain constrained.

So what should happen with services is transparency in the first instance, followed by review and evaluation, and then domestic reform. This work can be undertaken whether or not the current round of negotiations proceeds. But it will be more effective if the work is embedded in the negotiations.

Given the complex nature of the policy barriers, transparency (that is, documenting existing policy) is an important first step. In some developing economies, even this task will be prohibitively complex and costly in terms of bureaucratic resources. So there will be gains from international cooperation through capacity-building to provide support for this activity.

Similar arguments apply to policy review and evaluation. And it is important at this second stage to link the policy reviews to the goals of a country's development strategy.

While WTO members can contribute to capacity-building for policy transparency and policy review, the WTO through the structure of the GATS provides valuable guidance on the information that should be collected and reported in these stages. The relevant policy information is not simply the treatment of foreigners, but the policy applied to all potential entrants into a market. The references in the GATS to market access, national treatment and domestic regulation issues provide a structure for this information.

The same arguments apply yet again to reform. The main gains are from commitments on market access and domestic regulation; the main risks are from a focus on national treatment, which typically happens in both regional and multilateral trade negotiations. The GATS provides guidance on the distinction between market access, national treatment and domestic regulation, admittedly with some uncertainties in definitions that could be clarified (Adlung 2006).

Having decided on the priorities for reform, countries can commit to those changes in the WTO. This contribution is more valuable than negotiations with foreigners on the terms of their particular entry into markets. While additional pressure from abroad can help countries to overcome the domestic political constraints to reform, there is the risk that in the services area, other countries may make demands that are not in the reforming country's best interests. That evaluation is best done domestically, away from a negotiating arena.

Given the relatively high resource cost of making and implementing good policy, it is unlikely that all countries can or should move immediately to 'world's best practice' in all regulatory areas. The scope to make the transition to that practice is important. The WTO through the GATS provides options for scheduling policy changes, and thereby creating expectations about the direction of policy reform. But the challenge is to strengthen the scheduling process and avoid the lack of clarity that is a feature of current commitments (Adlung 2006).

Finally, in some cases, policy choices in one country spill over to welfare effects in another. For example, the application of systems of safety standards or testing procedures by one group of countries could affect demand for the exports of other countries. Competition policy choices such as merger approvals in one country can affect markets in other countries where merging firms compete.

These spillovers are best resolved through a commitment to openness in the application of solutions. For example, countries adopting systems of mutual recognition with respect to standards or testing could usefully agree to take in new members on the same terms as they themselves joined the arrangement.

Similarly, it is important in competition policy to consider the welfare of all affected consumers where mergers have cross-country effects. The WTO provides a forum for the design of arrangements in which non-founding members can have a say about the rules adopted and about the terms on which they may later participate.

9.5 Conclusion

So, to summarize, what should happen with services? Among the items that should be on the agenda are:

- Cooperation on transparency and review.
- Efforts to bind current policy.
- A focus on market access and domestic regulation in further liberalization.
- Clarity on scheduling.
- Specification of paths of evolution of regulatory reform.
- Capturing the spillovers in that work.

These are primarily matters of the design of domestic reform, not international negotiation on the exchange of commitments to provide foreigners with options for market entry. The WTO's contribution is through its principles not necessarily its traditional processes, and in that sense, services cannot be a deal-maker in the Doha Round of trade negotiations.

The question, in other words, is not what services can do for the WTO and its negotiations, but what the WTO and its principles can do for services reform.

Chapter 10

Services in PTAs: Donuts or Holes?[1]

Philippa Dee and Christopher Findlay

10.1 Introduction

There are at least four ways of assessing the services provisions of preferential trade agreements (PTAs):

- evaluating the rules;
- evaluating the commitments made under those rules;
- evaluating the extent to which the commitments constrain or change the *status quo*, given that there can be large gaps between bound and applied protection in the areas of both services and investment;
- evaluating whether any change to the *status quo* has economic significance.

Those who have evaluated the services provisions of preferential trade agreements according to the first two criteria have tended to see 'donuts'. Those who have evaluated them according to the second two criteria have tended to see 'holes'.

The purpose of this paper is to outline some of the evidence according to the four methods of evaluation, and to spell out the implications for the likely effects of an Australia–China preferential trade agreement.

---

[1] This is an edited version of Chapter 6 in Sisera Jayasuriya, Donald MacLaren and Gary Magee (2009), *Negotiating a Preferential Trading Agreement: Issues, Constraints and Practical Options*, Cheltenham UK: Edward Elgar: 97–128. The authors thank Ryo Ochiai for exceptional research assistance.

10.2 Evaluating the Rules

The standard way of evaluating the trading rules established by the services provisions of preferential trade agreements is to compare them to the rules established by the General Agreement on Trade in Services (GATS) under the WTO.

The GATS imposes one key discipline on all services trade — the most-favoured nation obligation. This requires a country to treat the services suppliers of all other countries equally. There is to be no discrimination among the various different foreign sources of services.

Beyond that, there are two other key disciplines that apply on a positive list basis, ie they only apply to selected services sectors that a country chooses to subject to those disciplines. The first is a national treatment obligation. This requires a country to treat the services suppliers of all other countries the same as its domestic suppliers. There is to be no discrimination between domestic and foreign suppliers. The second is a market access obligation. This requires a country to refrain from applying six specific types of quantitative restrictions on services suppliers, be they domestic or foreign suppliers. For example, there is to be no limit on the number of services suppliers, or on the value of services transactions.

A country may choose to 'schedule' a particular services sector, thus subjecting it to both these disciplines, but it is also allowed to list any 'limitations' on the application of the disciplines, reflecting restrictive policy measures that it wishes to retain. Countries can also be selective in which modes of service delivery they will subject to these disciplines. A country can selectively 'schedule', or refrain from 'scheduling', any of the four recognized modes of delivery:

- mode 1 — 'cross-border trade' — where both the producer and consumer stay in their home countries, and the services is often delivered electronically;
- mode 2 — 'consumption abroad' — where the consumer moves temporarily to the country of the producer;
- mode 3 — 'commercial presence' — where the producer establishes a permanent commercial presence in the country of the consumer;

- mode 4 — 'the movement of natural persons' — where the producer moves temporarily to the country of the consumer.

By recognizing all these modes of services delivery, the GATS recognizes that services transactions typically occur face to face, behind the border of the producing or consuming country. But under the positive list approach, countries have a great deal of discretion in whether to subject their services sectors to the disciplines of national treatment and market access in practice.

The GATS also recognizes that services are an area where market failures can occur. For example, there is a legitimate role for regulation of natural monopoly in some network industries, for regulation to protect against information asymmetries in the professions, for prudential regulation of financial services to ensure systemic stability, and for safety regulation in air passenger transport.

The GATS recognizes the right of individual governments to regulate. Non-economic objectives can be pursued, for example, through universal service obligations. Services provided by governments are quarantined. But GATS also requires that domestic regulatory regimes be the 'least burdensome' necessary to achieve their objectives. This provides a further WTO discipline on non-discriminatory measures that fall outside of the narrow scope of GATS 'market access' commitments, although the discipline is rather loose, especially since the definition of 'least burdensome' has yet to be decided by WTO members.

There is a presumption that the services provisions of PTAs will be GATS-plus. That is, they will impose rules at least as liberal as the GATS, and impose them on at least as many sectors. In part, this presumption is written into the GATS itself. For the services provisions of PTAs to be WTO-consistent, they need to have 'substantial sectoral coverage', and provide for the absence or elimination of 'substantially all discrimination', in the sense of the national treatment obligation. But note that there is no WTO requirement for PTAs to address non-discriminatory market access limitations, or to address domestic regulation. And enforcing WTO consistency has proved no easier in services than it has in goods.

In practice, when PTAs have included services provisions, they have tended to be of two types. GATS style agreements have included national treatment and market access obligations for services on a positive list basis. And they have included investment provisions only via the treatment of commercial presence in the services sector. By contrast, NAFTA style agreements have included national treatment and market access obligations for services on a negative list basis. That is, the obligations apply to all services sectors, except those nominated for exclusion in an annex of reservations and exceptions. And they have typically included a separate chapter on investment that imposes most-favoured nation and national treatment obligations on investment in all sectors (again, subject to reservations and exceptions), not just in services.

Both types of agreements cover obligations to facilitate the temporary movement of individual services suppliers, since this is one of the modes by which services are delivered. Some agreements of either type may also include a separate chapter on the movement of business persons. Such chapters may outline obligations such as limits on the use of economic needs tests for immigration purposes. These obligations typically apply to all business persons, not just services suppliers.

There are many more aspects to the rules governing services in the GATS and in PTAs. Good detailed discussion of all aspects is contained in three OECD documents (OECD 2002a, 2002b, 2002c), which examine the relationship between PTAs and the multilateral trading system for services, investment and labour mobility.

The discussion in those papers has been used to devise a template for scoring the services, investment and labour mobility provisions of PTAs. The purpose is to compare PTAs with each other and with multilateral disciplines under the WTO (not just the GATS agreement, but other relevant agreements such as the WTO agreement on Trade Related Investment Measures).

The templates for evaluating these dimensions of PTAs are shown in Tables 10.1, 10.2 and 10.3.[2] The top section of each template has been

---

[2] These templates were also used in Dee (2008b).

Table 10.1. Template for Scoring Cross-border Trade in Services

Category		*Score*
Form of Agreement		
Scope	Covers everything	1
	Excludes only air passenger transport or govt services	0.8
	Excludes air passenger transport and govt services (same as GATS)	0.75
	Excludes a little more than GATS (eg financial services)	0.5
	Excludes a lot more than GATS	0.25
	Endeavours with unspecified scope (cooperation or no detailed provisions)	0.2
	No services provisions	0
MFN	Negative list bindings	1
	Positive list bindings	0.75
	Best endeavours	0.25
	No commitment	0
MFN exemptions	None	1
	None for new bilateral agreements	0.5
	Some for new bilateral agreements	0.25
	For all existing and new bilateral agreements or no commitment on MFN	0
National treatment	Negative list bindings	1
	Negative list bindings – some sectors	0.75
	Positive list bindings	0.5
	Best endeavours	0.25
	No commitment	0
Market access (ie prohibition on QRs as in GATS)	Negative list bindings	1
	Negative list bindings – some sectors	0.75
	Positive list bindings	0.5
	Best endeavours	0.25
	No commitment	0
Local presence not required (right of non-estab.)	Has this provision	1
	Has this provision, but with some exemptions	0.5
	Doesn't have this provision	0
Domestic regulation	General provisions as in GATS plus necessity test (or equiv.)	1

Table 10.1.   Continued.

	General provisions as in GATS (transparency, not a disguised restriction)	0.75
	Measures in a reasonable and impartial manner	0.4
	Provisions for specific sectors eg professions	0.25
	No provisions	0
Transparency (scores additive)	Prior comment	0.3
	Publish (as in GATS)	0.4
	National inquiry point (as in GATS)	0.3
Recognition	General provisions as in GATS (nondiscrimination, based in international standards) plus provisions for all sectors	1
	General provisions as in GATS (nondiscrimination, based in international standards) plus provisions for specific sectors	0.75
	General provisions as in GATS (nondiscrimination, based in international standards)	0.5
	Provisions for specific sectors eg legal, engineering	0.25
	Encouragement	0.2
	No provisions	0
Monopolies and exclusive services providers	Stronger than general provisions in GATS	1
	General provisions as in GATS (not act inconsistently with commitments, not anticompetitive in other markets)	0.75
	General provisions as in GATS plus some exceptions	0.6
	Provisions for specific sectors eg telecommunications	0.5
	No provisions	0
Business practices	Stronger than the GATS	1
	General provisions as in GATS (consult with a view to eliminating)	0.75
	Provisions for specific sectors	0.5
	No provisions	0
Transfers and payments	No restrictions except to safeguard balance of payments	1
	Restrictions in other prescribed circumstances	0.5
	No provisions	0
Denial of benefits (ie rules of origin)	Denial only to persons that do not conduct substantial (or any) business operations in other party	1
	Tougher treatment to specific sectors	0.75
	Tougher treatment to all sectors	0.5
	Total denial if owned by third party, or no provisions to prevent denial	0

Table 10.1. Continued.

Safeguards	General provisions	0
	Provisions for particular sectors	0.25
	Future negotiations	0.5
	No provisions or banned	1
Subsidies	Provisions limiting their use	1
(may be in separate	Consultation	0.5
chapter but covers	Future negotiations to limit their use	0.25
services)	No provisions	0
Govt procurement	Provisions on non-discriminatory access	1
in services	Provisions for access in some sectors	0.75
(could be in	Future negotiations	0.5
separate chapter)	No provisions	0
Ratchet mechanism	All subsequent unilateral liberalization to be bound	1
	Sectoral exceptions to ratchet mechanism	0.75
	No mechanism	0
Telecomms	Interconnection (access to and use of PSTN and services	0.5
(scores additive)	by service suppliers of other party)	
	Unbundling	0.1
	Particular services (eg leased circuits, resale, number portability)	0.1
	Competitive safeguards	0.1
	Universal Service Obligations	0.1
	Allocation of scarce resources (eg spectrum)	0.1
Financial services	Prudential carveout	0.4
(scores additive)	Provision for recognition of prudential measures	0.2
	NT for access to payments and clearing systems	0.1
	New financial services	0.1
	Privacy	0.1
	Data transfer	0.1
Content of	For negative list agreements, look at non-conforming measures	
Agreement	For positive list agreements, look at specific, horizontal and MFN commitments.	
General	No modes excluded by one or more parties	1
reservations or	One mode excluded by one or more parties (eg mode 4)	0.5
exceptions – modes	Two or more modes excluded by one or more parties, or no provisions	0

Table 10.1. Continued.

General reservations or exceptions – measures	No measures (MFN, NT, MA) excluded by one or more parties	1
	One measure (eg MA) excluded by one or more parties	0.5
	More than one measure excluded by one or more party, or no provisions	0
Sectoral exclusions (out of 46 substantive sectors) (least generous treatment among members of FTA)	No sectors excluded by one or more parties	1
	1–10 sectors excluded by one or more parties (eg maritime, audiovisual)	0.8
	11–20 sectors excluded by one or more parties (eg maritime, audiovisual)	0.6
	21–30 sectors excluded by one or more parties	0.4
	31–40 sectors excluded by one or more parties	0.2
	More than 40 sectors excluded by one or more parties, or no provisions on services trade	0
Subnational exclusions	No measures at sub-national (state or provincial) level excluded	1
	Measures at local level excluded by one or more parties	0.7
	Measures at State level excluded by one or more parties	0.4
	Measures at all subnational levels excluded by one or more parties, or no provisions on services trade	0
Other general exclusions	No other general exclusions	1
	One other exclusion (eg for minorities, land purchases) by at least one party	0.5
	Two or more other exclusions (eg for minorities, land purchases) by at least one party	0

designed to compare agreements at the rule-making stage. Thus the top section of each template contains categories and scores for ranking the *form* of the agreement, as indicated in the relevant chapters.

The templates also contain a few broad summary measures to compare the levels of commitments contained in each agreement. Thus the bottom section of each template contains categories and scores for ranking the *content* of the agreement, as indicated in the relevant annexes of commitments, reservations or exceptions. However, the measures of content are relatively crude.

The first template deals with cross-border trade (defined as modes 1 and 2), but also picks up some of the more general features that appear in services chapters, such as provisions to deal with domestic regulation

Table 10.2.   Template for Scoring Investment

Category		Score
Form of Agreement		
Sectoral coverage	Beyond services (in separate chapter)	1
	Services only (mode 3 in services chapter)	0.5
	Based on bilateral treaties	0.4
	Endeavours without specified scope	0.25
	None	0
Scope of MFN, NT etc provisions (scores additive)	Establishment (ie greenfield)	0.3
	Acquisition (ie merger)	0.2
	Post-establishment operation	0.3
	Resale (ie free movement of capital)	0.2
MFN	Negative list bindings	1
	Positive list bindings	0.75
	Best endeavours	0.25
	No commitment	0
MFN exemptions	None	1
	None for new bilateral agreements	0.5
	Some for new bilateral agreements	0.25
	For all existing and new bilateral agreements, or no provisions to prevent exemptions	0
National treatment	Negative list bindings – all sectors	1
	Negative list bindings – some sectors	0.75
	Positive list bindings – all sectors	0.5
	Best endeavours	0.25
	No commitment	0
Nationality (residency) of management and board of directors (including exceptions)	Cannot restrict either	1
	Cannot restrict either, with sectoral exceptions	0.75
	Can partially restrict board of directors	0.5
	Can partially restrict management or both. Alternatively, sectoral promises to liberalize, but no general promise.	0.25
	No provisions limiting restrictions	0
Performance requirements	No local content, trade or other specified requirements (eg on tech transfer, or where to sell)	1
	No local content or trade requirements ie as in TRIMS	0.75
	Provisions more limited than TRIMS	0.5
	No provisions	0

Table 10.2.   Continued.

Transparency (in services or invest. chapter) (scores additive)	Prior comment	0.3
	Publish (as in GATS)	0.4
	National inquiry point (as in GATS)	0.3
Denial of benefits (ie rules of origin)	Denial only to persons that do not conduct substantial (or any) business operations in other party	1
	Tougher treatment to specific sectors	0.75
	Tougher treatment to all sectors	0.5
	Total denial if owned by third party, or no provisions	0
Expropriation etc (scores additive)	Minimum standard of treatment	0.2
	Treatment in case of strife	0.4
	Expropriation and compensation	0.4
Transfers and payments	No restrictions except to safeguard balance of payments	1
	Restrictions in other prescribed circumstances	0.5
	No provisions	0
Investor State dispute settlement	Yes	1
	No	0
Safeguards	General provisions	0
	Provisions for particular sectors	0.25
	Future negotiations	0.5
	No provisions	1
Subsidies (may be in separate chapter but covers investment)	Provisions limiting their use	1
	Consultation	0.5
	Future negotiations	0.25
	No provisions	0
Government procurement (could be in separate chapter)	Provisions on non-discriminatory access	1
	Provisions for access in some sectors	0.75
	Future negotiations	0.5
	No provisions	0
Ratchet mechanism	All subsequent unilateral liberalization to be bound	1
	Sectoral exceptions to ratchet mechanism	0.75
	No mechanism	0

Table 10.2. Continued.

Content of Agreement

General	No measures (MFN, NT, MA) excluded by one or more parties	1
reservations or	One measure (eg MA) excluded by one or more parties	0.5
exceptions	More than one measure excluded by one or more party, or no provisions	0
Sectoral exclusions (out of 46 substantive sectors)	No sectors excluded by one or more parties	1
	1–10 sectors excluded by one or more parties (eg maritime, audiovisual)	0.8
	11–20 sectors excluded by one or more parties (eg maritime, audiovisual)	0.6
	21–30 sectors excluded by one or more parties	0.4
	31–40 sectors excluded by one or more parties	0.2
	More than 40 sectors excluded by one or more parties, or no provisions on investment	0
Subnational exclusions	No measures at sub-national level excluded	1
	Measures at local level excluded by one or more parties	0.7
	Measures at State level excluded by one or more parties	0.4
	Measures at all subnational levels excluded by one or more parties, or no provisions on investment	0
Other general exclusions	No other general exclusions	1
	No other general exclusions, but some exclusions for some sectors	0.75
	One other exclusion (eg for minorities, land purchases) by at least one party	0.5
	Two other exclusions (eg for minorities, land purchases) by at least one party, or no provisions on investment	0

and monopolies. This template refers primarily to the services chapters of the agreements.

The second template deals with investment (defined as mode 3 plus portfolio investment). It notes whether agreements deal with investment in services only, or more generally. It also covers some of the issues such as investment protection that are peculiar to investment. This template captures the content of the services, investment, and possibly the dispute settlement chapters of the agreements.

Table 10.3. Template for Scoring Movement of Natural Persons

Category		Score
Form of Agreement		
Sectoral coverage	Beyond services and investment (separate chapter)	1
	Services and investment (in both services and investment chapters)	0.75
	Services only (mode 4 in services)	0.5
	Endeavours	0.25
	None	0
Scope	Allows permanent immigration	1
	Includes access to labour market	0.75
	Temporary movement only	0.5
	No clear scope	0.25
	None	0
Immigration	Requires changes to immigration procedures (eg visa quotas or eligibility criteria)	1
	Subject to existing immigration laws and procedures, or no provisions	0
MFN for mode 4 delivery	Negative list bindings	1
	Positive list bindings	0.75
	Best endeavours	0.25
	No commitment	0
MFN exemptions	None	1
	None for new bilateral agreements	0.5
	Some for new bilateral agreements	0.25
	For all existing and new bilateral agreements or no commitment on MFN	0
National treatment for mode 4 delivery	Negative list bindings	1
	Negative list bindings – some sectors	0.75
	Positive list bindings	0.5
	Best endeavours	0.25
	No commitment	0
Market access (ie prohibition on QRs as in GATS)	Negative list bindings	1
	Negative list bindings – some sectors	0.75
	Positive list bindings	0.5

Table 10.3.   Continued.

	Best endeavours	0.25
	No commitment	0
Domestic regulation	General provisions as in GATS plus necessity test (or equivalent)	1
	General provisions as in GATS (transparency, not a disguised restriction)	0.75
	Measures in a reasonable and impartial manner	0.4
	Provisions for specific sectors, eg professions	0.25
	No provisions	0
Transparency for mode 4 delivery (scores additive)	Prior comment	0.3
	Publish (as in GATS)	0.4
	National inquiry point (as in GATS)	0.3
Transparency for temp. movement of people (scores additive)	Expedite procedures	0.3
	Publish	0.4
	Answer queries or comments	0.3
Recognition	General provisions as in GATS (nondiscrimination, based in international standards) plus provisions for all sectors	1
	General provisions as in GATS (nondiscrimination, based in international standards) plus provisions for specific sectors	0.75
	General provisions as in GATS (nondiscrimination, based in international standards)	0.5
	Provisions for specific sectors eg legal, engineering	0.25
	Endeavours	0.2
	No provisions	0
Denial of benefits (ie rules of origin)	Denial only to persons that do not conduct substantial (or any) business operations in other party	1
	Tougher treatment to specific sectors	0.75
	Tougher treatment to all sectors	0.5
	Total denial if owned by third party or no provisions	0
Ratchet mechanism	All subsequent unilateral liberalization to be bound	1
	Sectoral exceptions to ratchet mechanism	0.75
	No mechanism	0

Table 10.3. Continued.

Content of Agreement — Service Delivery

General	No measures (MFN, NT, MA) excluded by one or more parties	1
reservations or	One measure (eg MA) excluded by one or more parties	0.5
exceptions	More than one measure excluded by one or more party, or no provisions on movement of people	0
Sectoral exclusions	No sectors excluded by one or more parties	1
(out of 46	1–10 sectors excluded by one or more parties (eg maritime, audiovisual)	0.8
substantive sectors)	11–20 sectors excluded by one or more parties (eg maritime, audiovisual)	0.6
	21–30 sectors excluded by one or more parties	0.4
	31–40 sectors excluded by one or more parties	0.2
	More than 40 sectors excluded by one or more parties, or no provisions on movement of people	0
Subnational	No measures at sub-national level excluded	1
exclusions	Measures at local level excluded by one or more parties	0.7
	Measures at State level excluded by one or more parties	0.4
	Measures at all subnational levels excluded by one or more parties, or no provisions on movement of people	0
Other general	No other general exclusions	1
exclusions	One other exclusion (eg for minorities, land purchases) by at least one party	0.5
	Two other exclusions (eg for minorities, land purchases) by at least one party, or no provisions on movement of people	0

Content of Agreement — Facilitation of Mobility

Skill coverage	All groups (including unskilled)	1
(least generous	All business persons, traders and investors, intra-corporate transferees, and professionals	0.5
treatment among		
members of FTA)	A subset of the above (eg specialists, managers and intra-corporate transferees)	0.25
	No groups	0
Short term entry	Over 90 days or no time limit mentioned	1
(least generous	Up to 90 days	0.75
treatment among	Up to 60 days	0.5
members of FTA)	Up to 30 days	0.25

Table 10.3. Continued.

	Unspecified	0.1
	No short term entry, or in the case of unbinding service provisions (eg endeavors)	0
Long term entry (least generous treatment among members of FTA)	5 years or more or no time limit mentioned	1
	Up to 4 years	0.8
	Up to 3 years	0.6
	Up to 2 years	0.4
	Up to 1 year	0.2
	Unspecified	0.1
	No long term entry, or in the case of unbinding service provisions (eg endeavors)	0
Quotas on numbers of entrants	No (or not mentioned)	1
	Yes, or in the case of unbinding service provisions (eg endeavors)	0
Local labour market testing or other criteria	All such tests prohibited or not required	1
	Some such tests prohibited or not required	0.5
	No prohibitions (or not mentioned or in the case of unbinding service provisions (eg endeavors)	0

The third template deals with the movement of people (defined as mode 4), but also picks up whether there are additional measures in the agreements to facilitate labour mobility, either for service providers, investors, or more generally. This template captures the content of the services, investment, and labour mobility chapters of the agreements.

These templates have been used to score all of the major agreements involving a pre-selected list of 73 countries in the years up to 2004. The 66 agreements, and their country membership, are shown in Table 10.4. Most of these agreements have been notified to the WTO, but some have not. The templates have also been used to score comparable WTO disciplines, where they exist. It was not possible to give a general score for the content dimension of the WTO agreements, as this depends on the commitments of each individual member country. Each agreement, whether a PTA or a WTO agreement, is given a score between 0 and 1 against each characteristic, where 0 is most restrictive and 1 most liberal. Summaries of the scoring exercise are shown on Tables 10.5 to 10.7.

Table 10.4. PTA Agreements

Agreement	Date	Membership dynamics
EEC/EU	1958	Austria (joined 1995), Belgium-Luxembourg, Denmark (joined 1973), Finland (joined 1995), France, Germany, Greece (joined 1981), Hungary (joined 2004), Ireland (joined 1973), Italy, Netherlands, Poland (joined 2004), Portugal (joined 1986), Spain (joined 1986), Sweden (joined 1995), United Kingdom (joined 1973)
EFTA	1960	Austria (left 1995), Denmark (left 1972), Finland (joined 1961, left 1995), Iceland (joined 1970), Norway, Portugal (left 1985), Sweden (left 1985), Switzerland, United Kingdom (left 1972)
CACM	1961	Costa Rica (joined 1962), El Salvador, Honduras, Nicaragua
EC–Switzerland	1973	EU membership, Switzerland.
EC–Iceland	1973	EU membership, Iceland
EC–Norway	1973	EU membership, Norway
Bangkok agreement	1976	Bangladesh, China (joined 2001), India, Korea, Lao PDR, Sri Lanka
LAIA	1981	Argentina, Bolivia, Brazil, Chile, Colombia, Ecuador, Mexico, Paraguay, Peru, Uruguay, Venezuela
Sparteca	1981	Australia, Fiji, New Zealand, PNG, Solomon Is.
US–Israel	1985	Israel, United States
CER	1989	Australia, New Zealand
Mercosur	1991	Argentina, Brazil, Paraguay, Uruguay
EFTA–Turkey	1992	EFTA membership, Turkey
CARICOM–Venezuela	1992	Dominican Republic, Venezuela
Chile–Colombia	1993	Chile, Colombia
EFTA–Israel	1993	EFTA membership, Israel
CEFTA	1993	Hungary, Poland
EFTA–Romania	1993	EFTA membership, Romania
Chile–Bolivia[b]	1993	Bolivia, Chile
EEA	1994	EU membership, Iceland, Norway
NAFTA	1994	Canada (joined precursor in 1988), Mexico, United States (joined precursor in 1988)
COMESA	1994	Egypt (joined 1998), Madagascar, Mauritius,
EC–Romania	1995	EC membership, Romania
SAPTA	1995	Bangladesh, India, Nepal, Pakistan, Sri Lanka
Bolivia–Mexico	1995	Bolivia, Mexico
Costa Rica–Mexico	1995	Costa Rica, Mexico
Colombia–Mexico–Venezuela	1995	Colombia, Mexico, Venezuela
CARICOM–Colombia	1995	Colombia, Dominican Republic

Table 10.4. Continued.

ASEAN Framework Agt on Services	1995	Indonesia, Lao PDR (joined 1997), Malaysia, Philippines, Singapore, Thailand
EC–Turkey	1996	EU membership, Turkey
Chile–Mercosur[a]	1996	Mercosur membership, Chile
Canada–Israel	1997	Canada, Israel
Israel–Turkey	1997	Israel, Turkey
Canada–Chile	1997	Canada, Chile
Bolivia–Mercosur[a]	1997	Mercosur membership, Bolivia
Andean (decision 439)	1998	Bolivia, Colombia, Ecuador, Peru, Venezuela
ASEAN Framework Agt on Investment	1998	Indonesia, Lao PDR (joined 1997), Malaysia, Philippines, Singapore, Thailand
Mexico–Nicaragua	1998	Mexico, Nicaragua
Chile–Mexico	1999	Chile, Mexico
EC–South Africa	2000	EC membership, South Africa
EC–Israel	2000	EC membership, Israel
Mexico–Israel	2000	Mexico, Israel
New Zealand–Singapore	2001	New Zealand, Singapore
EC–Mexico	2001	EC membership, Mexico
EFTA–Mexico	2001	EFTA membership, Mexico
India–Sri Lanka	2001	India, Sri Lanka
US–Jordan	2001	United States, Jordan
Mexico–Nth. Triangle	2001	El Salvador, Honduras, Mexico
EFTA–Jordan	2002	EFTA membership, Jordan
EC–Jordan	2002	EC membership, Jordan
Canada–Costa Rica	2002	Canada, Costa Rica
Japan–S'pore (services)	2002	Japan, Singapore
Central America– Republic of Chile[a]	2002	Chile, Costa Rica, El Salvador
Central America– Dominican Republic[a]	2002	Costa Rica, Dominican Republic (joined 2001), El Salvador (joined 2001), Honduras (joined 2001)
Panama–Central America[a]	2002	El Salvador, Panama
EFTA–Singapore	2003	EFTA membership, Singapore
EC–Chile	2003	EC membership, Chile
ASEAN–Chile	2003	ASEAN membership, China
Singapore–Australia	2003	Singapore, Australia
China–Hong Kong	2004	China, Hong Kong
US–Singapore	2004	United States, Singapore
US–Chile	2004	United States, Chile
EC–Egypt	2004	EC membership, Egypt
EFTA–Chile	2004	EFTA membership, Chile
Chile–Korea	2004	Chile, Korea
Mexico–Uruguay	2004	Mexico, Uruguay

[a] Not notified to WTO.

Table 10.5. Comparing PTAs and the GATS — Cross Border Trade and
General Measures

	GATS	*Averages across PTAs*		
		All agree-ments	*1994 and after*	*2000 and after*
Form of Agreement				
Scope	0.75	0.44	0.52	0.53
MFN	1	0.44	0.53	0.53
MFN exemptions	na	0.05	0.03	0.04
National treatment	0.5	0.45	0.56	0.56
Market access (ie prohibition on QRs as in GATS)	0.5	0.35	0.45	0.54
Local presence not required (right of non-establishment)	0	0.26	0.36	0.35
Domestic regulation	0.75	0.16	0.21	0.32
Transparency	0.7	0.26	0.35	0.43
Recognition	0.5	0.28	0.38	0.38
Monopolies and exclusive services providers	0.75	0.22	0.27	0.29
Business practices	0.75	0.08	0.13	0.11
Transfers and payments	1	0.30	0.41	0.44
Denial of benefits (ie rules of origin)	1	0.47	0.61	0.71
Safeguards	0.5	0.88	0.83	0.85
Subsidies	0.25	0.05	0.05	0.07
Government procurement in services	0.5	0.20	0.27	0.36
Ratchet mechanism	0	0.27	0.33	0.29
Telecommunications	0.5	0.23	0.32	0.35
Financial services	0.6	0.15	0.23	0.25
Simple average of above	0.59	0.29	0.36	0.39
Content of Agreement				
General reservations/exceptions — modes	na	0.49	0.60	0.63
General reservations/exceptions — measures	na	0.44	0.52	0.54
Sectoral exclusions	na	0.15	0.15	0.18
Sub-national exclusions	na	0.46	0.55	0.60
Other general exclusions	na	0.48	0.59	0.59
Simple average of above		0.40	0.49	0.51

Source: Author's own calculations.

The scoring shows that in virtually all dimensions, PTAs have
become more liberal over time, and with fewer exclusions. This is shown

Table 10.6. Comparing PTAs and the GATS — Investment

	GATS	Averages across PTAs		
		All agree-ments	1994 and after	2000 and after
Form of Agreement				
Sectoral coverage	0.5	0.56	0.67	0.71
Scope of MFN, NT etc provisions	1	0.59	0.72	0.81
MFN	1	0.49	0.55	0.59
MFN exemptions	na	0.16	0.19	0.20
National treatment	0.5	0.55	0.65	0.70
Nationality (residency) of management and board of directors (including exceptions in Annex)	0	0.11	0.14	0.10
Performance requirements	0.75	0.25	0.37	0.30
Transparency (in services or investment chapter)	0.7	0.33	0.45	0.54
Denial of benefits (ie rules of origin)	1	0.39	0.47	0.52
Expropriation etc	0	0.20	0.30	0.33
Transfers and payments	1	0.42	0.53	0.59
Investor State dispute settlement	0	0.24	0.35	0.34
Safeguards	0.5	0.94	0.93	0.91
Subsidies	0.25	0.05	0.04	0.05
Government procurement	0.5	0.20	0.27	0.28
Ratchet mechanism	0	0.27	0.36	0.34
Simple average of above	0.51	0.36	0.44	0.46
Content of Agreement				
General reservations/exceptions	na	0.51	0.60	0.63
Sectoral exclusions	na	0.21	0.24	0.30
Sub-national exclusions	na	0.54	0.65	0.77
Other general exclusions	na	0.42	0.49	0.52
Simple average of above		0.42	0.50	0.55

Source: Author's own calculations.

by the average scores across PTAs being higher for later subgroups of agreements than they are for the sample as a whole.

In many dimensions, PTAs are not as liberal on average as WTO agreements. This is only in part because the sample of PTAs includes agreements that have no substantive services provisions at all (note that it would involve selection bias to exclude such agreements from the

Table 10.7. Comparing PTAs and the GATS — Movement of People

	GATS	Averages across PTAs		
		All agreements	1994 and after	2000 and after
Form of Agreement				
Sectoral coverage	0.5	0.45	0.58	0.56
Scope	0.5	0.32	0.41	0.40
Immigration	0	0.02	0.00	0.00
MFN for mode 4 delivery	1	0.41	0.48	0.52
MFN exemptions	na	0.05	0.03	0.06
National treatment for mode 4 delivery	0.5	0.42	0.51	0.56
Market access (ie prohibition on QRs as in GATS)	0.5	0.38	0.47	0.54
Domestic regulation	0.75	0.16	0.21	0.32
Transparency of regulations governing service delivery via mode 4	0.7	0.30	0.41	0.48
Transparency of regulations governing temporary movement of persons	0	0.18	0.27	0.28
Recognition	0.5	0.27	0.36	0.35
Denial of benefits (ie rules of origin)	1	0.47	0.59	0.69
Ratchet mechanism	0	0.25	0.31	0.29
Simple average of above	0.50	0.28	0.36	0.39
Content of Agreement — Service Delivery				
General reservations/exceptions	na	0.43	0.51	0.52
Sectoral exclusions	na	0.17	0.19	0.22
Sub-national exclusions	na	0.49	0.60	0.65
Other general exclusions	na	0.51	0.63	0.67
Simple average of above scores		0.40	0.48	0.51
Content of Agreement — Facilitation of Mobility				
Skill coverage	na	0.31	0.36	0.39
Short term entry	na	0.50	0.63	0.69
Long term entry	na	0.46	0.58	0.60
Quotas on numbers of entrants	na	0.55	0.68	0.74
Needs test	na	0.00	0.00	0.00
Local labour market testing or other criteria	na	0.08	0.11	0.07
Simple average of above		0.32	0.40	0.41

Source: Author's own calculations.

sample). It is also because many PTAs are silent on issues such as domestic regulation, monopolies, private business practices, safeguards and subsidies. These are not areas where PTAs have forged ahead of WTO disciplines. But on the two core issues of market access and national treatment, PTAs are now more liberal on average than the WTO. This is largely because of the growing list of agreements that include these disciplines on a negative list rather than positive list basis.

Other writers have suggested that on core rules, at least, PTAs are generally GATS-plus. Stephenson (2002) has argued that the NAFTA-style agreements that characterize PTAs in the Western Hemisphere outperform the GATS in three key respects. First, the negative list approach promotes transparency. Second, she argues that it precludes the possibility of making binding commitments that lag actual practice (an assessment that will be examined in more detail in a later section), and hence promote stability. Finally, she argues that they promote more liberal commitments than the GATS, an assessment that is now examined in more detail.

10.3 Evaluating the Commitments

Again, the standard way of evaluating the trade commitments made under the services provisions of preferential trade agreements is to compare them to commitments made under the GATS.

It is often simply asserted that because negative list PTAs commit to market access and national treatment in all services sectors and modes of delivery except those specifically excluded, they must be more liberalizing than GATS schedules or positive list PTAs, which only commit to market access and national treatment in specifically nominated sectors. In principle, however, it is possible for a negative list agreement to be no more liberalizing than a positive list one, if the annexes of reservations and exceptions are sufficiently long. And some lists are quite long — Singapore's lists of reservations and exceptions in its negative list agreement with the United States run to 71 pages.

Accordingly, a definitive assessment requires a careful sector-by-sector and mode-by-mode comparison of the commitments actually made in PTAs, both positive and negative list, against the commitments made in GATS schedules. An early comparison along these lines was made by Dee (2005b), who compared the negative list commitments made by Australia and the United States in the Australia-US Free Trade Agreement (AUSFTA) with their positive list commitments under the GATS. The assessment concluded that the areas of overlap were considerable. AUSFTA did go further than GATS commitments, but the areas of additional market opening were relatively minor, and not generally in areas where there were significant barriers to begin with. This was consistent with the claim by the Australian Government that the major achievement of AUSFTA in the areas of services and investment was to prevent the introduction of any new discriminatory measures, rather than to roll back any existing ones.

A more widespread comparison along these lines has been done by Roy, Marchetti and Lim (2006).[3] The authors compared the commitments undertaken by 29 WTO Members (counting the EC as one) under mode 1 (cross-border supply) and mode 3 (commercial presence) in 28 PTAs negotiated since 2000, and compared these with both the prevailing GATS commitments and recent Doha Round offers of these countries.

The authors agree with the above assessment that PTAs appear to offer limited value added over GATS disciplines in the areas of rules governing safeguard mechanisms, subsidies, domestic regulation and the like. Their main contribution appears to be in their levels of commitments.

On commitments, the authors find that PTAs tend to go significantly beyond GATS offers in terms of improved and new bindings. Further, the proportion of new/improved commitments is generally much greater in PTAs (compared to GATS offers) than in GATS offers (when compared to existing GATS commitments). Some countries are described as showing spectacular improvements in their PTA commitments. Among them are countries that have signed a PTA with the United States. On average, these now have mode 1 and mode 3 commitments in more than 80 per cent of services sub-sectors, compared

---

[3] More recent evidence is reported in Chapter 14 of this volume.

to commitments in less than half of services sub-sectors in their GATS schedules/offers.

In most cases where PTA commitments improve on WTO commitments, it is primarily through new bindings rather than through improvements on existing bindings. Arguably, though, the commitments are more likely to imply real liberalization in the latter case than in the former. Exceptions to the general trend include China and India, whose PTA commitments (China's with Hong Kong and Macao, India's with Singapore) tend to take the form of improvements to sectors already committed under GATS schedules/offers rather than new bindings, and are mostly limited to mode 3.

The authors find that the countries that have a smaller proportion of new/improved commitments in PTAs have all used the positive list scheduling approach. This is not to say that all positive list agreements have led to lesser commitments than negative list ones. China's agreements with Hong Kong and Macao were positive list agreements that nevertheless provided significant new commercial opportunities. But those countries such as Australian and Singapore that have signed agreements of both types have made greater commitments in their negative list ones.

Finally, the authors note that PTAs have provided for advances both for sectors that have tended to attract fewer offers in the GATS (eg audiovisual, road, rail, postal–courier), as well as for sectors that were already popular targets for GATS offers (eg professional, financial services). One exception was health services, where PTA commitments did not appear to go significantly beyond GATS offers.

Overall, the authors conclude (p. 33) that

> PTAs generally have provided for significant improvements over GATS commitments, sometimes even leading to real liberalization of the market.

10.4 Evaluating the Extent of Real Liberalization

Comparing PTA commitments to actual regulatory policies to evaluate the extent of real liberalization is even more labour-intensive than comparing positive and negative list agreements. And it generally cannot be done in a mechanical fashion, because information about regulatory policies and the reasons for regulatory changes is spread unevenly around different sources. The sources need to be read and interpreted carefully, and there is still a danger that the results of any comparison will reflect paucity of information rather than anything else.

One recent such comparison has capitalized on a pre-existing database of actual regulatory practice that was compiled for a different purpose.[4] Barth *et al.* (2006) make use of a database on actual regulatory practice in banking as it stood around 2000, as reported in responses to a detailed World Bank survey. The database had been used previously to assess the impact of that regulation on banking performance (eg Barth, Caprio and Levine 2004). In the more recent exercise, Barth *et al.* (2006) compare regulatory practice with actual WTO commitments in the financial sector for 123 WTO Members.

The authors find significant differences between commitments and actual practice. Some of their examples are as follows.

- More than 30 WTO Members that prohibit foreign firms from entering through acquisitions, subsidiaries or branches in their WTO schedules allow such entry in practice.
- Six WTO Members do not allow foreign entry through subsidiaries or branches even though in their schedules they indicated they do. This anomaly may reflect the 'prudential carveout' in the GATS, whereby Members are not required to schedule limitations maintained for prudential purposes. However, it is highly questionable whether bans on foreign entry could be defended as purely prudential measures.
- A large number of WTO Members prohibit banks from engaging in insurance or securities activities in their schedules, but allow such activities in practice.
- 26 WTO Members in practice set the same minimal capital entry requirements for domestic and foreign banks, even though in their schedules they do not commit to such non-discriminatory treatment.

---

[4] Again, more recent evidence is reported in Chapter 14 of this volume.

The authors also look for evidence of statistically significant correlations between WTO commitments and regulatory practice. Even if the two do not match exactly, they expect the correlation to be positive. However, their finding does not bear this out.

> The results ... indicate that on average countries are more open based on actual practice than their WTO commitments. The difference in means between actual practice and commitments, moreover, is statistically significant. Also, there is no significant correlation between actual practice and commitments. These results hold for developing countries and countries with more than 2 million people, but not for the developed countries. The latter group of countries is on average less open based upon actual practice than commitments. (Barth *et al.* 2006, p. 25)

This last, rather explosive finding passes without further comment!

The authors also try to explain the gap between commitments and actual practice. One of their findings is that countries with greater foreign ownership of total bank assets also tend to have the biggest divergence between the indices for commitments and actual practice. Countries with greater foreign ownership also tend to display less actual discrimination against foreign banks, but tend to display more discrimination based on commitments. Lastly, developed countries that made commitments earlier in time tend to display less discrimination, while the opposite is the case for developing countries.

In general, therefore, the authors find many instances where WTO commitments are significantly less liberal than actual practice. They also find instances where WTO commitments are more liberal than actual practice, particularly in developed countries.

As evidence about whether PTAs promote real liberalization, the findings are merely circumstantial. However, if WTO commitments lag actual practice by a significant margin, then even if PTAs improve significantly on WTO commitments, they may still themselves lag actual practice.

Furthermore, if actual practice lags WTO commitments, as it appears to in a few cases, then there is clearly an enforcement problem that may also carry over to PTA commitments. One reason for the enforcement problem in a WTO context may be that trade partner countries are not equipped to check the compliance of all other WTO Members. Such a monitoring problem may be less severe in a PTA context. But another reason for an enforcement problem may be that trade commitments are made by trade negotiators who are divorced from what is really going on in their own countries. This problem may well carry over to PTAs, especially in countries where problems of coordination among different government ministries are endemic.

Roy, Marchetti and Lim (2006) also attempt to assess whether PTA commitments lead to real liberalization. They do not make direct comparisons with regulatory practice, but look for instances where PTA commitments are phased in over time, using the phasing mechanism as an indication that real liberalization is taking place. They note that the group of countries making such phased commitments is fairly widespread, although it appears that financial services and telecommunications dominate. Most phase-out commitments have been contracted by countries as part of a PTA with the United States, although not exclusively.

Certainly, the PTA experience with partners other than the United States can be dramatically different. It is widely recognized that in the ASEAN countries, both WTO commitments and PTA commitments can lag actual practice by a considerable margin.[5] And one of the recent PTAs to contain no services commitments whatsoever is that between ASEAN and China.

10.5 Evaluating the Economic Significance Real PTA Liberalization

It is sometimes claimed that because services trade barriers do not involve tariff revenue, that preferential services trade liberalization cannot impose losses on PTA members through trade diversion. This claim is made explicitly by Roy, Marchetti and Lim (2006), in their otherwise excellent paper, and is implied by the modelling treatment of services in papers such as Hertel (2000). The argument is fallacious, for the following reasons.

---

[5] See the discussion of the ASEAN Framework Agreement on Services by Stephenson and Nikomborirak (2002).

Some regulatory trade restrictions, particularly quantitative restrictions, create artificial scarcity. The prices of services are inflated, not because the real resource cost of producing them has gone up, but because incumbent firms are able to earn economic rents — akin to a tax, but with the revenue flowing to the incumbent rather than to government. Liberalization of these barriers would yield relatively small gains associated with better resource allocation, but also have redistributive effects associated with the elimination of rents to incumbents. Such rent-creating restrictions are tariff-like, with the redistribution of rent having effects similar to the redistribution of tariff revenue.

Alternatively, services trade restrictions could increase the real resource cost of doing business. An example would be a requirement for foreign service professionals to retrain in a new economy, rather than to pass an accreditation process. Liberalization would be equivalent to a productivity improvement (saving in real resources), and yield relatively large gains. This could increase returns for the incumbent service providers, as well as lowering costs for users elsewhere in the economy.

This distinction has two important implications. First, the gains from liberalizing cost-escalating barriers is likely to exceed the gains from liberalizing rent-creating barriers by a significant margin. Secondly, in the context of PTAs, the danger of net welfare losses from net trade diversion arises if the relevant barriers are rent-creating, since rent distribution can have the same effects as tariff redistribution (see also Pomfret 1997). So a key question for establishing the economic significance of any real services trade liberalization achieved in PTAs is whether it targets trade barriers that create rents or raise costs.

While many PTAs go further than the GATS, they have tended to be selective in two important ways:

- they have tended to be preferential, even in the provisions that go beyond goods trade; and
- they have tended to target only those provisions that explicitly discriminate against foreigners.

There are strong political economy explanations for both of these outcomes.

With some exceptions, recent PTAs have tended to do one of two things in the new age areas (including services) — either bind the *status quo*, or make concessions on a preferential basis, even when logic suggests they could sensibly be made non-preferentially.[6] One very clear reason for this outcome is that countries with strong 'offensive' interests in the Doha Round are unlikely to give away negotiating coin by making defensive concessions on a non-preferential basis within a PTA, prior to a Doha Round settlement. In particular, Roy, Marchetti and Lim (2006) note that the United States always lodges a broad exception for the market access obligation in its PTAs whose purpose is to ensure that those PTAs do not go beyond its market access obligations under the GATS.

Partly because they have been preferential, recent PTAs have tended to target only those provisions that explicitly discriminate against foreigners. This is because, in many cases, the only provisions that can feasibly be liberalized on a preferential basis are those that discriminate against foreigners.

But even without this feasibility constraint, there are economic and political economy forces that tend to limit concessions within PTAs to those that explicitly discriminate against foreigners. These were drawn from Dee (2007) and summarized in the previous chapter of this volume, so are not repeated here.

This focus on measures that discriminate against foreigners means that PTAs are not concentrating on the trade barriers that matter most in an economic sense. As noted earlier, the barriers that are easiest to liberalize on a preferential basis are explicit quantitative restrictions. These create artificial scarcity, and hence generate rents. For example, one popular target for liberalization in PTAs has been barriers in banking and telecommunications. The limited empirical evidence suggests that in these sectors (where explicit barriers to entry are rife), barriers appear to

---

[6] For example, two of Australia's concessions in the Australia-United States Free Trade Agreement were the lifting of Foreign Investment Review Board screening on inward foreign direct investment in non-sensitive sectors, and a commitment to provisions similar to those in the WTO Agreement on Government Procurement. Both measures were made preferentially, even though the arguments advanced by the Australian Government would have applied *a fortiori* to non-preferential liberalization.

create rents. In distribution services, where indirect trade restrictions also apply, barriers appear to increase costs. In air passenger transport and the professions, barriers appear to have both effects. In particular, discriminatory barriers in the professions appear to create rents, while the non-discriminatory restrictions (such as restrictions that require partnerships, and require both the investors and managers of professional firms to themselves be licensed professionals) increase costs.[7] And theoretical arguments suggest that barriers in maritime and electricity generation primarily affect costs.[8]

Dee (2007) shows that if an East Asian PTA managed to eliminate all discrimination against foreigners in these sectors where empirical evidence is available, the gains would be small compared to a moderately successful completion of the Doha Round. And they would be trivial compared to a comprehensive program of unilateral regulatory reform, one that instead targeted non-discriminatory behind-the-border restrictions on competition. The reason is that there appears to be a reasonably strong correlation in practice between measures that discriminate against foreigners and measures that create rents.

What then is the source of the interest in PTAs? As noted in the previous chapter, a major motivation by *demandeur* countries is to capture the first mover advantage. However, a PTA negotiation might give a first mover advantage to a supplier who is not competitive in world terms. The country giving the preference risks landing itself with a second class supplier who is difficult to budge.

10.6 Implications for an Australia–China Free Trade Agreement

China comes to PTA negotiations in services from a slightly different perspective to many other countries. Its first waves of reforms in services focused on domestic regulation — converting sectors that were once monopolized by State-owned enterprises into sectors where some

---

[7] Gregan and Johnson (1999), Kalirajan *et al.* (2000), Kalirajan (2000), Nguyen-Hong (2000), OECD (2005c), Copenhagen Economics (2005).
[8] Steiner (2000), Clark, Dollar and Micco (2004).

domestic competition could occur (Findlay and Pangestu 2004). It then went through the process of WTO accession, a process that saw it make significant commitments on all fronts, but with an important focus on removing discrimination against foreign suppliers (see also Mattoo 2004).

Despite the significant progress, Australian services providers have found that China still has significant barriers to trade. Australian officials have compiled a list of over 100 pages of services trade barriers that they would like to target in PTA negotiations, barriers that include derogations from national treatment, limitations on market access, and restrictions imposed by China's domestic regulatory regimes. The exercise has contributed greatly to transparency in China, since coordination problems among Chinese government departments have been rife, and individual departments have been unaware of the restrictions and limitations imposed by others.

The question remains what real liberalization is likely to be achieved in practice. At the time of writing, it is unclear even whether services will be listed on a positive or a negative list basis. For its part, Australia will maintain its strategy of binding the *status quo*. China has so far been unwilling to include services provisions in its PTAs at all, or has been unwilling to go beyond its existing WTO accession commitments, arguing (with some cause) that these have already imposed a significant adjustment burden.

Australian officials will press China to go at least a little further. And they will press on all fronts — national treatment, market access and domestic regulation. What is significant is that they will do so on a preferential basis. They do not see themselves as negotiating on behalf of the rest of the world. Even when they make requests concerning domestic regulation, they will not be asking China to deregulate. Rather, they will ask for a waiver or an exemption of the current regulation for Australia.

Whether such preferential relaxation of domestic regulation affects rents or costs in China depends to a large extent on whether supply conditions from the Australian end are competitive (eg Panagariya 2000, Francois and Wooten 2001). If supply conditions are competitive, then the potential cost saving for Australian producers will attract new entry to bid the prices down to match the lower costs, for the benefit of Chinese users. If the supply conditions are not competitive, then selected Australian producers may be able to pocket the cost savings, generating greater rents in Australia for no benefit to Chinese users. Given the 'client focus' of Australian trade officials, which sees them happy to negotiate on behalf of individual services suppliers, rather than necessarily ensuring open entry for all Australian suppliers, it is not difficult to conceive of situations where the latter might occur.[9]

Either way, Australia is clearly seeking a first mover advantage for its services in China, or in some cases a second mover advantage (behind Hong Kong and Macao). The gains to China are likely to be small, although so too are the adjustment costs. What is certain is that an Australia–China Free Trade Agreement will do nothing to further the cause of domestic regulatory reform in China. At worst, it may create a subset of Australian services suppliers earning rents in China, who then have an interest in opposing further regulatory reform.

---

[9] While these stated positions of Australian trade officials were accurate when this chapter was originally written, the Australian Government has since released a policy statement (DFAT 2011) which re-endorses somewhat the principle of non-discrimination: 'The Gillard Government will not make it a condition of agreement with another country that Australia be treated more favourably than its competitors. When a trading partner has already given Australia's competitors access to its markets on terms more favourable than those available to Australian exporters, the Australian Government will seek parity with those competitors. … While the Australian Government will not encourage its trading partners to exclude some competing countries from their trade liberalizing offers, Australia cannot insist that they embrace the principle of non-discrimination. If a trading partner were to provide access to Australian exporters on terms more favourable than those provided to our competitors the Australian Government would, consistent with the fundamental non-discrimination principle of the global trading rules, have no objection to those favourable terms subsequently being extended to all other countries' (p. 12). As at the end of 2012, the Australia–China Free Trade Agreement has still not been concluded.

Chapter 11

What Behind-the-Border Reforms in Services and Investment are Best Done through Trade Agreements?[1]

Philippa Dee

11.1 Introduction

What behind-the-border reforms in services and investment are best done through trade agreements? One way to answer this question is to think of trade agreements as being exercises in piecemeal reform, in the sense that they provide opportunities for reform, but in a constrained, partial manner. The key policy question is whether countries should unreservedly take advantage of these opportunities, despite the constraints, or whether the nature of the constraints should temper the way in which they go about the reforms.

The key policy dilemma originates in the theory of the second best. Lipsey and Lancaster (1956) noted that if, for institutional or other reasons, one of the conditions for economic efficiency cannot be achieved, then the other conditions may no longer be desirable. Their definition of piecemeal policy was a situation where it was still 'second best' optimal to achieve the other conditions, even though one could not be achieved. Examples of papers that have tried to characterize

---

[1] This is an edited version of Chapter 5 in Economic and Social Commission for Asia and the Pacific (ESCAP) (2009), *Challenges and Opportunities for Trade and Financial Integration in Asia and the Pacific*, Studies on Trade and Investment 67, ST/ESCAP/2563, Bangkok: ESCAP: 93–109. Available from http://www.unescap.org/tid/publication/tipub2563.asp.

315

piecemeal second best policy include Davis and Whinston (1965) and Boadway and Harris (1977).

In the context of goods trade, the principles of piecemeal reform are well understood. The economic cost of a tariff is a function, not just of the average level of tariff, but also of its dispersion. So a key guiding principle of piecemeal tariff reform is that it should not exacerbate the dispersion. Otherwise, partial reform may actually worsen economic well-being. In his seminal analysis, Corden (1971, 1974) therefore examined options such as the 'concertina' method — where high tariffs would be squeezed down to medium levels at the first stage, then these and the existing medium tariffs would be squeezed down to a lower level — and 'across-the-board' reductions — where each year, all tariffs would be reduced by an equal percentage.

This guiding principle is now sufficiently well accepted in trade negotiating circles that it has been embodied in a negotiating modality. In the Doha Round of non-agricultural market access negotiations under the World Trade Organization (WTO), tariff cuts would take place according to the so-called Swiss formula, which ensures that within each country, the highest tariffs would undergo the greatest percentage cuts. According to this 'tops down' formula, the partial reform achieved via the negotiations would reduce both the average level of tariffs, and their dispersion.

The aim of this chapter is to explore whether there are principles that can be brought to bear in negotiating the services and investment provisions of trade agreements, which can help to ensure that the partial reforms achieved under those agreements add to, rather than detract from, economic well-being. These principles might be seen as the services and investment equivalents of the tops-down principle for tariff reform. It is not the aim to go as far as developing a negotiating modality for services or investment — that would be premature. However, the principles developed here could be used by individual countries on a voluntary basis when undertaking negotiations in services and investment.

There are two possible levels of analysis. One is to compare trade agreements, as exercises in piecemeal reform, with other modes of liberalization. Should countries embrace trade agreements in services and investment whenever the opportunity arises, even though the liberalization achieved under them is likely to be constrained in various ways? Or should countries watch for instances when trade agreements might make things worse?

The second level of analysis is to consider which particular reforms should be included in trade agreements (the question posed in the title of the chapter). Should countries negotiate whatever they can within trade agreements? Or should they worry about which reforms will avoid losses and/or deliver the biggest gains? The chapter now proceeds with those two levels of analysis in turn.

11.2 Trade Agreements versus Other Modes of Liberalization[2]

Trade agreements can be either multilateral or preferential, but they typically involve the reciprocal exchange of trade concessions with one or more trading partners. They stand in contrast to unilateral liberalization, where a country 'goes it alone'.

In the context of goods trade, the benefits of reciprocity are well understood. The key economic benefit is that reciprocity helps to neutralize the negative terms of trade effects of unilateral tariff reform (eg Bagwell and Staiger 1999). It is also argued that reciprocity helps with the political economy of tariff reform — the benefits to exporting interests from a trading partner's concessions can be offset against the losses to import-competing interests from a country's own concessions (eg Baldwin and Robert-Nicoud 2008).

In the case of services and investment, the benefits of reciprocity for either the economics or the political economy of reform have yet to be established. This section explores these issues. But first it must establish exactly what types of partial reforms trade agreements can be expected to achieve in services and investment.

As noted recently (Dee and Findlay 2009):

---

[2] Parts of this section draw on Dee and Findlay (2009).

- when real liberalization of services and investment occurs in trade agreements, it tends to involve the removal of discrimination against foreigners;
- in preferential trade agreements (PTAs), this tends to be on a preferential basis, ie only for the particular partner country;
- therefore, when real liberalization of services and investment occurs in trade agreements, it tends not to involve the liberalization of restrictions that affect domestic and foreign players equally.

Further, the key to establishing the economic significance of any real services trade liberalization achieved in trade agreements is to establish whether it targets trade barriers that create rents or raise costs. The barriers that are easiest to liberalize on a preferential basis are explicit quantitative restrictions. These create artificial scarcity, and hence tend to generate rents. Thus for both PTAs and multilateral agreements, there are reasons to be cautious about the size of the potential gains. In both cases, there are also situations where the trade agreements could make things worse.

In the case of PTAs, the problem is that if concessions are made to a particular foreign trading partner, prior to removing non-discriminatory distortions and ensuring the general contestability of the market, then the concessions simply risk handing monopoly rents to foreigners. Furthermore, if the new trading partner has to incur sunk costs to enter the market, then a country risks landing itself permanently with a second class supplier who is difficult to budge (see also Dee and Findlay 2008, Marchetti and Roy 2008).

Multilateral trade agreements can avoid some of these problems, by opening a market to many foreign players simultaneously. But this does not mean that they are completely without problems.

At best, removing discrimination against all foreign suppliers simultaneously will not be sufficient to ensure the full benefits of market opening. It is useful to draw a comparison with the theory of goods trade. When goods are homogeneous and domestic and foreign varieties are perfect substitutes, removing all discrimination against foreign suppliers will be sufficient to ensure that the country can access goods at the lowest possible price (in this case, 'the' world price), even if domestic suppliers are still penalized by domestic distortions. However, services are typically highly differentiated, often being tailored to the needs of individual customers. In this case, simply removing discrimination against foreign suppliers will not be sufficient to ensure that a country can access goods at the lowest possible price. If domestic suppliers are still penalized by distortions, the prices of their services will remain 'too high', despite the foreign competition. The empirical analysis of Dee (2007) suggests that this latter problem can be highly significant in practice.

At worst, removing discrimination against all foreign suppliers simultaneously can move a country's resource allocation in the 'wrong' direction, risking an adverse overall economic outcome. If domestic suppliers are subject to domestic regulatory impediments, the resources devoted to domestic supply will be too small, and in a first best situation, the domestic sector should be bigger. However, subjecting the sector to more foreign competition, while keeping it subjected to its own domestic regulatory impediments, will tend to make the sector shrink rather than grow — domestic resource allocation is moved in the 'wrong' direction. This has the potential to make economic well-being worse (depending on whether the sector is a general equilibrium substitute to complement to other sectors in the economy) (see also Dee, Hardin and Holmes 2000).

Not only is this a potentially bad economic outcome, it is also a poor outcome in terms of domestic political economy. Potential domestic new entrants are a key group likely to be in favour of reform. Failure to lift the domestic regulatory impediments that hold them back therefore misses an opportunity to mobilize them as part of the pro-reform coalition.

To the extent that both PTAs and multilateral trade agreements focus on barriers to services trade and investment that create rents rather than raise costs, they both represent poor political economy in another sense. Often, the essence of barriers to services trade and investment is that they serve to protect incumbent service providers from any new competition, be it from domestic players or foreigners. Thus, incumbent service providers are often the most vociferous opponents of reform. Yet trade reforms that manage to lower cost structures have the potential to benefit even the incumbent service providers. Failure to lift the domestic regulatory impediments that hold them back misses an important opportunity to mobilize incumbents as part of the pro-reform coalition.

Indeed, the politics of regulatory reform is often the politics of incumbent versus a range of opposing interests — not just potential new entrants (either domestic or foreign), but also upstream supplying industries, downstream using industries, consumers, and sometimes even governments. Most of the protagonists are domestic. Trade negotiations are forums where the politics is domestic versus foreign. They are not forums that can mobilize the full range of domestic pro-reform interests.

The case for reciprocity in services and investment

In this respect, international reciprocity does not help greatly with the political economy of trade reform in services and investment. This is because the politics is primarily one of competing domestic interests, not domestic versus foreign interests (Dee and Findlay 2008).

Furthermore, international reciprocity does not help greatly with the economics of trade reform in services and investment. In goods trade, the adverse terms of trade effects occur because goods trade barriers operate at the border. However, the regulatory barriers to services and investment are primarily behind-the-border barriers, and their first round effects are primarily on domestic prices and costs. If unilateral trade liberalization has any impact on the terms of trade at all, it can often be positive rather than negative, particularly if the liberalization removes barriers that raise domestic costs. Thus there are no benefits from reciprocity *within* services, as there are no adverse terms of trade effects to be neutralized (Dee and Findlay 2008).

Nor are there likely to be significant benefits from reciprocity across sectors. One reason is that the most intensive users of services are often other services sectors. So the domestic benefits of services reform often flow to other services sectors, not to manufacturing or agriculture (see Dee and Findlay 2008 for more details).

11.3 What to Liberalize within Trade Agreements

Trade agreements may nevertheless provide useful venues to lock in certain types of reforms, despite all the qualifications noted above. A second key question is what types of reforms are best done within trade agreements.

An important first step, however, is to recognize how trade barriers in services and investment may interact with legitimate domestic regulation. This interaction can set additional limits on the extent of trade liberalization.

Limits to liberalization[3]

In many services sectors, there are legitimate reasons for domestic regulation. For example, a key reason for prudential regulation in banking and insurance markets is to guard against systemic instability of the financial system. A key reason for regulating transport industries is to ensure passenger safety. A key reason for having regulated access regimes in telecommunications is to avoid the inefficient duplication of infrastructure components that have 'natural monopoly' characteristics.

In services such as education and health, there are typically at least two key regulatory objectives. One is to deal with asymmetric information. Almost by definition, the clients of health firms or education institutions are not sufficiently trained to know whether the services they are receiving are of high quality. In some markets, this problem is dealt with after the event, via product liability legislation. In education and health markets, this option is typically deemed unsatisfactory, so quality is regulated before the event — via training and perhaps licensing/registration requirements for individual service providers, and by licensing and quality assurance processes for institutions.

Note, however, that regulated quality assurance processes are not the only solution to this problem. Reputation also has a role to play. Services providers who plan to be in a market for the long term cannot afford to

---

[3] Parts of this section draw on Dee (2009).

offer shoddy service for ever, or they will lose clients. They have an incentive to offer quality, and to establish a reputation for doing so.

A second key regulatory objective in education and health markets is to ensure equitable and affordable access, either for all, or for particular disadvantaged segments of society. Government provision is the traditional method of meeting this objective. Government subsidies to private institutions, and government subsidies (through scholarships and the like) to consumers, are also ways in which is it achieved. However, few governments can afford to subsidize everyone. So typically there are limits on who can get government funding, simply for budgetary reasons.

In some services sectors like banking and insurance, there is a relative clear-cut distinction between the regulatory instruments used for legitimate prudential reasons, and those that are deemed regulatory impediments to trade. The instruments commonly used for prudential purposes include minimum capital requirements, capital adequacy ratios, liquidity reserve ratios, possible coverage by an insolvency guarantee or deposit insurance scheme, and a required frequency of publication of financial statements.

While there are a few grey areas, in most cases regulatory restrictions affecting trade in banking and insurance services can be dismantled without jeopardizing prudential objectives, which are achieved using other means.[4] Of course, there is still a sequencing issue — it would be unwise to open financial markets without adequate prudential regulation and without adequate regulatory capacity to design and enforce it.

In health and education services, the distinction between instruments used to achieve quality and access objectives and those deemed to be regulatory barriers to trade is less clear-cut. Entry may be restricted to ensure that low-quality providers do not enter the market. Or entry may be restricted to protect incumbent service providers. Similarly, access to subsidies may be limited because governments cannot afford to subsidize everybody. Or access to subsidies may be limited in order to disadvantage new entrants.

---

[4] Dinh (2013) gives new insights on some of the grey areas in light of the global financial crisis.

Achieving quality objectives in health and education will inevitably mean that there are barriers to the entry and operation of at least some providers. However, a well-designed quality control framework will ensure that the providers who are locked out are the genuinely low-quality ones. The framework can afford to be relatively neutral in its treatment of domestic and foreign providers, or incumbents and new entrants.

Similarly, even in the most open health or education system, not all providers or clients will gain access to government subsidies. If the system is to not unduly constrain trade, then this denial of subsidies should be the same for domestically-owned and foreign providers. Ideally, to maximize efficiency, it should also be neutral with respect to incumbents and new entrants, finding some criteria other than incumbency as a mechanism to ration the subsidies. Governments may chose not to be neutral in their treatment of access to subsidies by domestic and foreign customers, however. For obvious reasons, they may choose to deny the right of foreign customers to local subsidies.

Because there are more targets than instruments in health and education, trade liberalization in these services could not be expected to lead to the compete removal of entry barriers or restrictions on access to subsidies. What trade negotiations might be expected to do is to ensure that they are reduced to levels that are 'no more burdensome than necessary', in the language of the GATS. Where the rationale for regulation is quality assurance, then the logical way to operationalize this necessity test is to define *minimum acceptable standards* of quality that meet the needs of both sides. To date, there has been little progress in operationalizing a necessity test for any services within the WTO. Arguably, more progress might be made within a PTA among partners whose levels of development were not too dissimilar.

What to liberalize?

As noted, trade agreements may provide useful venues to lock in certain types of reforms, despite all the qualifications noted above. The qualifications now include the fact that full liberalization might not be possible in situations where there is a 'targets and instruments' problem

— too few regulatory instruments available to achieve the desired targets.

If countries want to concentrate their trade negotiating efforts in areas that generate the biggest gains, they need to consider five characteristics of their own regulatory barriers:

- the 'height' of the trade barrier, that is, the extent to which regulatory restrictions have raised costs or created rents;
- the 'impact' of the barrier — whether the impact has been on costs or rents;
- the 'incidence' of the barrier — whether it applies only to foreign suppliers, or whether it also applies to domestic operators;
- the size of the affected sector; and
- the nature of its input-output linkages to other sectors.

All these factors will affect the overall economy-wide gains from reform. Some of the evidence on the first three characteristics was surveyed in Chapter 9 of this volume. More recent evidence in these three issues is reported in Dee (2013b).

The size of the affected sector

The size of the affected sector is sufficiently important that it can sometimes dominate the height of the barrier. In an economy such as Indonesia, for example, barriers to trade in telecommunications services are 'higher' than those in the distribution sector (ie wholesale and retail trade) — the height of the barrier in distribution is in fact quite modest. But the distribution sector is bigger, counting for around 15 per cent of the economy. Primarily because of this, the estimated gains from further reform in distribution are bigger than those in telecommunications, even once account is taken of the potential productivity boost that could come from greater business-to-business e-commerce (Dee 2008a).

Intersectoral linkages

Finally, a key consideration is which services sectors have strong intersectoral linkages to the sectors where a country's ultimate comparative advantage lies. Ghani (2009) draws a distinction between East Asia, where the ultimate comparative advantage is in manufactures, and South Asia, where the ultimate comparative advantage is in services itself (eg both ICT services and ICT-enabled services such as back-office professional services).

The services that have strong intersectoral linkages with manufacturing are areas such as transport, logistics and energy services. The services that have strong intersectoral linkages to services are most other services. Therefore, East Asia will get relatively large economy-wide gains from liberalizing and improving productivity in transport, logistics and energy (see Dee 2012b for the most recent evidence on this). South Asia will get relatively large economy-wide gains from liberalizing and improving productivity in most services sectors.

Sectoral priorities — principles of piecemeal reform

One important principle for piecemeal reform of services — the services equivalent of the 'tops down' principle — is to look for sectors where trade barriers tend to add to costs. These are typically not the areas where regulatory barriers have created artificial barriers to entry (although rents can still be converted to real resource costs in a number of ways, for example, by being capitalized into the cost of land). Instead, they tend to be areas where regulations create unnecessary procedures and red tape.

In the East Asian region, these services sectors also happen to be sectors with strong intersectoral linkages to manufacturing. Thus the sectoral priorities in East Asia should include the various links in the logistics chain — customs, transport (road, rail, air, maritime), distribution, and telecommunications, which is vital for e-commerce. They should also include energy services, particularly electricity, where poorly designed domestic regulation can add to costs. And they should also include some less obvious backbone services, such as legal and accounting services, where at least some regulatory restrictions also add to costs.

At least some of these services involve significant physical infrastructure, and it is also well-recognized that the availability of infrastructure is also critical to economic growth. Thus regulatory reforms that can improve the investment climate in these areas will have a doubly beneficial impact — increasing the resources available, as well as improving the productivity of the resources that are employed.

In South Asia, services trade reforms do not need to be quite so targeted, because of the relatively dense intersectoral linkages within the services area. But the transport and distribution sectors are areas where regulatory trade barriers in South Asia are high, and are likely to be adding unnecessarily to cost structures.

11.4 Concluding Comments

A second key principle for piecemeal reform of services — arguably even more important than the first — is to look more broadly than just removing discrimination against foreign providers. This means that trade negotiators and trade ministers should not 'let the tail wag the dog'.

- They should not pursue services trade for its own sake, but rather define their country's overall domestic reform objectives clearly, and let the trade policy initiatives fall naturally out of that.
- They should not get hung up on 'negotiating coin'.
- They should worry primarily about productivity in services, and let trade look after itself.

Part 4

Achieving Services Trade Reform through Domestic Reform

Chapter 12

The Role of Institutions in Structural Reform[1]

Philippa Dee

12.1 Introduction

The economic focus of structural reform is on behind-the-border impediments to the effective functioning of markets. The objective is to establish rules of competition and to remove barriers to competition in instances where competitive markets can be expected to guarantee the most efficient allocation of resources. Where markets alone cannot deliver efficient outcomes, or where there are additional policy objectives besides efficiency, the task of structural reform is to find ways of regulating the markets, or pursuing the additional policy goals, that do the least damage to economic efficiency.

The APEC Leaders' Agenda to Implement Structural Reform has prioritized a number of policy areas that are central to structural reform. A sound economic and legal framework and system of corporate governance are required to establish the rules for competition. Competition policy is required to ensure that there are no artificial barriers to competition, including anti-competitive business practices. Sound regulatory policies and competition policies are required to ensure that when markets are regulated, this is done in an unobtrusive manner. Lastly, sound public sector management is required to hold governments

---

[1] First published as Chapter 4 in Philippa Dee (2010), *Institutions for Economic Reform in Asia*, London and New York: Routledge: 36–52.

accountable for all the ways in which they affect markets, including through their own procurement practices.

Since the economic focus of structural reform is on behind-the-border measures, the political economy of structural reform is primarily domestic. But structural reform is not easy, because of the diversity of economic interests involved. These include the following.

- *Incumbent producers.* Their profits may suffer when reforms mean that they are faced with a more competitive environment. However, they may be driven to innovate to meet the new competitive challenges. They may also benefit from reforms that reduce their own costs. These may be reforms that release them from an unduly restrictive regulatory environment, or complementary reforms in other markets that reduce their input costs.
- *Potential new entrants (domestic or foreign).* Their profits are likely to grow when reforms provide additional business opportunities. These firms may also provide an important source of additional employment, helping to counteract the potential for employment opportunities to shrink in incumbent firms. Indeed, the experience in many economies undertaking reforms in telecommunications, for example, is that even if additional competition causes the incumbent firm to shrink, the overall size of the telecommunications sector can expand greatly.
- *'Upstream' industries that supply inputs to the reforming sector.* Their sales to the current incumbent may suffer, but their sales to new entrants are likely to grow. Importantly, the net effect on these firms depends on the size of the whole reforming sector, not just on the size of the current incumbent.
- *'Downstream' industries that buy inputs from the reforming sector.* If the only impediment to economic performance in the reforming sector is artificial barriers to competition, then downstream firms are likely to benefit when greater competition pushes down the prices of their inputs. If the reforming sector is also subject to soft budget constraints or inefficient cross-subsidies, the situation can be a great deal more complicated. A better policy setting may require the prices of inputs to downstream using industries to rise, so as to better match

production costs, while the distributional concerns are met in less distorting ways. However, there will be additional, indirect effects on these downstream firms. Even if the prices of some of their inputs rise, the better economy-wide allocation of resources may allow the prices of some other inputs to fall. The net effect depends on some quite complicated economy-wide interactions.

- *Consumers.* These are in a similar situation to downstream using industries. However, a further complication is that consumers are not just affected by the prices of the things they buy, but also by the sizes of the incomes they earn. So the net effect on consumers also depends on what happens to employment prospects, not just in the reforming sector, but elsewhere. It also depends on flow-on effects to the informal sector, and to profits, which also enter the incomes streams of at least some consumers. Once again, the net effect depends on some quite complicated economy-wide interactions.
- *Governments.* Particular parts of the bureaucracy can be adversely affected when the regulations they administer are simplified or abolished. For this reason, bureaucrats can be some of the most vocal opponents of efficiency-enhancing structural reforms. Government revenues can also be affected by structural reforms — not just tax revenues, but also the dividend streams from government-owned business enterprises. If government-owned enterprises are themselves the current incumbent firms, governments will have an interest in ensuring that structural reforms that reduce dividend incomes streams are also able to boost tax revenues to compensate. Yet again, the net effect depends on some quite complicated economy-wide interactions.

The role of institutions

If institutions are to support the structural reform process, they need to support both the economics and the political economy of structural reform. Structural reforms may deliver a better set of rules governing the operations of markets, and these new rules will require institutions to implement and enforce them. These institutions, which support the economics of reform, include competition policy regulators, national audit offices, and so on. The desirable characteristics of such institutions to implement and enforce the rules are outlined briefly in Section 12.4 below.

But if structural reforms are to happen at all, there needs to be institutions that can mediate among the diverse range of economic interests involved and build a coalition for reform. The chapter first discusses the political impediments to the adoption of structural reforms.[2] It then discusses the characteristics and functions of institutions that can help to overcome those political impediments. Finally, it gives examples of actual institutions from around the Asia-Pacific region that have these characteristics and perform at least some of these functions. These examples appear as detailed case studies in Dee (2010a).

12.2 Impediments to Structural Reform

There are at least three possible reasons why good structural reforms are not adopted.[3] Each has different implications for the type of regional cooperation that could help support the structural reform process.

- Governments do not know what is policy 'best' or 'better' practice, or lack the capacity to implement it. This argues for external assistance to governments to provide the expertise to undertake systematic reviews of existing policy arrangements, and to evaluate policy alternatives. It also argues for external assistance to build the capacity to implement better policies. Finally, it argues for an international exchange of policy experience to raise awareness of what constitutes better practice, and how to implement it. The APEC regional processes have been highly effective in providing a forum for such exchanges of policy experience to date.
- Governments know what is 'better' practice, but face political resistance from vested interests. This argues for government-sponsored policy reviews to analyse the gains and losses to all players, not just the vested interests, so as to help marshal countervailing interests in favour of reform. It also argues for an

---

[2] Parts of this chapter appeared in Chapter 2 of APEC (2007).

[3] The following taxonomy is due to Ross Garnaut.

international exchange of experience about how to handle vested interests, and how to strengthen domestic institutions in favour of the public interest.

- Governments do not want 'better' policy, because they rely on the rents from current policies for political funding purposes. In these circumstances, government itself is a vested interest, and will be resistant to initiating its own policy reviews that would expose the costs to others of current policies. However, there is a potential role for private (or otherwise independent) policy review institutions to carry out the necessary work of scrutiny, and to marshal countervailing interests in favour of reform.

In all three cases, there is a useful role for institutions that can undertake policy reviews. But the purpose of the reviews varies, depending on the nature of the problem. If the problem is one of identifying better policies, then the policy reviews provide a *technical* solution — they review current policy settings and identify better options. But if the problem is managing vested interests (which may include those within government), then the policy reviews are a *strategy* rather than a technical solution. The policy review institution can provide them as ammunition with which to manage vested interests and build a coalition in favour of reform, but there is no guarantee that the reviews will be decisive in any particular instance. Over time, however, they can help influence the terms of the debate. Each of these roles of policy review institutions is now discussed in turn.

Identifying better policy options

For a policy review process to make a useful contribution to identifying better policy options, there needs to be an orderly policy development process, and the policy review needs to be done early enough to articulate viable options before positions become locked in.[4] Quite often, policy making does not fit this model. Rather, policymaking often results from political imperatives calling for quick action, from deals with

---

[4] Parts of this section are taken from Coghlan (2000), PC (1998) and Banks (2003).

particular interest groups and from bargaining between political interests or parties. Sometimes these approaches result on good policy outcomes, but the risk of failing to do so is undoubtedly higher than in cases where a more open and orderly policy development process is adopted.

Figure 12.1 shows such an open and orderly policy development process. The figure presupposes having certain institutions, or at least institutional divisions. However, an orderly policy development process does not depend on having those exact institutions — other institutions could perform the same functions, depending on the system of government. What is important is the functions themselves.

When the system works in an ideal fashion, a great deal of policy development work takes place before a proposal is put to government. This includes the policy review, a sequential process of articulating the problem, assessing a range of options and recommending the best option or explaining why some other option is recommended. The essential elements of a policy review process are shown in Box 12.1. The last element, a strategy to implement the preferred option and then review its operation, provides an *ex post* check on policy performance.

The ideal policy development process also involves a great deal of consultation. Ideally, there would be two rounds of consultation with all relevant stakeholders, one at the inception of the policy review as the review panel or agency is starting to develop its ideas, and again after the preparation of a draft report that outlines the full analysis and possible policy solutions (sometimes, but not always, including a preferred solution at the draft stage). This consultation process helps the review agency to identify all the costs and benefits to each stakeholder, and provides an opportunity for the review panel to explain its preferred solution to stakeholders.

At the very end of the ideal process, a policy proposal is put to government by the responsible officials and Minister, and a decision is made as to the appropriate form of regulation or other policy action. In a parliamentary system, this decision is often made by Cabinet, a grouping of all government Ministers. When a Minister makes a submission to Cabinet, other Ministers can scrutinize the proposal, although this Cabinet scrutiny is typically not made public. In a presidential system,

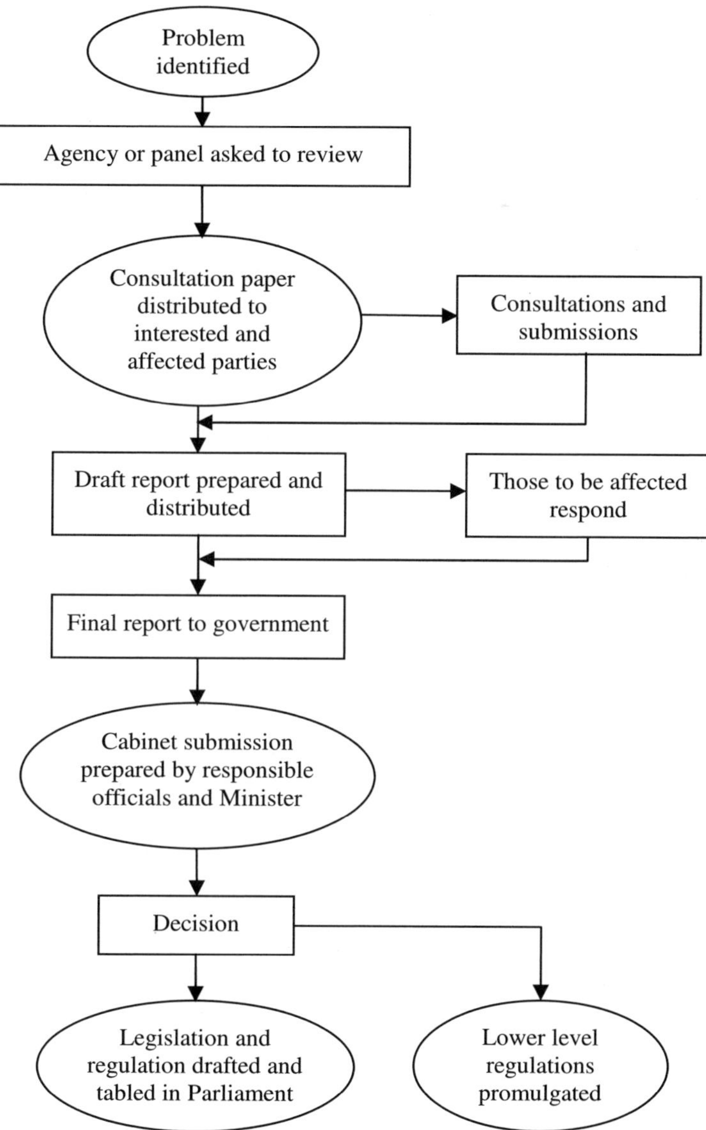

Figure 12.1. An Orderly Policy Development Process
Source: Adapted from Coghlan (2000).

Box 12.1   Elements of a Policy Review

A policy review may set out:

1. The problem or circumstances which give rise to the need for action

2. The desired objective(s)

3. The policy options (regulatory and non-regulatory) that may constitute viable means for achieving the desired objective(s)

4. An assessment of the impact (costs and benefits) on consumers, business, government and the community of each option

5. A consultation statement (the process and results of consultation with all stakeholders)

6. A recommended option

7. A strategy to implement (including consideration of appropriate enforcement mechanisms) and review the preferred option.

the decision may be made by the executive branch, with scrutiny only from within the presidential office.

If the decision is to implement 'black letter law', then legislation will be drafted and tabled in the legislature. This allows for public debate and scrutiny by members of both the ruling government and opposition parties. If the decision is to institute lower level regulations of any sort, these will typically not be tabled in the legislature.

As noted, sometimes the policy development process does not work in an orderly fashion, and a proposal is put to government without any prior policy review or consultation. In this case, there is very little scope for those other than the responsible Minister to have input into the decision-making process. And there is no public scrutiny, if at all, until after the decision is made.

No political system in the Asia-Pacific region measures up to the ideal in every respect. But many have at least some of the institutional elements that allow for prior policy review and consultation, as will be seen later. And the opportunity provided by policy reviews for transparent consultation is the key to their strategic role in managing vested interests.

Managing vested interests

An independent policy review process can help deal with vested interests in a number of ways.

First, policy reviews can help set the agenda — policy change will not happen if nobody talks about it. At this early stage, policy reviews do not need to provide policy recommendations. Indeed, to do so may be seen as pre-emptive of the subsequent policy development process. But they can carefully analyse the costs and benefits of current policy settings, and perhaps canvas some of the policy alternatives without taking a strong or preemptive stance on any particular one. The aim is to highlight who is losing from current policy settings, perhaps to quantify the size of those costs, and to show how the losers might be better off under policy alternatives. This can help alert the losers, who may be aware of the direct costs they face, but may be less aware of the indirect costs. Policy reviews can galvanize them to start pressuring for policy change, and provide ammunition for such a campaign.

Second, reviews can also set the parameters of the debate. Vested interests typically highlight the effects of policy changes on themselves alone. Policy reviews can establish analytical frameworks within which to examine the costs and benefits of current policy settings to all stakeholders — incumbents, new entrants, upstream and downstream industries, consumers and governments. Such frameworks may attract criticism, and lead to sometimes frustrating debates about the assumptions underlying them, and the relative sizes of the costs and benefits. But such frameworks make it much harder to ignore the interests of particular stakeholders altogether, particularly those, such as consumers, who may not be well-organized or are less able to represent themselves.

Third, a policy review process can help to depoliticize a debate. A highly politicized environment is not conducive to rational policy analysis. Nor is sound policy development helped by populist public sentiment that emphasizes slogans over analysis. Most governments will therefore find it in their own interests on occasion to take the heat off an issue by referring it for independent, objective study. The results of such study can then be brought back to the public at a later stage, to educate public opinion about the range of stakeholder interests involved.

Fourth, policy reviews can 'name and shame' the recipients of special deals. This needs to be done carefully, and as neutrally as possible, so as not to inflame the political debate or unduly threaten the credibility of the review institution. But vested interests often rely on a lack of transparency in their dealings with government. So reviews that expose the outcomes of those dealings can help to clarify the gainers from current policy settings, as well as the losers. This in turn can also start to put pressure on the political processes themselves.

Fifth, a policy review process can marshal countervailing interests against vested interests, and help to build a coalition in favour of reform. It may not always be obvious to governments in advance who the champions of structural reform might be. A carefully laid out policy review process that invites the participation of all interested parties can help the champions to self-select. It also provides a forum for groups of champions to identify their common interests, and to agree to cooperate in pro-reform strategies.

Sixth, policy reviews with a sufficiently broad purview can help to identify policy *combinations* that lead to so-called Pareto improvements, where at least some stakeholders are better off and none is worse off. It is sometimes possible to identify such 'virtuous cycles' of structural reforms. For example, manufacturing firms that are put under competitive pressure when their tariff protection is reduced may benefit in turn from transport reforms that reduce their input costs. Importantly, policy reviews can also identify options such as phased implementation or adjustment assistance, which can ease the burden on those that would otherwise lose from structural reform. Both the policy reviews and the review institutions can then achieve acceptance from particular vested interests, and the reviews can thus help to build a *grand* coalition in favour of reform.

Assisting policy coordination within government

A policy review process can help to build a pro-reform consensus outside of government. But Ministers with an economic reform agenda also have to build consensus within government.

Although the structures of government vary widely across the Asia-Pacific region, there are some broad elements in common. Most bureaucracies have at least some government departments with economy-wide responsibilities. These typically include the ministry in charge of tax policy. Sometimes they include a central agency in charge of government spending, or a single agency charged with overall responsibility for structural reform. These ministries tend to take a broad, horizontal view of economic issues.

There are also government departments in charge of overseeing sectional policies. These might include ministries in charge of telecommunications policy, industry policy, health policy, and so on. These ministries are responsible for administering and enforcing current policies, and are staffed with highly skilled and qualified specialists capable of performing these tasks. The interests of such ministries are often closely aligned with the interests of the producers in their respective sectors. It is not necessarily that the ministries are 'captured', just that they have a sectional rather than an economy-wide focus.

Thus Ministers with an economic reform agenda need to be able to harness the economy-wide views of the central agencies in the policy development process, while using the specialist skills and expertise of the sectoral agencies for both policy development and implementation. Coordination problems can arise when the narrower perspective of the sectoral line agencies means that they are against structural reform.

A policy review process can help with such coordination problems. An independent policy review agency can consult with various central and line government departments, just as it consults with all other potential stakeholders. This can alert the sectoral departments to broader economic considerations, just as it does to other stakeholders.

Some economies assign an active coordinating role to one of the central agencies with broad, horizontal portfolio responsibilities. If such agencies are armed with high-quality, independent policy reviews, this too can strengthen the public interest during the policy coordination process.

A final coordination problem is to ensure that sectoral departments abide by coordinated decisions, and implement the structural reforms as intended. Where a central agency has been assigned a coordinating role, it may be in position to exercise budgetary sanctions over line departments. But *ex post* policy reviews can also be used as way of exposing any non-performance by sectoral line agencies.

12.3 The Characteristics of Effective Policy Review Institutions

Keeping in mind the various uses of policy reviews, it is now possible to canvas the characteristics of effective policy review institutions.[5] There are three key attributes.

- *Statutory independence*. The review agency should not be bound by current government policy, as line government departments often are. In conducting its reviews, it needs to be able to provide a full critique of current government policy settings, as a necessary first step in developing and promoting structural reforms. The review agency need not be independent of government funding. Secure tenure arrangements for the individuals responsible for the reviews may be as important as the funding arrangements. The critical point is that the review agency should be able to be fearless in its criticisms.

  Further, the review agency should not have an implicit stake in the *status quo*, as regulatory agencies in charge of implementing current economic policy often do. At worst, such agencies may be captured by current vested interests. But even statutorily independent regulatory institutions can have a strong implicit stake in the regulatory *status quo*, as this is often required to implement current policy effectively. Ideally, therefore, a policy review agency should be independent of current regulatory agencies.

---

[5] Parts of this section draw on PC (1998).

- *An economy-wide view* — the review agency needs to look beyond narrow sectional interests, and to consider *net* gains to the economy as a whole. Tracing through all the economic effects of a particular reform on all the various stakeholders can require considerable analytical capacity. Ensuring that the review agency has access to analytical resources, including skills in partial and general equilibrium modelling and cost benefit analysis, can help to provide such analysis and ensure its credibility.

- *Transparent processes* — the review agency needs to ensure the transparency of the arguments and analysis put to it. It could do this, for example, by holding its consultations in the form of public hearings, or by publishing summaries of its consultations shortly afterwards. The agency's reports to government should also be made public, ensuring the transparency of its own advice to government. Transparent processes bolster the ability of at least some countervailing interests to marshal against particular vested interests, so helping to ensure that an economy-wide view will be taken by policy makers. This can also relieve the government from having to marshal those countervailing interests itself.

A requirement to take an economy-wide view is critical, and a requirement to maintain transparent processes and to consult widely is not enough, for two reasons. Without a requirement to take all views into account, a review agency may simply ignore some views. More importantly, one key group of stakeholders — consumers — rarely participate in public consultation processes. In many economies, consumer interest groups are active on consumer safety issues, but rarely participate on matters of economic efficiency. Having a review agency required to take an economy-wide view ensures that consumer interests are taken into account, as well as the interests of producers and upstream and downstream industries.

Such an agency cannot possibly undertake the policy development for every single policy proposal. But it is particularly useful in those policy areas where there are major potential efficiency or other payoffs to the community from change, but where existing entitlements create resistance to reform. As noted, referring such issues to a statutorily independent body can help to depoliticize them, and allow breathing space for more careful analysis.

The government need not be bound by the recommendations of such a review agency. Indeed, the independence of the agency may be assisted by removing it from any responsibility for downstream policy implementation. Nevertheless, a review agency can still have influence, even if it can sometimes be ignored, for several reasons:

- transparent processes have influence, and such an agency can identify the winners and losers from current policy setting; and
- ideas have influence, and such an agency can formulate reform proposals with high-quality intellectual backing.

A policy review institution will be subject to inevitable attack from vested interests, and so needs to protect its credibility in the face of such attacks. Credibility is enhanced if the organization has the resources to ensure that its analysis is of the highest quality. Credibility may also be enhanced if it can maintain the status of an 'honest broker', mediating among the special interests and making recommendations, but not becoming involved in the politics of the subsequent decision-making. If it is to remain 'above the fray', but if its ideas are to have influence, its ideas need to be championed, or at least debated, by others. Thus an educated and literate commentariat has an important role in adding credibility to an independent review institution. Alternatively, a review agency could credibly remain involved in the subsequent decision-making, so long as it had no clear conflict of interest. However, this involvement would divert resources from its review tasks. Finally, credibility can be built over time as each vested interest becomes the beneficiary of some reforms, even though it loses from others. Thus, even vested interests can come to recognize that they have a stake in the long-term survival of a policy review institution.

A statutorily independent review body is not the only type of organization that could carry out the review and consultation phases of policy development. Government departments can develop their own consultation mechanisms, such as holding round-tables of relevant stakeholders or asking for written submissions from interested parties, as input to their own policy development processes. Such consultations are facilitated by e-government initiatives, and may be effective in eliciting countervailing producer interests.

Inter-departmental committee processes convened by a central agency (such as a Finance Ministry or Presidential office) can also bring a number of stakeholder interests to bear by proxy, through the representative line departments. Inter-departmental processes can be important in themselves for ensuring policy coherence among the different departments. The process is assisted if a central coordinating agency has the authority to ensure that final committee decisions are honoured. Coordinating agencies that have control over the purse strings are generally in a strong position in this regard. So too are agencies that control access to leaders.

However, neither departmental consultations nor inter-departmental committees necessarily ensure that consumer interests are taken into account. Further, public consultation is often limited to the first round of consultation shown in Figure 12.1. Not often do government departments or inter-departmental committees circulate their own reform proposals for public comment once they have been tentatively formulated.

Another type of review mechanism is to convene a review panel of eminent persons on a once-off basis to consider a particular issue. Such panels often rely on the integrity of individual appointees for their independence and impartiality. For example, appointees who come from an independent judicial background may maintain that independence in a review context, while more overtly 'political' appointees may be neither independent nor impartial. Such panels also depend for their effectiveness on their terms of reference, which may direct them to take a broad or narrow focus on a particular issue. And terms of reference that are tailor-made to a particular issue are more likely to be manipulated than policy guidelines that need to be applied across a whole range of issues. Resourcing such panels with a well-trained secretariat from the bureaucracy can provide the skills to carry out economy-wide analysis, but is not sufficient to ensure that it is actually carried out. The commitment of panel members may suffer since their participation is on a one-off basis, especially if it is also part-time.

Finally, a bicameral system of government can sometimes provide one other important mechanism of policy review. Upper houses of government can sometimes instigate their own reviews of legislation before it is voted on in the upper house. The reviews may include public consultation, and may be a useful final screening mechanism. But they are typically highly charged politically, and occur too late in the policy development process to have a major influence on policy design.

12.4 Good Institutions to Implement and Enforce the Rules

Where rules have been developed to promote the greater good of the community as a whole, as opposed to sectional interests, it is important that they be administered and enforced by institutions that do not have conflicts of interest, and are not amenable to capture by sectional interests. Capture occurs when the regulator gets 'too close' to the regulated.

Some institutional strategies to guard against regulatory capture are (Banks 2003):

- *An independent regulator* — having a regulatory body that is formally (preferably statutorily) independent from both the regulated entities, and the government ministries that represent those entities;
- *Generic rather than industry-specific regulation* — often there are regulatory problems that are common across a number of industry segments (eg infrastructure industries with natural monopoly characteristics), and having generic rather than industry-specific regulation can help to prevent capture by any particular industry segment;
- *Adequate funding* — ensuring that the regulator is not dependent for its financial survival on kickbacks or excessive licence fees paid by the regulated;
- *Statutory guidance* — providing the regulator with statutory guidance about the overall objectives of the regulation, and whose interests are to be taken into account in implementing it;

- *Transparency* — requiring the regulator to have open and transparent processes, and to publish the basis of its regulatory decisions;
- *Review* — allowing those affected by regulatory decisions to ask for judicial and/or administrative review of those decisions; and
- *Accountability* — requiring that the regulator report regularly to the relevant Minister or to the legislature about its activities and financial performance.

While regulatory 'capture' is one problem, regulatory 'culture' is another. Recent experience of 'regulatory overreach' suggests that there can be more subtle pressures on regulators that can distort decision-making. These pressures include (Banks 2003):

- *Undue ambition* — for example, there is often insufficient recognition that monopolists have economic incentives to provide an economically efficient *structure* of prices by themselves, even if that price structure might be set at too high a *level* (Baumol, Bailey and Willig 1997).
- *Pressure from government* — even where governance arrangements involve statutory independence, governments may still exert some influence because they provide funding and over time can determine the functions and therefore the power of the regulator.
- *Populism* — like everyone else, regulators like to be 'popular'. Thus an action that is popularly perceived to be profiteering by a large firm may be inappropriately subjected to regulatory control, even if it is objectively efficient (eg where current profits are the reward for a past risky investment). Similarly, there may be pressures on regulators to manipulate asset valuations so as to avoid having to raise the retail prices of a regulated monopoly.
- *Technophilia* — when regulators are required to develop or endorse standards, they can be captured by those who value technology or elegant technological solutions for their own sake.
- *Risk aversion* — regulators face risks with asymmetric returns. It is rare that a regulator will be found deficient for over-regulation, partly because these costs are not generally or immediately apparent, but

will often face censure if a low-risk adverse outcome *is* realized (eg a child dies on play equipment).

- *Precedent* — regulators may be constrained by past decisions in which they have vested their reputation, and which firms have relied upon for key business decisions. This can lead to lock-in of poor implementation and enforcement.

These pressures reinforce that regulatory forbearance is likely to be the appropriate stance in situations in which market outcomes are only a little bit imperfect.

12.5 Regional Examples

Policy review institutions can support the political economy of structural reform in two distinct ways. They can provide a technical solution by helping to identify better policy options, and they can be part of a strategy to deal with vested interests, including those inside government. These dual roles suggest that there could be three key attributes of effective institutions — statutory independence, an economy-wide view, and transparent processes.

Regional examples of such institutions vary widely. However, they all bear at least some of the hallmarks of effective policy review institutions.

One clear example is the Council on Economic and Fiscal Policy in Japan. According to Hosen (2010), this was an institutional innovation of the Koizumi government in Japan designed primarily to deal with the predominance of vested interests in the previous policy making process, and the lack of transparency in that process. It has been instrumental in achieving structural reforms of pensions and medical care, among others.

One key attribute of the Council is its transparency — summary minutes of Council meetings are published within three days of Council meetings. This has helped to expose, and therefore neutralize, the special pleading of business vested interests. Another key attribute is the representation on the Council of government departments with broad portfolio responsibility, as well as two representatives each from academia and the business community. This has ensured an integrated approach to economic policy-making and helps to neutralize vested interests within the bureaucracy.

The Council was not designed to provide technical solutions by identifying policy options. So to date, the Council has not commissioned or undertaken extensive policy reviews on its own initiative. However, Japan faces the challenge of ensuring that the Council's role and influence survive beyond the Koizumi era. According to Hosen, one strategy has been to involve the Council in medium-term economic planning, particularly in the area of fiscal policy.

Another example is the Australian Productivity Commission. Rattigan (1986) describes how it began life in the 1920s as the Australian Tariff Board, and was expected to implement the then government's policy of tailor-making assistance to industry. Instead, considerations of how to design a rational assistance policy led the organization to consider the negative effects of tariffs on inputs, as well as the positive effects of tariffs on outputs. This in turn highlighted how assistance to manufacturing could act as a tax on efficient agricultural exporters — there was no such thing as 'assistance all round', contrary to government intentions. Thus, adopting an economy-wide approach led the organization to a quiet revolution in its own thinking, which was in turn reflected in its policy recommendations to government.

The institution's role has evolved since. Banks and Wonder (2010) describe how, as the deadening effects of high protection became clear, the organization was instrumental in arguing for reductions in industry assistance. In the 1990s, it turned its attention to the inadequate performance of Australia's government-owned enterprises in the infrastructure sector, arguing for reforms that would subject them to greater competition — either 'benchmark' competition with each other, or real competition through the entry of private suppliers into at least some segments of the market. After several name changes, the organization now advises on most areas of structural policy. It remains a purely advisory body. But the three key characteristics of an effective policy review organization are enshrined in its legislation. It was recently commended by the Australian Treasurer as a vital source of public information and advice to government on policy reforms needed to underpin Australia's long-term prosperity.

Llanto (2010) describes how the National Economic and Development Authority (NEDA) in the Philippines serves as the national and regional development plan and program coordinator among the various branches of government. It issues planning guidelines and conducts multi-sectoral and regional consultations for inputs to the Philippines Medium Term Development Plan. The NEDA Board is a cabinet level board composed of the major government departments and is chaired by the President of the Philippines. The NEDA Secretariat provides technical and secretariat services to the various NEDA committees. It has comprehensive information on the implementation of government policies and has the capacity to comment on policies issued by government. According to Llanto, NEDA has latent powers to lead the policy development process, but has not exercised these to date.

Another Philippine institution with a powerful coordinating and *ex post* review role is the Department of Budget and Management. Its public sector management framework has been developed with technical assistance from donors, who drew from the earlier experience of Australia in public expenditure management reform. The department requires various line agencies and corporations to adhere to performance-based or outcome-oriented budgeting, helping to ensure adherence to and implementation of government policies.

A third institution is the Philippines Institute of Development Studies, which has acted as an independent and impartial policy review institution and analyst for more than 25 years. It produces independent policy reviews, research and analysis, which are turned over to the public domain by way of publications, seminars, workshops, and testimony on hearings arranged by various Congressional committees. The organization is not resourced for conducting significant public consultations.

The Philippine examples described by Llanto illustrate how further useful work to support structural reform could take place within a medium-term economic planning framework. Old-fashioned economic planning is often seen as outmoded in an era of open markets and outward-oriented growth strategies, but a medium-term planning process could also provide a useful forum for detailed *ex ante* reviews of policy options, providing a lead in the policy development process. Such a medium-term focus can then bind successive governments and guard against excessive 'short-termism' in policy development.

Mid-term reviews carried out during the planning cycle could also provide an opportunity for *ex post* policy reviews. Thus a traditional planning process could potentially be transformed into a system of continuous rolling *ex ante* and *ex post* policy reviews. Indonesia's BAPPENAS is a traditional planning agency with the technical expertise to undertake detailed policy reviews. However, according to Soesastro, Aswicahyono and Narjoko (2010), it has not yet taken on a more pro-active policy review role. Malaysia is another economy in which the planning process could potentially be transformed into a process of critical *ex ante* and *ex post* policy reviews. According to Nambiar (2010), however, its planning process has been more concerned with ensuring the smooth implementation of given policies, and its policy development sometimes lacks transparency. According to Nitsmer (2010), Thailand could also benefit from a more transparent medium-term perspective in policy development to counter pressures of public opinion that is sometimes overly simplistic.

Other economies besides the Philippines have think-tanks that conduct impartial policy reviews and analysis. Other regional examples are the Centre for Strategic and Independent Studies in Indonesia, the Thai Development Research Institute, the Fiscal Policy Research Institute in Thailand, the Malaysian Institute of Economic Research, the Central Institute for Economic Management in Vietnam and the Chinese Academy of Social Sciences. These organizations vary in the extent to which they sit inside or outside formal government structures, the extent to which their contributions are used in the policy development process. But all have at least some of the characteristics of independent policy review institutions, and perform at least some of those functions.

The problem of developing a mandate for structural reform is not confined to democratically elected governments. China and Vietnam also face the problem of managing vested interests. Early in Vietnam's transition to a market economy, many reforms were seen as clear Pareto improvements — with at least some clear winners, and with no clear losers. According to Vo and Nguyen (2010), the reform process is now more difficult, with some of the government's priority reforms potentially creating losers as well as winners. One strategy that Vietnam has tried is a taskforce approach — putting together groups of experts from within and outside government to consider one particular area of reform. The approach has had mixed success. It has injected a much-needed economy-wide view, but has suffered problems of commitment from the taskforce participants. According to He (2010), China too is at the stage where reforms can potentially create losers as well as winners, and so it requires new strategies to deal with vested interests. China, along with Indonesia, also has problems of coordinating reforms among different parts of government, not just at the national level, but also regionally. For example, a lack of interdepartmental coordination has been identified as a major cause of policy incoherence in Indonesia's sugar trade policy (Stapleton 2006).

Structural reform is an ongoing process. Economic growth and technological change mean that there needs to be constant reassessments of whether and how markets can deliver efficient outcomes, whether the regulatory solutions to market failures are adequate, and whether the relative priorities given to economic and non-economic objectives are appropriate. In the best-managed economies, structural reform is never done.

Governments in all political systems require a mandate of some sort to undertake structural reforms, but a key question is how that mandate is cultivated. At one extreme, a government could choose to implement an economic reform agenda in a 'crash through or crash' style — simply implementing reforms until the cumulative opposition from vested interests and/or public opinion erodes their legitimacy. Alternatively, they could attempt to influence the terms of the debate.

A reform program that makes provision for an independent policy review process may be slower than a 'crash through or crash' program. But it is likely to be more sustainable in the longer term. This is because the reviews do not just identify reform options, they help 'sell' them in the face of opposition from vested interests, overly simplistic public opinion and/or bureaucratic or Ministerial resistance.

Chapter 13

Toward a Theory of Policy Efficiency[1]

Philippa Dee

13.1 Introduction

If South Asia is to survive and prosper in the 'new normal' global economic environment, its behind-the-border domestic reforms will be even more important than before. But these reforms are much more difficult and complex than initial market opening (Soesastro 2010). So it is timely to ask what lessons can be learned about how to 'get the job done'. The focus of Dee (2012) is on the processes and institutional arrangements that will help. In other words, it is about policy efficiency, a concept that is given a formal definition shortly.

While the focus of Dee (2012) is not primarily on the content of the reforms, their further necessity is undeniable. As Dasgupta, Pitigala and Gourdon (2012) observe, recovery from the global financial crisis in 2008–09 will involve a fundamental restructuring of the global economy. Under the 'new normal', the developed countries of Europe and North America will save more, spend less and grow more slowly. Their demand patterns will not provide the same impetus for export growth for South Asia and other developing regions, except perhaps in services. Global recovery will instead be led by emerging markets. This means that the South Asian region will have to look East. It will also have to look internally for sources of growth.

---

[1] This is an edited version of Chapter 1 in Philippa Dee (2012), *Economic Reform Processes in South Asia*, London and New York: Routledge: 1–22.

A 'look East' strategy can take advantage of South Asia's comparative advantage (relative to East Asia) in food, organic and inorganic materials, textiles, metal products and labour-intensive manufactures such as apparel, footwear, parts and jewellery, as well as in services. But if South Asia is to link into East Asia's existing production networks, it will have to significantly improve its transport and logistics services. Currently, the quality of these services is better than in some of the new low-income members of the Association of Southeast Asian Nations (ASEAN), but significantly poorer than in China or some of the original ASEAN members. It will also have to lower border trade barriers that remain well above those in East Asia, despite past reforms.

Looking internally will involve boosting intra-regional trade, as well as cultivating the large internal markets in the region. The uncharacteristically low levels of intra-regional trade currently are an indication of significant economic and political barriers — the region has one of the most fragmented markets in the world. Converting internal and regional markets into sources of growth will require tackling the physical, logistical and regulatory barriers to the movement of goods and services both within and between South Asian economies.

Under the 'new normal', South Asia will have to intensify its efforts at behind-the-border domestic reforms. But these are difficult. So what institutional mechanisms can the region use to make the job easier, and to improve the success rate?

13.2 Defining Policy Efficiency

As used here, the concept of policy efficiency applies to the policy making *process*. Policy efficiency ensures that difficult but worthwhile reforms are identified, prioritized, initiated, implemented and sustained. While it may be true that some reforms will generate larger economy-wide benefits than others, the concept of policy efficiency is not primarily about picking which ones are better. It is about ensuring that at least some worthwhile reforms are actually adopted, rather than staying on the economist's drawing board.

The concept of policy efficiency goes beyond economic 'business as usual'. Economists normally operate as policy draftspeople. They design policies that, according to theory and past evidence, will lead to improvements in economic well-being. They may identify which policies will generate larger net gains than others. They may also identify and rank possible adjustment costs. But implementation is not normally their concern. Implementation itself is left to politicians and bureaucrats. This study of which policies get adopted and which stay on the drawing board is left to political scientists.

The concept of policy efficiency also goes beyond political economy 'business as usual'. Studies of political economy will explain whether a policy is adopted or not as the outcome of a balance of interests — one group of voters versus another, politicians versus voters, politicians versus lobby groups, politicians versus bureaucrats, and so on. But the process is normally static. Each group's interests remain fixed, and there is no scope for learning, or for groups to change their minds about their policy priorities.

The concept of policy efficiency is related to the concept of 'political will'. Some definitions of political will are tautological — political will is what it takes to get a policy adopted, and if it is not adopted, this shows that political will is lacking. Other definitions of political will describe the environment in which policies are actually adopted. For example, Andrews (2008) talks about 'reform space' as an environment in which there is an *acceptance* of the need for reform, and the *authority* and *ability* to carry it out (see Figure 13.1).

Policy efficiency is about the cultivation of political will. It is about institutional mechanisms that help to create acceptance of the need for reform, that provide the authority for reformers to do their job, and that provide a learning environment where ability can be developed.

13.3 Achieving Policy Efficiency

Achieving policy efficiency means that reforms will move off the drawing board to be implemented and sustained over time.

     Services Trade Reform: Making Sense of It

Is there **acceptance**: Of the need for change and reform? Of the specific reform idea? Of the monetary costs of reform? Of the social costs for reformers? Do embedded incentive mechanisms facilitate or hinder acceptance, especially when transitioning from old to new?	
Is there **authority**? Does legislation allow people to challenge the *status quo* and initiate reform? Do formal organizational structures and rules allow reformers to do what is needed? Do informal organizational norms allow reformers to do what is needed?	
Is there **ability**? Are there enough people, with appropriate skills, to conceptualize and implement the reform? Are there the appropriate information sources to help conceptualize, plan, implement and institutionalize the reform?	Reform space, at the intersection of A, A, A, determines how much can be achieved

Figure 13.1. Reform Space
Source: Andrews (2008).

Understanding what it takes to achieve policy efficiency means understanding first what gets in the way of better policies being adopted.

An earlier volume (Dee 2010a) started with the following taxonomy of what gets in the way of better policies being adopted.

- Governments do not know what is policy 'best' or 'better' practice, or lack the capacity to implement it.
- Governments know what is 'better' practice, but face political resistance from vested interests.
- Governments do not want 'better' policy, because they rely on the rents from current policies for political funding purposes.

Thus the key problems were seen essentially as two-fold — ignorance, or vested interests (including those inside government). Thus policy efficiency could be promoted by institutional arrangements that helped to overcome these two problems. The earlier volume argued that in both cases, there was a useful role for policy reviews, and hence for institutions that could undertake them.

If the problem was one of identifying better policies, then the policy reviews could provide a technical solution — they could review current policy settings and identify better options. But if the problem was managing vested interests (including those within government), then policy reviews would be a strategy rather than a technical solution. They would provide ammunition with which to manage vested interests and build a coalition in favour of reform, although there would be no guarantee that the reviews would be decisive in any particular instance. Over time, however, they could help influence the terms of the debate.[2]

The earlier volume also argued that there are three key characteristics of effective policy review institutions:

- *Statutory independence* — the review agency should not be bound by current government policy, as line government departments often are. Further, the review agency should not have an implicit stake in the *status quo*, as regulatory agencies in charge of *implementing* current economic policy often do.
- *An economy-wide view* — the review agency needs to look beyond narrow sectional interests, and to consider net gains to the economy as a whole. Tracing through all the economic effects of a particular reform on all the various stakeholders can require considerable analytical capacity, so providing sufficient resources may be important for ensuring credibility of the analysis.
- *Transparent processes* — the review agency needs to ensure the transparency of the arguments and analysis put to it. The agency's reports to government should also be made public, ensuring the transparency of its own advice to government.

Transparent processes would bolster the ability of at least some countervailing interests to marshal against particular vested interests, so helping to ensure that an economy-wide view would be taken by policy

---

[2] The previous chapter in this volume outlined both these arguments in more detail.

makers. This could also relieve the government from having to marshal those countervailing interests itself.

Thus the earlier volume argued that sustainable economic reform required transparency and a process of coalition building. Furthermore, cultivating coalitions in favour of reform was not just a matter of compensating or 'buying off' losers (compare Haggard and Webb 1994b), although compensation clearly had a useful role (for example, Banks and Wonder 2010). Policy reviews also helped to overcome imperfect information (including information asymmetries), and possibly influence levels of commitment. In short, they were institutional mechanisms that promoted learning, and could thus persuade groups to change their minds about their policy priorities.

The earlier volume showed how policy reviews could occur both *ex ante* and *ex post*, contributing to an ongoing, rolling process of policy development and review. Obviously, a crisis situation may sometimes be sufficiently severe that such an orderly process of policy development was completely disrupted. Nevertheless, policy reviews during and after a crisis event could still help to correct policy mistakes at an early stage.

The earlier volume examined eight case studies of structural reforms in the East Asian region. Two case studies were from developed democracies in Japan and Australia. Four were from developing democracies in the Philippines, Indonesia, Malaysia and Thailand. Two were in developing countries, Vietnam and China, the central governments of which are not democratically elected but as the volume made clear, still have to manage a variety of vested interests and maintain a mandate for reform. The volume found that in each case, the reform process had been supported to a greater or lesser extent by indigenous institutions that undertook at least some of the functions, and had at least some of the characteristics, of effective policy review institutions.

Does this work in South Asia? A key purpose of Dee (2012) is to present a series of case studies of reform in South Asia to find out. The case studies are not designed to give a comprehensive coverage of reform *content* — they do not cover all major reforms in the region, nor are they absolutely comprehensive in the reforms they do cover. Their purpose is primarily to provide insights into the processes and institutions that have allowed these reforms to move off the drawing board.

At the outset, however, it is clear that in South Asia, politics has often played a more complex and influential role over economic outcomes than in East Asia. Before proceeding to the case studies, it is therefore useful to revisit the theoretical literature on the political economy of reform, in order to identify political constraints to achieving policy efficiency.

13.4 Political Constraints to Achieving Policy Efficiency

There have been two main waves of literature on the political constraints to achieving economic reform.

In the 1990s, a few efforts were taken to look back at case studies of past reforms in a range of countries, and to try to generalize about the conditions that contributed to success or failure. Many of the case studies were drawn from the Latin American experiences with macroeconomic crisis, or with the collapse of communism in Eastern European transition economies. Reviews along these lines are in Williamson (1994), Bresser Pereira *et al.* (1993) and Haggard and Webb (1994a).

Williamson (1994) set out to test 16 hypotheses about what made reform feasible and successful — see Table 13.1. While none of the hypotheses were shown to be necessary or sufficient, a few received strong support:

- the need for a strong political base;
- visionary leadership; and
- a coherent economic team.

Propositions that were disproved were that reform required authoritarian regimes, or that it was a right wing endeavour.

Of particular relevance here are the conflicting views of Jeffrey Sachs (from Williamson 1994) and Adam Przeworski (from Bresser Pereira *et al.* 1993) about the desirability of seeking broad public support for a reform agenda. Sachs' personal experience was primarily with the major

Table 13.1. Hypotheses about Reform

Hypothesis
1. Policy reforms emerge in response to crisis
2. Strong external support (aid) is an important condition for successful reform
3. Authoritarian regimes are best at carrying out reform
4. Policy reform is a right wing program
5. Reformers enjoy a 'honeymoon period' of support before opposition builds up
6. Reforms are difficult to sustain unless the government has a solid base of legislative support
7. A government may compensate for the lack of a strong base of support if the opposition is weak and frightened
8. Social consensus is a powerful factor impelling reform
9. Visionary leadership is important
10. A coherent and united economic team is important
11. Successful reform requires economists in positions of political responsibility
12. Successful reform requires a comprehensive program capable of rapid implementation
13. Reformers should mask their intentions to the general public
14. Reformers should make good use of the media
15. Reform becomes easier of the losers are compensated
16. Sustainability can be enhanced by accelerating the emergence of winners

Source: Williamson (1994).

macroeconomic crises of Bolivia, Poland, Russia, and elsewhere. In his view, reformers do not succeed by building social consensus. In deep crisis, there is no consensus to build on, only confusion and a range of conflicting opinions. In his view, it is at best a waste of time to seek a broad coalition for reform because most people do not understand what is required. Sachs therefore takes a rather patronizing and dismissive view of the general polity. He probably reflects the secret view of many professional economists — 'if only they would put me in charge, then everything would be alright'.

By contrast, Przeworski's experience with Polish reform makes him think that 'big bang' approaches to reform not only weaken democratic political institutions, they also make errors in economic policy more likely. In addition, he argues that these approaches end up threatening the sustainability of economic reforms. He documents this with his own experience of Polish reforms. Closer to the Asian region, there is a good example of big bang approaches threatening sustainability in the New Zealand experience with economic reforms.

Haggard and Webb (1994b) also stress the importance of the distinction between what it takes to initiate reforms, and what it takes to sustain them. When initiating reforms, they note that politicians can counter opposition with a range of tactics, such as using the technical expertise of their staff, their power over the agenda, broad political mandates, and by exploiting political and institutional circumstances. In the long run, they argue that reform must involve a process of coalition building.

While the earlier phase of literature was based on practical case studies, the more recent literature has delved into the theoretical basis for the inability to implement reforms, using game theory techniques. In an early review, Rodrik (1996) found myopia an unconvincing explanation for bad policy choices. But in papers by Fernandez and Rodrik (1991) and Dewatripont and Roland (1992), he pointed to imperfect information and time inconsistency (arising from inability to make credible commitments) as possible reasons.

The importance of information and commitment problems has been confirmed in the more recent theoretical literature, some of which has also focussed on political constraints. One of the most complete elaborations of the role of politics in economic policy making is by Persson and Tabellini (1995, 1999, 2002), in the context of monetary and fiscal policy making.

Some of their analysis is static (formalized as a one-period decision making horizon, as in Persson and Tabellini 2002). In the static analysis, the political problems that might get in the way of good economic policy making are the standard explanations from political economy — conflicting interests among voters, conflicting interests of voters and politicians, and conflicting interests among different politicians. But a static frame of analysis does not provide useful insights into how to promote learning.

More insightful for the current purpose is their dynamic analysis (formalized as a two-period decision making horizon, as in Persson and Tabellini 1999). Using this framework, they identify the following incentive constraints to achieving good policy outcomes.

Lack of credibility. Desirable policies may lack credibility because governments are unable to credibly commit to maintaining them over time (the time inconsistency problem).

Political opportunism. Desirable policies may not be adopted because governments may be prepared to 'do what it takes', including adopting bad policy, to get elected. This constraint operates if politicians value holding office *per se* (perhaps because of the perks it provides) and voters, although rational, are uninformed. This can lead to electoral cycles in policies *before* elections, so as to sway voter behaviour.

Political ideology. This may shape policy formation if different parties pursue different ideological platforms once in office, and if the election outcome is uncertain. In the theoretical models, this can lead to electoral cycles in policies *after* elections, as the winning party tries to influence economic outcomes (for example, by foreclosing the options of a future government of the opposite persuasion).

Divided government. If more than one group is involved in decision making (for example, in coalition governments, federal governments, or where governments are lobbied by special interests), this may lead to overspending. Each decision maker fully internalizes the benefits of public spending but only bears a fraction of the cost (the 'common pool' problem).

Pressure for redistribution. The obvious implication here is that each policy will be valued not only for its impact on economic efficiency, but also for its redistributive effects.

The authors also discuss what institutional mechanisms are useful for overcoming these incentive constraints. When the problem is lack of credibility arising from time inconsistency, the answer is to delegate the task to an independent policy maker, and/or to limit the scope of the task. Thus monetary policy is often delegated to an independent monetary authority (often a central bank), whose objective is stated in simple terms (for example, inflation targeting). Fiscal policy is rarely delegated, but may be subject to rules that limit spending levels.

Delegation of tasks to an independent authority can also help to overcome electoral cycles in policy making arising from either political opportunism or political ideology. Where ideology is the problem, there is also a case for institutional checks and balances that can moderate political conflict and policy extremism.

By contrast, the authors argue that an institutional solution to divided government is to centralize power in the hands of a single high-level decision maker. In fiscal policy, a two-stage budgeting strategy may help, where decisions about the size of the budget are made independently of its distribution.

13.5 The Role of (High Level) Bureaucracy

If delegation can help alleviate at least some of these incentive constraints to good policy, is it likely to take place in practice? In a further two papers, Alesina and Tabellini (2007, 2008) examine the role of the bureaucracy to answer this question. They find that the delegation of tasks that politicians are likely to prefer need not align with what voters would prefer. So this can become another impediment to good policy.

It is worthwhile examining these papers in more detail, for two reasons. The first is to get a flavour of the information problems that lead to this type of result. With an understanding of these information problems, it is possible to outline what types of learning might help — and whether policy reviews might provide that learning. The second is to better understand the role of high level bureaucracy in policy making. Some South Asian countries have inherited well-developed bureaucratic structures from their British colonial past. As the case studies in this volume make clear, these bureaucracies have played an important role, for good and ill, in South Asian policy development.

In the theoretical papers of Alesina and Tabellini (2007, 2008), both politicians and bureaucrats are held accountable to voter interests, but by different mechanisms. Politicians are held accountable to the electorate, at election time — a now-standard treatment of political behaviour. By contrast, top level bureaucrats (ie those most likely to be involved in policy development, as opposed to implementation) are held accountable by their professional peers, or by the public at large, for how they fulfil the goals of their organization (which at least initially align with the goals of the electorate). Thus bureaucrats are motivated by 'career concerns' — their perceived ability at meeting organizational goals. This 'career concern' model of bureaucratic behaviour has also been used by Holmstrom (1999) and Dewatripont, Jewitt and Tirole (1999 a, b).[3]

This difference in accountability mechanisms leads to different behaviour — politicians put in effort so as to maximize their probability of re-election; bureaucrats put in effort so as to maximize their perceived ability. In any given situation, there is no clear presumption that politicians will try harder than bureaucrats, or vice versa — that depends on the relative rewards to each group from their effort. However, in some circumstances, politicians will ease off, because they have met their re-election threshold, while bureaucrats will keep on trying.

Given this difference in behaviour, the authors first consider the question of which tasks, in what circumstances, *should* be delegated to bureaucrats rather than politicians.

They find that bureaucrats are preferable for difficult tasks, for which ability is more important than effort. This is because, by undertaking objectively more difficult tasks, bureaucrats are seen by their peers to have higher perceived ability (by contrast, anyone can do simple tasks). Bureaucrats fully internalize the benefits of this higher perceived ability, and 'rise to the challenge'. By contrast, politicians only want to overcome their re-election threshold.

The authors note that this tends to be consistent with allocations in the real world. While the problem of time inconsistency is a well-known reason for monetary policy to be delegated to bureaucrats (ie central bankers), many countries also delegate microeconomic regulatory tasks to government departments or to competition authorities under only very general 'public interest' guidelines. This gives these delegated

---

[3] In other papers, politicians and/or bureaucrats are seen to be motivated by objectives other than voter welfare. In Maskin and Tirole (2004), political incumbents aim to please the voters while bureaucrats (judges) have intrinsic motivations. In Besley and Coate (2003) and Schultz (2004), both bureaucrats and politicians have intrinsic motivations. In the limit, it is easy to see how good policy choice can be perverted if motivations are not aligned. A tougher but more subtle task is to identify situations where there are problems in achieving good policy choices even when politicians' and bureaucrats' hearts are in the right place, and then to identify when and how institutional innovations can assist in overcoming these principal–agent problems.

bureaucrats considerable scope for policy development, not just implementation.

An East Asian example that possibly reflects a combination of time inconsistency and complexity motives is the development of public expenditure management reforms by the Department of Budget and Management in the Philippines (Llanto 2010). This is by no means the only example of where bureaucrats have tried to develop a medium-term budget planning framework as a way of disciplining the short-termism of politicians (another example is mentioned in Hosen 2010). But as the Philippine example makes clear, developing an effective budgetary management framework that 'has teeth' by being linked directly to policy development is a complex process. In the Philippines, it required developing a medium-term expenditure framework, an organizational performance indicator framework and an accountability, monitoring and evaluation framework, and entrenching these planning tools throughout the public service.

Alesina and Tabellini (2007) also consider the role of governments in achieving redistribution, something that has been a high priority in development models in South Asia. Here, a particular form of information asymmetry plays a key role in the outcome. If the electorate is more uncertain about the opposition's future redistributive policies than those of the incumbent, then this confers an incumbency advantage. This in turn reduces the politician's effort in redistributive tasks, relative to non-redistributive (eg efficiency improving) tasks. The politician can reduce effort, but by redistributing towards a majority of voters can still be re-elected, even if some voters lose. Nevertheless, there is no clear presumption that voters at the constitutional stage would prefer bureaucrats rather than politicians to undertake the redistribution.[4] Politicians themselves will have a strong preference to retain redistributive tasks, precisely because they can reduce effort while still pleasing the majority.

---

[4] If voters are risk averse and the bureaucrats can be trusted to be fair (providing equal distribution), then the bureaucrats are probably preferred. This is because bureaucrats will put in more effort, and will not expose voters to the risk of being in the minority.

Alesina and Tabellini (2008) consider more generally what delegation of authority politicians are actually likely to choose on an ongoing basis, as opposed to what voters would choose at the constitutional stage. Typically, politicians would not make the same choices as voters. Firstly, politicians would tend to delegate tasks requiring costly effort to bureaucrats, while retaining tasks that provide rents of office (an excess of the rewards of office over the costs of effort). Secondly, as just noted, there is a bias against delegating tasks that involve redistribution, since they involve an incumbency advantage and lower equilibrium effort. Thirdly, there is also likely to be a bias against delegating tasks when politicians can extract rents from lobby groups, rather than simply redirecting a given amount of effort because of them. This is more likely when there are several competing lobby groups, willing to fight each other for political favours. Finally, there are offsetting considerations in whether politicians will delegate more risky tasks. One the one hand, bureaucrats can act as risk takers (or 'scapegoats') for politicians. On the other hand, riskier tasks are associated with greater rents of office.

13.6 Easing the Political Constraints to Policy Efficiency

If independent policy reviews are to influence actual policy choices, they must do two things:

- they must identify better policy options;
- they must raise the cost to incumbent politicians of not adopting those better options, even if those options entail more effort, or otherwise reduce the rents of office.

The analysis of Alesina and Tabellini (2007, 2008) suggests at least two key ways in which policy reviews can improve the accountability of politicians to voter wishes, thereby achieving these objectives. One involves providing better information to incumbent politicians. Another involves providing better information to the political opposition (which in single-party states may be different factions within the Party).

In the above theoretical models, bureaucrats are good at pursuing efficiency objectives while politicians are also in a position to effect compensation to losers. According to Alesina and Tabellini (2008), this is almost what defines the distinction between politicians and bureaucrats. When policies designed to promote efficiency also have redistributional consequences (as they almost invariably do in the realm of structural reform), then at least some political delegation may be required to ensure than the necessary compensation of losers takes place, either directly or by bundling policies. The downside to full political delegation is that politicians' effort is lower than bureaucratic effort would be, either because bundling dilutes politicians' incentives,[5] or because structural reforms tend to be difficult.

One important agenda-setting role of policy reviews is to re-evaluate the assignment of policy targets and instruments. With suitable reassignment, a better division of labour can be achieved between bureaucratic and political effort that mitigates this tendency of politicians to reduce effort. When structural reform policies have both efficiency and equity implications, politicians may try less hard than bureaucrats to achieve the efficiency gains, but manipulate the redistributional implications to ensure re-election. If an additional policy instrument were brought to bear to meet the redistributional goals, the structural reform policy could be delegated to bureaucrats, who could pursue the efficiency gains without the same compromises.

Nambiar (2010) and Nitsmer (2010) provide two East Asian examples of the ways in which efficiency goals can be compromised in the process of compensating particular groups. Nambiar (2010) describes several examples of what has been an almost endemic problem in Malaysian policy making, whereby virtually every economic policy has had a New Economic Policy dimension. This has meant that in virtually every policy area, the pursuit of efficiency goals has been compromised by elements that purport to promote Bumiputera interests. It would have been far less damaging economically to assign one or a few policies

---

[5] Politicians are not judged separately on their performance on each task; they may put a lot of effort into one task, but still lose the election because they cannot perform the other. Recognition of this risk induces them to reduce effort on both tasks.

(such a skills and management training) to promote Bumiputera participation in economic activity, and to leave the design of other policies free to maximize efficiency gains. One important function of independent policy reviews would be to canvas this reassignment.

Similarly, Nitsmer (2010) documents how the achievement of efficiencies in urban transport in Thailand has been compromised by price controls and other measures that are purportedly to help the poor. In practice, they have diluted incentives to invest in infrastructure to such an extent that the poor now have the least access to public transport of any group. One important function of independent policy reviews in this case would be to highlight the unintended consequences of trying to achieve two targets with a single instrument.

Thus one way that incumbent politicians can be persuaded to adopt better policies, even if those policies require more effort, is if they can be persuaded that those policies can be safely delegated to bureaucrats, in situations where bureaucrats can be trusted to rise to the challenge. Separating efficiency from redistributional issues, and assigning different policy instruments to each, is one way in which politicians can be persuaded to delegate questions of efficiency (especially if they are difficult), while allowing them to retain power over redistribution.

In the above theoretical models, another factor that tends to blunt politicians' effort is the incumbency advantage that arises from voters being more uncertain about the opposition's future redistributive policies than those of the incumbent. As Alesina and Tabellini (2007, p. 176) note, this means that

> it is in the interest of politicians to pretend that they are ideologically biased in favour of specific groups or policies, even if in reality they are purely opportunistic. The ideology of politicians is like their brand name: it keeps voters attached to parties and reduces uncertainty about how politicians would act once in office.

Policy reviews can highlight policy alternatives that yield greater efficiency gains than current policies, and/or have distributional consequences that benefit a different set of economic agents. If this information can be used by opposition parties to create a credible threat to do better than the incumbents if elected, then this can demolish any incumbency advantage. Indeed, one reason why structural reform is not solely a right wing endeavour is because such credible threats have sometimes induced left wing parties to co-opt right wing agendas to stay in power.

Schultz (2004) is explicit about access to information being the key to the incumbency advantage. He argues that the electorate at large has insufficient incentives to become informed about complicated political or economic issues, while politicians are briefed by experts and bureaucrats and it is their job to gather information and make decisions.

Independent policy reviews can widen the information base to the electorate at large, and also to the opposition. In at least some political climates, this can help to create a credible threat that the opposition will implement better policies than the incumbent, thus encouraging the incumbent to try harder. Note that this makes it doubly important that the policy review institutions are seen as being independent. To have influence, they need to be of use to both the political incumbents and the opposition.

But the above analysis also confirms the types of political circumstance in which independent policy reviews will be less effective in creating a credible threat. One is if politicians, both incumbent and opposition, are unduly ideological. In this case, they will not be persuaded by new arguments, information or policy options that do not accord with their preconceived political platforms. At the other extreme, independent policy reviews will also be less effective if politicians, both incumbent and opposition, are seen by the electorate as being unduly opportunistic. In this case, whatever political promises they make will not be seen as credible.

Those East Asian case studies in Dee (2010a) where policy reviews have been less effective in influencing actual policy choices can be seen to fit this pattern. In the Philippines and Thailand, the political elites have tended to be opportunistic, and policy think tanks have struggled to find the kind of influence over policy choice that they have (sometimes) enjoyed in Indonesia or Australia (although note that this has not prevented reforms being initiated from within the Philippine bureaucracy). In Malaysia, by contrast, the ideological commitment to the New Economic Policy framework also made policy choice fairly impervious to independent policy analysis.

13.7 Application to South Asia

South Asia provides a new set of reform experiences with which to test the institutional and political influences on policy efficiency. The three countries examined here (India, Pakistan, Sri Lanka) share some broad similarities. All inherited British colonial institutional structures. All turned from inward looking import substitution to an outward looking development model. All experienced macroeconomic crises in the late 1980s or early 1990s, which provided a strong impetus for their reform efforts. All shared the involvement of international institutions in constructing their structural reform programs. But in all three countries, the reforms had strong home-grown dimensions, and thus considerable domestic ownership.

How do these reform experiences shed light on the sources of policy efficiency? The reminder of this section looks broadly at the extent to which the South Asian case studies confirm or contradict the above hypotheses about what promotes policy efficiency, and what constrains it. As noted earlier, the selection of case studies was based not on the content or importance of the reforms, but on what they revealed about policy efficiency, particularly in the face of political constraints. The final section summarizes the individual case studies in more detail, to provide guidance to readers on where further evidence on policy efficiency can be found.

The earlier experiences of reform in Latin America and Eastern Europe suggested that strong success factors were visionary leadership, a strong political base and a coherent economic team. The South Asian case studies in this volume confirm the importance of visionary leadership. Although not national leaders themselves at the time, Manmohan Singh in India and Shaukat Aziz in Pakistan provided the vision for successful reform efforts in the 1990s, and were supported by their national leaders. In Sri Lanka, the reforms of 1989–90 were the product of a strong executive presidency.

Where these visionary leaders were able to assemble a strong and coherent team, the reforms tended to be better thought out and more rigorously implemented, also contributing to their success and longevity. Reforms in Pakistan and Sri Lanka were sometimes the product of leaders operating as a one-man band and as a result, the reforms were not always well-formulated, and did not always survive in implementation.

But the successful reforms in South Asia have rarely been the product of a strong political base. Instead, they have often come from coalition governments, or otherwise arisen during times of great social and political instability. Politics may have constrained the reform process, but it certainly has not prevented it.

Good information and analysis about reform options has clearly helped the reform process. For a start, the availability of high quality indigenous studies of reform options helped to establish critical domestic ownership in India, despite the involvement of the International Monetary Fund and the World Bank. India also has well-established mechanisms for independent formulation of reform options by highly qualified experts through its committee system in the case of banking reforms, and through its Finance Commissions in the case of fiscal policy reforms. By contrast, trade policy formulation has been left primarily in the hands of a line government department, which has not been as successful in formulating options proactively, or analysing their effects. In Pakistan and Sri Lanka, one of the key weaknesses of the reform efforts pushed by one-man bands or small teams has been the poor quality of policy development. Where reforms have been more successful (as in financial sector reforms in Pakistan), it has been because the visionary leaders have assembled teams of qualified experts to carry out detailed policy formulation.

There are a few instances in the cases studies where governments have agreed to delegate tasks to experts and to impose rules, so as to overcome commitment problems or to counter undue political opportunism. The most striking example is the enactment of fiscal responsibility legislation by the central government and 26 out of 28 state governments in India. The legislation imposed substantially harder budget constraints than previously, although it still allowed 'flexibility' that has been exploited in the recent past. Another example of delegation is the establishment of an independent regulatory agency for telecommunications in India, and the side-lining of the line government department previously responsible.

There are also examples where policy advisors have been able to offer new assignments of policy targets and instruments. An example from India is the ongoing efforts of banking review committees to relax the initially very stringent priority sector norms, to allow banks to make credit allocations on the basis of risk assessment, and to persuade politicians to use fiscal rather than credit allocation instruments to achieve redistribution objectives. In the absence of quick opportunities to do so, decision-makers have resisted such a wholesale reassignment, but the bureaucrats and politicians have jointly found a way to relax the priority sector norms. This is an example of partial success at a reassignment of policy instruments. It is also an example of how politicians in India have tended to minimize the extent of dramatic breaks with the past.

A further useful role for high level bureaucracy is in making information about policy options available to opposition parties, so as to reduce incumbency bias. Clearly, the lengthy and relatively open processes of consultation and policy debate in India have contributed in this way in at least some spheres. In banking, for example, there has been continuity across different regimes of independent policy advisory institutions, and even of individual committee chairs, ensuring that politicians of all persuasions have been able to access and process the policy advice without the advice becoming politicized. In Pakistan, by contrast, loud reform announcements have often been made but bureaucrats have tended to change along with governments, so the bureaucracy has been more politicized and less in a position to service incumbent and opposition parties equally. A similar politicization of the bureaucracy occurred during the second wave of Sri Lanka's reforms. There was also a tendency for politicians to bypass the administrative system altogether. Not only did the bureaucracy lose the opportunity to serve the politicians impartially, there was decay over time in their capacity to undertake technical assessments of the costs and benefits of reforms.

The South Asian region provides some interesting examples of managing vested interests and building coalitions in favour of reform. As noted, the policy making process in India often involves lengthy periods of public discussion and debate after recommendations are made, and before a decision is taken. Coalition building appears to have been a strength of Indian policy making, and one of the successful strategies appears to have been for politicians to stress the consistency of proposed reforms with the traditional development model. The lengthy process of debate has allowed new ideas to be gradually coopted into the existing consensus. As a result, reform has been incremental and dramatic changes have been avoided, but the reforms have had legitimacy and therefore longevity. But as noted, a weakness has sometimes been in the analysis and formulation of the reform proposals themselves.

In Pakistan, and to a lesser extent Sri Lanka, the reform process has involved periods of much less active coalition building in favour of particular reforms. In the first wave of Sri Lankan reforms, consensus was obtained partly by offering compensation to potential losers. But in both countries, policy U-turns have been more frequent as new leaders have stalled or reversed the reforms of their immediate predecessors, even though there may have been a broad political consensus about the ongoing need for reform.

Thus there have been some notable political constraints on policy efficiency in South Asia. One feature of the region has been the preponderance of coalition governments, particularly in India and Sri Lanka. But while coalitions may imply divided government and make achieving reforms more difficult, coalitions can also increase or dampen the extent to which the government is driven by ideology or opportunism. One of the reasons put forward for why India has been able to sustain reforms in a period of coalition governments is that the regional coalition partners have been opportunistic but ideologically neutral, forcing a degree of pragmatism on the two major parties and moderating their ideological stances. So the problem of divided government has been offset by a reduction in political ideology. In Sri Lanka, by contrast, when a left leaning major party was in coalition with left leaning minor parties, there was not the dilution of ideology as in India. As a result, coalition politics proved a stronger barrier to reform.

Clearly, much of the politics in the region has been far too complicated to be summarized in simple terms of ideology versus opportunism. For example, ethnic and social tensions have been a dominant force in Sri Lankan politics, sufficiently strong to lead to violence and civil war. Pakistan has had a similarly turbulent political history, with military coups, cross-border tensions with neighbouring India and extremist insurgency being just some of the elements involved. Yet it is no coincidence that the most successful period of economic reform in Pakistan was during the military-cum-civilian government of Pervez Musharraf. In the early years, the military government was less driven by ideology or opportunism, but rather by the imperative to secure economic development. This was the period when the strongest reform push occurred. Over time, however, the military-cum-civilian government needed to secure legitimacy and became more opportunistic to buy support. And whatever else can be said of Pakistan's civilian governments, they have been ideologically opposed to their military predecessors. So in recent times Pakistan has experienced policy cycles as civilian governments have halted or reversed the policies of their military predecessors.

The South Asian experience shows how the political climate can condition and constrain policy efficiency. But even in difficult political circumstances, there have been institutional strategies that have helped to ensure that at least some reforms have moved off the drawing board. Indeed, it has been through a process of policy review and analysis, involvement of stakeholders and coalition building that South Asian governments have been able to sustain reform efforts in the absence of a strong political base. Coalition government have sometimes injected a useful amount of pragmatism, but high quality policy analysis and public debate have also played a vital role, as in East Asia.

Yet a weakness has sometimes been in the formulation and analysis of the policy proposals themselves. And academics and think tanks have sometimes been 'missing in action' in providing objective, independent reviews and helping to manage vested interests (for example, in Indian trade policy making).[6] The more active involvement of academics and think tanks could be a particularly useful counterweight to an overly politicized bureaucracy. The academics and think tanks do not need to appeal to or 'educate the public' in a populist fashion — Pakistan's experience shows that this is not sufficient to sustain reforms. What is needed is to inform opinion makers and influential people of all political persuasions — to raise the level of debate. Politicians may not always be receptive. But ideas do have influence, as some of the case studies show. With the power of ideas, reforms can be initiated and sustained even by politicians who have a weak political base. This is the powerful message that South Asia's reform experience can offer the rest of the world. Thus if regional cooperation is to improve policy efficiency, along the lines suggested by Drysdale (2010), it should focus particularly on building the technical and strategic policy review capacity of these institutions.

13.8 Summary of South Asian Reform Case Studies

Husain and Kumar (2012) argue that a comparison of the reform experiences of India and Pakistan since 1991 provides a controlled experiment in the influence of political factors. In most dimensions, the reform experience of the two countries was similar. They shared a common history, culture and politics for many centuries. They inherited the same governance and institutional frameworks from the British colonial period. Their economic policies were broadly comparable. Both embarked on a broadly similar reform path in 1991 in the face of economic crisis. In India, the reform process has been sometimes slow and halting, but the movement forward has been perceptible and the fear of complete reversal has remained insignificant. In Pakistan, by contrast, reform effort has been characterized by discontinuity and disruption.

Husain and Kumar argue that many aspects of the policy making process have been similar in the two countries, and cannot account for the difference in outcomes. Instead, the difference lies in the political

---

[6] Note that independence is a function of tenure as much as it is of funding. The think tanks in East Asia have sometimes played a very influential role in the technical and strategic aspects of policy development, despite government funding.

realm. In India, the pattern has been for the dominant development paradigm to co-opt ideas from other development models so as to win broad political support and to maintain a degree of policy flexibility. They contrast this with the 'bridge-burning' of Pakistan's political rivals, as each successive government sought to distance itself from its predecessors. Reforms have not been sustained for long enough to generate the wide-spread benefits that could ensure their legitimacy and irreversibility.

Banking sector reforms in India show how the process has tended to be slow and incremental. Drawing on models by Lindblom (1959, 1979), Vaidya (2012) stresses how in practice, the limits of knowledge and experience make it impossible for policy makers to fully optimize their policy choices. Instead, they will tend to draw on past experiences in their own and other countries to identify better options that lie in the near neighbourhood of the *status quo*. Such incremental changes are not likely to rock the political consensus, and can be easily reversed if they prove to have unintended consequences. The resulting reform process may look like 'muddling through', but it avoids serious lasting mistakes.

India's banking sector reforms have been slow and cumbersome. Once the need for reform is recognized, the government or the central bank typically sets up a committee involving experts, public servants and sometimes representatives of the private sector to devise a reform roadmap. The roadmap is then put into the public domain for extensive debate by government, academics and the press. After consultation, the government typically accepts some of the committee's recommendations. Vaidya argues that the committee process can be seen as a way of coming up with a finite set of feasible policy options. The final policy action is the consensus arrived at through the political system. The result has been incremental reform.

This task force approach has also been used in Vietnam (Vo and Nguyen 2010), where commitment problems arose when task force members were appointed on a once-off and often part-time basis. In India, the same committee chair has often been asked to address the same or similar problem as few years down the line. The 'repeated games' have ensured greater commitment and continuity across reviews.

Banking sector reforms also illustrate the way that the Indian political process has dealt with economic reforms that challenge the prevailing development model. Since 1967–68 the Reserve Bank of India has specified that certain priority sectors should have assured access to credit. The first formal guidelines specified agriculture, small scale industry and exports as priority sectors, to which a certain minimum proportion of total bank credit should be directed. While these sectoral priorities accorded with the prevailing development model, the priority sector norms led to inefficiencies in credit markets and inflexibility in bank operations. In 1991 it was argued that fiscal policy rather than credit allocation rules should be used to achieve redistribution. However, this wholesale switch was deemed to be untenable politically, so the worst consequences of the credit allocation rules were instead alleviated by a dramatic expansion in the number of sectors designed as priority sectors. Thus reform was achieved, not in a first-best way, but equally not in a way that challenged the prevailing development model that accorded high priority to redressing inequality. By contrast, reform of security interest legislation has been achieved more directly, because it has not challenged the prevailing development model to the same extent.

From the 1950s to around 1980, the fiscal deficits of the central government in India experienced political cycles. Srivastava and Sarma (2012) find that deficits were higher around election years, though the cycles were asymmetric — the reductions in non-election years were smaller than the increases, leading to an accumulation of government debt relative to gross domestic product (GDP). Since about 1980, and the growing importance of coalition politics, political cycles have essentially disappeared. Instead, the deficits have remained high even in non-election years, indicating the importance of structural rather than political factors, in particular the growth of interest payments relative to GDP.

At the federal level, India had an elaborate legislative system of budgetary control, but this did not prevent the accumulation of deficits over many years. At the peak in 2004–05, the combined fiscal deficit of the central and state governments reached 14 per cent of GDP, while that of the central government alone was 8 per cent of GDP. A harder budget constraint was needed, and this was delivered in the form of fiscal responsibility legislation, currently enacted by the central government and 26 out of 28 state governments. Key players in framing and implementing these reforms were the central government and the Twelfth Finance Commission. The central government enacted its own legislation, while the Twelfth Finance Commission developed the constraints and time paths to apply to both the centre and the states. The commission also developed incentive mechanisms to persuade the states to follow with their own legislation.

The Indian constitution makes provision for Finance Commissions periodically to address the issue of vertical as well as horizontal fiscal imbalances. This resource-sharing role is common to many such institutions in federated states. But the Indian constitution also allows the Commission to consider any other matters in the interests of 'sound finance'. It is this broader mandate that has allowed the Commissions to play an influential role in framing tighter fiscal disciplines and suggesting incentives for their adoption. The global financial crisis has provided a strong reminder of the desirability of leaving policy space for countercyclical fiscal policy. It is expected that the Thirteenth Finance Commission will play a role in amending the rules to provide such space in a sensible fashion.

Prior to 1991, foreign direct investment (FDI) flows into India were encouraged on a selective basis, primarily to encourage foreign technical collaboration. Sahoo (2012) shows that since the major reforms of 1991, FDI policy has become considerably more liberal, although prior government approval is still required for some types of investment, and FDI is still prohibited in a few sectors.

In India, FDI reforms were one area where the 1991 economic crisis proved definitive. One of the economic problems was the large accumulation of external debt, default on which would have brought an unacceptable loss of face. So attracting non-debt-creating sources of finance became a priority. The gainers from easing FDI restrictions were many; the losers were few, and their adjustment problems were eased by other reforms that took place at the same time.

While reform of FDI restrictions has proved relatively uncontroversial, there are significant challenges if India is to keep pace with China in continuing to attract FDI. Chief among these are addressing infrastructure bottlenecks and dealing with inflexible labour laws. The latter reforms will be particularly difficult, as they cannot be achieved by the exercise of discretionary powers, but will require legislative amendments. Such reforms will require all the policy efficiency that India can muster.

Trade policy in India has proved more resistant to reform than FDI policy. Nataraj (2012) describes the relatively elaborate trade policy making machinery that was originally designed to promote exports while protecting import-competing industries. This was not the ideal platform for launching comprehensive trade reform, and the 1991 crisis did not prove as definitive as it did in the case of FDI reform. The government has been careful to build a political consensus for ongoing trade reform efforts, but detailed, objective analysis of the likely costs and benefits of reform options has been lacking, and the analysis that has been provided by non-government organizations and business groups has tended to reinforce a defensive stance.

Further reform is likely to require that trade policy debates be elevated above the level of line government departments. It is also likely to require that open and formal mechanism of consultation be established in a way that would provide incentives for stakeholders and observers to undertake the necessary detailed, objective analysis.

While the reform process in Pakistan has suffered discontinuity and disruption, some notable progress has been made on financial sector reforms under the governments of Nawaz Sharif (1990–93 and 1997–99) and particularly Pervez Musharraf (1999–2007). The nationalization of Zulfqar Ali Bhutto had produced a financial sector with poor service quality and a weak financial position. Nasir (2012) describes how Sharif began the process of privatization and liberalization, and the Musharraf government followed with the major institutional reforms that have transformed and modernized the sector.

A critical success factor was Musharraf's Prime Minister, Shaukat Aziz, who was himself a successful banker and saw financial sector reform as key to the long-run performance of the whole economy. He appointed a team of professionals to design and implement an ongoing reform program, and had the full support of the President, who allowed the reforms to proceed without interference. This sustained effort, maintained during one of Pakistan's more long-serving governments, has paid dividends. It stands in contrast to the implementation failures elsewhere, as reform efforts have been undermined by political imperatives and a lack of commitment by the leadership.

The chequered reform experience in Sri Lanka described by Weerakoon (2012) provides a number of lessons. It shows that adjustment assistance to those hurt by reforms can be a useful mechanism to garner support, even in a society where distributional concerns are sufficiently acute to have led to violence. But adjustment assistance requires fiscal space. Thus structural reforms are harder in circumstances where fiscal restraint is also required.

Sri Lanka's experience also illustrates how first-generation reforms — cutting tariffs, scrapping exchange controls and abolishing administrative red tape — tend to be easier than second generation reforms. First, they are 'stroke of a pen' reforms that can generally be carried out within the discretion of government and do not require legislative changes. Second, when implemented in particularly poorly performing economies, they can sometimes generate true Pareto improvements, where at least some groups gain and no group loses (see also He 2010).

By contrast, second generation reforms are harder. As Weerakoon notes, this is because they often involve a fundamental realignment in the functions of the state. In this context, failure to reform public sector institutions can mean that even well-intentioned policy initiatives can be ineffective. Where public sector institutions have become prey to vested interests and/or politicized, they become vulnerable to political disruptions of the sort experienced in Sri Lanka. The technocracy can then no longer provide the competence or continuity to carry reform effort forward through changes of government, so the effort becomes much harder to sustain.

The South Asian experience shows how the political climate can condition and constrain policy efficiency. Even with the best institutional arrangements for policy review and analysis, involvement of stakeholders, and political accountability, political conflicts can sometimes stymie reform efforts. Thus bad politics will not help produce good economics.

But there are feedback loops. Not only does the political climate condition what is possible in the economic front, but the economic climate can also condition what is possible politically. Khan (2012) argues that an improvement in economic relations between India and Pakistan could be a powerful confidence-building measure to promote better political relations. This is consistent with the view that economic diplomacy matters, not just in terms of what economic outcomes it delivers, but also as an element of international diplomacy more broadly (see also Drysdale 1988).

Chapter 14

Promoting Domestic Reforms through Regionalism[1]

Philippa Dee and Anne McNaughton

This presumption [that international trade is the main vehicle for transmitting reforms and increasing economic freedom] is so ingrained, for economists in particular, that it is hard to know its precise historical origin. (Gassebner, Gaston and Lamla 2008, p. 1).

To date, the available, limited, evidence suggests that, with the exception of the European Union, most services policy reform has been unilateral. (Francois and Hoekman 2010, p. 678)

14.1 Introduction

As the first quotation above illustrates, there is a strong presumption among economists that trade and economic reform are linked. One particular corollary is that domestic reforms are promoted by regionalism, because regionalism promotes trade. Yet the second quotation above suggests that strong empirical evidence for the second proposition is lacking. The purpose of this chapter is to examine in some detail both the theoretical arguments and empirical evidence on this issue, drawing on the relevant economic, political and legal literatures. It concludes with some proposals on how to use regional institutions to better support domestic reform efforts.

---

[1] This is an edited version of ADBI Working Paper No. 312, Asian Development Bank Institute, Tokyo, October 2011. Forthcoming in conference volume for ADBI Annual Conference 2010, 'The Political Economy of Asian Regionalism'.

The proposition that domestic reform might be promoted through regionalism can be either a tautology or an impossibility, depending on how the terms are defined. This chapter takes a broad definition of domestic reform, one that is independent of at least some notions of market integration. Domestic reform is defined as behind-the-border reform, and it comprises two key elements:

- contestability — where market competition determines economic outcomes in all circumstances where competition is appropriate; and
- appropriate regulation —where well-designed regulation guides market outcomes in those cases where market forces alone cannot be guaranteed to deliver the best outcomes

Appropriate regulation is required in cases of market failure, where 'natural' monopoly, asymmetric information and/or externalities prevent markets from delivering efficient outcomes. Appropriate regulation may also be required where governments have additional objectives besides efficiency, such as equity, safety, diversity, and so on.

Contestability requires that *market participants* not be able to manipulate the terms of entry into, or operation within, markets to their own advantage by restricting competition. This is the role of competition policy, narrowly defined — to prevent anti-competitive practices by the private sector. But in the Asian region, anti-competitive *government* practices are arguably a much more important impediment to the efficient operation of markets. Thus the objective of domestic reform should be two-fold (Dee 2010a):

- to remove government legislation, regulation and bureaucratic practice that restricts competition for no good public purpose; and
- to ensure that where government intervention is required to safeguard legitimate objectives (including, but by no means limited to, preventing anti-competitive practices by the private sector), the government intervention is no more burdensome than necessary to achieve those objectives.

This chapter also needs a definition of regionalism. It takes an equally broad definition of this concept — closer regional interaction. In the economic sphere, this closer interaction can be market-driven or institution-driven. Over the last three decades of the 20th century, Asian economic interaction was primarily market-driven. In the first decade of the 21st century, trade agreements have begun to have sufficient 'bite' to promote institution-driven economic interaction (Baldwin 2006). But trade agreements are not the only institutions that promote closer regional interaction. There is an alpha-numeric soup of institutional arrangements — ASEAN, ASEAN+3, ASEAN+6, EAS (East Asian Summit), ARF (ASEAN Regional Forum), APEC — that are designed to promote closer interaction, not just for economic but also for political and security purposes.

So the question implicit in the title of this chapter has two possible interpretations. The first is whether market-led regionalism creates sufficient dynamics to promote domestic reform, without the assistance of regional institutions. However, in very open economies it may be difficult in practice to distinguish unilateral reform that has been spurred by market-led regionalism from that spurred by other factors (such as purely domestic competitive factors). So this interpretation of the question borders on the tautological. The second interpretation is whether any of the current raft of regional institutions can further promote domestic reform. This chapter concentrates on the second interpretation — whether domestic reform is better promoted by regional institutions, rather than unilaterally by market factors (including market-led regionalism).

The next section of this chapter examines the theoretical arguments on why formal regional agreements might usefully promote reform. The arguments are both political and economic. All have been used at various times to argue that formal regional agreements help to promote trade reform *at* the border. Some of these arguments extend to reforms behind the border.

The following section examines the empirical evidence, including case studies and econometric evidence from both the economic and political/legal literature. Some evidence is circumstantial — looking at what has happened in countries that have entered regional arrangements

— and some is more direct — looking in detail at the commitments made in regional agreements. The empirical evidence tends to support the finding in the second quotation above — that few regional arrangements other than the EU have successfully promoted domestic reform.

The chapter next examines the reasons for these findings. Various writers have offered a range of reasons why non-EU trade agreements have not promoted domestic reform. This chapter also examines the political and legal literature for the fundamental reasons why the EU has succeeded. Contrary to some popular conceptions, the key is not, or not solely, the existence of a supra-national institutional framework. This is fortunate, since is it widely agreed that the Asian region has no taste for such a framework. But other elements of the recipe for success are transferrable. The final section of this chapter therefore makes suggestions for how Asian regional institutions could internalize some of these lessons on how to promote domestic reform.

14.2 Theoretical Arguments

Political economy arguments

One central reason from the political economy literature as to why trade agreements can promote domestic reform is that some binding external mechanism helps to overcome the time-inconsistency problem formalized by Kydland and Prescott (1977). This problem is the inability of political institutions to bind themselves for future periods given that they are exposed to the strategic behaviour of private agents (eg electoral bribes and lobbying by vested interests). So what governments say now that they will do may not be what they actually do in the future – they cannot make credible commitments. In these circumstances, governments may agree *ex ante* to restrict their powers in the public interest. This explains why governments agree, for example, to delegate monetary policy to independent central banks.

It is also why governments may not rely on unilateral action to achieve either trade reform or behind-the-border reform, but rather bind themselves in a formal treaty with trading partners. This rationale is recognized in the legal literature (eg Pauwelyn 2005) as well as in the economic and political economy literature (eg Martin 2001). Legal scholars tend to stress that such arrangements also protect the commitments from the 'instability' of 'representative democracy' — in other words, the problem of strategic behaviour is not just a problem of vested interest groups but a problem of democracy more broadly. Thus, for example, Tallberg (2002) uses the time inconsistency problem to explain why the EU member states have chosen to delegate authority to supranational institutions beyond direct democratic control.

An interesting variant of the commitment argument is that reform can occur within a regional trade arrangement as a precursor to the 'main event' — WTO membership. Ethier (1998, 1999, 2001) has formalized variants of this argument. His models are explicit attempts to capture some of the salient features of 'third-wave' or 'new age' preferential trade agreements (PTAs). These agreements first emerged in the 1990s and were not only about merchandise trade, but also included areas such as services, investment, competition policy, government procurement, e-commerce, labour and environmental standards.

Ethier observes that many 'new age' agreements are between small 'outside' countries that are not yet members of the world trading system,[2] and larger 'inside' countries that are. The small, outside countries want to reform their internal economies so that they can be accepted as members of the global trading system. Ethier asserts that the sign of successful reform is whether these countries attract foreign direct investment. Their problem is how to signal a credible commitment to reform in advance.

The outside country's solution is to sign a PTA with an inside country involving enough trading concessions to the insider country so that it will in turn have an incentive to act as an enforcer and retaliate if the outside country deviates from its reform commitment. The aim is not necessarily to receive enormous concessions from the inside country in return. All that is required is a small trade concession, so that multinationals have an incentive to locate in the outside country. Ethier (2001) also examines in

---

[2] Ethier (2001) identifies these as countries that until recently adopted basically-autarkic, anti-market policies.

detail the incentives of the large inside country to accede to such an arrangement, even in preference to pursuing further multilateral reform.

Finally, he shows that a world equilibrium on which small countries compete for investment in this fashion is beneficial, because it internalizes an externality. The global interest calls for successful reform to be as widespread as possible, but if there are agglomeration economies, then multinationals will want to cluster their foreign investments together. A global web of bilateral PTAs, initiated by outside countries' competition for investment, internalizes the externality.

This theoretical framework explains a number of US bilateral trade agreements as 'dress rehearsals' for WTO accession. But note that it is essentially WTO accession that is driving the reform, not the PTA *per se*. This point is recognized by Lewis (2008), for example, who argues that Lao PDR undertook its domestic reforms unilaterally to link its domestic policies and laws to proposed WTO commitments (despite that fact that Lao PDR also signed a bilateral trade agreement with the United States). Hence it was WTO membership, and its protections of a rules-based trading system, that drove the reform.

A second reason often cited by economists, but rooted in political economy, is that concession trading can somehow help to neutralize domestic vested interests. It is difficult for governments to build support for liberalization in the face of pressures from vested interests, particularly those in import-competing industries. Participation in regional arrangements may help to build support for liberalization, because exporters who would gain from greater access into overseas markets can counter the pressure from those in import-competing industries, who would lose from lower import protection at home. This argument is found in World Bank (2000) and in Hoekman and Mattoo (2011), for example.

A third rationale, closely related to the commitment argument, is the 'skyhook' argument. Governments may be happy to take decisions in the public interest that upset particular vested interests, but find it convenient to blame third parties so as to escape electoral punishment (eg Tallberg 2002). The third parties may be trading partner governments (in PTAs) or supranational institutions (in the EU).

A final line of argument is one that stresses the administrative efficiency of taking detailed reform proposals out of the political sphere. Politicians (as principals) assign the detailed rule-making to agents, who then develop and apply their policy-relevant expertise, saving politicians' time for more general policy decisions. This argument has been used to explain the delegation of powers to supranational institutions in the EU (Tallberg 2002), and the delegation of trade negotiation and rule-making to trade officials in Geneva (Pauwelyn 2005). In the context of domestic reform, it begs the question of why delegation to an external agent is preferable to delegation to a domestic bureaucracy that is, in at least some political systems, supposed to be apolitical.

There is at least one political economy argument for why a multilateral or plurilateral forum may be inimical to domestic reform. If the reform takes place multilaterally, the possibility of exchanging concessions across sectors in the future may induce countries to withhold reforms today. Harms, Mattoo and Schuknecht (2003) claim that this explains the low level of WTO commitments by some countries in financial services, because the financial services agreement was concluded in a separate single-sector negotiation after the Uruguay Round, and participants must have had a reasonable expectation of future multi-sectoral negotiations. They also note that there is a general incentive to retain negotiation coin, and forgo the benefits of unilateral liberalization, by countries that face high entry barriers (including behind-the-border barriers) into their overseas export markets and have sufficient bargaining power to extract concessions from their trading partners.

Economic arguments

Bagwell and Staiger (1999) show that multilateral trade commitments can help internalize an externality associated with tariff protection. Countries imposing the tariffs can shift some of the cost of those tariffs onto their trading partners because their tariffs can alter world prices and generate a terms of trade decline for their trading partners. Conversely, unilateral reform can generate a terms of trade decline for the reforming country, preventing it from reaping all of the gains from reform. Bagwell and Staiger show that the WTO principles of reciprocity and non-discrimination help to neutralize the world price implications of tariff negotiations and thus allow efficient outcomes. They also note, however, that exceptions to the most-favoured nation principle for the purpose of creating a PTA revive the local-price externality, thus frustrating the ability of a multilateral system governed by reciprocity to deliver an efficient outcome.

It is not clear that this terms-of-trade argument extends beyond tariff reforms. Dee and Sidorenko (2006) point out that empirically, the terms of trade effects of unilateral behind-the-border reforms are likely to be minimal or even positive, so trade agreements may not be necessary to ensure efficient outcomes. In the context of cross-border trade in services (rather than goods), Francois and Hoekman (2010) argue that the WTO, with its principles of reciprocity and non-discrimination, may not be sufficient. They cite the work of Antràs and Staiger (2007), who look at the problem of the relationship-specific investments that might be required between domestic and foreign firms involved in the trade of customized inputs (eg producer services), and the opportunity for post-contractual opportunism that this provides. If firms cannot credibly commit to a price in advance, the volume of trade will be too low from the perspective of international efficiency when governments set trade policy unilaterally. By expanding the volume of trade in the customized input, trade agreements can potentially move countries toward the international efficiency frontier. But this beneficial outcome only comes about if governments have no political economy (distributional) motives, but are only concerned with maximizing real national income (efficiency).[3]

It is possible to find arguments for why trade may be inimical to domestic reform. Gassebner, Gaston and Lamla (2008) argue instead that freer trade may reinforce a *status quo* bias in domestic policies. Freer trade will benefit the specific factor in the exporting sector. But diversity of economic institutions (domestic reform in one country, lack of reform in the other) may be the source of the gains from trade. If the specific

---

[3] The argument of Bagwell and Staiger (1999) in the context of simple tariff reform does not depend on the motives of government.

factor in the exporting sector is politically influential, they may lobby for trade reform but against domestic reform, even if the two together would generate a higher benefit to the economy as a whole. They cite India as a possible example of this phenomenon. This argument would also explain why many of the regional trade agreements between developing countries in the East Asian region are heavy on merchandise trade reform but (the titles of chapters in the trade agreements notwithstanding) light on other types of reform (Ochiai, Dee and Findlay 2010).

A different kind of economic argument is a 'spillovers' argument articulated by Kawai and Wignaraja (2011) and Czaga (2004), among others. Kawai and Wignaraja (2011) argue that East Asia's market-led integration and its development of production networks and region-wide supply chains has begun to require not just further liberalization of trade and FDI, but also the harmonization of policies, rules and standards governing trade and investment, as well as the protection of investment and intellectual property rights. Thus liberalization at the border has begun to create pressure for harmonization behind the border. They argue that Asian policy makers view PTAs as vehicles to support this harmonization effort. They are thus part of the policy framework to deepen production networks and supply chains formed by global multinationals and emerging Asian firms. The Japanese support for the development of an ASEAN Economic Community through its funding of the Economic Research Institute for ASEAN and East Asia is consistent with this idea.

Kawai and Wignaraja (2011) also note that the region's response to the Asian financial crisis has demonstrated how Asian economies can cooperate to address common challenges. The key product of that cooperation was the Chang Mai initiative — a multilateral currency swap arrangement among ASEAN, China, Hong Kong, Japan and Korea to manage regional short-term liquidity problems. Nevertheless, this arrangement was not used during the recent global financial crisis. The authors also note that Asian countries have been attracted to PTAs because of slow progress in the WTO Doha negotiations. In those negotiations, developed countries are being asked to liberalize agriculture while developing countries are being asked to liberalize industrial goods and services. To date the negotiations have focused on agriculture and industrials, with not much effort being devoted to behind-the-border issues.

14.3 Empirical Evidence

Given the variety of theoretical arguments why regional institutions may promote domestic reform, one would expect the empirical evidence to bear them out. The purpose of this section is to canvas the empirical literature.

Case studies

Individual case studies establish that regionalism is neither necessary nor sufficient for domestic reform. Several examples can be cited to show that formal regional agreements are not necessary.

Martin (2001) shows that while East Asian reformers have successfully made many of the reforms to domestic and trade policies required to secure export and income growth, there has been no single approach to achieving this. China's reform process focused mainly on unilateral reform and WTO accession. Martin argues that several East Asian transition economies (Cambodia, Lao PDR, Myanmar and Vietnam) used accession to the ASEAN Free Trade Agreements as part of their reform strategy, though he notes that some of the exceptions allowed under the original liberalization commitments were excessive. He notes that Vietnam's and Lao PDR's bilaterals with the United States required more extensive reforms. But as noted above, these were essentially dress rehearsal for WTO accession. WTO accession has also been a key driver of unilateral reform in Cambodia.

Francois (2005) argues that EU accession would not exert much pressure on Turkey to restructure its transport, because Turkey has to a large extent undertaken the required reforms and put in place the required regulatory frameworks unilaterally.

While these examples show PTA membership or accession is not necessary for domestic reform, the experiences of Canada and Mexico show that it is not sufficient.

Barichello (2004) argues that the effect of NAFTA or its predecessor CUSTA on domestic agricultural policy reform in Canada has been minimal. He notes that the negotiations were conducted specifically to avoid sensitive non-tariff barriers. In one instance CUSTA actually led to an increase in protection from non-tariff measures. In contrast, the Uruguay Round Agreement was associated much more closely with actual or potential policy reforms. And there was significant unilateral reform in the form of substantial cuts in budgetary support, driven by the domestic imperative to eliminate budget deficits.

Francois (1997) notes that Mexico's reform process started well before NAFTA. Starting with its WTO accession, Mexico began a major restructuring program in the 1980s. This included reforms of trade, intellectual property rights, foreign exchange restrictions, foreign investment, and privatization. Francois also notes that formal consultation mechanisms with the United States were also in place before the NAFTA negotiations. Graham and Wada (2000) identify a trend break in the pattern of US FDI into Mexico in 1989. Over 1966–88, the stock of US FDI grew at 3.1 per cent a year; over 1989–98 it grew at 5.6 per cent a year. They argue that this was not caused by NAFTA or the series of bilateral deals between the US and Mexico that preceded it, but as a response to Mexico's unilateral reforms.

More tellingly, Tornell, Westermann and Martínez (2004) document how Mexico failed to attain rapid growth in the 1990s, and that after 2001 its GDP and exports stagnated. They argue that the lack of growth cannot be blamed on NAFTA or the other reforms that were implemented. The source of the problem was a lack of structural reform after 1995, as well as Mexico's response to the peso crisis — a deterioration in contract enforceability and an increase in non-performing loans.[4]

While PTAs may be neither necessary nor sufficient for domestic reform, what is the preponderance of empirical evidence? It comes in

---

[4] Francois (1997) notes that the crisis did not lead to the re-imposition of exchange controls or a dramatic increase in protection, in part because of strong intervention by the United States and the IMF — in this qualified sense, NAFTA did provide a policy anchor to the reforms already in place. But NAFTA had not led to further structural reforms.

two types — broad-brush econometric exercises, and more detailed comparisons of PTA commitments with domestic policies.

Broad-brush econometric evidence

Evidence from economic papers

The empirical findings of Gassebner, Gaston and Lamla (2008) are in line with their theoretical arguments. Using a panel of 144 countries over 1995–2006, they find that empirically, economic reforms are not driven by greater trade openness. They also find that reforms are not habit-forming — instead there is a *status quo* bias. But they do find evidence of the importance of reforms in other countries. The important mechanism is not international trade, but geographical and cultural proximity. Countries that are more integrated in the process of the global exchange of information also tend to be more reform-minded. Finally, they find that EU membership also helps.

Harms, Mattoo and Schuknecht (2003) examine empirically what drives (the lack of) liberalization commitments in financial services trade (an example of a behind-the-border commitment made through a trade agreement). They find empirical evidence to support the idea that members of international trade coalitions in agriculture and textiles held back financial services commitments, possibly to use them as bargaining chips in future negotiations.

Evidence from legal and political papers

The EU is supposedly the archtypical example of a formal regional agreement that has generated domestic reform. What does the EU-focussed literature say? For empirical evidence on this score, we need to turn to the legal rather than the economic literature, for the following reason.

The EU Treaty is a negative list agreement — everything is liberalized unless otherwise stated. This is in contrast to positive list agreements, such as the specific commitments of the General Agreement on Trade in Services (GATS) under the WTO, where nothing is liberalized unless otherwise stated. Furthermore, the EU Treaty covers a wide range of areas and unlike most negative list PTAs, does not have detailed annex lists of exceptions and reservations,[5] though it allows general exceptions on grounds such as public morality, public policy, public security or public health (similar to the Article XX exceptions of the GATT, though in the EU Treaty the details vary depending on the area covered).

Therefore, one measure of actual reform in the EU is provided by the enforcement of these original broad commitments through dispute resolution, rather than by the gradual accumulation of more ambitious commitments. And in the early years, despite their obligations under the Treaties, Member states were not dismantling trade barriers, either at or behind their borders (McNaugton 2011), so dispute resolution was the key mechanism by which actual reform took place. Seminal empirical work in this area is by Stone Sweet and Brunell (1998).

They conceive of European integration as a response to the demands of those individuals and companies who need European rules (ie a more reformed regime), and those who are advantaged by European law and practices compared with national law and practices. Thus from a legal perspective, they argue that integration depends on the development of more liberal rules to govern transnational activities, the capacity of supranational organizations to respond to those demands, and a stable and effective means of resolving legal disputes.

Furthermore, they argue that to the extent that the legal system actually removed national barriers to exchange within the EU (a process known in legal circles as *negative integration*, and in trade circles roughly equivalent to the adoption of negative list liberalization

---

[5] Becoming a member of the EU is like becoming a member of a club: the state does not get to pick and choose which parts of the treaties it will bind itself to. However, in particular instances — the United Kingdom's and Northern Ireland's refusal to adopt the Euro, for example — *all* the Member States agree upon the primary provisions of EU law in relation to the Euro *and then* they all agree to a Protocol under which, in this case, the United Kingdom and Northern Ireland can 'opt in' at a later stage, upon notifying the Council of Ministers of their intention to do so. So in an EU context, the exercise of state sovereignty and the adoption of treaty provisions operate differently from in 'mainstream' public international law, including that of the WTO and regional trade agreements.

commitments that immediately require the elimination of all non-conforming measures), it put pressure on governments to adopt EU market regulations (known in legal circles as *positive integration*, and in trade circles roughly equivalent to the development of EU directives and other secondary legislation to provide a reformed behind-the-border regulatory structure, such as through harmonization, to ensure that the benefits of liberalization were realized).[6]

To test this proposition, Stone Sweet and Brunell (1998) undertake regression analysis over the period 1961 to 1992 to test whether the extent of transnational dispute settlement (measured by the annual number of so-called Article 177 references, whose significance is explained in a later section) is influenced by the level of transnational activity (measured by annual levels of intra-EU trade) and the number of European rules (measured by the annual number of directives and regulations promulgated by the European Commission). Note that according to the EEC Treaty, all national measures restricting trade were required to be abolished by the end of 1969, and by virtue of the doctrine of direct effect initiated in 1963 (the significance of which is also discussed later), traders could then ask national judges not to apply such measures. Given the time period covered by their regressions, it seems that the argument is a two-fold one. Where trade was already significant, traders had an incentive to ensure that negative integration actually occurred, and hence mounted dispute action when they perceived that it had not. As the negative integration further spurred trade, this first incentive was strengthened. It also provided pressure to create additional directives and regulations to further promote transnational activity (though econometrically the authors do not correct for the resulting endogeneity of either their measure of intra-EU trade or European rules), and thus further dispute settlement to enforce the additional rules.

They find that both variables have a significant positive effect on dispute settlement. However, adding EU rules to the regression does not explain a great deal more of the variation in dispute settlement activity than trade volumes alone (the adjusted R squared in both cases is 0.92). Thus it might appear that additional rules and directives have not

---

[6] See Stone Sweet (2010) for a summary in precisely these terms.

generated much additional reform. This does not mean that behind-the-border reform has not occurred. The original Treaty itself contained commitments across a broad range of behind-the-border matters. In fact, Stone Sweet and Brunell (1998) present data on both the extent and subject matter of dispute resolution activity over time. They show that in the 1971–5 period, more than half the references concerned just two sectors — the free movement of goods and agriculture. In the 1991–5 period, these two areas accounted for only 27 per cent of total references, while areas such as establishment (ie commercial presence), transport, competition, social provisions, social security, taxes and the environment had grown in relative importance.

What the finding does suggest is that it was the actions of individuals involved in trade that drove the liberalization. The activity of the European Commission in generating additional directives and regulations was much less important (though still statistically significant). In fact, the use of directives reached its peak between 1986 and 1992, and thereafter the Commission found it increasingly difficult to promote integration through direct legislation (McNaughton and Furlong 2008).

Pitarakis and Tridimas (2003) undertake much more careful econometric analysis, paying particular attention to directions of causality (and hence the endogeneity of intra-EU trade). They confirm that legal challenges to instances of incompatibility between EU law and national law (a process they call legal integration) has significantly boosted EU trade. Interestingly, Carrubba and Murrah (2005) also find that public support for EU integration and public political awareness also boost the use of the legal system to support economic integration.

Not only has the subject matter of challenges to national legislation become broader over time, so too has the legal interpretation of what constitutes a regulatory impediment to economic integration. Because the Treaty obligations are based on the principle of negative integration, (ie the removal of barriers to trade) and are broad-brush, it has been through judicial interpretation and the accretion of case law that regulatory barriers have been defined. Barnard (2010) documents how a gradual widening of interpretation has occurred across all the key pillars of EU integration — free movement of goods, free movement of services (including establishment), free movement of persons, and free movement of capital. Interpretations initially focussed on 'non-discrimination', but the case law then widened to include barriers to 'market access' — regulatory measures that may not explicitly discriminate against foreign sources of goods, services, people or capital, but which nevertheless impede their access. Most recently, the concept has widened even further to any measure that is a 'restriction on' or 'obstacle to' free movement.

In the area of goods, under the so-called *Dassonville* formula, for example, 'all trading rules' that are 'capable of hindering, directly or indirectly, actually or potentially' intra-EU trade are considered as having an effect equivalent to quantitative restrictions, and are therefore prohibited. The jurisprudence has also tackled the problem of goods having to meet the regulatory requirements of more than one regulator. The *Cassis de Dijon* decision replaces dual regulation of a product (by home and host states) with single (home state) regulation, which the host country is required to respect under the principle of mutual recognition. Under this principle there is a *presumption* of the equivalence of the regulatory measures.

A wide variety of national rules have been judged to be restrictions on the freedom to provide services — authorization requirements, translation requirements, requirements to swear an oath of allegiance, maximum or minimum staffing levels, minimum fees, rules regulating gambling, and advertising restrictions.[7] In the case of people movement, the interpretation is now even wider — there is no longer a requirement for the movement to be linked to economic activity.

The original Treaty provisions on the movement of capital were weaker that those elsewhere, because capital movements were seen to be closely linked to the stability of economic and monetary policy. It was not until 1992 (with the advent of the Single Market) that capital movements were finally liberalized, and not until 1995 that barriers were allowed to be the subject of transnational dispute settlement actions (and thus subject to judicial interpretation) in the same way as barriers to goods, people or services. But the jurisprudence has developed along

---

[7] Note, however, that with the final version of the recent Services Directive, the EU has stopped short of allowing the regulation in the country of origin to automatically prevail when services are traded cross-border (McNaughton 2011).

similar lines to that for services. The free movement of capital was a condition of entry into the first stage of monetary union.

Evidence from examining PTAs

The above econometric evidence is relatively broad-brush — it tests for links between trade and domestic reform, without looking systematically at the influence of regional trade agreements. A great deal of literature examines the effects of having a PTA in place. A relatively small but growing literature looks beyond the existence of PTAs, to examine the effects of their detailed provisions. We now consider each type of evidence in turn.

Econometric evidence from looking at the existence of PTAs

A vast literature examines empirically the link between the existence (or much more rarely, the content) of PTAs and measures of economic performance. The most well-known framework is the gravity model, which explains bilateral flows of merchandise trade, and is often used to test for the influence of having a PTA in place. But to the extent that merchandise trade flows are affected by the presence of PTAs, they are likely to be driven in the first instance by commitments on border trade measures such as tariffs, as much as by any commitments on behind-the-border reforms. So this literature is not the best source of evidence on the existence of behind-the-border reform commitments in PTAs.

The gravity model framework and its successors have also been used to explain bilateral foreign direct investment (FDI). This evidence is more likely to indicate the presence and effectiveness of behind-the-border reforms, because at least some of the key barriers to FDI, both pre- and post-establishment, operate behind the border. Unfortunately, there is little comparable evidence on bilateral services trade, which is governed by a raft of behind-the-border regulation, because there is little bilateral data available on services trade flows.

The study of FDI that probably comes closest to establishing a link between PTAs and domestic reform is Park and Park (2008). They argue that while PTA membership can be an important factor in attracting FDI, it cannot be a sufficient condition — PTA membership should be accompanied by domestic reform measures. This is essentially an empirical test of Ethier's argument that was summarized above. But they also say that PTA membership works by being a commitment device for the domestic reform, so it is the domestic reform that is attracting the FDI, not the PTA membership. They show that both reform and PTA membership boost FDI, but do not examine empirically the interaction between reform and PTA membership.

Dee (2008b) does a careful mapping of PTA provisions on cross-border trade in services, investment and the movement of people, and looks at their impact on FDI. She uses a specification of the behaviour of FDI taken from theoretical models that jointly explain patterns of trade and FDI, and allow for complex network patterns of both. She finds evidence that patterns of FDI (and trade by implication) in the Asian region are driven by fundamentals, in a way that makes use of fine divisions of comparative advantage, but is also subject to considerations of economies of scale and transport costs. This is in contrast to investment patterns in some other regions (such as in Latin America, where distance and risk considerations are found to dominate). The resulting network patterns of investment in Asia do not appear to have been driven by the investment and services provisions of PTAs signed with the bilateral providers of FDI. But the network nature of regional investments in Asia means that individual members have been insulated from any investment diversion when their FDI source countries have signed PTAs with third countries. This is because the investment that the sources make in third countries can be a general equilibrium complement to bilateral investment within the overall Asian network. So PTAs are seen as being neither a threat nor a promise to FDI in the region.

Many more such studies of the effects of PTA membership on trade and investment flows can be cited. But most only look at the existence of PTA membership, and do not distinguish the behind-the-border features, as Dee (2008b) does. And at best, the evidence these studies provide is only circumstantial.

Evidence from looking at the detailed provisions of PTAs

It is not possible to tell whether PTAs have promoted domestic reforms, simply by looking at the PTA commitments themselves. This is because:

- PTA commitments may simply reproduce commitments made in the WTO; and
- even when they go beyond WTO commitments, they may still lag actual practice.

It is incredibly time-consuming for 'outsiders' (ie those outside of the trade negotiation fraternity) to compare PTA commitments with WTO commitments. It is not sufficient to look at chapter titles, nor even the broad content of the chapters in each agreement, because the devil is in the detail — particularly in the detailed annexes of reservations and exceptions, as well as in the product classifications used to describe the goods and services for which commitments are being made. Further, in some chapters, such as those on intellectual property, the language is highly technical and legalistic, and difficult for non-specialists to understand. In other chapters, the commitments being made are 'soft' (for example on a 'best endeavours' basis), so it is not at all clear that they should be counted as substantial commitments. One comprehensive comparison of a single PTA, the Australia–US Free Trade Agreement, with the WTO commitments of its two partner countries confirms that a great deal of the PTA was already committed in the WTO (Dee 2005b). A more selective comparison, limited to services commitments, made for a number of East Asian Free Trade Agreements comes to a similar conclusion, particularly for the less developed members (Fink and Molinuevo 2007).

It is even more time consuming to compare PTA commitments with actual practice. The tariff schedules of most countries are publicly available, so it is reasonably straightforward to compare PTA tariff commitments with actual practice. But for virtually all behind-the-border areas, actual practice is defined in a complex web of legislation, regulation, and formal and 'informal' bureaucratic practice. Collecting information on all the strands of this web is a truly major undertaking. As will be seen, there is growing evidence that PTA commitments can lag actual practice, sometimes by a considerable margin, particularly in developing countries. Accordingly, it is not possible to take exercises that just look at provisions (eg Fink and Molinuevo 2007, Kawai and Wignaraja 2011, Plummer 2007) to impute actual reform.

Studies that have made systematic comparisons of PTA commitments with either WTO commitments or actual practice are not yet comprehensive, but are slowly growing in number. This section will concentrate on reporting comparisons that have been made for commitments in services and investment. In part, this is because these areas are where most comparisons have been made to date. Nevertheless, the commitments in services are highly relevant to the broader issue of whether PTAs promote domestic reform. This is because restrictions on trade in services usually take the form of domestic regulation, as services tend to be highly regulated, reflecting a variety of important public policy objectives (Czaga 2004).

The services agenda (broadly defined, and including commercial presence) is also aligns relatively closely with the revealed integration objectives in the East Asian region. The ASEAN Economic Community Blueprint — a document outlining the priorities for economic integration in that region — contains reasonably 'hard' targets for services, investment, and transport and information infrastructure, while those in areas such as competition policy, consumer protection and intellectual property rights are weaker and/or on a 'best endeavours' basis. Kawai and Wignaraja (2011) stress the importance in the East Asian region for harmonizing the policies, rules and standards governing trade and investment. But harmonization is an agenda that even the EU has not achieved, having moved instead to the weaker and more decentralized principle of mutual recognition.

Comparing PTA commitments with WTO commitments

Roy, Marchetti and Lim (2006) compare the commitments undertaken by 29 WTO Members (counting the EC as one) for cross-border supply and commercial presence in services in 28 PTAs negotiated since 2000, and compare these with both the prevailing GATS commitments and the Doha Round offers at the time of those countries.

The authors find that PTAs appear to offer limited value added over GATS disciplines in the areas of rules governing safeguard mechanisms, subsidies, domestic regulation and the like. Their main contribution appears to be in their levels of commitments. A more detailed summary is given in Chapter 9 of this volume. Overall, the authors conclude (p. 33) that

> PTAs generally have provided for significant improvements over GATS commitments, sometimes even leading to real liberalization of the market.

Fink and Jensen (2009) also examine the services commitments in PTAs negotiated in the 1990s and 2000s. They come to a similar conclusion to Roy, Marchetti and Lim (2006) — in areas where there are no WTO disciplines, there tend not to be rules in PTAs either (safeguards, subsidies, procurement, domestic regulation). They also find that the tendency is for PTAs to have more commitments in sectors where countries have also made more extensive commitments in the GATS. Sensitive sectors such as health, transport and financial services as well as the movement of natural services suppliers tend to be subject to the fewest commitments.

But Adlung and Morrison (2010) have looked at evidence of where the services provisions in PTAs fall short of the same countries' GATS commitments. They find that instances of such 'negative preferences' can be found in most recent agreements, including those involving some of the largest WTO members. Of the 56 PTAs whose contents (including sectoral classification) are compared with GATS commitments, 46 (or 80 per cent) contain some form of GATS-minus commitments in either their horizontal or sectoral sections. The authors also document some of the GATS-minus components in three particular agreements — the Economic Partnership Agreement between the EU and the CARIFORUM States, the AUSFTA agreement between Australia and the United States, and the China–ASEAN Agreement. They conjecture that such GATS-minus commitments are mutually conceded in 'sensitive' sectors or tacitly accepted in view of 'side-payments' in what they call non-WTO currency (including development finance).

Comparing PTA commitments with actual practice

One recent comparison of PTA commitments with actual practice has capitalized on a pre-existing database of actual regulatory practice that was compiled for a different purpose. Barth *et al.* (2006) make use of a database on actual regulatory practice in banking as it stood around 2000, as reported in responses to a detailed World Bank survey. The database had been used previously to assess the impact of that regulation on banking performance (eg Barth, Caprio and Levine 2004). In the more recent exercise, Barth *et al.* (2006) compare regulatory practice with actual WTO commitments in the financial sector for 123 WTO Members.

The authors find significant differences between commitments and actual practice. A more detailed summary is given in Chapter 9 of this volume. In general, the authors find many instances where WTO commitments are significantly less liberal than actual practice. They also find instances where WTO commitments are more liberal than actual practice, particularly in developed countries.

As evidence about whether PTAs promote real liberalization, the findings are merely circumstantial. However, if WTO commitments lag actual practice by a significant margin, then even if PTAs improve significantly on WTO commitments, they may still themselves lag actual practice.

Furthermore, if actual practice lags WTO commitments, as it appears to in a few cases, then there is clearly an enforcement problem that may also carry over to PTA commitments. One reason for the enforcement problem in a WTO context may be that trade partner countries are not equipped to check the compliance of all other WTO Members. Such a monitoring problem may be less severe in a PTA context. But another reason for an enforcement problem may be that trade commitments are made by trade negotiators who are divorced from what is really going on in their own countries. This problem may well carry over to PTAs, especially in countries where problems of coordination among different government ministries are endemic.

Some recent, much more comprehensive evidence along similar lines is cited by Hoekman and Mattoo (2011). They report on research by

Borchert, Gootiiz and Mattoo (2010) that has collected information on actual policies in the major services sectors of 102 countries — 78 developing countries and 24 OECD countries. This information has been compared with GATS commitments for the 93 WTO members in the sample. The comparison shows that there is a very significant gap between applied and 'bound' policies (the commitments) because most services liberalization around the world has been undertaken unilaterally. The Uruguay commitments are on average 2.3 times more restrictive than currently applied policies. Borchert, Gootiiz and Mattoo (2010) also look at the Doha Round offers made by 62 WTO members. They find that the best offers submitted so far improve on current GATS commitments by about 10 per cent, but remain on average twice as restrictive as actual policies.

According to Hoekman and Mattoo (2011), there are some PTAs that have induced significant market opening. They cite the example of the liberalization of telecommunications in several Central American countries as a result of the CAFTA agreement with the United States. But their general assessment is that although recent PTAs have wider sectoral coverage of services, they do not appear to have induced significant change in applied policies.

Roy, Marchetti and Lim (2006) also attempt to assess whether PTA commitments lead to real liberalization. They do not make direct comparisons with regulatory practice, but look for instances where PTA commitments are phased in over time, using the phasing mechanism as an indication that real liberalization is taking place. They note that the group of countries making such phased commitments is fairly widespread, although it appears that financial services and telecommunications dominate. Most phase-out commitments have been contracted by countries as part of a PTA with the United States, although not exclusively.

Dee (2011) tracks actual policy changes in four services sectors in the ten ASEAN countries between 2008 and 2010, and gains some insight into how much has been driven by commitments under the ASEAN Framework Agreement on Services (AFAS). A brief summary of the policy changes affecting trade in medical, health, banking and insurance services in ASEAN countries during 2008–10 is shown in Tables 14.1

and 14.2. The table shows that there has been at least some progress in all four sectors.

Not surprisingly, some of the recent policy changes in banking and insurance services involved a tightening of prudential regulation in response to the global financial crisis. Prudential regulation has a legitimate purpose of ensuring systemic stability. It is generally not regarded as a barrier to trade in financial services, and for this reason it is carved out of the GATS. Nevertheless, Vietnam appears to have instituted stricter licensing requirements for banks to an extent that goes beyond purely prudential oversight. Within ASEAN, this is an isolated example of possible overreaction to the global financial crisis. In addition, both Brunei and Vietnam have required (or clarified) that foreign bank branches must lend against their local capital rather than their parent capital. This is a 'grey area' measure — while it further constrains the activities of foreign bank branches, it also gives the local prudential authorities some control over the capital reserve requirements of foreign branches, rather than having to rely on the prudential oversight of the authorities in the branches' home countries.

The tables also show the extent to which countries in the region have instituted genuine trade reforms in response to commitments made under AFAS or the GATS. In banking, both Thailand and Vietnam have instituted multilateral reforms in line with commitments under the GATS, while Thailand has also relaxed restrictions on hiring foreign personnel on a preferential basis under its AFAS commitments. In insurance, Vietnam expects to implement a package of reforms in the near future in line with its WTO commitments. In health services, Indonesia has relaxed the minimum bed size for foreign-invested hospitals on a preferential basis. In medical professional services, Cambodia has implemented a mutual recognition agreement with its ASEAN neighbours. In all other respects, the reforms recorded in Tables 14.1 and 14.2 are unilateral and non-preferential, or if they have a regional dimension, it is because of geographical constraints rather than preferential commitments.

Some of the more notable unilateral reform efforts are the relaxations of interest rate controls in Cambodia and Vietnam. Malaysia also awaits

Table 14.1.   ASEAN's Progress in Liberalizing Trade in Healthcare Services 2008–10

	Medical Professionals	*Health Services*
Brunei	None.	None.
Cambodia	New mutual recognition agreement signed with ASEAN countries in 2009.	None.
Indonesia	Law no. 44/2009 covers medical professionals for hospitals. Hospitals can employ foreign medical professionals, but the employment must be intended for the purpose of knowledge and technology transfers. This rules out foreigners in unskilled positions. Permenkes no. 028 issued on 4 January 2011 says clinics cannot hire foreign healthcare workers. Foreign equity limits for medical and dental clinics (specialist only) have been raised from 65% to 67%. Those for nursing have been raised from 49% to 51% in Medan and Surabaya, and from zero to 49% in the rest of Indonesia.	Law no. 36/2009 on health requires all foreign healthcare facilities to obtain operating licence. Law no 44/2009 on hospitals regulates their establishment and management and introduces mandatory accreditation every 3 years. Foreign equity limits for hospitals and medical laboratories have been raised from 65% to 67%. The minimum size of foreign hospitals has been lowered from 300 to 200 beds for ASEAN investors, though the hospitals still have to be specialist. Foreign medical professionals can be employed in hospitals and medical laboratories, but this must be intended for the purpose of knowledge and technology transfer. This now rules out foreigners in unskilled positions. Universal services obligations have been spelt out in law.
Lao PDR	None.	None.
Malaysia	PROSPECTIVE: The Malaysian National Healthcare Financing Scheme (similar to Australia's Medicare system) may finally be implemented. The government is keen to push tele-medicine, and has also been promoting medical tourism. It has been promoting the recruitment of foreign doctors and specialists and establishing new medical colleges and twinning programs to raise the ratio of doctors per head of population.	None.
Myanmar	Same as for health services.	Some easing of cross-border trade. Some joint venture hospitals have been established since 2008.

Table 14.1.   Continued.

Philippines	The process for issuing employment permits to foreign nationals has been extended from 1 to 3 working days. Otherwise, the lack of progress in liberalization stems from the constitutional provision that the practice of all professions in the Philippines shall be limited to Filipino citizens.	A major policy change is the suspension for one year of the need to obtain a Certificate of Need, the only restriction on new entry of private hospitals. The DOH Administrative Order No. 2007-0027 created the improved quality assurance and monitoring program for clinical laboratories in the Philippines and rendered obsolete the DOH-BHFS Circular No. 3 Series of 2003, which suspends issuance of permit to new entry of laboratories. The process for issuing employment permits to foreign nationals has been extended from 1 to 3 working days. In 2009, the Health and Wellness Alliance of the Philippines was established to organize industry and government stakeholders involved with global healthcare and wellness services, tourism and retirement. PROSPECTIVE: There are emerging demands for the amendment of the Republic Act 4226 or the Hospital Licensure Act to expand the coverage of the law to include health facilities other than hospitals.
Singapore	None.	None.
Thailand	HORIZONTAL: The Working of Alien Act 1978 has been replaced by the Working of Alien Act 2008. Among other things, it extends the validity period of the work permit from not exceeding one year to not exceeding two years. However, non-immigrants visas are normally granted for one year.	Same as for medical services.
Viet Nam	None.	The Health Insurance Law took effect on 1 July 2009, aiming to ease the load on provincial and central hospitals, and expand policyholder categories to include drug addicts and people with congenital defects who were previously excluded.

Source: Dee (2011).

Table 14.2. ASEAN's Progress in Liberalizing Trade in Financial Services 2008–10

	Banking	*Insurance*
Brunei	Since the Ministry of Finance issued clarification on lending in 2009, foreign banks can only lend against local capital. PROSPECTIVE: With effect from 1 January 2011, the Monetary Authority Brunei Darussalam will be establish as a Statutory Body to regulate the banking, finance and insurance sector, independent of the Ministry of Finance.	None.
Cambodia	An amendment was made in September 2009 to liberalize interest rate setting. NOTE: Both the minimum capital requirement and the reserve requirement were changed in 2009 in response to the global financial crisis.	None.
Indonesia	None. NOTE: Changes to banking industry regulation concerned a few prudential measures.	None. NOTE: The only change in insurance regulation during 2008-2010 concerned prudential measures.
Lao PDR	None.	New Law on Investment Promotion 2009 means that 100% foreign ownership is allowed, the minimum foreign equity in joint ventures has been reduced from 30% to 10%, and the term of licences has been extended from 50 to 99 years. However, the government does not want to issue new licences because of the small size of the market. PROSPECTIVE: The Law on Insurance is expected to be amended to be more appropriate to the current situation of a more liberalized and open economy to the world and regional integration. In the coming years, the scope of the compulsory insurance-based social security system will be extended.

Table 14.2.   Continued.

Malaysia	In Nov 2010, the central bank announced several measures to curb property speculation as well as to address the rising household debt problem. Among these, the monetary regulator imposed a maximum loan-to-value ratio of 70%, which will be applicable to the third house financing facility taken out by a borrower. PROSPECTIVE: The Central Bank of Malaysia is currently preparing for a 'new' Financial Sector Masterplan, which would further liberalize the banking and securities markets.	None.
Myanmar	None.	Myanmar Insurance can supply insurance services including quasi-medical insurance for expatriates going abroad. In 2008 quasi-medical insurance did not exist.
Philippines	None.	None.
Singapore	None.	None.
Thailand	The Bank of Thailand has permitted commercial banks to employ personnel of ASEAN nationality with unlimited numbers in any positions, but foreign institutions face consideration on a case-by-case basis. This policy change implements commitments under AFAS. A foreign bank with branches in Thailand is allowed to establish up to 2 additional branches by the approval of the Bank of Thailand. This implements commitments under the GATS.	None.
Viet Nam	In mid 2010, the Government removed the control over the lending interest rate (commercial banks could arrange the lending interest rate with customers), but the State Bank used some administrative procedures to impose the borrowing rate below 14% (the rate that commercial banks in the Vietnam banking association have committed). Circular 09 sets out stricter requirements for shareholders,	PROSPECTIVE: The draft amendment and supplement to the Law on Insurance Business would recognize the cross-border provision of insurance services by foreign insurance organizations and individuals. It would also recognize the right to set up branches of foreign non-life insurance enterprises in Vietnam. It would also abolish ceding percentages. All are in accordance with Vietnam's WTO

Table 14.2. Continued.

especially founding shareholders, who wish to establish a joint stock commercial bank, and new longer timeframes of the application process for a licence. Prior to 2010, foreign bank branches could lend against the parent capital but from 2010, branches have to lend against their own chartered capital, not their parent capital. PROSPECTIVE: Under the Law on Credit Institutions which will take effect on 1 January 2011, the prime interest rate structure is abolished. The prime rate was eliminated as unreflective of the supply-demand relationship on the market and was viewed as interventionist by financial markets. NOTE: Certain prudential requirements have been raised, including the minimum capital adequacy ratio.	commitments. It would expand the range of recognized insurance products and insurance enterprises.

Source: Dee (2011).

a new Financial Master Plan that will further liberalize the banking and securities markets in the near future. Lao PDR has implemented a package of reforms in the insurance sector, although at the same time, the government does not want to issue any new licences. While this moratorium is explained because of the small market size, it also has the potential to offer protection to the existing government–foreign joint ventures. In Myanmar there has been a slight expansion in the range of insurance products on offer, although there has been no weakening of the monopoly position of Myanmar Insurance.

In the fields of medical and health services, there have been significant reforms in Indonesia and the Philippines, and a slight easing in Myanmar. In Indonesia, new legislation has been introduced to fill the significant gaps in the regulatory framework (Dee 2009). In a few cases, the introduction of explicit legislative guidelines has the potential to limit practices (such as the hiring of foreigners into relatively unskilled positions) that might have occurred otherwise. In most cases, however, the legislation will have somewhat reduced the scope for bureaucratic discretion. It also tightens the quality assurance framework in Indonesia by making the hospital accreditation process mandatory every three years. Finally, the Indonesian legislative reforms have also been accompanied by a slight easing of foreign equity limits. In the Philippines, there has been a lifting of the regulatory restrictions on the entry of new hospitals and medical laboratories. In Myanmar there has been a growth in cross-border trade in medical and health services and some limited evidence of foreign investment occurring.

Thus there is evidence of worthwhile reform efforts in all four services. Some has been driven by AFAS or WTO commitments but in general, the more significant reforms have taken place unilaterally.

A further key question is whether the recent reforms have made a significant difference. This is indicated in Figures 14.1 and 14.2, for domestic and foreign medical services providers respectively. These figures compare the overall prevalence of restrictions in 2008 and 2010. The differences reflect the reforms summarized in Table 14.1. The reforms have made only a slight difference to the overall prevalence of restrictions on foreign suppliers, and no difference to the prevalence of restrictions on domestic suppliers.

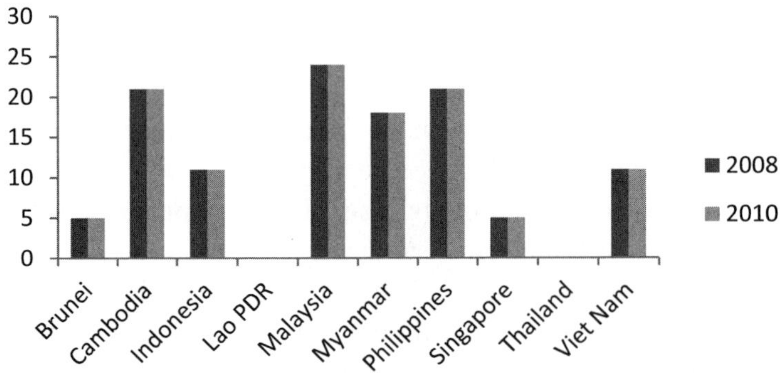

Figure 14.1. Changes in ASEAN's Restrictions on Domestic Medical Services Over Time (prevalence in per cent)
Source: Dee (2011).

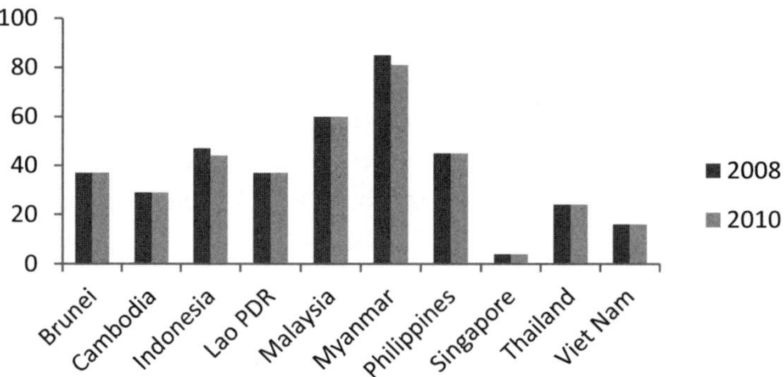

Figure 14.2. Changes in ASEAN's Restrictions on Foreign Medical Services Over Time (prevalence in per cent)
Source: Dee (2011).

Comparable figures for the other three sectors are not reproduced here, but tell a similar story. In health services, recent reforms have removed the last restrictions facing domestic suppliers. But the prevalence of restrictions against foreign health services providers is still quite high, and the recent reforms since 2008 have made only slight inroads into those trade barriers. In banking also, the reforms have made only a slight difference to the overall prevalence of restrictions. In some countries, such as Vietnam, banking reforms in some dimensions (as easing of interest rate controls) have been offset by a tightening in others (more stringent non-prudential licensing requirements). Thus there is evidence that ASEAN countries are still using unnecessary regulatory restrictions in place of better-targeted prudential requirements. Finally, there has been very little reform of regulatory restrictions on trade in insurance services during 2008–10. In Lao PDR, legislative reforms have been essentially negated by the recent moratorium on granting new licences. Insurance is a sector that is typically under pressure during WTO accession negotiations, so some ASEAN countries have already undergone market opening in this context. Other ASEAN countries will need to accelerate their reform efforts in this sector if the ASEAN Blueprint targets are to be met.

To summarize, empirical evidence to show conclusively whether formal regional institutional arrangements promote domestic reform is hard to come by. This is because the required research is incredibly labour intensive, and requires monitoring actual policy changes, not simply recording PTA commitments. The most compelling evidence to date is more circumstantial. In services, a sector that accounts for well over 50 per cent of most economies, where the trade barriers are overwhelmingly regulatory, even the best WTO Doha Round offers are on average twice as restrictive as actual practice. PTAs tend to improve on WTO commitments in services, at least in terms of sectoral coverage, if not in the depth of sectoral commitments or the disciplines on safeguards, subsidies, procurement and domestic regulation. But even if they improve on WTO commitments by a substantial margin, they are still likely to lag actual practice. It is on the basis of this and other evidence summarized above that Francois and Hoekman (2010) draw their conclusion — except in the EU, services trade reform has been primarily unilateral.

14.4   Why Has Reform Been Unilateral Outside the EU?

If PTAs have not succeeded in promoting regulatory reform in services outside of the EU, it is not because the reforms do not generate economic benefits. Francois and Hoekman (2010) survey recent econometric evidence showing that openness in a range of producer or intermediate services sectors is linked to productivity improvements and increased export performance in manufacturing. They also survey recent studies that have shown links between services sector liberalization and economic growth. Prospective studies have also highlighted the potential gains from future services trade reform. As noted by Francois and Hoekman (2010), these studies tend to show that services liberalization can generate much larger welfare gains that goods liberalization. One reason for this finding is that regulatory barriers in services can create deadweight costs, not just allocative inefficiencies of the sort generated by tariffs. Accordingly, services liberalization can generate larger welfare gains than tariff reform.

A recent example of such prospective studies is that by the APEC Policy Support Unit (2011) into the impacts and benefits of structural reforms in the transport, energy and telecommunications sectors in APEC member economies. It found that US\$ 175 billion a year in additional real income (in 2004 dollars) could be generated from further reforms in the APEC region. APEC-wide, the projected gains from these structural reforms are almost twice as big as the gains from further liberalization of merchandise trade. Yet the sectors where the structural reforms occur are less than a quarter of the size of those engaged in merchandise trade. When structural reforms lead to lower real production costs, even by half as much as the report estimates, they create a return to reform effort that is much greater than that from border trade reforms.

So why have trade agreements (other than the EU) failed to deliver services reform (and by implication, other types of structural reform)? Hoekman, Mattoo and Sapir (2007) speculate on the reasons, some of which are relevant to domestic reform more broadly. They note that despite significant unilateral reform, barriers to trade and FDI still remain. One explanation is the standard political economy problems of resistance by vested interests. But the authors note that in the case of services (and other behind-the-border reforms more generally), the reciprocity mechanisms that have traditionally been used to counter the resistance by incumbent producers are much less effective. One of the key reasons is that in services, the balance is tilted in favour of incumbents because of regulatory concerns — it is hard to design trade commitments that distinguish or separate protectionist policies from those that have a legitimate domestic efficiency or social equity rationale. Hoekman and Mattoo (2011) also note that export interests may be weaker in services because services markets tend to be either very open or very closed, and in neither situation do exporters have a strong incentive to mobilize politically.

The desire to retain regulatory autonomy has clearly been a major consideration in services negotiations. The GATS explicitly recognizes the right to regulate. And as Francois and Hoekman (2010, p. 681) observe

> The EU experience illustrates the difficulty for (unwillingness of) polities to converge on common norms and to allow for 'regulatory arbitrage' even in situations where in principle all are agreed that common minimum standards exist.

This argument would also suggest a limited role for regional agreements to push domestic reforms more generally in those areas involving cross-border trade, when domestic regulatory regimes go head-to-head. They may have more success in promoting reforms in those areas involving FDI, where host country regulations unambiguously apply.

While these authors point out one of the key limits of reciprocity in dealing with the political economy resistance to reform, various authors have pointed out the limits of reciprocity in dealing with the economic externalities associated with reform. The arguments by Antràs and Staiger (2007) and Dee and Sidorenko (2006) have already been summarized above. In a similar vein, Hoekman and Mattoo (2011) note that when reforms reduce deadweight costs, the benefits of reform are fully internalized and the pressure for reform will be unilateral. Blanchard (2007) notes that when firms can deliver services via FDI, governments have less incentive to manipulate the terms of trade on cross-border trade, so once again, reciprocity is not needed.

Yet there is agreement that the EU alone has generated significant policy reforms. But it is *sui generis* — one of a kind. So what is it about the EU agreement that has contributed to its success? And what lessons if any can been drawn about the factors that can facilitate domestic reforms elsewhere?

14.5   What is Special about the EU?

As noted above, the original EU Treaty contained broad commitments to the four freedoms — the free movement of goods, persons (both natural and legal), services and capital. The real liberalization came in the enforcement of those broad commitments, a process that also led to increasingly broad definitions of what was meant by a violation.[8]

It is important to understand the process by which this came about. The legal literature points to two key decisions of the European Court of

---

[8] As noted above, the interpretation of violations became broader in the sense that it moved away from the notion of discrimination to one based on impediments to free movement. But in another respect, the interpretation of violations became narrower, because judicial interpretations of allowable derogations also became broader (Barnard 2010).

Justice. The first was the seminal decision in *Van Gend en Loos* (Case 26/62, Van Gend en Loos v. Nederlandse Administratie der Belastingen, 1963 E.C.R.) in which the European Court of Justice developed the doctrine of 'direct effect'. The other key decision was that in *Costa v. ENEL* (Case 6/64, Costa v. ENEL, 1969 E.C.R. 585) in which the Court developed the doctrine of 'supremacy'.

Under the doctrine of 'direct effect', certain provisions of the EU Treaty have direct legal effect such that individuals and enterprises can claim Treaty-based rights in member state courts, prevailing over contrary national rules. This doctrine meant that individuals and enterprises did not have to wait for the European Commission to challenge contrary state rules — they could take action themselves in their own national courts.

Under the doctrine of 'supremacy', Treaty law took primacy over national law. This doctrine leveraged off the doctrine of 'direct effect'. In *Van Gend en Loos,* the Court ruled that member states had 'limited their sovereign rights', and effected a permanent transfer of power to the 'new legal order' of the Community. The Court then relied on this point in establishing the doctrine of supremacy in *Costa v. ENEL.* As noted by Persaud and Goebel (1997), this was at the core of all other Court doctrines, because it achieved the binding nature of the Court's own judgements.

The Van Gend en Loos judgement laid down certain criteria for Treaty provisions to have direct effect (the provisions needed to be clear, precise and absolute in their terms, aimed at achieving individual rights, and did not necessarily require Community or member state legislation for their effective application). Over time, the Court has found that Treaty provisions having direct effect include those that define three of the four freedoms — Article 30 on the free movement of goods; Articles 48 on free movement of workers and 49 on the right of establishment; and Article 56 on the freedom to provide services. Other Treaty provisions have been found also to have *horizontal* direct effect, meaning that an individual or enterprise can appeal to EU law in a case against another individual or enterprise, not just against a member government. Treaty provisions in this category include Articles 101 and 102 on competition law and Article 157 on the right of equal pay for equal work between men and women.

The doctrine of direct effect has allowed individuals and enterprises to challenge a wide variety of national measures in their own courts or in the courts of other member states. As noted above, in trade matters these dispute settlement proceedings tended to be aimed initially at rules that discriminated on the basis of nationality. Over time, the Court's interpretations of what constituted a Treaty violation widened to include a range of rules that could not be objectively justified on grounds of compelling state interests (Persaud and Goebel 1997).[9]

The reason that we know so much about the power of this appeal mechanism is that national judges can send questions — preliminary references — to the European Court of Justice so as to obtain an interpretation of EU law when this is relevant to the resolution of a dispute in the national court.[10] The European Court of Justice responds with a preliminary ruling that the national judge is expected to apply to resolve the case. The vast majority of preliminary references involve an allegation on the part of an individual or enterprise that a specific national law or practice in the same country is incompatible with EU law (McNaughton 2011, Stone Sweet and Brunell 2011). So even if dispute settlement takes place in a decentralized manner in national courts, it leaves a shadow at the Community level in the form of preliminary references, and centralized data on these are available. The data show that the number of such cases has grown steadily, from 147 in the period 1961–70 to 1,084 in the period 1991–5 (Stone Sweet and Brunell 1998). The subject matter of these cases has also broadened, as was noted earlier. Furthermore, the preliminary ruling mechanism has been the key mechanisms through which the interpretation of what constitutes a Treaty violation has evolved over time.

In what way does this mechanism differ from the standard dispute settlement mechanisms embodied in trade agreements (either regional or through the WTO)? Stone Sweet, one of the pre-eminent legal scholars in

---

[9] The doctrine of direct effect has also been extended beyond Treaty provisions, and also applies to certain Community directives.

[10] Lower national courts *can* refer such questions at their discretion; national courts of last resort are *required* to request the assistance of the European Court of Justice.

the field, gives a legal perspective on this issue (Stone Sweet 2010, Stone Sweet and Brunell 2011).

He argues that the European Court of Justice and the WTO Appellate Body are in fact similar, in that both are more than mere agents of the contracting States in a principal–agent relationship. They are what he calls Trustee Courts of their respective treaty systems. He defines a Trustee Court according to three criteria:

- the court is the authoritative interpreter of the regime's law, and has the authority to review the legality of acts taken by the contracting States under the regime's law;
- the court's jurisdiction with regard to the contracting States is compulsory; and
- it is difficult, or impossible as a practical manner, for the contracting States, as principals, to reverse the court's important rulings on Treaty law.

He notes that unlike a simple agent, a Trustee Court has the authority to govern the principals themselves. It also has the power to expand or contract its own 'zone of discretion'. Classic examples of the use of these powers in the EU context are the doctrines of supremacy and direct effect. Also in an EU context, Stone Sweet argues that the Member States conferred such authority on the European Court of Justice 'in order to help them overcome acute commitment problems associated with market and political integration' (Stone Sweet and Brunell 2011, p. 4).

While Stone Sweet and Brunell (2011) claim that the WTO Appellate Body has similar powers, Pauwleyn (2005) argues that there are notable checks and balances on its behaviour. The Dispute Settlement Understanding explicitly guards against judicial activism, by prohibiting panels and the Appellate Body from adding to or diminishing the rights and obligations of WTO Members. Pauwleyn (2005, p. 49) also argues that the Dispute Settlement Body exercises political control over dispute settlement:

As the umbilical cord between the political and judicial branch, it is a crucial interface and forum of contestation or voice to which both panels and the Appellate Body are most receptive.

Van den Broek (2009) also notes that current WTO dispute remedies are less than ideal. Compensation is often unrealistic because the defendant WTO member has to agree to it. Retaliation (raising levels of protection against imports from the defendant WTO member) involves shooting oneself in the foot. He argues that these aspects of WTO dispute settlement penalize the least developed WTO members in particular, a conjecture borne out by statistics on who uses the WTO dispute settlement process.[11]

Stone Sweet and Brunell (2011) consider how the European Court of Justice has dealt with the issue of legitimacy that its Trustee status creates. They argue that one strategy it uses to establish and maintain legitimacy is 'majority activism' — the Court's rulings tend to line up with the actual practice found in the majority of member states. The Court also has a clear mandate — to construct and consolidate a transnational, 'European' identity, in part in opposition to nationalism. Its majority activism clearly serves that purpose. The authors argue that because the WTO has no comparable identity construction mandate, it has not developed a variant of majority activism as a way of securing its legitimacy, though they argue that perhaps it should.

The impression that one gets from reading this legal literature is that the differences between the European Court of Justice and the WTO Appellate Body are differences of degree rather than kind. To the extent that there are analytically identifiable differences, they tend to support the more popular notion that more has been possible in the EU because the ultimate goal has been not just the furthering of prosperity, but the prevention of world wars. Pauwleyn (2005) also notes differences in the degree of judicial activism. But here it is important to recall the distinction between a negative list agreement (such as the EU Treaty) and a positive list agreement (such as the GATS). There may have been more judicial activism in the EU because the nature of the agreement allowed more scope for it.

---

[11] Of the 356 complaints brought between 1995 and 2006, 227 were brought by high income WTO members and only 1 was brought by a least developed country.

Nevertheless, there is a significant political economy difference between dispute settlement in the EU and the WTO that has received little attention in most of the legal literature. The doctrine of direct effect empowered a whole new set of domestic interests in favour of reform. As Burley and Mattli (1993) note, *importers* who objected to paying customs duties on their imports could invoke the Treaty of Rome to force their governments to remove them.

According to the standard political economy argument for regional rather than unilateral action, the interests of a country's exporters (in opening up foreign markets) need to be pitted against those of its import-competing industries (in keeping protection at home). The presumption is that the interests of consumers do not count politically because of the collective action problem of mobilizing large numbers of consumers with individually small stakes in the outcome.

At an economic level, this argument fails to recognize that exports are not *per se* 'good' in an economic sense (the mercantilist fallacy) — it depends on the price at which they can be sold.[12] At a political level, this argument fails to recognize that there can be powerful domestic business interests that align with those of consumers — importers who sell directly to consumers, businesses that use imports as intermediate inputs and are equally hurt by import protection, or exporters who are hurt indirectly by the real currency appreciation that import protection tends to generate.

The doctrine of direct effect empowered at least some of those domestic pro-reform business interests. The significance can be illustrated in the context of the example developed by Krugman (1997, p. 118):

> When the United States recently imposed utterly indefensible restrictions on Mexican tomato exports, an Administration official remarked off the record that Florida has a lot of electoral votes while Mexico has none. The economically correct rebuttal to this sort of thing is to point out that the other 49 states contain a lot of pizza lovers: the politically effective answer is to subject U.S.–Mexican trade to a set of rules and arbitration procedures in which the Mexicans do too have a vote.

---

[12] Multilateral action can nevertheless help to overcome terms of trade externalities, as noted earlier.

What the doctrine of direct effect does is give the pizza lovers in the other 49 states a voice by proxy, by empowering tomato importers, who make money by selling to pizza shops, to complain about the actions of the Administration officials. So the politics of fighting protection is internalized, and no longer subject to concerns about loss of sovereignty.

Burley and Mattli (1993) note that this empowerment in turn contributed to the legitimacy of the European Court of Justice. The Court was seen as siding with the 'little guy' against state bureaucracies, the 'people' against the 'power elites'. And this was a powerful antidote to charges of antidemocratic activism.

Burley and Mattli (1993) also point out the more general benefits of depoliticizing a reform debate by framing it according to non-political criteria. In the case of the EU, with the forum being the European Court of Justice, the external frame of reference for debate was often the rule of law. In other forums (some of which will be discussed shortly), the external frame of reference may be economic growth and efficiency. Even when the politics of reform is entirely internal, it is useful to have a forum that can provide and safeguard such a non-political frame of reference. Burley and Mattli (1993, p. 72) describe the process as follows:

> Even an economic decision that has acquired political significance is not the same as a 'purely' political decision and cannot be attacked as such. It retains an independent 'non-political' rationale, which must be met by a counterargument on its own terms. Within this domain, then, contending political interests must do battle by proxy. The chances of victory are affected by the strength of that proxy measured by independent non-political criteria.

The argument so far suggests that the unique feature of the EU that helped it to promote economic reform in sensitive, behind-the-border areas was that it overcame the problem of loss of sovereignty by internalizing the political battle to domestic interests, and yet still provided a non-political frame of reference for the debate.

Dee (2010a) provides a number of case studies from around the East Asian region to demonstrate that this has been a common feature of institutional arrangements that have proved effective at promoting structural reform in that region. When it comes to structural reform, the vested interests with the strongest stakes in the outcomes are primarily domestic — very often the interests of incumbent producers against potential new entrants (domestic as well as foreign), consumers, and upstream and downstream industries. The key to promoting reform is to mobilize domestic pro-reform champions to act as a countervailing force against vested interests. One way to do this is to provide an independent, non-political forum and a frame of reference that stresses economy-wide benefits. A further characteristic stressed by Dee (2010a) is that the forum should be transparent, in the sense of making public the arguments of the respective interests, and also making public any recommendations to government. In this way, the special pleading of vested interests can be revealed for what it is. Equally importantly, the pro-reform champions can also self-select on any particular issue.[13]

Examples of institutions that have promoted reforms in this way include the Productivity Commission and its predecessors in Australia (Banks and Wonder 2010) and the Council on Economic and Fiscal Policy in Japan (Hosen 2010). McNaugton (2011) shows, for example, that the concerns that the EU Services Directive are intended to address are being dealt with domestically in Australia by the Council of Australian Governments and the research and recommendations of the Productivity Commission. Institutional examples from the Philippines (Llanto 2010) and Indonesia (Soesastro, Aswicahyono and Narjoko 2010) illustrate how useful work to support structural reform could potentially take place within a medium-term economic planning framework. Old-fashioned economic planning is often seen as outmoded in an era of open markets and outward-oriented growth strategies, but a medium-term planning process can also provide a useful forum for detailed *ex ante* reviews of policy options, providing a lead in the policy development process. Such a medium-term focus can then bind successive governments and guard against excessive 'short-termism' in policy development.

Many East Asian economies also have influential think-tanks that conduct impartial policy reviews and analysis, and therefore provide an

---

[13] Note that under the processes of the European Court of Justice, even the issues self-select.

open, independent forum in which the views of vested interests are subject to scrutiny using an economy-wide frame of reference. These organizations vary in the extent to which they sit inside or outside formal government structures, and the extent to which their contributions are used in the policy development process. But all have at least some of the characteristics of effective policy review institutions— independence, an economy-wide view, and transparent processes.

The problem of developing a mandate for structural reform is not confined to democratically elected governments. China and Vietnam also face the problem of managing vested interests. One strategy that Vietnam has tried is a taskforce approach — putting together groups of experts from within and outside government to consider one particular area of reform (Vo and Nguyen 2010). According to He (2010), China too is at the stage where reforms can potentially create losers as well as winners, and so it requires new strategies to deal with vested interests.

In none of these East Asian examples has an institution been given the powers of a Trustee Court to bind the actions of the government. This is the essence of the East Asian distaste for supranational institutions — no East Asian government would be willing to limit its sovereign rights in this fashion. But this does not mean that institutions with only advisory powers cannot influence policy outcomes. The country case studies in Dee (2010a) demonstrate that they can, because ideas have influence by shaping debates, and transparent processes have influence by marshalling the winners as well as the losers from reform.

14.6 How to Shape Regional Institutions to Promote Domestic Reform?

The preponderance of evidence is that signing more PTAs will not promote domestic reform. The chapters may be written and the agreements signed, but the content will continue to be relatively empty so long as governments feel that such agreements impinge unduly on their sovereignty and their right to regulate. And one key reason that governments will continue to feel this way is that there is very little in PTAs to help governments deal with the domestic politics of reform.

Nor can great hope be placed in current WTO processes. Pauwelyn (2005) gives a careful examination of the likelihood of ongoing WTO success, particularly given its ever broader agenda. He concludes that (p. 58):

> The so-called bicycle club of trade must be disbanded. It takes exporters and producers as the core constituency of the system and assumes that, to keep their support, the world trade system requires ever more liberalization; otherwise, the bicycle will fall over. To survive as a legitimate organization, the WTO must extend its base to include consumers and citizens. It must, in other words, play out its strongest card: that genuine free trade benefits the masses, not the few. … The proxy of exporters/producers allegedly representing majority interests is no longer needed and can, in any event, no longer suffice.

It is instructive to look at recent proposals for how to restructure and revitalize the WTO. The immediate issues include whether to break away from a 'single undertaking' (the decision-making rule that nothing is agreed until everything is agreed), the consensus rule, or to allow more plurilateral rather than multilateral agreements.[14] Examples of these kinds of proposals are found in the Sutherland Report (2004) and the Warwick Commission (2007).

The proposals also include the idea that WTO members should grant direct effect to WTO treaty obligations, so that individuals and enterprises can take action in national courts in the event of non-compliance by a WTO member. On the face of it, this looks like a promising move, since the doctrine of direct effect was instrumental in the EU's success in achieving domestic reform. To date, not even the EU has granted direct effect to WTO obligations, on the grounds that unless all other WTO members gave direct effect in the same way to the same provisions, the EU might put itself at a disadvantage *vis-à-vis* the other WTO members (eg van den Broek 2009). The move may well also create uncertainty for EU traders, because EU courts might have to give preference to WTO measures at the expense of *EU* measures. The general granting of direct effect by all members would overcome the EU's first objection.

---

[14] The current WTO agreement on Government Procurement is plurilateral.

But Trachtman (1999) disagrees with the proposition that WTO members should grant direct effect to WTO obligations. He argues that the currently weak enforcement mechanisms help the WTO to achieve democratic legitimacy — something that Stone Sweet and Brunell (2011) argue is currently lacking. Trachtman (1999, p. 678) argues that 'direct effect without more direct democratic participation in formulation of the directly effective law raises as many issues as it resolves'.

Pauwelyn (2005) makes a similar argument. He argues that the current WTO does not allow sufficient democratic participation (not just of the members states, but also of the various private interests within them) to ensure the loyalty required for members to put up with the more legalistic system that the WTO has become. This is in contrast to the EU, where progress was slow and incremental, but where loyalty was more or less maintained (see also the seminal analysis of the EU by Weiler 1991).[15] Giving direct effect to WTO obligations would be a mistake, because it would achieve efficiency without loyalty.

Pauwelyn (2005) reviews the other major proposals that have been put forward to reform the WTO, not just in terms of the compliance it achieves, but more broadly. If a lack of democratic participation is the problem at the moment, then the solution is not to divorce trade negotiations even more from the 'rough and tumble' of representative democracy (eg Weiler 2001, Bhala 2001), nor is it to dispense with the current consensus rule (eg Sutherland Report 2004). But nor does he think that the current dispute settlement process should be weakened (eg Barfield 2001). As a legal scholar and former Legal Officer with the WTO Secretariat, the lesson he draws from the history of the WTO is that to be effective, it needed an independent and automatic enforcement mechanism — particularly once it started dealing with non-tariff barriers and behind-the-border measures.

---

[15] When the doctrines of direct effect and supremacy were first developed, there were only six Member States of what is now the EU, and the legislative voting pattern in the Council of Ministers was by unanimity. Since then, there have been changes in the voting patterns in the Council, with the introduction and then modification of Qualified Majority Voting. In addition, a 'co-decision' procedure has been introduced for legislation, under which both the EU Parliament and the Council of Ministers must consent to a measure for it to be adopted. These changes have contributed to the further/deeper integration of the EU legal system, and to further reforms at the domestic level in EU member states.

As noted above, Pauwelyn (2005) argues that the problem of the WTO is that it remains focused primarily on non-discrimination instead of economic efficiency, and on the interests of producers instead of the interests of consumers. As such, it has been ripe for exploitation by special interests. Examples cited by Pauwelyn are the protectionist agreements on agriculture, antidumping and the former agreement on textiles, and win-lose agreements (which benefit some countries at the expense of others) such as TRIPS.

So Pauwelyn's solution is to propose more politics and participation in the WTO, not less. And he gives a number of concrete WTO-specific proposals to provide more capital city input into Geneva processes, and to give a broader range of actors a voice in WTO issues, if not a seat at the table. Van den Broek (2009) also urges a greater role for non-state actors in bringing pressure for WTO compliance via the 'mobilization of shame'. Pauwelyn also proposes a slight weakening of discipline (and more options for exit) by dispensing with the single undertaking and by not requiring a consensus of all WTO members that a new plurilateral agreement can be added to the WTO system.

If the current configuration of exporter and import-competing producer interests can no longer secure further trade liberalization in the WTO, as the current fate of the Doha Round suggests, then it is even less likely to secure deeper domestic reforms in either the WTO or in regional trade negotiating forums. These current forums are simply not equipped to help governments fight the necessary domestic political battles. The above proposals are worth considering if the WTO is to make progress on its current agenda. But in the context of a much broader agenda — domestic reform — a key question is whether it would be sufficient to give a greater range of domestic interests a voice in a forum in which other governments also sit, or whether it would be even better to remove the other government(s) from the table.

The above economic arguments suggest that a reciprocity mechanism is weak or ineffective in achieving behind-the-border reform. So it does not help to have another government at the negotiating table, especially when this raises concerns about loss of sovereignty, to compound the problem of lack of democratic legitimacy. But this does not mean that regional institutions, or even the WTO for that matter, cannot assist domestic governments to push a domestic reform agenda.

This has been recognized recently by Hoekman and Mattoo (2011) in the context of services trade liberalization. They argue that a concerted, international effort to pursue regulatory cooperation could help to push the reform process along both unilaterally and in market access negotiations. They argue that two types of cooperation are needed. The first is international assistance with diagnosing prevailing policies (or the lack of them) and using this analysis to devise strategies for reform. This process could help to identify a menu of regulatory options for countries to consider. Aid for trade initiatives could also help with the implementation. A second type of cooperation is between regulators, explicitly focused on addressing regulatory externalities that impede trade. An example would be initiatives to improve the international mobility of workers, as international experience suggests that this requires the regulatory cooperation of both the home and host countries.

Dee and Findlay (2008) proposed a similar agenda, but also noted that further progress would be needed on domestic reform *before* further progress could be expected in market access negotiations. This would be the only way to overcome the quite legitimate concerns of developing countries that they were 'not yet ready' for services trade liberalization.

Drysdale (2010) addresses more directly the kinds of regional institutions and mechanisms that could best support a domestic reform agenda. He stresses the importance of ownership of the reform agenda, something that is not helped if the reforms are seen to be dictated by outside organizations or by trading partner governments. He proposes regional support for those home-grown institutional mechanisms (such as those cited above) that help to generate successful domestic reforms. The key elements of regional support are capacity building and providing forums for experience-sharing. The domestic activities needing such support are *domestic* efforts to diagnose current policies and develop policy alternatives, in transparent *domestic* forums that allow the views of vested interests to be met and challenged by domestic pro-reform champions. The evidence above suggests that it was this aspect of the EU that accounts for its success in achieving domestic reform. So this aspect is worth the support of regional institutions.

Which members of the alpha-numerical soup of Asian regional institutions are best-placed to carry out this support? Drysdale (2010) and Soesastro (2010) point out that of all the current regional institutions, APEC has the track record of regional experience-sharing and mentoring. It has the sanction, through the Leaders' Agenda to Implement Structural Reform (signed in 2004). And it has started to develop the delivery mechanisms, for example through the establishment of the APEC Policy Support Unit. This is not to say that other regional institutions could not also start usefully working in this direction. What is critical is to recognize that the key to achieving domestic reform is to win the domestic political battle. This is what regional institutions need to support.

References

Adams, R., Dee, P., Gali, J. and McGuire, G. (2003) 'The Trade and Investment Effects of Preferential Trading Arrangements — Old and New Evidence', Productivity Commission Staff Working Paper, Canberra: Productivity Commission.

Adlung, R. (2006) 'Services Negotiations in the Doha Round: Lost in Flexibility?', *Journal of International Economic Law*, 9(4): 865–93.

Adlung, R. and Morrison, P. (2010) 'Less than the GATS: "Negative Preferences" in Regional Services Agreements', *Journal of International Economic Law*, 13(4): 1103–43.

Alesina, A. and Tabellini, G. (2007) 'Bureaucrats or Politicians? Part I: A Single Policy Task', *American Economic Review*, 97(1): 169–79.

Alesina, A. and Tabellini, G. (2008) 'Bureaucrats or Politicians? Part II: Multiple Policy Tasks', *Journal of Public Economics*, 92(3–4): 426–47.

Anderson, J.E. and Neary, P.J. (1994) 'Measuring the Restrictiveness of Trade Policy', *World Bank Economic Review*, 8(2): 151–69.

Anderson, J.E. and Neary, P.J. (1996) 'A New Approach to Evaluating Trade Policy', *Review of Economic Studies*, 3(2): 107–25.

Andràs, P. and Staiger, R. (2007) 'Offshoring and the Value of Trade Agreements', Centre for Economic Policy Research Discussion Paper 6966, London: Centre for Economic Policy Research.

Andriamananjara, S. (2002) 'On the Size and Number of Preferential Trading Arrangements', *Journal of International Trade and Economic Development*, 11(3): 279–95.

Andrews, M. (2008) 'Creating Space for Effective Political Engagement in Development', in S. Odugbemi and T. Jacobsen (eds) *Governance Reform Under Real-World Conditions: Citizens, Stakeholders and Voice*, Washington DC: World Bank: 95–113.

APEC (Asia-Pacific Economic Cooperation) (1995) *Foreign Direct Investment and APEC Economic Integration*, Singapore: APEC Economic Committee.

APEC (1996) *Guide to the Investment Regimes of Member Economies*, Singapore: APEC Committee on Trade and Investment.

APEC (2007) *2007 APEC Economic Policy Report*, Singapore: APEC Secretariat.

APEC Policy Support Unit (2011) The Impacts and Benefits of Structural Reforms in the Transport, Energy and Telecommunications Sectors in APEC Economies, Singapore: APEC Secretariat.

Arndt, C. and Pearson, K. (1996) 'How to Carry Out Systematic Sensitivity Analysis via Gaussian Quadrature and GEMPACK', GTAP Technical Paper No. 3, West Lafayette IN: Center for Global Trade Analysis, Purdue University.

Bagwell, K. and Staiger, R. (1998) 'Will Preferential Arrangements Undermine the Multilateral Trading System?', *Economic Journal*, 108(449): 1162–82.

Bagwell, K. and Staiger, R. (1999) 'An Economic Theory of the GATT', *American Economic Review*, 89(1): 215–48.

Baldwin, R. (1994) *Towards an Integrated Europe*, London: Centre for Economic Policy Research.

Baldwin, R. (1996) 'A Domino Theory of Regionalism', in R.E. Baldwin, P. Haapranta and J. Kiander, J. (eds) *Expanding European Regionalism: The EU's New Members,* Cambridge: Cambridge University Press: 25–48.

Baldwin, R. (1999) 'Frictional Trade Barriers, Developing Nations and a Two Tiered World Trading System', paper prepared for CEPR Workshop on New Issues in the World Trading System, London, 19–20 February.

Baldwin, R. (2006) 'Managing the Noodle Bowl: The Fragility of East Asian Regionalism', CEPR Discussion Paper No. 5561, London: Centre for Economic Policy Research.

Baldwin, R. (2011) '21st Century Regionalism: Filling the Gap between 21st Century Trade and 20th Century Trade Rules', mimeo (version dated April 2011), Geneva: Graduate Institute.

Baldwin, R.E. and Kimura, F. (1998) 'Measuring US International Goods and Services Transactions', in R. Baldwin, R. Lipsey and J. Richardson (eds) *Geography and Ownership as Bases for Economic Accounting*, Chicago: University of Chicago Press: 9–48.

Baldwin, R. and Robert-Nicoud, F. (2008) 'A Simple Model of the Juggernaut Effect of Trade Liberalization', CEP Discussion Paper No. 845, London: Centre for Economic Performance, London School of Economics.

Baldwin, R.E. and Venables, A.J. (1995) 'Regional Economic Integration', in G. Grossman and K. Rogoff (eds) *Handbook of International Economics, Vol. III*, Amsterdam: Elsevier: 1597–644.

Baltagi. B., Egger, P. and Pfaffermayr, M. (2007) 'Estimating Models of Complex FDI: Are There Third-country Effects?', *Journal of Econometrics*, 140(1): 260–81.

Banks, G. (2003) 'The Good, the Bad and the Ugly: Economic Perspectives of Regulation in Australia', speech delivered to the Conference of Economists 2003, Business Symposium, Hyatt Hotel, Canberra, 2 October.

Banks, G. and Wonder, B. (2010) 'The Policy Determinants of Structural Reform in Australia', in P. Dee (ed.) *Institutions for Economic Reform in Asia*, London and New York: Routledge: 63–87.

Barfield, C. (2001) *Free Trade, Sovereignty, Democracy: The Future of the World Trade Organization*, Washington DC: The American Enterprise Institute Press.

Barichello, R. (2004) 'NAFTA and Domestic Agricultural Policy Reform: Observations from Canada', Working Paper No. 2004-08, Vancouver: Food and Resource Economics, University of British Columbia.

Barnard, C. (2010) *The Substantive Law of the EU: Four Freedoms,* Third Edition, Oxford: Oxford University Press.

Barth, J. R., Caprio Jr, G. and Levine, R. (2004) 'Bank Regulation and Supervision: What Works Best?', *Journal of Financial Intermediation,* 13(2): 205–48.

Barth, J., Marchetti, J., Nolle, D. and Sawangngoenyuang, W. (2006) 'Foreign Banking: Do Countries' WTO Commitments Match Actual Practices?', Staff Working Paper ERSD-2006-11, Economic Research and Statistics Division, Geneva: World Trade Organization.

Baumol, W., Bailey, E. and Willig, R. (1997) 'Weak Invisible Hand Theorems on the Sustainability of Multiproduct Natural Monopoly', *American Economic Review*, 67(3): 350–65.

Berden, K., Francois, J., Tamminen, S., Thelle, M. and Wymenga, P. (2009) *Non-Tariff Measures in EU–US Trade and Investment — An Economic Analysis*, Rotterdam: ECORYS Nederland BV.

Besley, T. and Coate, S. (2003) 'Elected Versus Appointed Regulators: Theory and Evidence', *Journal of the European Economic Association*, 1(5): 1176–1206.

Bhagwati, J., Krishna, P. and Panagariya, A. (1999) *Trading Blocs: Alternative Approaches to Analyzing Preferential Trade Agreements*, Cambridge and London: The MIT Press.

Bhala, R. (2001) 'The Power of the Past: Towards *De Jure Stare Decisis* in WTO Adjudication (Part Three of a Trilogy)', *George Washington International Law Review* 33(3 & 4): 873–978.

Blanchard, E. (2007) 'Foreign Direct Investment, Endogenous Tariffs, and Preferential Trade Agreements', *B.E. Journal of Economic Analysis and Policy: Advances in Economic Analysis and Policy*, 7(1): 1–50.

Blomström, M. and Kokko, A. (1997) 'How Foreign Investment Affects Host Economies', Policy Research Working Paper No. 1745, Washington DC: World Bank.

Boadway, R. and Harris, R. (1977) 'A Characterization of Piecemeal Second Best Policy', *Journal of Public Economics*, 8(2): 169–90.

Bond, E. and Syropoulos, C. (1996) 'The Size of Trading Blocks, Market Power and World Welfare Effects', *Journal of International Economics*, 40(3–4): 411–37.

Bora, B. and Guisinger, S. (1997) 'Impact of Investment Liberalization in APEC', mimeo, Adelaide: School of Economics, Flinders University.

Borchert, I., Gootiiz, B. and Mattoo, A. (2010) 'Restrictions on Services Trade and FDI in Developing Countries', mimeo, Washington DC: World Bank.

Borchert, I., Gootiiz, A. and Mattoo, A. (2012a) 'Guide to the Services Restrictions Database', Policy Research Working Paper 6108, Washington DC: World Bank.

Borchert, I., Gootiiz, A. and Mattoo, A. (2012b) 'Policy Barriers to International Trade in Services', Policy Research Working Paper 6109, Washington DC: World Bank.

Boumellassa, H., Gouel, C. and Laborde, D. (2007) 'Bilateral and Sectoral Investment Relations at a World Scale — Impact on Trade', Report prepared by CEPII for the Commission of the European Union, Directorate-General for Trade, Paris: Centre D'études Prospectives Et D'informations Internationales.

Boylaud, O. and Nicoletti, G. (2000) 'Regulation, Market Structure and Performance in Telecommunications', Working Paper 237, ECO/WKP (2000)10, Economics Department, Paris: OECD.

Bresser Pereira, L.C., Maravall, J.M. and Przeworski, A. (1993) *Economic Reforms in New Democracies: A Social-democratic Approach*, Cambridge: Cambridge University Press.

Brown, D., Deardorff, A., Fox, A. and Stern, R. (1995) 'Computational Analysis of Goods and Services Trade Liberalization in the Uruguay Round', in W. Martin and L.A. Winters (eds) *The Uruguay Round and the Developing Economies*, World Bank Discussion Paper No. 307, Washington DC: World Bank: 365–80.

Brown, D., Deardorff, A., Fox, A. and Stern, R. (1996) 'The Liberalization of Services Trade: Potential Impacts in the Aftermath of the Uruguay Round', in W. Martin and L.A. Winters (eds) *The Uruguay Round and the Developing Economies*, Cambridge: Cambridge University Press: 292–315.

Brown, D., Deardorff, A., Stern, R. (1996) 'Modelling Multilateral Trade Liberalization in Services', *Asia Pacific Economic Review*, 2(1): 21–34.

Brown, D., Deardorff, A. and Stern, R. (1997) 'Some Economic Effects of the Free Trade Agreement between Tunisia and the European Union', in A. Galal and B. Hoekman (eds) *Regional Partners in Global Markets: Limits and Possibilities of the Euro-Med Agreements*, London: Centre for Economic Policy Research: 71–97.

Brown, D., Deardorff, A. and Stern, R. (2000) 'CGE Modelling and Analysis of Multilateral and Regional Negotiating Options', paper presented at conference on Issues and Options for the Multilateral, Regional and Bilateral Trade Policies of the United States and Japan, University of Michigan, Ann Arbor, 5–6 October.

Brown, D., and Stern, R. (2001) 'Measurement and Modelling of the Economic Effects of Trade and Investment Barriers in Services', *Review of International Economics*, 9(2): 262–86.

Burley, A.M. and Mattli, W. (1993) 'Europe before the Court: A Political Theory of Legal Integration', *International Organization*, 47(1): 41–76.

Carrubba, C. and Murrah, L. (2005) 'Legal Integration and Use of the Preliminary Ruling Process in the European Union', *International Organization*, 59(2): 399–418.

Chanda, R. (2001) 'Movement of Natural Persons and the GATS', *The World Economy*, 24(5): 631–54.

Clark, X., Dollar, D. and Micco, A. (2004) 'Port Efficiency, Maritime Transport Costs, and Bilateral Trade', *Journal of Development Economics*, 75(2): 417–50.

Coghlan, P. (2000) 'The Principles of Good Regulation', in Productivity Commission and Australian National University *Achieving Better Regulation of Services*, Conference Proceedings, Canberra: Productivity Commission.

Conway, P., Janod, V. and Nicoletti, G. (2005) 'Product Market Regulation in OECD Countries: 1998 to 2003', ECO/WKP(2005)6, Paris: OECD.

Cooper, R. (1988) 'Survey of Issues and Review', in L. Castle and C. Findlay (eds) *Pacific Trade in Services*, Sydney: Allen and Unwin: 247–62.

Copenhagen Economics (2005) Economic Assessment of the Barriers to the Internal Market for Services, Copenhagen: Copenhagen Economics.

Corden, M. (1971) *The Theory of Protection*, Oxford: Clarendon Press.

Corden, M. (1972) 'Economies of Scale and Customs Union Theory', *Journal of Political Economy*, 80(3): 465–75.

Corden, M. (1974) *Trade Policy and Economic Welfare*, Oxford: Clarendon Press.

CSI (Coalition of Service Industries) (2002) 'Trade Remedy System under the WTO Framework: Functions and Mechanism', statement by Robert Vastine, President of CSI, at 2002 Annual Conference of the Advisory Committee of the Shanghai WTO Affairs Consultation Center and 2002 WTO Forum, Shanghai, 5–7 November.

Czaga, P. (2004) 'Regulatory Reform and Market Openness: Understanding the Links to Enhance Economic Performance', OECD Trade Policy Working Papers No. 9. Paris: OECD.

Dasgupta, D., Pitigala, N. and Gourdon, J. (2012) 'South Asia's Economic Prospects from Global Rebalancing and Integration', in P. Dee (ed.) *Economic Reform Processes in South Asia*, London and New York: Routledge: 23–42.

Davis, O.A. and Whinston, A.B. (1965) 'Welfare Economics and the Theory of the Second Best', *Review of Economic Studies*, 32(1): 1–14.

Deardorff, A. (1985) 'Comparative Advantage and International Trade and Investment in Services', in R. Stern (ed.) *Trade and Investment in Services: Canada/U.S. Perspectives*, Toronto, Canada: Ontario Economic Council: 39–71.

Deardorff, A. and Stern, R. (1994) 'Multilateral Trade Negotiations and Preferential Trading Arrangements', in A. Deardorff and R. Stern (eds) *Analytical and Negotiating Issues in Global Trading System*, Ann Arbor: University of Michigan Press: 53–85.

Deardorff, A. and Stern, R. (2005) 'Empirical Analysis of Barriers to International Services Transactions and the Consequences of Liberalization', in P.Dee and M. Ferrantino (eds), *Quantitative Methods for Assessing the Effects of Non-tariff measures and Trade Facilitation*, Singapore: APEC Secretariat and World Scientific Publishing: 549–609.

Dee, P. (2003) 'Modelling the Policy Issues in Services Trade', *Économie Internationale*, (94–95): 283–300. Reproduced as Chapter 3 in this volume.

Dee, P. (2005a) 'A Compendium of Barriers to Services Trade', mimeo prepared for World Bank, Canberra: The Australian National University, available at http://crawford.anu.edu.au/pdf/staff/phillippa_dee/Combined_report.pdf.

Dee, P. (2005b) 'The Australia–US Free Trade Agreement: An Assessment', Pacific Economic Papers No. 345, Canberra: Australia–Japan Research Centre, Australian National University.

Dee, P. (2007) 'East Asian Economic Integration and its Impact on Future Growth', *The World Economy,* 30(3): 405–23.

Dee, P. (2008a) 'Benchmarking and Assessing Indonesia's Regulation of Services', mimeo prepared for the World Bank, Canberra: The Australian National University.

Dee, P. (2008b) 'Multinational Corporations and Pacific Regionalism', in J. Palacios (ed.) *Multinational Corporations and the Emerging Network Economy in Asia and the Pacific,* London and New York: Routledge: 232–266.

Dee, P. (2009) 'Services Liberalization toward the ASEAN Economic Community', in J. Corbett and S. Umezaki (eds) *Deepening East Asian Economic Integration,* ERIA Research Project Report 2008 No. 1, Jakarta: Economic Research Institute for ASEAN and East Asia: 58–96.

Dee, P. (2010a), *Institutions for Economic Reform in Asia*, London and New York: Routledge.

Dee, P. (2010b) 'Services Liberalization Toward the ASEAN Economic Community', in S. Urata and M. Okabe (eds) *Tracing the Progress Toward the ASEAN Economic Community*, ERIA Research Project Report 2009, No. 3, Jakarta: Economic Research Institute for ASEAN and East Asia: 28–124.

Dee, P. (2011) 'Services Liberalization Towards an ASEAN Economic Community', in S. Urata and M. Okabe (eds) *Towards a Competitive ASEAN Single Market: Sectoral Analysis*, ERIA Research Project Report 2010 No. 3, Jakarta: Economic Research Institute for ASEAN and East Asia: 17–136.

Dee, P. (2012a) *Economic Reform Processes in South Asia*, London and New York: Routledge.

Dee, P. (2012b) 'Services Liberalization: Impact and Way Forward', paper prepared for ASEAN Economic Community Mid-Term Review, Jakarta: Economic Research Institute for ASEAN and East Asia.

Dee, P. (2013a) 'Barriers to Trade in Healthcare Services in ASEAN Countries', in P. Dee (ed.) *Priorities and Pathways in Services Reform: Part 1 — Quantitative Studies*, World Scientific Studies in International Economics 26, Singapore: World Scientific (forthcoming).

Dee, P. (2013b) *Priorities and Pathways in Services Reform: Part 1 — Quantitative Studies*, World Scientific Studies in International Economics 26, Singapore: World Scientific (forthcoming).

Dee, P. (2013c) 'Does AFAS have Bite? Comparing Commitments with Actual Practice', mimeo, Canberra: Australian National University.

Dee, P. and Dinh, H. (2013) 'Impact of Regulatory Barriers to Trade in Insurance Services', in P. Dee (ed.) *Priorities and Pathways in Services Reform: Part 1 — Quantitative Studies*, World Scientific Studies in International Economics 26, Singapore: World Scientific (forthcoming).

Dee, P. and Findlay, C. (2008) 'Services: A "Deal-Maker" in the Doha Round?', in B. Blonigen (ed.) *Monitoring International Trade Policy: A New Agenda for Reviving the Doha Round,* London: Centre for Economic Policy Research and Kiel: Kiel Institute for the World Economy: 49–63. Reproduced in edited form as Chapter 9 in this volume.

Dee, P. and Findlay, C. (2009) 'Services in PTAs — Donuts or Holes?', in S. Jayasuriya, D. MacLaren and G. Magee (eds) *Negotiating a Preferential Trading Agreement: Issues, Constraints and Practical Options*, Cheltenham: Edward Elgar: 97–128. Reproduced in edited form as Chapter 10 in this volume.

Dee, P. and Gali, J. (2005) 'The Trade and Investment Effects of Preferential Trading Arrangements', in T. Ito and A. Rose (eds) *International Trade in East Asia*, Chicago: University of Chicago Press: 133–70.

Dee, P., Geisler, C. and Watts, G. (1996) 'The Impact of APEC's Free Trade Commitment', Industry Commission Staff Working Paper, Canberra: Productivity Commission.

Dee, P. and Hanslow, K. (2001) 'Multilateral Liberalization of Services Trade', in R. Stern (ed.) *Services in the International Economy*, Ann Arbor: University of Michigan Press: 117–39. Reproduced in edited form as Chapter 4 in this volume.

Dee, P., Hanslow, K. and Phamduc, T. (2003) 'Measuring the Cost of Barriers to Trade in Services', in T. Ito and A. Krueger (eds) *Trade in Services in the Asia-Pacific Region*, NBER-East Asia Seminar on Economics, Volume 11, Chicago: University of Chicago Press: 11–43. Reproduced in edited form as Chapter 5 in this volume.

Dee, P., Hardin, A. and Holmes, L. (2000) 'Issues in the Application of CGE Models to Services Trade Liberalization', in C. Findlay and T. Warren (eds) *Impediments to Trade in Services, Measurement and Policy Implications*, London and New York: Routledge: 267–86. Reproduced as Chapter 2 in this volume.

Dee, P., Hardin, A. and Schuele, M. (1998) 'APEC Early Voluntary Sectoral Liberalization', Productivity Commission Staff Working Paper, Canberra: Productivity Commission.

Dee, P., Le, T.D. and Dang, T.H. (2005) 'Evaluating Vietnam's WTO Accession Offer in Services', paper prepared for World Bank capacity-building program, Canberra: Australian National University.

Dee, P. and Nguyen-Hong, D. (2003) 'Domestic Regulatory Reform and Liberalization of Trade in Infrastructure Services', in A. Sidorenko and C. Findlay (eds) *Regulation and Market Access*, Canberra: Asia Pacific Press: 78–105.

Dee, P. and Sidorenko, A. (2006) 'The Rise of Services Trade: Regional Initiatives and Challenges for the WTO', in C. Findlay and H. Soesastro (eds) *Reshaping the Asia*

Pacific Economic Order, London and New York: Routledge: 200–26. Reproduced as Chapter 8 in this volume.

Dewatripont, M., Jewitt, I. and Tirole, J. (1999a) 'The Economics of Career Concerns, Part I: Comparing Information Structures', *Review of Economic Studies*, 66(1): 183–98.

Dewatripont, M., Jewitt, I. and Tirole, J. (1999b) 'The Economics of Career Concerns, Part II: Application to Missions and Accountability of Government Agencies', *Review of Economic Studies*, 66(1): 199–217.

Dewatripont, M. and Roland, G. (1992) 'Economic Reform and Dynamic Political Constraints', *Review of Economic Studies*, 59(4): 703–30.

DFAT (Department of Foreign Affairs and Trade) (1999), *Global Trade Reform: Maintaining Momentum*, Canberra: Ausinfo.

DFAT (2011) 'Gillard Government Trade Policy Statement: Trading Our Way to More Jobs and Prosperity', Canberra: Department of Foreign Affairs and Trade.

Dinh, H. (2013) 'Impact of Regulatory Barriers to Trade in Banking Services', in P. Dee (ed.) *Priorities and Pathways in Services Reform: Part 1 — Quantitative Studies*, World Scientific Studies in International Economics 26, Singapore: World Scientific (forthcoming).

Disclosure (1999) *Global Researcher — Worldscope database*, January, United States: Disclosure.

Donovan, D. and Mai, Y.H. (1996) 'APEC Trade Liberalization: The Impact of Increased Capital Mobility', *Australian Commodities* 3(4), Canberra: ABARE: 520–6.

Doove, S., Gabbitas, O., Nguyen-Hong, D. and Owen, J. (2001) 'Price Effects of Regulation: International Air Passenger Transport, Telecommunications and Electricity Supply', Productivity Commission Staff Research Paper, Canberra: Productivity Commission.

Drake, W. and Nicolaïdis, K. (1992) 'Ideas, Interests, and Institutionalization: "Trade in Services" and the Uruguay Round', *International Organization*, 46(1): 37–100.

Drysdale, P. (1988) *International Economic Pluralism*, Sydney: Allen and Unwin.

Drysdale, P. (2010) 'Introduction', in P. Dee (ed.) *Institutions for Economic Reform in Asia*, London and New York: Routledge: 1–5.

EC (European Commission) (2003) 'The Doha Development Agenda After Cancun', 25 September 2003, Brussels: European Commission Directorate-General for Trade.

Ethier, W. (1982) 'National and International Returns to Scale in the Modern Theory of International Trade', *American Economic Review*, 72(3): 389–405.

Ethier, W. (1998) 'Regionalism in a Multilateral World', *Journal of Political Economy*, 106(6): 1214–45.

Ethier, W. (1999) 'Multilateral Roads to Regionalism', in J. Piggott and A. Woodland (eds) *International Trade Policy and the Pacific Rim*, New York: St Martin's Press: 131–52.

Ethier, W. (2001) 'The New Regionalism in the Americas: A Theoretical Framework', *North American Journal of Economics and Finance*, 12(2): 159–72.

Ethier, W. and Horn, H. (1991) 'Services in International Trade', in E. Helpman and A. Razin (eds) *International Trade and Trade Policy*, Cambridge MA: MIT Press: 223–44.

Fernandez, R. and Rodrik, D. (1991) 'Resistance to Reform: *Status Quo* Bias in the Presence of Individual-specific Uncertainty', *American Economic Review*, 81(5): 1146–55.

Findlay, C. (2008) 'Transport Services', in A. Mattoo, R. Stern and G. Zanini (eds) *A Handbook of International Trade in Services*, Oxford: Oxford University Press: 356–88.

Findlay, C. and Pangestu, M. (2004) 'Services Sector Reform Options: The Experience of China', mimeo, Adelaide: University of Adelaide.

Findlay, C. and Warren, T. (2000) Impediments to Trade in Services: Measurement and Policy Implications, London and New York: Routledge.

Fink, C. and Jansen, M. (2009) 'Services Provisions in Regional Trade Agreements: Stumbling Blocks or Building Blocks for Multilateral Liberalization?', in R. Baldwin and P. Low (eds) *Multilateralizing Regionalism: Challenges for the Global Trading System*, Cambridge and New York: Cambridge University Press: 221–61.

Fink, C., Mattoo, A. and Rathindran, R. (2002) 'Liberalizing Basic Telecommunications: Evidence from Developing Countries', paper presented at OECD–World Bank Services Experts Meeting, OECD, Paris, 4–5 March.

Fink, C. and Molinuevo, M. (2007) 'East Asian Free Trade Agreements in Services: Roaring Tigers or Timid Pandas?', Trade Issues in East Asia, Washington DC: World Bank.

Francois, J. (1990) 'Trade in Producer Services and Returns Due to Specialization under Monopolistic Competition', *Canadian Journal of Economics*, 23(1): 109–24.

Francois, J. (1997) 'External Bindings and the Credibility of Reform', in A. Galal and B. Hoekman (eds) *Regional Partners in Global Markets: Limits and Possibilities of the Euro-Med Agreements*, London: Centre for Economic Policy Research: 35–48.

Francois, J. (1999) 'A Gravity Approach to Measuring Services Protection', mimeo, Rotterdam: Erasmus University.

Francois, J. (2005) 'Accession of Turkey to the European Union: Market Access and Regulatory Issues', in B. Hoekman and S. Togan (eds) *Turkey: Economic Reform and Accession to the European Union*, Washington DC: World Bank and Centre for Economic Policy Research: 123–46.

Francois, J. and Hoekman, B. (1999) 'Market Access in the Service Sectors', mimeo, Tinbergen Institute, cited in B. Hoekman (2000) 'The Next Round of Services Negotiations: Identifying Priorities and Options', *Federal Reserve Bank of St Louis Review*, 82(4): 31–47.

Francois, J. and Hoekman, B. (2010) 'Services Trade and Policy', *Journal of Economic Literature*, 48(3): 642–92.

Francois, J., McDonald, B. and Nordstrom, H. (1995) 'Assessing the Uruguay Round', in W. Martin and L.A. Winters (eds) *The Uruguay Round and the Developing Economies*, Discussion Paper 307, Washington DC: World Bank: 117–214.

Francois, J. and Shiells, C.R. (1994) 'AGE Models of North American Free Trade', in J. Francois and C.R. Shiells (eds) *Modelling Trade Policy: Applied General Equilibrium Assessments of North American Free Trade*, Cambridge: Cambridge University Press: 3–44.

Francois, J. and Wooten, I. (2001) 'Imperfect Competition and Trade Liberalization under the GATS', in R. Stern (ed.) *Services in the International Economy*, Ann Arbor: University of Michigan Press: 141–56.

Fujita, M., Krugman, P. and Venables, A. (1999) *The Spatial Economy: Cities, Regions and International Trade*, Cambridge MA: MIT Press.

Gassebner, M., Gaston, N. and Lamla, M. (2008) 'The Inverse Domino Effect: Are Economic Reforms Contagious?', KOF Working Paper No. 187, Zurich: KOF Swiss Economic Institute.

Ghani, E. (2009) 'Is Service-led Growth a Miracle for South Asia?', in World Bank *Service-led Growth in South Asia*, Washington DC: World Bank: 17–70.

Gehlhar, M. (1997) 'Historical Analysis of Growth and Trade Patterns in the Pacific Rim: An Evaluation of the GTAP Framework', in T. Hertel (ed.) *Global Trade Analysis: Modelling and Applications*, Cambridge: Cambridge University Press: 349–63.

Gehrels, F. (1957) 'Customs Union from a Single-country Viewpoint', *Review of Economic Studies*, 24(1): 61–4.

Golub, S. (2003) 'Measures of Restrictions on Inward Foreign Direct Investment for OECD Countries', OECD Economic Studies No 36, Paris: OECD.

Gonenc, R. and Nicoletti, G. (2000) 'Regulation, Market Structure and Performance in Air Passenger Transport', Working Paper No. 254, ECO/WKP(2000)27, Economics Department, Paris: OECD.

Gordon, R.H. and Bovenberg, L. (1996) 'Why is Capital so Immobile Internationally? Possible Explanations and Implications for Income Taxation', *American Economic Review*, 86(5): 1057–75.

Graham, E. and Wada, E. (2000) 'Domestic Reform, Trade and Investment Liberalization, Financial Crisis, and Foreign Direct Investment in Mexico', *The World Economy*, 23(6): 777–97.

Gregan, T. and Johnson, M. (1999) 'Impacts of Competition Enhancing Air Services Agreements: a Network Modelling Approach', Productivity Commission Staff Research Paper, Canberra: Productivity Commission.

Grossman, G. and Helpman, E. (1991) *Innovation and Growth in the Global Economy*, Cambridge: MIT Press.

Haggard, S. and Webb, S. (1994a) Voting for Reform: Democracy, Political Liberalization and Economic Adjustment, Oxford: Oxford University Press.

Haggard, S. and Webb, S. (1994b) 'Introduction', in S. Haggard and S. Webb (eds) *Voting for Reform: Democracy, Political Liberalization and Economic Adjustment*, Oxford: Oxford University Press: 1–36.

Hanslow, K., Phamduc, T. and Verikios, G. (1999) 'The Structure of the FTAP Model', Research Memorandum, Canberra: Productivity Commission, available from http://www.crawford.anu.edu.au/staff/pdee.php.

Hanslow, K., Phamduc, T., Verikios, G. and Welsh, A. (2000) 'Incorporating Barriers to FDI into the FTAP database', Research Memorandum, Canberra: Productivity Commission.

Hardin, A. and Holmes, L. (1997) 'Services Trade and Foreign Direct Investment', Industry Commission Staff Research Paper, Canberra: Productivity Commission.

Harms, P., Mattoo, A. and Schuknecht, L. (2003) 'Explaining Liberalization Commitments in Financial Services Trade', Policy Research Working Paper No. 2999, Washington DC: World Bank.

Harrison, J. and Pearson, K. (1996) 'Computing Solutions for Large General Equilibrium Models using GEMPACK', *Computational Economics*, 9(2): 83–127.

He, F. (2010) 'China's Economic Reform: Success, Problems and Challenges', in P. Dee (ed.) *Institutions for Economic Reform in Asia*, London and New York: Routledge: 195–211.

Heckscher, E. [1919] (1949) 'The Effect of Foreign Trade on the Distribution of Income', reprinted in H. Ellis and A. Metzler (eds) *AEA Readings in the Theory of International Trade*, Philadelphia: Blakiston: 272–300.

Helpman, E. (1981) 'International Trade in the Presence of Product Differentiation, Economies of Scale, and Monopolistic Competition: A Chamberlinian–Heckscher–Ohlin Approach', *Journal of International Economics*, 11(3): 304–40.

Hertel, T. (1997) *Global Trade Analysis: Modelling and Applications*, Cambridge: Cambridge University Press.

Hertel, T. (2000) 'Potential Gains from Reducing Trade Barriers in Manufacturing, Services and Agriculture', *Federal Reserve Bank of St Louis Review*, July/August: 77–104.

Hertel, T., Walmsley, T. and Itakura, K. (2001) 'Dynamic Effects of the "New Age" Free Trade Agreement between Japan and Singapore', *Journal of Economic Integration*, 16(4), 446–84.

Hillberry, R., Anderson, M., Balistreri, E. and Fox, A. (2001) 'The Determinants of Armington Taste Parameters in CGE Models, or "Why You Love Canadian Vegetable Oil"', paper presented to Fourth Annual Conference on Global Economic Analysis, Purdue University, West Lafayette, 27–29 June.

Hindley, B. and Smith, A. (1984) 'Comparative Advantage and Trade in Services', *The World Economy*, 7(4): 369–90.

Hoekman, B. (1995) 'Assessing the General Agreement on Trade in Services', in W. Martin and L.A. Winters (eds) *The Uruguay Round and the Developing*

Economies, World Bank Discussion Paper No. 307, Washington DC: World Bank: 327–64.

Hoekman, B. (2006) 'Trade in Services, Economic Growth and Development, and International Cooperation: A Survey of the Literature', mimeo, Washington DC: World Bank.

Hoekman, B. and Mattoo, A. (2011) 'Services Trade Liberalization and Regulatory Reform: Re-invigorating International Cooperation', Policy Research Working Paper 5517, Washington DC: World Bank.

Hoekman, B., Mattoo, A. and Sapir, A. (2007) 'The Political Economy of Services Trade Liberalization: A Case for International Regulatory Cooperation', *Oxford Review of Economic Policy*, 23(3): 367–91.

Hoekman, B. and Primo Braga, C. (1997) 'Protection and Trade in Services: A Survey', *Open Economies Review*, 8(3): 285–308.

Holmes, L. and Hardin, A. (2000) 'Assessing Barriers to Services Sector Investment', in C. Findlay and T. Warren (eds) *Impediments to Trade in Services: Measurement and Policy Issues*, London and New Work: Routledge: 52–71.

Holmstrom, B. (1999) 'Managerial Incentive Problems: A Dynamic Perspective', *Review of Economic Studies*, 66(1): 169–82.

Hosen, M. (2010) 'Accelerating Economic Reform in Japan: The Role of the Council on Economic and Fiscal Policy', in P. Dee (ed.) *Institutions for Economic Reform in Asia*, London and New York: Routledge: 53–62.

Huang, Y. (2005) 'Are Foreign Firms Privileged by Their Host Governments? Evidence from the 2000 World Business Environment Survey', Working Paper 4538-04, Cambridge MA: MIT Sloan School of Management.

Huff, K.M. and Hertel, T. (1996) 'Decomposing Welfare Changes in the GTAP Model', GTAP Technical Paper 5, West Lafayette IN: Department of Agricultural Economics, Purdue University.

Husain, I. and Kumar, R. (2012) 'Comparing Structural Reforms in India and Pakistan', in P. Dee (ed.) *Economic Reform Processes in South Asia*, London and New York: Routledge: 43–60.

IC (Industry Commission) (1991) *Availability of Capital*, Report No. 18, Industry Commission, Canberra: Productivity Commission.

ICAO (International Civil Aviation Organization) (2004) *Database of the World's Air Services Agreements*, Doc 9511, 2004 edition, CD-Rom.

ITU (International Telecommunications Union) (2006) *ICT Statistics Database*, available at http://www.itu.int/ITU-D/icteye/Indicators/Indicators.aspx.

Johnson, H. (1960) 'The Economic Theory of Customs Union', *Pakistan Economic Journal*, 10(1): 14–32.

Johnson, M., Gregan, T., Gentle, G. and Belin, P. (2000) 'Modelling the Benefits of Increased Competition in International Air Services', in C. Findlay and T. Warren (eds) *Impediments to Trade in Services: Measurement and Policy Implications*, London and New York: Routledge: 119–151.

Jomini, P., McDougall, R.A., Watts, G. and Dee, P. (1994) 'The Salter Model of the World Economy: Model Structure, Database and Parameters', Canberra: Productivity Commission.

Jones, R. and Scheinkman, J. (1977) 'The Relevance of the Two-sector Production Model in Trade Theory', *Journal of Political Economy*, 85(5): 909–35.

Kalinova, B., Palerm, A. and Thomson, S. (2010) 'OECD's FDI Restrictiveness Index: 2010 Update', Working Paper on International Investment, Paris: OECD.

Kalirajan, K. (2000) 'Restrictions on Trade in Distribution Services', Productivity Commission Staff Research Paper, Canberra: Productivity Commission.

Kalirajan, K., McGuire, G., Nguyen-Hong, D. and Schuele, M. (2000) 'The Price Impact of Restrictions on Banking Services', in C. Findlay and T. Warren (eds) *Impediments to Trade in Services: Measurement and Policy Implications*, London and New York: Routledge: 215–30.

Kang, J. (2000) 'Price Impact of Restrictions on Maritime Transport Services', in C. Findlay and T. Warren (eds) *Impediments to Trade in Services: Measurement and Policy Implications*, London and New York: Routledge: 189–200.

Karsenty, G. (2000) 'Assessing Trade in Services by Mode of Supply', in p. Sauvé and R. Stern (eds) *GATS 2000: New Directions in Services Trade Liberalization*, Washington DC: Brookings Institution: 33–56.

Karsenty, G. (2002) 'Trends on Services Under the GATS: Recent Developments', paper presented at the WTO Symposium on Assessment of Trade in Services, Geneva, 14–15 March.

Kawai, M. and Wignaraja, G. (2011) 'Asian FTAs: Trends, Prospects and Challenges', *Journal of Asian Economics*, 22(1): 1–22.

Keller, W. (1980) *A General Equilibrium Approach*, Amsterdam: North–Holland.

Kemp, S. (2000) 'Trade in Education Services and the Impacts of Barriers to Trade', in C. Findlay and T. Warren (eds) *Impediments to Trade in Services: Measurement and Policy Implications*, London and New York: Routledge: 231–44.

Khan, M.S. (2012) 'India–Pakistan Trade: A Roadmap for Enhancing Economic Relations', in P. Dee (ed.) *Economic Reform Processes in South Asia*, London and New York: Routledge: 191–206.

Kimura, F., and Baldwin, R.E. (1998) 'Application of a Nationality-adjusted Net Sales and Value-added Framework: The Case of Japan', in R. Baldwin, R. Lipsey and J. Richardson (eds) *Geography and Ownership as Bases for Economic Accounting*, Chicago: University of Chicago Press: 49–82.

Kocherlakota, N. (1996) 'The Equity Premium: It's Still a Puzzle', *Journal of Economic Literature*, 34(1): 42–71.

Konan, D. and Maskus, K. (2006) 'Quantifying the Impact of Services Liberalization in a Developing Economy', *Journal of Development Economics*, 81(1): 142–62.

Krishna, P. (1998) 'Regionalism and Multilateralism: A Political Economy Approach', *Quarterly Journal of Economics*, 113(1): 227–51.

Krugman, P. (1979) 'Increasing Returns, Monopolistic Competition, and International Trade', *Journal of International Economics*, 9(4): 469–79.

Krugman, P. (1991) 'Increasing Returns and Economic Geography', *Journal of Political Economy*, 99(3): 483–99.

Krugman, P. (1993) 'Regionalism versus Multilateralism: Analytical Notes', in J. de Melo and A. Panagariya (eds) *New Dimensions in Regional Integration*, Cambridge: Cambridge University Press: 58–79.

Krugman, P. (1997) 'What Should Trade Negotiators Negotiate About?', *Journal of Economic Literature*, 35(1): 113–20.

Krugman, P. (1998) 'What's New about the New Economic Geography', *Oxford Review of Economic Policy*, 14(2): 7–17.

Kydland, F. and Prescott, E. (1977) 'Rules Rather Than Discretion: The Inconsistency of Optimal Plans', *Journal of Political Economy*, 85(3): 473–92.

Leamer, E. and Levinsohn, J. (1994) 'International Trade Theory: The Evidence', NBER Working Paper No. 4940, Cambridge MA: National Bureau of Economic Research.

Lee, H. and van der Mensbrugghe, D. (2001) 'Interactions Between Direct Investment and Trade in the Asia-Pacific Region', paper presented at the Fourth Annual Conference on Global Economic Analysis, Purdue University, 27–29 June.

Levy, P. (1997) 'A Political-economic Analysis of Free-trade Agreements', *American Economic Review*, 87(4): 506–19.

Lewis, D.J. (2008) 'Integration of Landlocked Countries into the Global Economy and Domestic Economic Reforms: The Case of Lao People's Democratic Republic', Asia-Pacific Research and Training Network on Trade Working Paper Series No. 58, Bangkok: Asia-Pacific Research and Training Network on Trade.

Lewis, K. (1999) 'Trying to Explain Home Bias in Equities and Consumption', *Journal of Economic Literature*, 37(2): 571–608.

Lindblom, C.E. (1959) 'The Science of Muddling Through', *Public Administration Review*, 19(2): 79–88.

Lindblom, C.E. (1979) 'Still Muddling, Not Yet Through', *Public Administration Review*, 79(6): 517–26.

Lipsey, R. (1957) 'Mr Gehrels on Customs Unions', *Review of Economic Studies*, 24(2): 211–14.

Lipsey, R. (1958) 'The Theory of Customs Unions: A General Equilibrium Analysis', PhD Thesis, London: University of London.

Lipsey, R. and Lancaster, K. (1956) 'The General Theory of Second Best', *Review of Economic Studies*, 24(1): 11–32.

Llanto, G. (2010) 'The Policy Development Process and the Agenda for Effective Institutions in the Philippines', in P. Dee (ed.) *Institutions for Economic Reform in Asia*, London and New York: Routledge: 88–105.

Low, P. and Mattoo, A. (2000) 'Is There a Better Way? Alternative Approaches to Liberalization under GATS', in P. Sauvé and R. Stern (eds) *GATS 2000: New*

Directions in Services Trade Liberalization, Washington DC: Brookings Institution: 449–72.

Malcolm. G. (1998) 'Adjusting Tax Rates in the GTAP Database', GTAP Technical Paper No. 12, Centre for Global Trade Policy Analysis, West Lafayette IN: Purdue University.

Marchetti, J. and Roy, M. (2008) 'Services Liberalization in the WTO and in PTAs', in J. Marchetti and M. Roy (eds) *Opening Markets for Trade in Services: Countries and Sectors in Bilateral and WTO Negotiations*, Cambridge: Cambridge University Press: 61–112.

Markusen, J. (1981) 'Trade and the Gains from Trade with Imperfect Competition', *Journal of International Economics*, 11(4): 531–51.

Markusen, J (1989) 'Trade in Producer Services and in Other Specialized Intermediate Inputs', *American Economic Review*, 79(1): 85–95.

Markusen, J. (1995) 'The Boundaries of Multinational Enterprises and the Theory of International Trade', *Journal of Economic Perspectives*, 9(2): 169–89.

Markusen, J., Rutherford, T. and Hunter, L. (1995) 'Trade Liberalization in a Multinational Dominated Industry', *Journal of International Economics*, 38(1–2), 95–117.

Markusen, J. Rutherford, T. and Tarr, D. (1999) 'Foreign Direct Investment in Services and the Domestic Market for Expertise', paper presented at Second Annual Conference on Global Economic Analysis, Denmark, 20–22 June.

Martin, W. (2001) 'Trade Policy Reform in the East Asian Transition Economies', Policy Research Working Paper No. 2535, Washington DC: World Bank.

Maskin. E. and Tirole, J. (2004) 'The Politician and the Judge: Accountability in Government', *American Economic Review*, 94(4): 1034–54.

Mattoo, A. (2004) 'China's Accession in the WTO: The Services Dimension', in D. Bhattasali, S. Li and W. Martin (eds) *China and the WTO: Accession, Policy Reform, and Poverty Reduction Strategies*, Washington DC: World Bank.

Mattoo, A. and Fink, C. (2002) 'Regional Agreements and Trade in Services: Policy Issues', World Bank Policy Research Working Paper No. 2852, Washington DC: World Bank.

Mattoo, A. and Sauvé, P. (2010) 'The Preferential Liberalization of Services Trade', NCCR Trade Regulation Working Paper No. 2010/13, Bern: Swiss National Centre of Competition in Research.

Mattoo, A. and Wunsch-Vincent, S. (2004) 'Pre-empting Protectionism in Services: The GATS and Outsourcing', *Journal of International Economic Law*, 7(4): 765–800.

Mayer, W. (1974) 'Short-run and Long-run Equilibrium for a Small Open Economy', *Journal of Political Economy*, 82(5): 955–68.

McDougall, R.A. (1993) 'Incorporating International Capital Mobility into Salter', Salter Working Paper No. 21, Canberra: Productivity Commission.

McGuire, G. (1998) 'Australia's Restrictions on Trade in Financial Services', Productivity Commission Staff Research Paper, Canberra: Productivity Commission.

McGuire, G. and Schuele, M. (2000) 'Restrictiveness of International Trade in Banking Services', in C. Findlay and T. Warren (eds) *Impediments to Trade in Services: Measurement and Policy Implications*, London and New York: Routledge: 201–14.

McGuire, G., Schuele, M. and Smith, T. (2000) 'Restrictiveness of International Trade in Maritime Services', in C. Findlay and T. Warren (eds) *Impediments to Trade in Services: Measurement and Policy Implications*, London and New York: Routledge: 172–88.

McKibbin, W. and Vines, D. (2000) 'Modelling Reality: The Need for Both Inter-temporal Optimization and Stickiness in Models for Policy-making', *Oxford Review of Economic Policy*, 16(4): 106–37.

McKibbin, W. and Wilcoxen, P.J. (1996) 'The Role of Services in Modelling the Global Economy', *Asia Pacific Economic Review*, 2(2): 3–13.

McNaughton, A. (2011) 'Integrating Services Markets: A Comparison of EU and Australian Experiences', *Australian Journal of International Affairs*, 65(4): 454–68.

McNaughton, A. and Furlong, P. (2008) 'The EU Services Directive', mimeo, Canberra: Australian National University, forthcoming in C. Findlay (ed.) *Priorities and Pathways in Services Reform: Part 2 — Political Economy Studies*, World Scientific Studies in International Economics 26, Singapore: World Scientific.

Melvin, J. (1969) 'Increasing Returns to Scale as a Determinant of Trade', *Canadian Journal of Economics*, 2(3): 389–402.

Melvin, J. (1989) 'Trade in Producer Services: A Heckscher–Ohlin Approach', *Journal of Political Economy*, 97(5): 1180–96.

Miroudot, S., Sauvage, J. and Shepherd, B. (2010) 'Measuring the Cost of International Trade in Services', MPRA Paper No. 27655, Munich Personal RePEc Archive, online at http://mpra.ub.uni-muenchen.de/27655/.

Mundell, R. (1964) 'Tariff Preferences and the Terms of Trade', *Manchester School of Economic and Social Studies*, 32(1): 1–13.

Mussa, M. (1974) 'Tariffs and the Distribution of Income: The Importance of Factor Specificity, Substitutability, and Intensity in the Short and Long Run', *Journal of Political Economy*, 82(6): 1191–204.

Nagarajan, N. (1999) 'The Millennium Round: An Economic Appraisal', Economic Papers No. 139, Directorate General for Economic and Financial Affairs, Brussels: European Commission.

Nambiar, S. (2010) 'Enhancing Institutions and Improving Regulation: The Malaysian Case', in P. Dee (ed.) *Institutions for Economic Reform in Asia*, London and New York: Routledge: 121–44.

Nasir, Z.M. (2012) 'Financial Sector Reforms in Pakistan', in P. Dee (ed.) *Economic Reform Processes in South Asia*, London and New York: Routledge: 154–72.

Nataraj, G. (2012) 'Policy Efficiency of Trade Reforms in India', in P. Dee (ed.) *Economic Reform Processes in South Asia*, London and New York: Routledge: 136–53.

Neary, P. (1999) 'Discussion of Economic Policy and the Manufacturing Base: Hysteresis in Location (by A. Venables)', in R. Baldwin and J. Francois (eds) *Dynamic Issues in Commercial Policy Analysis*, Cambridge: Cambridge University Press: 196–201.

Neary, P. (2001) 'Of Hype and Hyperbolas: Introducing the New Economic Geography', *Journal of Economic Literature*, 39(2): 536–61.

Nguyen-Hong, D. (2000) 'Restrictions on Trade in Professional Services', Productivity Commission Staff Research Paper, Canberra: Productivity Commission.

Nitsmer, P. (2010) 'Gridlock: Regulatory Regimes in the Thai Passenger Transport Sector', in P. Dee (ed.) *Institutions for Economic Reform in Asia*, London and New York: Routledge: 145–65.

Novy, D. (2009) 'Gravity Redux: Measuring International Trade Costs with Panel Data', Warwick Economic Research Paper No. 861, Department of Economics, Warwick: University of Warwick.

Obstfeld, M. and Rogoff, K. (2000) 'The Six Major Puzzles in International Macroeconomics: Is there a Common Cause?', NBER Working Paper 7777, Cambridge MA: National Bureau of Economic Research.

Ochiai, R., Dee, P. and Findlay, C. (2010) 'Services in Free Trade Agreements', in C. Findlay and S. Urata (eds) *Free Trade Agreements in the Asia Pacific*, Singapore: World Scientific: 29–80.

OECD (Organization for Economic Co-operation and Development) (2000) 'Quantification of the Costs to National Welfare of Barriers to Trade in Services: Scoping Paper', TD/TC/WP(2000)32, Working Party of the Trade Committee, Paris: OECD.

OECD (2002a) 'The Relationship between Regional Trade Agreements and the Multilateral Trading System: Services', TD/TC/WP(2002)27/FINAL, Paris: OECD.

OECD (2002b) 'The Relationship between Regional Trade Agreements and the Multilateral Trading System: Investment', TD/TC/WP(2002)18/FINAL, Paris: OECD.

OECD (2002c) 'Labour Mobility in Regional Trade Agreements', TD/TC/WP(2002)16/FINAL, Paris: OECD.

OECD (2003) 'Service Providers on the Move: Labour Mobility and the WTO General Agreement on Trade in Services', *OECD Policy Brief*, Paris: OECD.

OECD (2004) 'The Economy-wide Effects of Services Trade Barriers in Selected Developing Countries', TD/TC/WP(2004)42, Paris: OECD.

OECD (2005a) 'Indicators of Regulatory Conditions in the Professional Services', 2 December 2005, accessible at

http://www.oecd.org/document/24/0,2340,en_2649_37421_35858776_1_1_1_37421,00.h
tml.

OECD (2005b) 'Indicators of Regulatory Conditions in Seven Non-manufacturing
Sectors', 2 December 2005, accessible at

http://www.oecd.org/document/32/0,2340,en_2649_37421_35791136_1_1_1_37421,00.h
tml.

OECD (2005c) 'Modal Estimates of Services Barriers', TD/TC/WP(2005)36, Paris:
OECD.

OECD (2011) 'The Impact of Trade Liberalization on Jobs and Growth: Technical Note',
OECD Trade Policy Working Papers, No. 107, Paris: OECD.

Ohlin, B. (1933) *Interregional and International Trade,* Cambridge, MA: Harvard
University Press.

Panagariya, A. (2000) 'Preferential Trade Liberalization: The Traditional Theory and
New Developments', *Journal of Economic Literature*, 38(2): 287–331.

Park, I. and Park, S. (2008) 'Reform Creating Regional Trade Agreements and Foreign
Direct Investment: Applications for East Asia', *Pacific Economic Review*, 13(5):
550–66.

Pauwelyn, J. (2005) 'The Transformation of World Trade', *Michigan Law Review*,
104(1): 1–65.

PC (Productivity Commission) (1998) *Annual Report 1997–98*, Canberra: Productivity
Commission.

PC (2000) *Broadcasting*, Report No. 11, Canberra: Productivity Commission.

Persaud, I. and Goebel, R.J. (1997) 'Achieving Full Effectiveness of Community Law:
The Court of Justice's Third Stage of Enforcement Rules', *American Society of
International Law Proceedings*, 91: 159–65.

Persson, T. and Tabellini, G. (1995) 'Double-edged Incentives: Institutions and Policy
Coordination', in G. Grossman and K. Rogoff (eds) *Handbook of Development
Economics, Volume III*, Amsterdam: Elsevier Science: 1973–2030.

Persson, T. and Tabellini, G. (1999) 'Political Economics and Macroeconomic Policy', in
J.B. Taylor and M. Woodford (eds) *Handbook of Macroeconomics, Volume I*,
Amsterdam: Elsevier Science: 1397–1482.

Persson, T. and Tabellini, G. (2002) 'Political Economics and Public Finance', in A.J.
Auerbach and M. Feldstein (eds) *Handbook of Public Economics, Volume III*,
Amsterdam: Elsevier Science: 1549–1659.

Petri, P.A. (1997) 'Foreign Direct Investment in a Computable General Equilibrium
Framework', paper presented at the Making APEC Work: Economic Challenges
and Policy Alternatives conference, Keio University, Tokyo, 13–14 March.

Pitarakis, J.Y. and Tridimas, G. (2003) 'Joint Dynamics of Legal and Economic
Integration in the European Union', *European Journal of Law and Economics*,
16(3): 357–68.

Plummer, M.G. (2007) '"Best Practices" in Regional Trading Agreements: An
Application to Asia', *The World Economy*, 30(12): 1771–96.

Pomfret, R. (1997) The Economics of Regional Trading Arrangements, Oxford: Claredon Press.

Rattigan, A. (1986) *Industry Assistance: The Inside Story*, Melbourne: Melbourne University Press.

Riezman, R. (1979) 'A 3x3 Model of Customs Unions', *Journal of International Economics*, 9(3): 341–54.

Rodrik, D. (1996) 'Understanding Economic Policy Reform', *Journal of Economic Literature*, 34(1): 9–41.

Roy, M., Marchetti, J. and Lim, H. (2006) 'Services Liberalization in the New Generation of Preferential Trade Agreements (PTAs): How Much Further than the GATS?', Staff Working Paper ERSD-2006-07, Economic Research and Statistics Division, Geneva: World Trade Organization.

Rybczynski, T. (1955) 'Factor Endowment and Relative Commodity Prices', *Economica*, 22(4): 336–41.

Sahoo, P. (2012) 'Foreign Direct Investment in India: Unfinished Agenda', in P. Dee (ed.) *Economic Reform Processes in South Asia*, London and New York: Routledge: 109–35.

Sampson, G. and Snape, R. (1985) 'Identifying Issues in Trade in Services', *The World Economy*, 8(2): 171–82.

Sauvé, P. (2002) 'The Relationship Between Regional Trade Agreements and the Multilateral Trading System — Services', Working Party of the Trade Committee, Trade Directorate, Paris: OECD.

Schultz, C. (2004) 'Information, Polarization and Accountability in Democracy', mimeo, Institute of Economics, Copenhagen: University of Copenhagen.

Sidorenko, A. and Findlay, C. (2002) 'Horizontal versus Sectoral Disciplines for Services Regulation', in S. Stephenson, C. Findlay and S. Yi (eds) *Services Trade Liberalization and Facilitation*, Canberra: Asia Pacific Press: 164–81.

Sidorenko, A. and Findlay, C. (2003) 'The Costs and Benefits of Health Services Trade Liberalization: The Case Study of Australia, Singapore and Malaysia', Report for the APEC Project CTI 17/2002T, May, Singapore: APEC Secretariat.

Snape, R. (1998) 'Reaching Effective Agreements Covering Services', in A. Krueger (ed.), *The WTO as an International Organization*, Chicago and London: University of Chicago Press: 279–92.

Soesastro, H. (2010) 'A Strategy for Regional Cooperation to Promote Structural Reform', in P. Dee (ed.) *Institutions for Economic Reform in Asia*, London and New York: Routledge: 212–17.

Soesastro, H., Aswicahyono, H. and Narjoko, D.A. (2010) 'Economic Reforms in Indonesia after the Economic Crisis', in P. Dee (ed.) *Institutions for Economic Reform in Asia*, London and New York: Routledge: 106–120.

Sourdin, P. (2013) 'Impact of Air and Maritime Restrictions on International Transport Margins', in P. Dee (ed.) *Priorities and Pathways in Services Reform: Part 1 —*

Quantitative Studies, World Scientific Studies in International Economics 26, Singapore: World Scientific (forthcoming).

Srivastava, D.K. and Sarma, J.V.M. (2012) 'Monitoring Fiscal Performance in India', in P. Dee (ed.) *Economic Reform Processes in South Asia*, London and New York: Routledge: 86–108.

Stapleton, T. (2006) 'Institutional Determinants of Indonesia's Sugar Trade Policy', *Bulletin of Indonesian Economic Studies*, 42(1): 95–103.

Steiner, F. (2000) 'Regulation, Industry Structure and Performance in the Electricity Supply Industry', Working Paper No. 238, ECO/WKP(2000)11, Economics Department, Paris: OECD.

Stephenson, S. (2002) 'Regional versus Multilateral Liberalization of Services', *World Trade Review*, 1(2): 187–209.

Stephenson, S. and Nikomborirak, D. (2002) 'Regional Liberalization in Services', in S. Stephenson, C. Findlay and S. Yi (eds) *Services Trade Liberalization and Facilitation*, Canberra: Asia Pacific Press: 89–124.

Stolper, W. and Samuelson, P. (1941) 'Protection and Real Wages', *Review of Economic Studies*, 9(1): 58–73.

Stone Sweet, A. (2010) 'The European Court of Justice and the Judicialization of EU Governance', *Living Reviews in European Governance*, 5(2): 1–50.

Stone Sweet, A. and Brunell, T.L. (1998) 'The European Court and the National Courts: A Statistical Analysis of Preliminary References, 1961–95', *Journal of European Public Policy*, 5(1): 66–97.

Stone Sweet, A. and Brunell, T.L. (2011) 'How the European Legal System Works: Override, Non-Compliance, and Majority Activism in International Regimes', mimeo, http://works.bepress.com/alec_stone_sweet/39 (accessed 1 April 2011).

Sutherland Report (2004) *The Future of the WTO: Addressing Institutional Challenges in the New Millenium*, The Sutherland Report: A Report of the Consultative Board to the Director-General, Supachai Panitchpakdi, Geneva: World Trade Organization.

Takeshi, K. and Golub, S. (2006) 'OECD's FDI Regulatory Restrictiveness Index: Revision and Extension to More Economies', Working Paper on International Investment, Paris: OECD.

Tallberg, J. (2002) 'Delegation to Supranational Institutions: Why, How, and with What Consequences?', *West European Politics*, 25(1): 23–46.

Tornell, A., Westermann, F. and Martínez, L. (2004) 'NAFTA and Mexico's Economic Performance', CESifo Working Paper No. 1155, Munich: CESifo (University of Munich and Ifo Institute).

Trachtman, J.P. (1999) 'Bananas, Direct Effect and Compliance', *European Journal of International Law*, 10(4): 655–78.

Trewin, R. (2000) 'A Price-impact Measure of Impediments to Trade in Telecommunications Services', in C. Findlay and T. Warren (eds), *Impediments to Trade in Services: Measurement and Policy Implications*, London and New York: Routledge: 101–18.

United Nations (1994) *World Investment Directory Latin America and the Caribbean*, New York: United Nations.

Vaidya, R.R. (2012) 'The Process of Banking Sector Reforms in India', in P. Dee (ed.) *Economic Reform Processes in South Asia*, London and New York: Routledge: 61–85.

Van den Broek, N. (2009) 'Enforcing WTO Compliance Through Public Opinion and Direct Effect: Two Proposals to Enhance the Compliance Perspectives for Least Developed WTO Members', *Frontiers of Economics and Globalization*, 6: 444–62.

Verikios, G. and Hanslow, K. (1999) 'Modelling the Effects of Implementing the Uruguay Round: A Comparison using the GTAP Model under Alternative Treatments of International Capital Mobility', paper presented at Second Annual Conference on Global Economic Analysis, Denmark, 20–22 June.

Viner, J. (1950) *The Customs Union Issue*, New York: Carnegie Endowment for International Peace.

Vo, T.T. and Nguyen, T.A. (2010) 'Institutional Changes for Private Sector Development in Vietnam', in P. Dee (ed.) *Institutions for Economic Reform in Asia*, London and New York: Routledge: 165–94.

Warren, T. (2000) 'The Impact on Output of Impediments to Trade and Investment in Telecommunications Services', in C. Findlay and T. Warren (eds) *Impediments to Trade in Services: Measurement and Policy Implications*, London and New York: Routledge: 85–100.

Warwick Commission (2007) The Multilateral Trade Regime: Which Way Forward? The Report of the First Warwick Commission, Coventry: University of Warwick.

Weiler, J.H.H. (1991) 'The Transformation of Europe', *Yale Law Journal*, 100(8): 2403–83.

Weiler, J.H.H. (2001) 'The Rule of Lawyers and the Ethos of Diplomats: Reflections on the Internal and External Legitimacy of WTO dispute Settlement', *Journal of World Trade*, 35(2): 191–207.

Welsh, A. and Strzelecki, A. (2000) 'Estimating Domestic and Foreign Returns to Capital for the FTAP Model', Research Memorandum, Canberra: Productivity Commission.

Weerakoon, D. (2012) 'Sri Lanka's Economic Reform Process: Progress and Constraints', in P. Dee (ed.) *Economic Reform Processes in South Asia*, London and New York: Routledge: 173–90.

Williamson, J. (1994) *Political Economy of Policy Reform*, Washington DC: Institute for International Economics.

Winters, A., Walmsley, T., Wang, Z.K. and Grynberg, R. (2001) 'Negotiating the Liberalization of the Temporary Movement of Natural Persons', Report to the Commonwealth Secretariat, London: Commonwealth Secretariat.

Winters, L.A., Walmsley, T., Wang, Z.K. and Grynberg, R. (2003) 'Liberalizing Temporary Movement of Natural Persons: An Agenda for the Development Round', *The World Economy*, 26(8): 1137–61.

World Bank (2000) *Trade Blocs*, World Bank Policy Research Report, Oxford: Oxford University Press.

World Bank (2001) *World Development Report 2000/2001: Attacking Poverty*, New York: Oxford University Press.

World Bank (2006) *Tunisia Agricultural Policy Review*, Report No. 35239-TN, Washington DC: World Bank.

World Bank (2008) Tunisia Global Integration: A New Generation of Reforms to Support Employment, Washington DC: World Bank.

WTO (World Trade Organization) (1995) 'Regional Trading Arrangements and the World Trading System', Geneva: WTO.

WTO (2005) Trade Policy Review, Report by Secretariat, Tunisia, WT/TPR/S/152, Geneva: WTO.

WTO (2009) *Trade Policy Review — Malaysia*, WT/TPR/S/225, Geneva: WTO.

Zissimos, B. and Vines, D. (2000) 'Is the WTO's Article XXIV a Free Trade Barrier?', CSGR Working Paper No. 49/00, Centre for the Study of Globalization and Regionalization, Warwick: University of Warwick.